Speech Dynamic Communication

Third Edition

Third Edition

Speech
Dynamic
Communication

MILTON DICKENS
University of Southern California

Harcourt Brace Jovanovich, Inc.
New York Chicago San Francisco Atlanta

PHOTO CREDITS

pp. 2–3, 22 (bottom), 66, 214, 316–17: EPA/Newsphoto

pp. 7, 16, 30–31, 90 (top right), 129, 137, 153, 155, 158, 164–65, 208–09, 235, 240, 250–51, 254, 260, 278–79, 283, 311, 326–28: Michael V. Sedano

p. 18: UPI/FDR Library, Hyde Park, N.Y.

p. 22 (top, center): Lynda Gordon

pp. 23, 48–49, 64, 90 (left center, right center), 107, 173, 180–81, 224, 231–32, 258, 324, 342–43: Glenn E. Hall

pp. 52–53: Carl Iwasaki, *Life* Magazine, © Time Inc.

p. 90 (bottom right): Herb Taylor/EPA Newsphoto

pp. 148–49, 321: Andrew Sacks/EPA Newsphoto

p. 215: Elliott Erwitt/Magnum

p. 225: Leonard Freed/Magnum

p. 264: Don Wilkinson

pp. 268, 320: Bruce Anspach/EPA Newsphoto

pp. 306, 357: Wide World

p. 330: Harvey Stein

p. 332: Bruce Davidson/Magnum

p. 338: Charles Gatewood

p. 341: Constantine Manos, © 1969 Magnum

p. 348: Robert Karam/EPA Newsphoto

p. 354: NC News/EPA Newsphoto

p. 360: Eve Arnold/Magnum

ISBN: 0–15–583193–3

Library of Congress Catalog Card Number: 73–15373

Printed in the United States of America

Preface

This third edition, like the previous ones, is intended to serve the needs of students taking a basic course for nonspeech majors. Those students need and expect to receive practical training that will increase their effectiveness in the speaking-listening situations they will encounter during their student years and during their future careers.

The underlying philosophy of the book remains unchanged. Twenty years ago in the preface to the first edition I said, "Public speaking is presented as a dynamic process of communication between speaker and listeners, not as a static, one-sided performance by the speaker. Hence the title, *Speech: Dynamic Communication*." At that time I was intrigued by the fact that I could find only one speech textbook that attempted to define its field. So I created a definition of speech in which communication was the key term, and I warned students that the definition was deceptively simple. Now, two revisions later, I have spelled out some of the practical implications of that definition in the opening chapter. In doing this, I present some of my current thinking on modern communication theory (instead of reserving it for the last chapter as I did in the second edition). Instructors who used the second edition will find that this major change means the deletion of most of former chapters 1 and 20 in favor of new materials and functions for the opening chapter.

A second major change is the addition of a chapter on listening.

At the time of publication of the previous editions, I did not believe that sufficient research had been done on listening to justify a separate chapter. Obviously, I now believe that research has begun to catch up with teaching needs.

A third major change is a revised and expanded chapter on group discussion, placed at the end (instead of in the opening section) of the book. This new chapter is a guide to leadership and participation in basic types of group discussion. It is a marriage of the practical and the theoretical. Thus, this chapter could reasonably be read as a how-to-do-it guide for chairing a committee, participating in a panel, or using parliamentary procedures in a club meeting. With equal logic, it could be read as an extended illustration of such abstract concepts as symbolic interaction, process, or information retrieval.

Users of the second edition will notice many other changes in the book, including the reduction from twenty chapters to eighteen to make room for the addition of new materials. And, of course, the entire book has been updated, especially the excerpts from contemporary speakers, the lists of speech topics, and the suggested schedule of class assignments in the appendixes.

Almost all of the photographs are new, but the past policies governing pictures have been retained and more rigorously enforced: pictures should usefully illustrate, not merely decorate, the accompanying text; photos should comprise mostly candid shots of students, rather than familiar pictures of prominent people.

The writing style remains informal and is addressed directly to students; the goal is readability and clarity without the sacrifice of accuracy or substance. Technical terms and references to scientific journals are used only when they are clearly required or serve a special teaching purpose.

My principal indebtedness in preparing this revision is to Glenn E. Hall, who assisted in nearly all phases of the work, who provided many of the photographs, and who should be credited as collaborator on Appendix A. Special acknowledgment is given to Michael Sedano, who contributed the greatest number of the photographs and who made useful suggestions regarding textual materials. Some of my ideas on teaching basic speech are blended with those of my faculty colleague James H. McBath, with whom I have coauthored two books. My thanks are given again to Frederick Williams, whose contributions to the second edition often carry over into this third edition.

Jennette Dickens, my wife, objects to my including the customary "without whom. . . ." I will honor this suggestion just as I have honored her many practical contributions included in the text.

Milton Dickens

Contents

four
AUDIENCE RESPONSES

five
SPEAKER-LISTENER INTERACTION

APPENDIXES

Speech
Dynamic
Communication
Third Edition

A speech is neither an act, nor a solo, nor an exhibition. It is an enlarged conversation between speaker and audience.

The Study of Speech Communication

one

TOPICAL PREVIEW

1
Communicating Through Speech

"THE SIMPLE ACT OF TALKING"

You learned to talk as a child; you have been talking ever since. Learning to talk was a remarkably haphazard performance: you learned from your parents, grandparents, cousins, schoolteachers, playmates, and assorted strangers—from practically anybody; you learned from TV, radio, and movies; you were influenced by reading everything from comic books to classics. Not surprisingly, therefore, you have acquired all sorts of speaking habits (including habitual attitudes)—some good, some bad, and others in-between. And sometimes, because you are so used to them all, you cannot tell which is which. You want to recognize and capitalize on the effective habits, improve the indifferent ones, unlearn and replace the undesirable ones. In short, you want to become a better talker. And that is exactly what this book is all about. You should realize immediately, however, that "the simple act of talking" is not simple at all; it is perhaps the most complex and difficult form of human behavior. You must broaden your notion of what is required to become a better talker. Let us begin by analyzing a deceptively simple definition.

DEFINITION OF SPEECH COMMUNICATION

For our purposes *speech* is the *communication* of thought and emotion by means of voice, language, and/or bodily action. By speech we can mean conversation, discussion, public speaking, reading aloud, acting, or even booing, heckling, sign language, or talking to yourself.

BASIC COMMUNICATION CONCEPTS

The key word in the above definition is *communication*. You have heard or seen this popular word used or abused many times. The failure of almost any type of public policy is explained as "a communication breakdown"; personal problems of all sorts are reduced to "We simply cannot communicate with one another any more." Several definitions are offered below, beginning with an extremely broad one, then narrowing to the particular type of communication to be studied in this book. The discussion accompanying each definition will provide you with a theoretical frame of reference and an introduction to some basic concepts that have important practical values.

1. Communication is the process by which one thing affects another.

This definition is drawn from the field of cybernetics, which is based on mathematical theory.[1] Cybernetics deals with control and communication between or among men, animals, insects, vegetables, machines, and all systems in nature. It may be difficult for you to conceive of a rosebush in your garden "communicating" with a bumblebee or of a computer "communicating" with an unmanned spacecraft sending photographs and other data from Jupiter back to earth, but from the viewpoint of cybernetics such communication does occur. The rosebush communicates with the bumblebee when it releases the nectar the bee seeks. The spacecraft is controlled by signals transmitted from the computers. In both examples, there has been transmission of "information"; there has been communication.

This definition of communication contains two concepts that we will discuss here.

---

[1] Thus, Weaver defines communication at the machine level as ". . . the procedures by means of which one mechanism (say automatic equipment to track an airplane and to compute its probable future positions) affects another mechanism (say a guided missile chasing this airplane)." Claude E. Shannon and Warren Weaver, *The Mathematical Theory of Communication,* University of Illinois Press, 1949, p. 95.

This composite of Eric Hoffer suggests that a speech never stands still; it constantly changes as you speak or listen. So do not study these pictures separately; study them "separately together."

First, examine the concept "process." A process is a dynamic, ongoing, ever-changing event or happening. It never stands still. The importance of this viewpoint to the study of speech communication has been stressed by the title of this book: speech is viewed as dynamic (like a motion picture), not static (like a snapshot). This process-centered concept was vividly expressed some 2,500 years ago when Heraclitus remarked that you can never step in the same river twice—the river is constantly changing and so are you.

The phrase "one thing affects another" provides a criterion for deciding whether communication has occurred. Suppose you are talking with a friend on the telephone and suddenly your receiver goes dead; your friend might go right on talking, but for you communication ceases when you can no longer hear what he is saying. Now suppose that you are talking with your friend in a living room where he is comfortably reclining on the couch. You are in the midst of a somewhat confused description of the plot of a movie you saw last night when suddenly you notice that your friend has fallen sound asleep. You would have to conclude that you failed to communicate because for a while you were literally talking to yourself.

2. Human communication is the process by which one person affects another.

This definition is presented to illustrate the task of narrowing the preceding definition. We have eliminated "communication" between inanimate objects and lower forms of life, but the scope is still too broad. The definition includes transmission of both symbolic and non-symbolic transfer of "stimuli." Thus if a robber sneaks up behind his victim and knocks him unconscious by hitting him with a club, we must say that the robber has "communicated" since he has certainly "affected" his victim. So we must narrow the definition further to symbolic behaviors. In this book we will not be interested in hitting one another with clubs but we will include the study of verbal attacks.

3. Human communication is the process by which one person affects the behavior of another through signs or symbols.

This definition includes all kinds of symbolic communication—speech, writing, music, fine arts, dance, architecture, and others. The added terms "signs or symbols" are variously defined by writers in the field of communication. Their usage here is as follows. Signs and symbols are alike in that they are anything that stands for or represents something else. A sign has a direct or natural relation to the thing signified (the referent); a symbol has an arbitrary or conventional relation. Thus smoke can be a nonverbal sign of fire; the spoken or written word *fire* is arbitrarily related to its referent by agreement among English-speaking people. Man creates symbols that not only represent observable phenomena, such as a fire, but also abstractions, such as "eternity." This ability to create abstract symbols is unique to man and is the most clear-cut criterion that distinguishes him from all other living things.

Do not suppose that all signs are bodily movements or that "the language of gesture" is a set of signs with universal meanings. Most of our gestures are symbols; that is, they have arbitrary meanings. Anthropologists have reported that common gestures, such as nodding or shaking the head, beckoning, or waving farewell, have different (even contradictory) meanings in different cultures. You must begin to think of your speech communication in the context of your society.

Our third definition confronts us with another difficult problem: Should we confine our definition to a process requiring two or more people? If so, we exclude the notion of one person "talking to himself" and thus affecting his own subsequent behaviors. This dilemma becomes especially sticky when we think of the fact that a speaker hears himself while talking to another person or persons —he is a member of his own audience and his self-feedback affects his behavior. Furthermore, speakers, actors, and oral readers frequently practice aloud beforehand for the explicit purpose of improving their later public performance. These (and many similar) examples prove that we should not confine our definition only to a process requiring two or more people, but rather to the whole range of human speech communication.

4. Intraindividual human communication is the process by which the thoughts and feelings of one person affect his behavior by means of signs and symbols transmitted and received by that same person.

A little of the theoretical rationale for this definition is indicated in the previous paragraph. But the inclusion of the definition in this textbook is based upon practical considerations.

A basic principle of effective speaking is that you should have something worthwhile to say. "What you say" is a product of your experiences, including reading, talking, and thinking. Usually you read and write silently, but sometimes you pause and read a sentence aloud, just to test "how it sounds" or perhaps to secure an opinion from somebody else. While you are reading, writing, or thinking, you may be surprised (if you check up on yourself) at how often you talk to yourself *sotto voce*—you find yourself talking in an undertone, whispering, or silently forming words with your mouth and lips. In short, much of your preparation of a classroom talk is itself an exercise in communication.

At this point, you may well ask an important question: "What about silent thinking?" Psychologists and other researchers have explored this question for many years. About sixty years ago, John B. Watson, father of behaviorism, advanced the theory that thinking is subvocal talking, and that talking is simply thinking aloud. Most psychologists are unwilling to go that far; the prevailing view is that language and thought are closely related but not necessarily identical. They all agree that language symbols are important tools for thinking—especially for complex or abstract thinking.

You will notice that the processes of planning the content of a talk are closely related to the processes used when giving the talk. First you talk it over with yourself, later you talk it over with your classmates. While talking with your classmates you are also listening to yourself. You think the thought as you express it thus improving your ability to show that you are "thinking on your feet," not parroting empty words.

As you broaden your goal of becoming a better speaker, you will also notice that the close relationship between speaking and thinking means that much of the training in this book will be training in how you think. In order to become a better speaker, you must also become a better thinker.

The fourth definition, however, is not restricted to the communication of thinking; the complete term is "thoughts and feelings." When you "have an idea," what you have is a mixture of thoughts and feelings. A person's thoughts and feelings are not two discrete types of human behavior that can occur in separation or alternation. Research in psychology, medicine, and physiology indicates that brain waves (indicators of thinking) go on twenty-four hours a day; likewise, glandular, circulatory, and respiratory functions (indicators of feelings or emotions) are continuous signs of being alive. You cannot turn off either one like a faucet. Maybe you have been in the habit of praising or condemning a public speaker for making "an entirely emotional speech" or "an entirely intellectual speech"; you may have supposed that you would practice these two kinds of speeches in a speech class. You could not do this even if you tried. Every idea that you talk about is a product of and an expression of you constantly thinking and constantly feeling. Of course, your classmates may try to evaluate a given talk from the standpoint of its logical appeal or emotional appeal but they are only looking at the two sides of the same coin. And research has shown that their evaluations differ so widely that they might as well have flipped that coin.[2]

However, you began this book with the quite accurate expectation that the focus would be on improving your ability to talk to other people. So let us define that.

5. Interindividual human communication is the process by which the thoughts and feelings of one person affect the behavior of another by means of signs or symbols transmitted by one person and perceived by another.

When you compare this definition with the previous one, the main question, in abbreviated form, may be put: "How does the intra become inter?" When you reflect upon "the simple act of talking" to someone else, an experience that you have always taken for granted, it is transformed into one of mankind's grandest achievements. Thinking and feeling require an individual brain, nervous system, glandular mechanisms, and so on. Contrary to John Donne, each person is physiologically an island. I can communicate with

[2] Randall C. Ruechelle, "An Experimental Study of Audience Recognition of Emotional and Intellectual Appeals in Persuasion," Speech Monographs, Vol. XXV, No. 1 (March 1958), pp. 49–58.

myself about my toothache and about my experiences with the world surrounding me. I assume that you can do the same things. But how can you or I be sure? How can we know that our sensations, thoughts, and feelings are the same or at least similar? How can we bridge the physiological and physical gap that separates us? The answer is that we try to compare our experiences by means of signs and symbols. Communities have developed languages that comprise thousands of words and dozens of grammatical rules governing the sequences of words. These language systems are often awkward and inadequate. None is simple and infallible. Learning to communicate with others is a lifelong task.

Together, we will concentrate on one basic type of language system, speech communication. Probably you now agree that the definition of this term on page 6 is indeed "deceptively simple." The practicality of our discussion in this section will come home to you many times as you progress. For example, every speaker, inexperienced or experienced, is constantly shifting back and forth between intra- and interindividual communication (although not calling them by such fancy names, you may say). So let us conclude this section by bringing the concepts down to a speaker's common experience, delightfully described by Supreme Court Justice Robert H. Jackson,

> I used to say that, as Solicitor General, I made three arguments of every case. First came the one that I planned—as I thought, logical, coherent, complete. Second was the one actually presented —interrupted, incoherent, disjointed, disappointing. The third was the utterly devastating argument that I thought of after going to bed that night.[3]

THE PROCESS OF SPEECH COMMUNICATION

In talks before your classmates you will go through the same experiences described by Justice Jackson—first you prepare a talk, then you give it, and afterwards you criticize yourself. It is useful to spell out the process in somewhat greater detail. In doing so, we are constructing a communication model which means that we divide the complete act into several major steps arranged in a selected sequence. This analytical approach can help you to understand how the whole process works or fails to work, but you must constantly remind yourself that the process of oral communication can be taken apart only in theory. Do not study the parts separately;

---

[3] Robert H. Jackson, "Advocacy Before the Supreme Court: Suggestions for Effective Case Presentations," *American Bar Association Journal,* Vol. XXXVII (November 1951), p. 803.

study them *separately together,* supplying in your imagination the sense of something in motion, something ever-changing. If you are visually minded, you may enjoy sketching some diagrams of your own.

The Speaker Has an Idea

Suppose that you are assigned to give a classroom talk and that you begin thinking about it silently in the privacy of your own room. You may ask yourself, "What shall I talk about?" Perhaps you think of three possibilities and you mentally weigh their pros and cons. Presently you choose what seems to be the best topic. Then you ask yourself, "What are the main points I want to make?" While answering your own question, you call upon your memory of past experiences and try to anticipate the future reactions of your instructor and classmates. Much of your behavior up to this point may be described as an inner dialog. You are mentally manipulating signs and symbols in the form of electrochemical impulses in your brain and nervous system and simultaneously experiencing feelings or emotions. These various complex activities are represented below in greatly simplified form by a diagram. The circle represents you, an integrated person (or personality); the arrow is intended to suggest the intraindividual communication going on within a single human being.

The Speaker Puts the Idea into Words

Of course the previous step overlaps this one because you were mentally putting ideas into words as you engaged in silent thought. Here we will go a step further by examining how you put your ideas into words adapted to your future audience. As you are trying to think through your coming classroom talk, you will probably make some written notes. When you read these notes, you have gone outside of yourself. Reading your own notes is basically the same as reading words written by another person. The signs and symbols are now received in the form of reflected light waves impinging on the retina and conducted thence to your brain by afferent nerve fibers. The notes you are writing are, however, the beginnings of an outline to be used when you deliver the talk. You are aware that any given idea can be expressed in different ways. Your way of wording an idea is not likely to correspond exactly with the wording your listeners would use. Your problem is to find the right words to bridge the gap between you and your audience. In doing this, you should practice aloud. As you listen to your own voice, you are receiving the signs and symbols in the form of sound waves impinging on the eardrum. The diagram below retains the inner arrow and adds an outside arrow to symbolize the behaviors of reading your own notes and hearing your own voice.

The Speaker Transmits to the Listeners

When you give the talk in class, your part of the transaction is that you now use vocal and other physical movements to transmit the signs and symbols in essentially the same way as when practicing in your room. You may speak louder because you now have an audience and you want to be clearly heard. (In some nonclass situations the reach of your voice may be extended electronically by such means as telephone, radio, or television.) The next diagram shows that internal behaviors are still going on and you are still hearing your own voice, but we add a new arrow to indicate your additional behaviors due to your awareness that you are no longer talking exclusively to yourself but also to other persons. You are endeavoring to bridge the gap. The reactions of anyone in your audience are reserved for analysis in the next section.

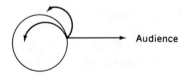

Audience

The Listeners Perceive

Now the listeners join the communication process and play an active, not a passive role. Assuming that they can hear your voice, understand your language, and see your appearance and bodily movements, they attach meaning to these signs and symbols. We are calling this internal behavior "perception." The meaning they receive may not correspond with the meaning you intended. So we know that your idea is not "delivered" as a parcel is delivered, nor is it transferred directly from your brain to theirs, nor does your thinking and feeling automatically become the listeners'. What happens can be more accurately described as the arousing or stirring up of thinking and feeling. You can start this process, but the listeners must complete it. Your hope is that the listeners' perception will be approximately what you intended. Meanwhile, you cannot directly observe their intraindividual behaviors. The diagram below shows the close resemblance between the listeners' inner reactions and your own behaviors in our first diagram.

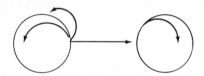

The Listeners Overtly Respond

In addition to their inner behaviors, the listeners also overtly respond. In some situations the audience may applaud or boo before a speaker can utter his first words. In the classroom, audience reactions are not so readily apparent, but they are there just the same. Listeners may smile, laugh, nod or shake their heads, wriggle restlessly, or yawn. Research indicates that student speakers are surprisingly accurate in judging fellow students' attitudes from such clues.[4]

And of course, in a conversation or group discussion, the listeners are likely to react promptly by talking. In such instances, an important point is underscored: a speaker is not only a transmitter but also a receiver, and the listeners are not merely passive receivers. You can think of anyone who communicates as a sort of "transceiver." This point is shown in the next diagram. Here you notice that the speaker is thinking about his speech and simultaneously responding to the feedback from his audience.

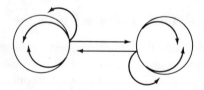

[4] Milton Dickens and David H. Krueger, "Speakers' Accuracy in Identifying Immediate Audience Responses During a Speech," *Speech Teacher,* Vol. XVIII, No. 4 (November 1969), pp. 303–07.

The Listeners Affect One Another

We will add a final significant variable—if you have more than one listener, a process of audience interstimulation and response occurs. Thus people tend to laugh louder in a group because they hear the others' laughter. Sometimes a person whispers his reactions to a friend seated next to him. Public speakers sometimes even arrange to have a few "claquers" scattered through the audience with instructions to start applauding each time the orator pauses after a climactic statement, and usually most of the audience almost automatically join the applause. In more ordinary cases, the mere presence of others usually censors an individual's behavior—he does not want to appear conspicuous or eccentric. The final diagram shows the interstimulation in an audience; to avoid cluttering the diagram some of the arrows previously shown are omitted, but you can supply them in your mind's eye.

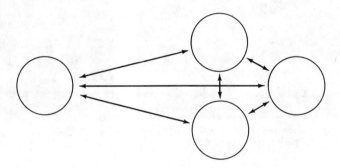

If you glance back and forth between the diagram and the picture on pages 2 and 3, you see that the pictures almost literally bring the diagram to life. You can visualize how, by means of an interchange of signs and symbols, the thoughts and feelings of one person become intermingled with those of others.

THE COMMUNICATIVE ATTITUDE

Everything in this chapter suggests that becoming a better speaker may include more than you originally supposed. You are not here to learn the art of saying nothing well, nor to practice putting on some sort of performance or act. You are here to improve yourself, but you realize that you cannot divorce the how-you-say-it from what you say, what you are, and to whom you say it. You must develop yourself as a whole person and practice becoming a more effective individual. You are here to improve your mastery of

Campus rallies are reminders that the goal of becoming a better speaker should be broadened. Your goal is to become a better communicator as a member of a community.

spoken language symbols, which are simultaneously the chief tools of your own thinking and the chief tools for intermingling your ideas with those of other people. In short, you are here to develop yourself as a member of a community.

A speaker has a communicative attitude when he thinks of himself and his listeners as participating in a single group. He does not think in terms of "they, the audience" and "I, the speaker." He has the "you and I" attitude toward each speaking situation. When you are speaking you want your listeners to feel that they are as much a part of the process as you are. You want to create the feeling that "all of us here are thinking this through together." The ability to heighten the listeners' awareness of their participation may be termed *communicativeness*.

If a speaker has a communicative attitude it will always show. His whole mood and manner will reveal it in a dozen subconscious ways. For example, he will tend to choose and prepare his subject matter with the idea of having something to share. While he is speaking his bodily alertness, his facial expression, and the variations in his voice will all be subtly improved if he speaks for communication. In addition to relying on these subconscious signs, however, a speaker can deliberately practice two specific sets of speaking habits to enhance his communicativeness. The first of these is *eye contact* (often called directness); the second is *references to audience*.

Eye Contact

Beginning speakers often try to avoid the eyes of their listeners. Instead of looking at the audience, they keep their eyes glued to their notes, the floor, the walls, or the ceiling. Communication with the listeners is impaired because the effect is that of speaking *at* them or *over* them or *away from* them, rather than *to* them or *with* them.

In general, the rule is this: While you are speaking maintain direct eye contact with your listeners, looking from one individual to another, unless you have reasons for looking elsewhere. Usually you should look about slowly; if your eyes keep darting rapidly from place to place, the effect may seem furtive or shifty. If the audience is fairly large or scattered, be careful to include persons from all parts of the group. Do not form the habit of concentrating most of your attention on one side of the room, for instance, or on just the first rows.

On some occasions, of course, there is good reason for looking away from your audience. Perhaps you are describing a tall building; so you look upward as a gesture to convey the effect of height. Perhaps you are telling a story and you wish to mimic somebody whose eyes were downcast or glazed. Perhaps you want to cite statistics or give a quotation, and to emphasize your accuracy, you may read from your notes. Thus communicativeness does not require that you should never look away from your audience.

Some students complain that catching someone's eye distracts them and causes them to forget what they are saying. The answer is: It all depends upon what you are used to doing. If you form the habit of maintaining eye contact, it seems distracting *not* to catch the listeners' eyes.

References to Audience

Show your awareness of the audience's participation by mentioning it from time to time. Such references may take a variety of forms. You should adapt the expression of your own ideas in terms of your listeners' reactions. "Before the meeting I was talking with several members of your club and they convinced me that the...." "I see that some of you are looking puzzled—let me put my point another way...." Sometimes you should refer to the name or the activities of the group. "I do not have to stress the importance of service to you members of Rotary...." Sometimes you can even call individual members of the audience by name. "During dinner I was introduced to Dr. Kenneth Shanks, chairman of your membership committee, who told me that...." In your speech class it is good practice to name individuals occasionally. "Miss Williamson, you are an education major, and this means...." "As we all heard the other day, Fred Bowman loves trout fishing, so he will be especially interested to know that...." In general, it is wise to word your ideas in terms of "you and I," "we," "us," "our," "as you know," "let's think about this together," and the like.

Franklin D. Roosevelt was acknowledged, even by his political enemies, to have been the most effective American speaker of his generation. When trying to characterize his effectiveness, people often used the term "communicativeness." When he was talking in person to individuals or small groups, President Roosevelt was noted for his eye contact, facial animation (he was the news photogra-

Franklin D. Roosevelt is shown here during one of his "Fireside Chats." He talked in a conversational voice to the millions of radio listeners; his wording also revealed his you-and-I attitude.

phers' delight), and variety of voice. He retained his communicative qualities even when addressing huge crowds or broadcasting to millions via radio. This was shown not only in all aspects of his delivery, but also in his choice of ideas and illustrations and in his choice of words, especially in his audience references. Study the following typical excerpts from Roosevelt speeches.

> . . . for I propose to follow my custom of speaking frankly to the nation concerning our common problems. . . .

> We gave warning last November that we had only just begun to fight. Did some people really believe that we did not mean it? Well, I meant it, and you meant it. . . .

> If I have spoken to you seriously tonight, it is because I believe that you too, are thinking of. . . .

> That is why I came to you . . . with a simple plea for your assistance . . . in working out our common problems. . . .

These audience references provide clues to a broad practical philosophy of communicating through speech (almost a review of this chapter). Recently, a political scientist put it this way:

> Franklin Roosevelt was fond of quoting "the missus" . . . sharing Eleanor's reports on typhoid fever . . . and unemployment. . . . H. G. Wells admiringly called Roosevelt "a ganglion for reception, expression, transmission, combination, and realization." In other words, FDR *listened*—and having listened, he adroitly undertook the politics of persuasion.[5]

SUMMARY

Early in this course you should broaden your idea of what is required to become a better speaker. Speech communication is a dynamic, ongoing, ever-changing process, a concept that is also applicable to all things in nature, animate or inanimate. Speaking requires the use of verbal and nonverbal signs and symbols that are the chief tools for your silent thinking, as well as the chief tools for intermingling your inner thoughts and emotions with those of other people. The study of basic communication concepts shows the importance of maintaining the "you and I" attitude in all speaking situations. You nurture communicativeness by practicing eye contact and references to your listeners. Your overall goal should be to develop yourself as a member of a community.

---

[5] James David Barber, "Tone-deaf in the Oval Office," *Saturday Review/World* (January 12, 1974), p. 10.

TOPICAL PREVIEW

I   Public speaking versus conversation
    A   Differences between public speaking and conversation
    B   Resemblances between public speaking and conversation
    C   Relation to confidence and poise

II   The problem of stage fright
    A   How prevalent?
    B   How difficult?

III   Attitudes that build confidence and poise
    A   Communication as interaction
    B   Learning from your listeners
    C   Confidence as emotional control

IV   Practices that build confidence and poise
    A   On days prior to the talk
    B   On the day of the talk
    C   While speaking

V   Summary

2
Gaining Confidence and Poise

PUBLIC SPEAKING VERSUS CONVERSATION

Suppose that you and one of your friends, who is a member of the football team, arrive early for class. Your friend has just returned from the big intersectional game and begins telling you how the game looked from a player's point of view. This, you would say, is a conversation. As he talks two more members of the class arrive and join you in listening to his account of the game. Let us imagine that others arrive by twos and threes and that all are eager to hear the exciting details. Your friend is so engrossed in his story that as more students join the group he simply raises his voice a bit and continues to talk. Now at what point does your friend's report cease to be conversation and become "a speech"? Would it be when the fifth person joins the group? Or the tenth, the thirteenth, the twentieth?

Differences Between Public Speaking
and Conversation

Consider the progressive sequence of pictures on pages 22–23. Let us agree that the first photograph of the two students shows "a conversation." You would probably also say that the last photo of the commencement address is a clear example of "making a speech."

Two students chatting between classes. This is conversation.

Here are four students talking. Is this still a conversation?

A professor holds a seminar. Is it still conversation?

A professor holds a class session on the lawn. Students often interrupt with questions or comments. When the professor or a student talks, is he conversing or is he making a speech?

This lady is speaking at a dinner meeting of a fairly large organization. Is she conversing or making a speech?
A commencement address—you would probably say that this is a clear example of making a speech.

Now let us analyze the entire sequence for the purpose of testing the hypothesis that there are no fundamental differences between conversation and public speaking.

The most obvious difference between pictures in the sequence is the increasing number of people. As we have already seen, however, this increase is not fundamental. An audience comprises one or more persons. The pictures are alike, then, in that all contain audiences, although of different sizes.

With an increase in size of the group, a speaker is likely to talk louder. However, exceptions are commonplace. You have probably heard your next-door neighbors raise their voices to a shout during a family quarrel. Vice versa, you have frequently heard speakers use quiet conversational tones when talking to an audience of hundreds by means of a public address system, or to millions via radio and television.

In larger groups the speakers usually stand in front of the listeners in order to make it easier for them to be seen and heard. The fourth and fifth photos remind you of how often the standing-sitting variable fluctuates.

The degree of formality offers no useful criterion. A student interview with the dean in his office can be more formal (and sometimes more formidable) than any talk given in a speech class.

A more interesting and complex variable is that of speaker-listener interaction. Thus you may argue that the first and second photos show situations where all the students talk and listen in alternation, whereas in public speaking one person does all the talking. But the several pictures raise some important questions. Even in conversations involving two or four or half a dozen participants, one person may do almost all of the talking. In the seminar shown in the third picture, the students usually take part by frequently interrupting the professor with questions, objections, or comments; the same thing is true of the class meeting on the lawn. Furthermore, in all the pictures, we know that the listeners are constantly "talking back" mentally, as well as by facial expressions and other overt responses.

You may always have supposed that there is a vast difference between conversation and public speaking. We now submit that none of the apparent differences is either inevitable or fundamental. They are differences of degree only, not of kind.

Resemblances Between Public Speaking and Conversation

All speaking situations, such as those illustrated by the photographs, have the fundamental characteristics described in our definition of speech and the definition of interindividual communication from which it was derived (pages 6–11). In each situation thought and emotion are communicated between speaker and listener through the same media (light and sound waves) and by the same kinds of signs and symbols (voice, language, and bodily action).

In both conversation and public speaking the transactions are always between or among individuals. A *group* cannot talk; only the individuals comprising the group can talk. Only the individuals can listen. There is no such thing as a "group mouth" or a "group ear" or a "group brain and nervous system." But you may object, "Individuals behave differently when they are in groups." Of course they do. The basic model of this interstimulation and response was illustrated by the diagram and the discussion on page 15. So when you give a classroom talk, do not think of your classmates as some mysterious "thing" called an audience. Instead, think of yourself as conversing with some friends who are interacting with you and with one another. What you are doing may be called public speaking, if you wish, but it is more usefully described as enlarged conversation.

The resemblances between conversation and public speaking are even illustrated by modern mass communication. Dr. Frank Baxter, award-winning pioneer in educational television, remarked in a personal conversation:

> If you think you are speaking to an audience of millions, it's enough to curdle anyone's liver. But I have learned to think of it differently. There is no such thing as *an* audience of 50 million people. There are innumerable little audiences, averaging perhaps 2.8 persons each, who are listening to you in their own living rooms on their own terms.

Relation to Confidence and Poise

Let us apply the above discussion to the problem of what is usually called stage fright. The author has talked about this problem with hundreds of students over the years, and has yet to find one who says that he is tense or nervous in an ordinary conversation with a friend; only a small percentage say that they are bothered by anxieties about an ordinary rap session or even a committee meeting; however, almost all of them have complained of some degree of psychological discomfort when called upon to do what they call "making a speech." The foregoing observations are corroborated by experimental research. A good example is the large-scale research conducted by McCroskey, involving several thousand beginning students.[1] One of McCroskey's findings was that significantly less

---

[1] James C. McCroskey, "Measures of Communication-Bound Anxiety," *Speech Monographs*, Vol. XXXVII, No. 4 (November 1970), pp. 269–77.

apprehension was shown on tests using words like "conversation" and "group discussion," than on tests using words like "public speaking" or "giving a speech." Such findings may be applied to the third and fourth pictures in the sequence. If one of the participants suddenly thought, "I'm making a public speech," the chances are that he would at once feel self-conscious and nervous; but as long as he thinks he is "conversing" or "discussing," he experiences no such sensations.

THE PROBLEM OF STAGE FRIGHT

If you are bothered by the expectation of some tension or nervousness, you have plenty of company. Many speech instructors at many schools over a long period of time have administered questionnaires at the beginning of a term, asking students to indicate what they hope to gain from the course. They have consistently found that about a third of the students list "gaining confidence and poise" as their number one goal, and that up to 90 percent of them list it among their top ten goals. That is why this chapter is included so early in this textbook. The great majority of students want to know the nature of the problem and what to do about it. This chapter will provide some guidelines based on scientific research and on the testimony of generations of experienced speakers.

How Prevalent?

In a pioneering research Gilkinson developed a test which he gave to 420 beginning speech students. Among other findings he reported that only 6 percent said yes to the item "Speaking in public is a pleasurable experience unaccompanied by any doubts or fears." [2] Dickens and Parker secured pulse and blood pressure readings immediately before and after classroom talks by 100 students; approximately 94 percent showed fluctuations from normal.[3] Using recently developed sophisticated equipment, Behnke and Carlile reported that "virtually every" student tested before, during, and after a classroom talk showed an elevated heart rate.[4] Various other tests and surveys have also shown that probably about 90 percent of all

[2] Howard Gilkinson, "Social Fears as Reported by Students in College Speech Classes," *Speech Monographs*, Vol. IX (1942), p. 147.
[3] Milton Dickens and William R. Parker, "An Experimental Study of Certain Physiological, Introspective and Rating-Scale Techniques for the Measurement of Stage Fright," *Speech Monographs*, Vol. XVIII, No. 4 (November 1951), pp. 251–59.
[4] Ralph R. Behnke and Larry W. Carlile, "Heart Rate as an Index of Speech Anxiety," *Speech Monographs*, Vol. XXXVIII, No. 1 (March 1971), pp. 65–69.

students experience some degree of nervous or emotional reaction toward speechmaking.

Immediately, however, it should be pointed out that these reactions are slight or moderate in the great majority of cases. This fact is clearly shown in the studies by McCroskey. His basic test for measuring college students' "feelings about communicating with other people" was given to 1,434 students at one university and 2,479 at another. These scores reveal an approximately normal distribution; that is, when presented as a graph they show the familiar bell-shaped "normal curve." Thus for about two-thirds of the students, the degree of apprehension may be described as slight or moderate. Only small percentages are found at either extreme of the scale. In another large-scale study Phillips administered a questionnaire to 4,500 students.[5] This was followed up by interviewing several hundred of them. About 5 percent were judged to be seriously disturbed by the prospect of taking a speech course. At Phillips' university, however, speech was required, indicating that the percentage would be much smaller where the course is an elective.

Thus the problem of stage fright is common to most beginning speakers. It is usually a perfectly natural and normal response to a somewhat new and challenging social situation.

How Difficult?

Over two thousand years ago Plutarch recorded that when Demosthenes, the most famous orator of ancient Greece, first addressed the people he was afflicted by "weakness in his voice, a perplexed and indistinct utterance and a shortness of breath. . . . So that in the end, being quite disheartened, he forsook the assembly." And Cicero, most famous of the ancient Roman orators, confessed through the words of Crassus:

> Assuredly, just as I generally perceive it to happen to yourselves, so I very often prove it in my own experience, that I turn pale at the outset of every speech, and quake in every limb and in all my soul.

Similar testimony has been added throughout the subsequent centuries by famous speakers, actors, musicians, and other public performers. Contrary to popular belief, however, these testimonies appear to be the exceptions. Research indicates that very few prominent and experienced speakers regularly suffer severe stage fright.

[5] Gerald M. Phillips, "Reticence: Pathology of the Normal Speaker," *Speech Monographs*, Vol. XXXV, No. 1 (March 1968), pp. 39–49.

Knisely, using a controlled interview technique, studied the stage-fright experiences of sixty highly experienced and successful speakers, all nationally prominent people. He found that fourteen of them (23.3 percent) never experience stage fright.[6] Wrenchley, in an entirely independent study, probed the careers of thirty other experienced speakers and reported that seven (also 23.3 percent!) had no stage fright.[7] Furthermore, Knisely found that of those who experienced stage fright the great majority described it as a mild nervous tension which disappeared soon after the beginning of a talk. Only three or four of the sixty could be said to find stage fright a continuing problem. They too, of course, were going ahead with regular and successful speaking engagements.

Speech communication teachers often request student evaluations of the class at the end of the term (anonymous, of course). Among the favorable comments are many mentions of gaining confidence in speaking both in and outside of class. More significant is the fact that most students do not touch upon this problem which so many of them had worried about during the first week; instead, they discuss such things as being able to organize their ideas more logically or to use words with greater precision. Even more satisfying to the instructor is the fact that frequently they go beyond the listing of personal benefits and write of an increased awareness of their role as a communicator in their community.

The candid camera shots on pages 30–31 show how a student during a period of about four minutes, while giving his first talk, visibly gained confidence as he shifted from talking to his notes and began talking to his listeners. Directly compare his appearance as he started talking (first photo) and as he concluded (fourth photo). The second and third shots suggest that improvement was by degrees. He began with the attitude of "I guess I think" and about three minutes later showed the first signs of the "you and I" attitude.

Students frequently testify that in the beginning they overestimated the difficulty of the problem of stage fright. One such student was asked at the first class meeting what he hoped to gain from the course, and he replied, "The most important thing is to learn to stand before an audience without being petrified." After giving his final speech, he exclaimed, "Four months ago I wouldn't have believed I could possibly do it!"

So, how difficult is the control of stage fright? Only as difficult as you make it.

---

[6] Wade A. Knisely, "An Investigation of the Phenomenon of Stage Fright in Certain Prominent Speakers," unpublished doctoral dissertation, University of Southern California, 1950.

[7] Elma D. Wrenchley, "A Study of Stage Fright Attacks in a Selected Group of Experienced Speakers," unpublished Master's thesis, University of Denver, 1948.

ATTITUDES THAT BUILD CONFIDENCE AND POISE

Almost any task can be made difficult if you keep telling yourself that it is difficult. If you are convinced that giving a classroom talk will be a frightening experience, probably it will be. The first major step toward gaining confidence and poise is likely to be the changing of some of your attitudes toward speechmaking. Concomitantly, you begin a practice program as is described presently. Just now, let us consider attitudes.

At this early stage we will use the term attitude in a broad non-technical sense, sometimes using roughly synonymous words, such as expectation, belief, feelings, or conviction. The attitudes discussed below should not be thought of as single entities—attitudes work in combinations and clusters.

If you do not consider stage fright a serious problem, you may read this chapter only to gain perspective and a sympathetic understanding of the problems of other people. If you have long-held, deeply-rooted misconceptions about speechmaking, you will need a little more time. You can make a start, however, right now.

Communication as Interaction

You already realize that giving a talk is not something the speaker does all by himself. You are not about to learn some completely new, unusual, almost abnormal behavior called "delivering a public speech." You are here to improve and enlarge your communicative abilities. You are not going to stand in splendid isolation and put on some kind of act or solo performance. Your talk is a process of speech communication, not an exhibition. You will participate in a number of interesting classroom projects, beginning with informal conversational ones, and progressing by natural stages through other less familiar speaking situations.

At the end of Chapter 1 the "you and I" attitude was recommended. At the beginning of this chapter you were encouraged toward a conversational attitude. In the give-and-take of an ordinary conversation you can easily recognize the two-way nature of the process; in larger groups you may become self-conscious and self-centered but the "two-wayness" is still there just the same. You are no longer talking to yourself as you did while practicing; you are now participating in a dialog with your classmates. If you become completely absorbed with your listeners and the ideas you are trying to share with them, you automatically crowd out such self-conscious thoughts as "How am I doing." Your attitude shifts from "me" to "them."

A comparison of the first and last pictures shows that this student gained confidence during a talk of about four minutes. He began with the attitude of "I guess I think,"...

As a starter, begin making friends with your classmates. You may find yourself doing this without even trying. But if you think you do not make friends easily, this class offers an opportunity for improvement. Friendliness begins with a genuine interest in other persons. Make a deliberate effort to chat with each of your classmates either in or outside the classroom. Listen with attention when a colleague is talking, and compliment him when he has done a good job. Everything you undertake in this course becomes easier when you know that you are doing it among friends. In learning to make a friend and to be one, you take a long stride toward a fuller understanding of the interactive processes that are occurring when you give a talk before a class or anywhere else.

Learning from Your Listeners

An unusual feature of a course in speech communication is that you receive personal evaluations and criticisms of your behaviors from your instructor and classmates. This feature is welcomed by some students but it shakes the confidence of many others. If you are in the latter category, you must build some new attitudes.

Negative feelings are expressed in a variety of ways: I look awkward when I get up to speak. My posture feels strange and unnatural. My face feels frozen. My smile is sickly. I am afraid of making embarrassing slips of the tongue. They will notice if my hands or knees tremble. What if I should forget? I am confused and don't know what I'm saying. I am afraid that I will make a fool of myself. Fears of this nature reflect the natural desire to make a good impression on others.

First of all, you should know that you look better than you feel. Dickens, Gibson, and Prall in a research study had forty students give short talks before an audience of sixty-one speech teachers. The teachers rated the students on how fearful they appeared to

and progressed by degrees to the beginnings of the "you and I" attitude.

be (one way of measuring poise). Then immediately after speaking, each student completed a test on how fearful he felt (one way of measuring confidence). When the listeners' ratings were compared with the speakers' self-ratings, it was found that the teachers over-estimated the students' confidence much more frequently than they underestimated it. In other words you are likely to appear more poised than you feel, even when judged by experts.[8]

After participating in the first few class projects, you will probably find that your expectations regarding personal criticisms in the class bear little resemblance to what actually occurs. When you listen to a colleague you will mostly be interested in what he talks about and what he says about it; you will be but slightly interested in looking for minor faults or mistakes. The same things are true of your instructor and most of your classmates when they listen to you. They will not be much impressed by such incidentals as slips of the tongue. If there are more important communication weaknesses, these will be evaluated as opportunities for improvement. Your instructor will appreciate your strong points and give credit when it is due. A few words of praise act like a tonic in building your confidence and poise. Later in the course you are likely to ask specifically for negative criticisms because you will have learned that overcoming faults is necessary for improvement. And the realization that you are steadily improving is a powerful confidence-builder.

Before long, you will come to accept criticism as an integral part of the course; you would feel shortchanged without it. By the end of the term you will probably be among the majority who single out the instructor's criticism as the most valuable part of their training.

[8] Milton Dickens, Francis Gibson, and Caleb Prall, "An Experimental Study of the Overt Manifestations of Stage Fright," *Speech Monographs,* Vol. XVII, No. 1 (March 1950), pp. 37–47.

Confidence as Emotional Control

We now say something that may startle you: Your speech goal is not to eliminate all nervousness or tension! As students sometimes bluntly say, "I find that I give a better talk when I come to class scared." Putting it yet another way: A sure method for antagonizing listeners is by revealing an attitude of overconfidence.

Before gaining much actual experience, some youthful would-be orators enjoy daydreams as charming as those in James Thurber's "The Secret Life of Walter Mitty." They envision some happy day when they will stride coolly and confidently before a huge and unruly crowd, deliver an eloquent address, and stand unmoved during the tremendous ovation that follows. With growing experience, however, they will learn that such a complete absence of emotion tends to make the speaker careless, condescending, or arrogant. Speaking experience will teach you that a certain amount of the right kind of tension is helpful.

In visualizing yourself as you will become by the end of this course, you should picture a person who has made great strides in emotional adjustment while facing an audience. You will feel more confident. You will appear more poised. Do *not* visualize yourself as strolling nonchalantly in front of a group and addressing them with no more tension than you would feel in saying, "Good morning," to your family as you join them for breakfast. Such a goal is possible but undesirable.

You want to *control* stage fright, not to eliminate it. You will learn to put your emotions to work, not to stifle them. Your nervous and emotional tension will be like the steam in a boiler. You will learn to release it so that it will give your speaking greater drive or punch.

Control involves more than a reduction of the frequency and severity of stage fright. There is a qualitative change as well. It is difficult to express this change in written words, but we may suggest it by saying that, over a period of time, the before-speaking sensations undergo a transition from a feeling of panic to a feeling of being keyed up. This keyed-up feeling may be unpleasant or pleasant or a mixture of both. The speaker is unafraid; he notes his inner tensions objectively and with satisfaction, knowing they will make him more alert, more vigorous, and more dynamic. He knows that soon after getting his speech under way he will forget these tensions, and he may even experience an overall sense of exhilaration.

Thus your objective in this class is not to become immune to the stimulus of an audience, but to develop emotional control. This objective may be usefully subdivided into three specific goals: (1) to effect a transition from the feeling of fear or panic to one of being keyed up; (2) to prevent the tension from becoming too severe immediately before speaking; (3) to learn how to release the tension effectively after the speech has begun.

PRACTICES THAT BUILD CONFIDENCE AND POISE

There are two keys to gaining confidence and poise. The first of these is a change of attitudes which has been discussed in the preceding section. The second key is practice. In his study of prominent speakers, Knisely reported:

> The one clear-cut and positive trend was that in fifty cases of the fifty-seven who had earlier experienced the problem, stage fright disappeared or diminished after the beginning of regular and frequent "practical" speaking careers. This phenomenon tended to occur regardless of the other known variables. In most cases, the results were reported as having occurred within less than a year after the beginning of intensive speaking series.

The same phenomenon has repeatedly been reported by speech teachers, as well as by members of organizations such as the Toastmaster and Toastmistress Clubs, where members have banded together for the purpose of practicing public speaking without the regular guidance of professional teachers. This class provides you with an opportunity to become gradually accustomed to facing a small audience, to gain experience through a series of classroom talks, to secure feedback from classmates, and to receive guidance from your instructor. Thus the process of building new attitudes will be blended with the process of putting them into practice.

This entire book emphasizes practical practices. At this juncture, therefore, we will describe a program particularly relevant to gaining confidence and poise. This program comprises specific procedures, many of which have been successfully used by public speakers for centuries, and many of which you should make habitual. You will, of course, adapt the following suggestions to your particular needs.

On Days Prior to the Talk

a. Choose a subject of special interest to you. Have you ever had an unusual experience that has affected you ever since? Tell the class about it. Have you come across information that has been invaluable to you? Share it with them. Do you believe deeply in some cause? Make an honest plea for it. If you can find a subject in which you are so interested that you can lose yourself in it, then self-consciousness is automatically reduced to a minimum.

b. Know your subject thoroughly. Some insidious siren seems to beckon beginning speakers to the *Reader's Digest* for speech subjects and then impels them to limit their study of the subject to that one condensed article. The *Reader's Digest* was never intended for such use. Do not try to give a digest of a digest. In the beginning speak only about subjects upon which you have a background of personal experience. Personal experience should often be reinforced by additional study, for you want to begin your speech knowing more about your subject than anyone else present, and knowing that you know it. Naturally you should not try to tell everything you know in one short talk; but confidence springs from the very fact that you couldn't possibly tell all you know on the subject in the time allowed. One of the highest compliments anyone can pay a speaker is to say he certainly knows what he's talking about. It is within your power to earn that compliment.

Begin your preparation early. Do not wait until a vacant period just before your speech class. Do not tire yourself by working far into the preceding night. You should give yourself several days for your speech so that your thinking on the subject will have time to mature. Talk about your subject with your friends; think about it while riding the bus; give it a chance to grow.

c. Learn the idea sequence of your talk. Out of all you know about a subject, you must make choices of which items to discard, which to use. Once chosen, the points must be arranged in sequence. Write them on a card and study them. You will soon learn that you cannot get lost as long as this card is available. It becomes your first important protection against the common fear, "What if I should forget?"

d. Practice aloud. Detailed suggestions for practicing aloud are given in the next chapter. Of special importance here, however, is that you practice extemporaneously from a single card of notes. Talk loud enough so that you become used to your own voice. Run through all of the items on the card, wording each one in much the same fashion as you word your ideas during a conversation. Revise the card if that seems needed. Then talk through it several more times. Do not try to use the same words each time. Changing wording is an ordinary experience in daily conversations, for instance, when a friend says, "Would you mind stating that again?" You restate it, probably in different words.

It is sometimes hard to convince a beginner that the best way to prevent forgetting is *not* to memorize. He thinks he would feel a lot safer if he wrote the entire speech and committed it to memory. But that is the hard way. It stands to reason that if a set of words has not been memorized, it cannot be forgotten—there are no words to forget. "But," you object, "if I don't memorize, I won't be able to say anything." Actually, it doesn't work out that way—as you will discover from class discussions and other early projects.

On the Day of the Talk

a. Chat with others.   If you are scheduled to speak in class today, come a bit early and sit down next to an acquaintance. Talk with him and keep your mind off your speech. Talk with people as they arrive. Keep your mind on them. Such talk will remind you that public speaking is simply enlarged conversation. Chat with friends individually or in small groups before you make your talk; you will do exactly the same thing a little later when you make it.

b. Concentrate on the proceedings.   When the class gathers, there will be remarks by the instructor or others before you give your talk. Follow these proceedings with interest. Pay attention and be genuinely absorbed in what is said and done. Above all, watch carefully for something that you can use as part of your opening remarks. This watching serves a dual purpose. It keeps your mind off yourself, preventing the build-up of undue tension, and it provides you with one of the best possible types of opening remarks.

c. Stretch and yawn.   If you feel "butterflies" fluttering during this period, watch for an opportunity to stretch. The muscles of the arms, shoulders, and neck can always be tensed and relaxed energetically in this fashion without attracting attention. And usually it is possible to yawn once or twice surreptitiously behind your hand or handkerchief. Yawning relaxes the jaws and throat, and will improve your voice quality when you begin.

d. Breathe slowly and regularly.   You can always force yourself to breathe slowly, a little more deeply than usual, and *regularly*. Regular breathing results in a notable calming effect on the whole body.

e. Walk to the platform confidently.   When you have been called upon or introduced, do not drag toward the front of the room as if you were approaching a scaffold, but walk briskly. Regardless of how you think you feel, walk as though you were completely poised and confident.

f. Pause before starting.   Approach the spot from which you plan to speak so that your last step will be toward the audience. Then pause, take a comfortable stance, look directly at one or two friends or acquaintances in the group, smile at them, and start talking.

While Speaking

a. Look at individuals. Do not try to look at your audience as a whole; keep on looking at and talking to the several individuals whom you know—possibly the same ones with whom you were chatting just before the meeting. Talk loud enough to be heard but make the talk enlarged conversation.

b. Move about. Plan to move about a good deal during the first minute or so. Find easy, natural things to do. Readjust the speaker's stand; open and close a book; if you can make use of a simple chart, walk to the chalkboard and draw one; use gestures to describe the shape or size of some object you have mentioned. The way to relax here is through purposeful physical action. During the first one or two talks, if it will make you feel at home, lounge upon the speaker's stand. Of course, you will want to discard such crutches as soon as possible, but at first get rid of pent-up energy. This prevents you from "freezing up."

c. Concentrate on your subject and audience. Your major purpose is to communicate your ideas as effectively as possible. Keep talking to and watching your listeners as you do in conversation. Here is where your oral practice pays off; it makes it possible for you to concentrate on the thoughts instead of on the words.

d. If for any reason your mind goes blank, you are still all right. First, repeat your last statement. Usually the repetition will put you back on the track of your thought. Second, if you are still lost consult your notes; consult them deliberately and then go ahead. Third, don't be afraid to take the audience into your confidence—as a last resort, grin at them and say, "Well I'm stuck. I had something planned to say at this point but just can't remember it. I guess all of you have been in the same boat at some time." Then repeat your last statement again or jump to your next point. Usually you can go on talking conversationally until the thread of your thought returns. When an experienced speaker forgets, he is not disturbed. He is likely to say, "Let's see now, there was something else I wanted to say to you about this matter . . . Oh yes, it was. . . ." You will learn by experience that forgetting is not a serious problem.

SUMMARY

A solid foundation on which to build a program for gaining confidence and poise is the concept that classroom talks are more usefully described as enlarged conversation rather than as public speaking. The control of stage fright is further assisted by an understanding that it is a common and normal experience, and that beginners tend to exaggerate the seriousness and difficulty of the problem. There are two keys to gaining confidence and poise: attitudes and practices. Three desirable attitudes are that classroom talks should be recognized as interactions, not exhibitions; that critical responses from listeners are a necessary step toward improvement; and that the objective is to control rather than stifle emotional response to an audience. The other key is frequent planned practice. Planning should include specific practices during the advance preparation of a talk, immediately before speaking, and while speaking.

TOPICAL PREVIEW

I Where to begin

II Steps in preparation
    A Analyze the audience
    B Choose the subject
        1 Appropriate early subjects
        2 Testing speech subjects
    C Determine the purpose
    D Gather the materials
    E Build the outline
        1 The beginning, middle, and end
        2 The speech unit
    F Practice the delivery
        1 Place
        2 Use of notes
        3 Wording
        4 Voice
        5 Posture and movement

III Summary

Preparing the First Speeches

WHERE TO BEGIN

Every speech, whether it be by a freshman addressing his class or by the President of the United States addressing Congress, includes all the fundamentals of speechmaking: communication, thought and emotion, voice, language, bodily action, speaker, audience, and occasion. But no one can master all the fundamentals at once; certainly you cannot before you give your first talk. Recognizing that fact, we will begin with the minimum information necessary to you for the preparation and presentation of your first speeches; but at the same time we will try to give you a perspective on the entire process. The study in expanding detail of that process will continue throughout this book and this course.

STEPS IN PREPARATION

The process of preparing a speech may be divided into six steps.

1. Analyze the audience.
2. Choose the subject.
3. Determine the purpose.

4. Gather the materials.
5. Build the outline.
6. Practice the delivery.

Analyze the Audience

Whether or not the speaker communicates anything, how well he communicates, and what he communicates can be decided only by the listeners. No other standard of speaking effectiveness will make sense. The verdict of the audience may be wrong, but it is still the verdict. The audience is the speaker's supreme court. Thus Chapters 1 and 2 stressed that students of speech communication should begin early to develop an interactive you-and-I attitude. This attitude requires interest in and knowledge about the members of the audience. Securing information about the listeners should be the first step in speech preparation; the application of that information should modify every remaining step.

Your speech communication class will be your only audience for a while. Size up your classmates, individually and collectively. You can tell by simply looking around you that the class comprises X number of women and Y number of men. You can roughly estimate their average age, noting perhaps one or two exceptions. You can tell by appearance most of the ethnic origins. You can sometimes make deductions about backgrounds or life-styles from dress and hairstyles.

Next, as recommended in Chapter 2, you begin getting acquainted and making friends. Memorize everyone's name. Chat with everyone individually or by twos and threes whenever the opportunity permits. Exchange information about home towns, majors, extracurricular activities, or views on current topics of campus interest. If all or most class members show an interest in the other persons, an *esprit de corps* soon develops.

Your instructor may conduct an anonymous class poll to discover additional information, such as political and religious preferences, and attitudes toward a list of persistent or current social problems. Thus all members will have useful data about their "laboratory" audience.

Meanwhile, begin to pay closer attention to the reactions of listeners in other classes, at informal student gatherings, at campus rallies, and at off-campus meetings. Clues regarding what to observe are often provided by audience pictures throughout this book. Then in later chapters, especially Chapter 11, we will be ready to broaden and systematize this important matter of audience analysis.

Choose the Subject

APPROPRIATE EARLY SUBJECTS   "What shall I talk about?" may
be a troublesome question. Your trouble may be that you are not sure
just what you are looking for. One student, for example, associated
"speech" with the speeches he could recall from his elementary
and high school studies. They were Patrick Henry's "Give Me
Liberty," Lincoln's "Gettysburg Address," Webster's "Reply to
Hayne," and a few others. In searching for similar subjects to use
in the classroom he was stalled, and no wonder. A few minutes
of conversation with his instructor revealed that the student was
working part time as a shoe salesman. Why not talk about selling
shoes? "You mean *that* would be acceptable for a *speech?*" he asked
in astonishment. Well, he worked out a talk with the title "If the
Shoe Fits," which proved to be an amusing and provocative discussion of the psychology of salesmanship.

Let us take a few more examples of typical subjects that have
been successfully used by speech students. A music major talked on
"The Most Important Musical Instrument," which turned out to be
the conductor's baton; the student explained what a symphony
conductor must be able to do. A history major talked on "Benedict
Arnold Was *Not* a Traitor." A young woman discussed the local
marriage course, and asked, "Can Marriage Be Taught?" A skin-
diving enthusiast described his sport, exhibited the necessary para-
phernalia—goggles and flippers—and finally produced an enormous
live lobster which he had caught the previous day. "What's Wrong
with Our High Schools?" was discussed by a student teacher who
thought he knew, and who had a thought-provoking opinion. An
advertising major criticized television commercials, using the title
"At Laughably Low Prices." A political science major with a talk on
"How to Win a Public Opinion Poll" made his class ponder an aspect
of democracy. "The Worst Speech I Ever Heard" was vividly described by a student who hoped to do better. A chess hobbyist talked
on "How Bobby Fischer Climbed to the World Championship,"
offering an opinion on the breaking of the chess-title monopoly of
Russian grandmasters. A car-repair experience stimulated one student to delve into the general problem of "Unscrupulous Auto
Mechanics." "An Alcoholic in the Family" was described by a student who was not a heavy drinker but had to live with one.

Additional lists of suggested subjects are provided at appropriate
times later in this text. Such lists are intended to be suggestive, not
prescriptive. As you read the samples, you will be stimulated to
think of similar subjects of your own.

The finding of subjects is your responsibility. You are going to
talk about your own experiences or ideas, your own thoughts and

feelings. You are the only person who knows what they are. You must make the choices. Your instructor will be glad to help, but do not expect him to do the job for you.

TESTING SPEECH SUBJECTS Once you have a list of possible speech subjects, how can you choose among them? The first speech topic should usually be one where you can draw mostly on your personal experience. There are two main tests: Are you interested in it? Can you interest the audience in it? As you progress in the course you will want to discuss subjects of increasing difficulty, seriousness, and significance. In assessing the comparative merits of future speech subjects, the following seven tests are helpful:

1. Does the subject reflect my personal interests and qualifications?
2. Can I relate the subject to the interests of the audience?
3. Does the subject suggest a clear-cut, specific speech purpose?
4. Is it appropriate to the assigned class project?
5. Can the subject be adequately handled within the time limits?
6. How much information about the subject do I already have?
7. Is additional information available?

Determine the Purpose

Many speakers, even experienced ones, are, to quote Owen Young, "in the same boat with Christopher Columbus. He didn't know where he was going when he started. When he got there he didn't know where he was, and when he got back he didn't know where he had been." Such speakers are apparently just out for a verbal walk. They may enjoy it, but the audience is not likely to. The listeners do not like aimless meandering. They expect a speaker to have a definite purpose. You should have a specific goal in mind as a guide when you begin preparing a talk. And your goal is not simply "to talk about" a general topic for three to five minutes.

Whatever the specific purpose of any speech may be, there is an overall purpose common to all speeches—to get an audience response. For practical use, let us break down that overall purpose into four general purposes:

General Purpose	Audience Responses Sought
To entertain	Favorable attention; enjoyment
To inform	Clear understanding; learning
To stimulate	Strengthening of a belief
To convince	A change of belief

Sometimes we seek only to influence the audience's thoughts and feelings. At other times we seek, in addition, to produce overt action as a part of the response. For example, in a talk to entertain we may want not only silent appreciation but also laughter and applause; in a talk to inform, not only covert learning, but also overt demonstration (as in answering examination questions correctly); in talks to stimulate or convince, not only belief, but also action (in such form as voting or giving money or signing a petition).

But a general purpose is not enough. Your speech must have a specific purpose. Thus, don't be content to say, "My purpose is to inform." And it doesn't help much to add "about football." Be as specific as possible, such as, "My purpose is to make clear to my audience the differences between the I formation and the wishbone T."

Gather the Materials

Your next move is to take an inventory of the knowledge you already have about the subject. This may be enough. If you are a member of the football team, for example, it is likely that you already have an extensive knowledge of the I formation and the wishbone T. As a rule, however, you will need to supplement your current knowledge by further research.

The three main methods for gathering speech materials are observation, conversation, and reading. If you are qualified to give a talk on some aspect of electronic computers, you should probably draw largely upon your observations of the machines in action. If you choose to speak on student attitudes toward space travel, you might secure your best materials by conducting an informal poll through conversations with various student leaders. On most subjects, however, you should read as widely as possible. On almost any current subject you can readily find a variety of books, magazine articles, or newspaper reports. Read from more than one source. In many cases you will want to cite your sources during the speech, so be careful to take notes on your exact references as well as on the materials themselves.

Build the Outline

1. THE BEGINNING, MIDDLE, AND END   An elderly preacher, renowned for his sermons, was asked how he made them so effective. "Well," he replied, "first, I tell them what I'm going to say; then I say it; then I tell them what I have said." He had a good basic outline that illustrates the first important principle of outlining: there should be a beginning, a middle, and an end. These three parts have been traditionally called introduction, body, and conclusion. The beginning, middle, and the end have different functions which are discussed in detail in Chapters 6 and 7. Your first classroom talks are likely to be relatively brief and limited to one main point.

The functions of the three divisions may be suggested as follows: introduction (How should I get into my main point?); body (How should I develop the point?); conclusion (How can I cinch it?). Negatively put: introduction (Don't just stumble into a discussion of your main point); body (Don't ramble); conclusion (Don't leave your discussion dangling in midair).

2. THE SPEECH UNIT   You begin by thinking about your subject until you can decide on what the main point of the talk will be. Then put that in the form of a short declarative statement. For your first class talk, be sure there is only one main point; and be careful not to make it too broad or ambitious. Then pick one or more items from your available materials that will develop or support your main point. Perhaps the easiest way to select those materials is to speak the main statement aloud and immediately add, "For example, . . ." That is likely to suggest an anecdote or quotation or some facts or figures. *A statement and one or more items of support, together with necessary transition statements, constitute a "speech unit," which is the basis of all speech organization.*

Let us illustrate by means of a pair of contrasting examples. The main point is exactly the same in both cases. The first example shows an ineffective way of organizing the speech unit; the second shows an effective way.

INTRODUCTION

STUMBLING
INTO THE
MAIN POINT

In trying to find a topic for today I thought of about half a dozen of them. Main points, I mean. But I couldn't think of anything that would interest very many of you. Finally I thought of an idea that applies to all of us. And that point is that there is no use trying to please everybody.

NO TRANSITION

BODY

WEAK SUPPORT
OF POINT

This is an important and interesting topic. I believe that the point is a true one. After all, human nature is human nature. On most questions, some people believe in one side, other people believe the opposite side, and still others believe yet another side. If you cater to one group, you will probably antagonize the others. If you try to reconcile all the contradictory points of view, you will probably be accused of being an appeaser. Furthermore, you cannot appease them all without sacrificing your real principles. And, after all, what is more important than one's prin-

STRAYING
FROM
POINT

ciples? They are the real lamps by which our feet should be guided. If we are willing to depart from our principles, we cannot be trusted. Therefore, you might better decide from the start upon your basic principles; chart your course like a mariner who wishes to cross a stormy sea; and take a consistent stand regardless of what other people think. Too many people try to steer their ships in terms of what the neighbors will say. But if we try to be guided by what the neighbors say, we will constantly have to turn the steering wheel because some of our neighbors will say one thing while at the same time another neighbor will say something else.

CONFUSED AND
CONFUSING
METAPHOR

NO TRANSITION

CONCLUSION

DANGLING

There are a lot more things that might be said about the topic. But I guess all of you have had plenty of experiences that prove my point.

The main point is supported mostly by restating the point, and to some extent by a weak explanation. The sequence of sentences is logical only in a loose, free-associational sense. The sample illustrates a typical, ineffective development of an idea.

For contrast, consider another way of developing the same talk.

INTRODUCTION

MAIN POINT

There is no use trying to please everybody.

TRANSITION

Aesop illustrated this point hundreds of years ago when he related the fable of the farmer who made a journey in company with his son and his mule.

BODY

SUPPORT
(anecdote)

This farmer and his son and the mule started their journey by walking along the public road in single file. Presently they passed a group of neighbors, and the farmer overheard someone say, "Look at those stupid people—walking when one of them might just as well ride the mule." Not wishing to be considered stupid by his neighbors, the farmer mounted the mule, and the journey was continued. Soon they passed another group of travelers, and the farmer was shocked to hear one of them remark, "There goes an example of a

CHRONOLOGICAL
SEQUENCE

father who likes to pose as a king—he rides in comfort but forces his young son to trudge in the heat and dust." Sensitive to such criticism, the farmer at once changed places with his son. This was all right until they passed another pair of travelers. One of them said to the other, "Just observe that ridiculous picture—a healthy, strapping boy riding the mule while his poor old father must walk." Much chagrined, the farmer thought of another solution; he mounted behind his son and both of them rode. But shortly they encountered another group, and this time the farmer flinched at the criticism, "Seldom will you see worse cruelty—two big strong men riding that exhausted little animal." So the farmer and his son dismounted, secured the mule's feet with a rope over a timber, and began carrying the mule. They were crossing a bridge where the mule, upside down, looked into the water with alarm and began to kick so vigorously that all three members of the party toppled off into the water.

BUILDING
TOWARD THE
POINT

TRANSITION

The moral of Aesop's fable is clear.

CONCLUSION

CLOSES WITH
A SNAP

If you try to please everybody, you usually end up by pleasing nobody.

This talk consists of a single *unit*, the principal parts of which are one main *point* and one *support*. The point is in the form of a *statement* and the support is in the form of an *anecdote*. The point is also in the form of a *restatement* at the end of the unit. Point, support, and restatement are linked together by *transitions*.

You will see that a brief one-unit talk does not require an elaborate outline. As you think through the organizational plan, you should sketch the plan on a sheet of scratch paper. In the Aesop example you first write down the statement of the main point, using special care as to the exact wording. As soon as you have decided to develop the main point by means of the fable, you think through the sequence of events as the farmer progresses along the road, and you may need to juggle the sequence until you think you have it right. Then you review possible ways of concluding the talk. Thus, your finished outline would consist of three statements and a few substatements. Something like this:

I. There is no use trying to please everybody.
    (Transition)

II. Aesop's fable.
    A. They lead the mule.
    B. Farmer rides.
    C. Son rides.
    D. Both ride.
    E. They carry the mule.
   (Transition)
III. If you try to please everybody, you usually end up by pleasing nobody.

You should not suppose, of course, that the best way to open a talk is always by stating your main point; or that the only way to develop a point is always by relating an anecdote; or that the best way to conclude is always by restating your main point. Suppose you began by implying or leading toward the main point, "I recently read in sometimes tedious detail all of the promises made in the platforms of both the Democratic and Republican parties. I had an overall reaction to both of the platforms. That reaction was expressed hundreds of years ago when Aesop wrote a fable about the farmer who. . . ." Then you relate the fable. You close by returning to the political platforms and how they contain contradictory promises in an effort to please everybody.

In the beginning you should avoid complicated outlines (they will be analyzed in Chapters 6 and 7) and focus on the use of two organizational concepts discussed immediately above: the basic plan (introduction, body, conclusion), and the speech unit (point, support, transitions).

Practice the Delivery

Special emphasis in this chapter is given to your development of a practice program, and most of the suggestions below deal with details. But do not dismiss them as trivial or suppose that they are "mere" skills. Your noblest aspirations and most significant thoughts are communicated to others through signs and symbols—voice, language, and bodily actions. Mastery of such tools is basic to all forms of communication. In the beginning, Einstein had to master the skills of simple arithmetic. Even the mighty Beethoven at some early stage had to master the keyboard and even learn to operate the foot pedals of a piano. Winston Churchill practiced his historic World War II speeches aloud, still struggling with some articulatory difficulties that he had not systematically attacked during his student years.

The importance of "mere" skills is illustrated in the pictures on pages 48–49 of a typical first classroom talk. This student discussed an interesting subject and had worthwhile ideas about it. But as you can see, he kept his eyes glued to his too-copious notes, he did not

move away from the lectern, his posture was poor, and he did not know what to do with his hands. These details were rapidly corrected, and a few weeks later his communicativeness became so much improved that he laughed heartily when shown these pictures.

1. PLACE   Your object should be to work out a habitual practice routine that will be tailor-made for your temperament. We will describe a possible routine, indicating various alternative details. Give it a trial, making adjustments as experience reveals the procedures that work best for you.

Suppose you are scheduled to give a three-minute talk on Friday. Complete your outline by Wednesday and practice aloud from it several times that day. Do the bulk of the practice Thursday. Run through the talk only once on Friday, an hour or two before you are to give it. In general, several shorter practice periods are better than one long period.

When you are ready to begin practice, choose a place suited to your temperament. You may prefer to practice in the privacy of your own room or perhaps an available empty classroom. You may wish to tape-record your efforts and play-back immediately after each rehearsal. However you should keep your audience in mind. It may be helpful to rig up a dummy as a reminder, or you may find that you do better by enlisting the services of a classmate or other friend to be your audience and perhaps also your critic.

2. USE OF NOTES   The first time or two you practice aloud, you may wish to use the entire outline that you have prepared. Then transfer or condense it onto one or two cards; cards are easier to

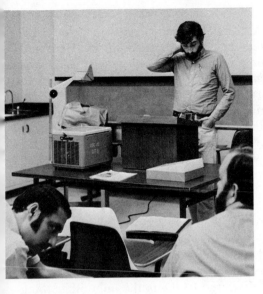

In his first classroom talk this student is notebound—he never looks at his listeners.
He never moves from behind the rostrum.
And he does not know what to do with his hands.

handle and not as conspicuous as sheets of paper. The four by six size is good—big enough to hold a good many notes yet small enough for easy handling. For a brief talk, the outline or notes will usually go on one card, two at most. You should be able to see the whole structure at a glance so that you will always have the pattern of your ideas clearly before you. Perhaps print them in large letters for easier reading. Resist the urge to make your notes too detailed. Recall that the entire outline for the Aesop talk is brief enough to be typed on one side of one card. And after a couple of oral practices, you may not need the entire outline—perhaps only a few key words or phrases.

3. WORDING Glance at the first item of your notes, look at your imaginary audience, and begin talking. Talk your way through the outline this first time regardless of difficulties. Refer to the notes as frequently as you wish, but keep your eyes toward the "audience" the rest of the time. Your first problem will be that of language—putting your ideas into words. As you take up each item in the outline, word your thought as you would in conversation. At first your flow of words will probably be hesitant and awkward, but stagger on. If in wording an idea you reach a dead end, go back and approach the idea from a slightly different angle. If you pause while struggling for the right words, don't worry. Just pause. But let the pause alone. Don't give way to the temptation to fill it with "and" or "uh" or other meaningless sounds.

After the first time through, sit down and think about the outline—possibly make a few adjustments in it. Then get up and start again. Time this trial. Eventually, you must develop a sense of speech timing, but it comes only from much practice with the clock. On this second trial, you will find that you are more fluent. Here and there you will find a word or phrase coming out exactly as it was the first time. That is all right, but make no conscious attempt to use the same words as before; avoid word for word memorization. If you stall occasionally while groping for the right word later on when you are giving the talk to the class, the pause can increase your effectiveness, can show your audience that you are thinking and not just reciting like a myna bird. The second time through, you should not refer to the notes so frequently. An occasional glance should suffice.

4. VOICE As soon as the words begin to flow a little better, you can begin giving some attention to your voice. First, talk loud enough to be heard—just a little louder than in ordinary conversation. Don't shout or strain. Avoid letting your voice die away at the ends of clauses or sentences. Variety of tone is the only other thing to watch in the beginning. Try to avoid speaking at the same rate or in a monotone. In conversation you vary your tone, its pitch and loudness, and you change speed. Try for that conversational variety as you practice.

5. POSTURE AND MOVEMENT After several trial runs you will have limbered up your vocabulary, freed yourself from over-dependence on the outline, and become accustomed to hearing your voice. You can then consider the third element of your delivery: bodily action. For this part of your practice, a large mirror is helpful.

See to it that your posture is good; look alert and yet at ease. It would be nice if this could be achieved by saying, "just stand naturally." Your habitual posture will feel natural to you, yet your habitual posture may be very bad. Stand in front of the mirror and experiment. Find a way of standing that looks natural and at the same time feels comfortable. If in doubt, check the result later with your instructor. When you get up in front of the audience for the first time or two, you may forget your practiced posture and succumb to the temptation of leaning on the speaking stand for support. Lounging on the stand is, of course, not recommended for continued use, but it may be all right at first to put yourself at ease. It is better to look slouchy and at ease than to give the impression that rigor mortis has set in.

Next, practice changing your position before the mirror. During a speech it is wise to move about once in a while in order to punctuate thought, help hold the listeners' attention, and reduce nervous tension. Put a chair in front of the mirror and practice moving about the chair. Stand behind it and talk; rest the right hand lightly on the chair back as you move from behind and forward to the left.

Then try again with the left hand on the chair as you move forward to the right. Adjust your movements until they look natural to you in the mirror.

A common problem at first is that you don't know what to do with your hands. Look again at the pictures of the student giving his first classroom talk. In addition to his hands' difficulty, he was note-bound throughout the talk. He should have looked at his listeners, and he did do this in his next talk. Immediately, he had less trouble with his hands, and he also showed some animation in voice and facial expression. He was no longer talking to his notes; he began interacting with his classmates.

Do not worry yet about gestures. If you feel the urge to gesture, go ahead. Otherwise, practice allowing your arms to hang relaxed at your sides. You may also rest hands or forearms lightly on the rostrum but do not clutch it. For variety you may occasionally clasp your hands behind your back—but again, lightly—and do not make this your predominant position.

You will discover that you cannot do everything at once. You need time and practice. When you rehearse give your attention each time to a single problem. How many times should you rehearse a given speech? From three to a dozen. You needn't expect to attain perfection. Progress is enough.

Now let us go back to the speech you were preparing for Friday. Rehearse about four times Wednesday, about six times Thursday, and once Friday morning. Then when you get up to give the talk, *forget all about the delivery details you were practicing!* Keep your mind concentrated only on the thought and the audience. The goal of this type of practicing is to make your delivery mechanisms habitual, so that when you are speaking you have only the ideas and the audience to think about. Eventually your delivery will take care of itself.

SUMMARY

The major steps of speech preparation are analyzing the audience, choosing the subject, determining the purpose, gathering the materials, building the outline, and practicing the delivery. All six of these steps will be studied in gradually expanding detail throughout this course. In preparing the first speeches two things are especially useful. First, you should learn to outline a speech unit consisting of a statement and supports. Second, you should establish a routine for practicing aloud, speaking extemporaneously from brief notes.

An outline is to speech construction as a blueprint is to building construction. This picture of President Eisenhower provides an example of a key-word outline that is condensed from a detailed one.

Speech Construction

TOPICAL PREVIEW

I   Importance of speech purpose

II Avoiding common mistakes
    A   Attempting too much
    B   Attempting too little
    C   Attempting the wrong thing

III Choosing the general purpose
    A   One purpose only
    B   Factors influencing choice
        1   Audience attitudes toward topic
        2   Other factors

IV Stating the general purpose

V   Making the general purpose specific
    A   Stating the specific purpose
    B   Centering the purpose on the audience
    C   Making the specific purpose concrete

VI Summary

Speech Purposes

IMPORTANCE OF SPEECH PURPOSE

The importance of aiming every speech toward a definite goal seems obvious, yet students often prepare and deliver speeches without ever consciously thinking about speech purpose. A typical example was the student who gave a talk advocating that cola drinks and coffee should be forbidden because they contain caffeine, and caffeine is harmful to health. The audience responded to the talk with a mixture of boredom, irritation, and confusion. The instructor questioned the speaker.

"Bill, what was your speech purpose?"

"Well, I wanted to show the dangers of cola drinks and coffee."

"Then your purpose was not to entertain us?"

"No."

"Was it to inform?"

"Well, yes, I think so."

"What did you want us to learn?"

"About those dangers."

"But we already knew about them, Bill. All of us knew that these drinks contain caffeine, and that caffeine is sometimes harmful."

"I suppose you're right."

"Was your purpose to convince?"

"Yes, that's it, to convince."

"Convince us that we should stop drinking coffee?"

"Yes."

"But you didn't say that. You said that these drinks should be forbidden. Did you mean forbidden by law?"

"I thought so."

"But you didn't describe such a law. Is a law pending?"

"I don't know."

"Apparently you hadn't thought about the purpose of your speech until now."

"I guess not."

This example shows that a purposeless speech is usually a futile speech, and that a speaker should always determine in advance the audience response he hopes to get. A well-chosen speech purpose guides a speaker through all the steps of speech preparation and presentation, keeping him steadily on a course, constantly reminding him of his goal. A poorly chosen speech purpose misleads a speaker, dissipating his efforts.

AVOIDING COMMON MISTAKES

Attempting Too Much

Perhaps the most common error among beginning speakers in choosing a speech purpose is that of attempting to get audience responses that could not possibly be achieved. The error may take any of several forms.

Select a speech subject that can be adequately presented within the time limit. Suppose your general purpose is to inform, and your time limit is three minutes. One student actually undertook to explain the Einstein theory in that time! Could you clarify the psychology of learning in three minutes? No. Could you cover "How to Study" in three minutes? No. What could you hope to cover? Something like "The Best Study Method I Have Found"? Probably.

Speakers sometimes attempt subjects that are too broad for a single speech regardless of time. There is no use in trying to cover "The History of Religion" in one talk—that could scarcely be covered in a year's course in college. You would have to plan carefully in order to do justice to "The History of Our University Chapel" in one speech of ordinary length.

Sometimes a speaker exhorts the audience to an action that is beyond its power. Does your proposal cost money? Does it take time? Does it require special skills? Does it assume special knowledge? Such questions highlight the importance of considering carefully exactly what lies within the power of a given group to perform in reference to your subject. If, for example, you are a member of the executive council of an organization and a disturbing problem has arisen, much time may be wasted by members speaking in favor of actions that a reading of the society's constitution would reveal as beyond the council's legal authority.

Finally, a speaker may attempt more than his status or his own speaking abilities make possible. A speaker who is highly respected by a group can attempt a more difficult purpose than someone who is unknown or disliked. An expert can attempt more than a novice. The trouble is that some beginning speakers lack insight into their own limitations. One student takes a course in psychology and immediately imagines that he can tell other people how to live their lives. Another student makes a hit with one audience and imagines that he is a born speaker. A little bit of knowledge or a little bit of success may therefore be a dangerous thing. Or, to reinforce one platitude with another, fools rush in where angels fear to tread.

Attempting Too Little

Sometimes a speaker attempts too little. Be wary of such topics as "My Most Enjoyable Summer Vacation." A speaker should avoid trivial purposes. Of course, triviality is often a matter of opinion. A member of the faculty might consider trivial a talk to convince an audience that dormitory rules for freshmen women should be changed; a freshman woman might rightly entertain an opposite opinion. Nevertheless, endless amounts of time are wasted at all sorts of meetings by speakers whose apparent purposes are not worth achieving. At the salesmen's meeting of a large company one salesman spends thirty minutes advocating a small change in procedure that would have been granted immediately on a simple one-sentence request. In club meetings everywhere hours are wasted by members strenuously trying to convince the group regarding some unimportant refinement of parliamentary procedure.

A speaker may attempt too little because he fails to adjust his purpose to audience knowledge or attitudes. You decide to inform your audience about Abraham Lincoln. But what do you do? You recite briefly the highlights of Lincoln's career with which every listener is already familiar. You should go beyond the audience's existing knowledge and inform them of some aspect of Lincoln's life that is new to them. Or you are asked to give a classroom talk with the general purpose to convince, and you prove to your listeners that they should drive safely. But all of them would agree with your proposition without your making the speech. You should attempt more—assume that they believe in safe driving and go on from there. Perhaps you could convince them that certain traffic regulations should be changed. In any speech where your purpose includes overt action, you attempt too little if you ask the auditors to do something they have already done. For example, a minister worked himself into a lather in a lengthy sermon summoning his audience to join the church, when at least 95 percent of his congregation were already members.

Finally, a speaker may attempt too little because he is too lazy to attempt more. Information may be minimum, or proofs may be thin, because the speaker did not give enough time to research and thought.

Attempting the Wrong Thing

Sometimes a speaker's purpose is inappropriate to the audience or occasion.

A local lawyer was asked to deliver a Memorial Day address at a famous country cemetery. After a few words at the beginning in which he touched upon the day and the honored dead, he launched into a discussion of public policies and ended with a political harangue urging his audience to vote for his party at the next elections. The audience was offended. His speech purpose was inappropriate to the occasion.

A university professor wrote an important scientific book that received a lot of publicity. He was invited to speak before the Kiwanis Club of his city. He read a learned scientific paper. The audience slept. Two days later most of them could not even describe his general topic. His speech purpose was inappropriate to the interests of his audience.

A government official was speaking before a convention of the local medical society. He tried to convince the doctors that they should support a plan to provide complete medical care at public expense. The speech purpose was inappropriate to the doctors' attitudes toward socialized medicine. All the speaker succeeded in doing was to antagonize the doctors, setting their opposition more firmly than before. If he had attempted to inform them about, let us say, the costs of medical care, leaving them with a clear understanding of the problem, he would probably have secured a response consistent with his beliefs and eventual hopes. He might have indirectly helped his cause instead of directly hurting it.

A young woman who was a brilliant student in a university was invited to speak before an influential women's club. She gave a well-documented lecture on the failures of American women to make proper use of the right to vote. Most of the audience were irritated by the speech; some were even insulted. The speech purpose was inappropriate to the attitudes of an audience toward a speaker much younger than themselves. The same speech would probably have been successful if it had been given by a mature woman with a record of achievement in civic affairs.

CHOOSING THE GENERAL PURPOSE

In order to avoid the common mistakes just described, you must determine speech purposes by a careful and systematic method. The first step is to choose one of the four general speech purposes discussed in Chapter 3: to entertain, to inform, to stimulate, to convince. The value of this first step is that it immediately narrows the field for your search. There are thousands of responses that human beings might make; you would waste your time trying to review them all. Therefore you begin by considering four basic types of response suitable for speaking situations.

One Purpose Only

The four general speech purposes are closely related, and therefore students often think that two or three or even all four may be successfully accomplished by one talk. For example, a student had just heard a television speech by the Attorney General. "The speech was certainly informative," he said; "it contained plenty of new facts and ideas. But it was entertaining, too: it was cleverly worded and had some humor. It was also stimulating; it reinforced a lot of beliefs. And the speech was convincing; it changed my mind on at least one question. Therefore the speech had all four general purposes." Not at all. A more careful analysis showed that the Attorney General's purpose was to convince—he would have been satisfied with nothing less. The entertaining, informative, and stimulating elements of his speech were means, not ends.

A single speech should have a single purpose, and everything the speaker says should be a means to that end. Catching and holding audience interest can be an end in itself or can be a means to some other end. Likewise, presenting information may be either an end or a means. The same is true of building new beliefs or reinforcing existing beliefs. When the relationship between ends and means is understood, it is no longer difficult to choose only one general purpose for a speech. For instance, you would not say, "My purpose is to entertain and inform with facts about the Panama Canal." Instead you would choose as your purpose either to entertain or to inform, demoting the other to a supporting role.

Factors Influencing Choice

1. AUDIENCE ATTITUDES TOWARD TOPIC In choosing a general speech purpose the most important factor should be the attitudes of your audience toward your subject. Let us work through a hypothetical case.

If you were to discuss a proposal for a new high school building in a small town, what would be the attitudes toward this proposal by various groups? Favorable attitudes would probably be found in most of the students who would be going to school in the new building, in the teachers, and in the children's parents, especially if they owned but little property. These attitudes might be lukewarm or strong, depending largely on the age and condition of the existing building, the amount of overcrowding, and whether or not nearby towns have newer buildings.

Unfavorable attitudes could be expected from people who pay high taxes but have no children in school, from groups fighting for tax reductions, or from groups advocating other community improvements that would have to compete for funds with the school proposal.

The undecided vote could be subdivided. First, there might be those who are completely neutral, that is, interested but open-minded. Common sense tells us, however, that it is difficult to know enough about a controversy to be interested in it without forming active opinions about it, and therefore the number of true neutrals would probably be small.

The second subdivision would include those people who have certain prejudices for and other prejudices against the proposal. Conflicting implies a balance of forces as contrasted with neutral, which implies an absence of forces. Conflicting attitudes might be expected in taxpayers with children in school, and in businessmen wondering if the extra costs of a school building would be offset by the extra income attracted to the community by a school improvement.

People would be indifferent toward the proposal either through lack of personal interest or lack of information. Lack of personal interest would be found among itinerant workers who do not expect to make this town their permanent home. Lack of information might be found among citizens with no children in school and with little property.

With the foregoing probabilities in mind, what should be your general speech purpose? Well, first you have to consider your own honest convictions. Assume that you favor the construction of the new school.

If the attitudes of most of your listeners were also favorable, your purpose should be further to stimulate them to support the proposal for a new building. You would want to reinforce their convictions and secure overt action—get them to vote, or to sign a petition, or to go out among their neighbors and secure more converts.

If the audience were opposed, your purpose would be to inform or convince. If they were strongly opposed, you might decide to shake their convictions with new information, paving the way for future talks which might carry the purpose another step forward. If opposition were not strongly entrenched, you might try to change their beliefs. It is unlikely in any case that you could produce actual overt action. That response should be left to future speakers.

If the audience were undecided, your general purpose would hinge on your analysis of the reasons for that indecision. Probably your purpose would be to convince. If the audience members were uninformed or apathetic, your purpose would become to entertain, to arouse attention and interest. If the attitudes of the audience were mixed, you would have to decide in which proportions. You might have to sacrifice the hope of convincing some of your listeners in order to persuade the remainder.

2. OTHER FACTORS Although audience attitudes toward your topic will usually be of greatest importance in choosing a general speech purpose, other factors will also influence your choice. The nature of the occasion may suggest the most appropriate purpose. An after-dinner speech suggests entertaining; a study club, informing; a ceremonial, stimulating; a debate, convincing. Common traits and interests may indicate the best choice of purpose. If your subject were household accidents, for example, the speech purpose would be influenced by the audience's age, sex, family status, or occupation. Audience attitudes toward you, the speaker, may bear upon the purpose. Thus if you had reason to believe that they would be prejudiced against you because of your age or sex or race, you might decide to entertain or inform rather than attempt to convince. Therefore, taking into account your subject, occasion, audience, and yourself, but paying attention particularly to the probable attitudes toward your topic, you make a choice of general speech purpose.

STATING THE GENERAL PURPOSE

You should write down your general purpose: to entertain, to inform, to stimulate, to convince, or a synonym for one of the four. Synonyms are useful in giving more exact shades of meaning in some cases.

However, the statement of your general purpose is only the first portion of what will become your full statement of speech purpose. The full statement, as we will presently see, requires the addition of specific details. Therefore the wording of the general purpose should lead naturally into statement of specific details.

Following are some examples of statements of general purposes, showing use of possible synonyms, and suggesting how specific details will be added to complete the statements.

1. Entertain

    To entertain my audience with ...
    To get my audience to pay favorable attention to ...
    To arouse the interest of my audience in ...
    To get my audience to laugh about ...

2. Inform

    To inform my audience about ...
    To get my audience to understand clearly ...
    To show my audience how to ...
    To get my audience to learn that ...

3. Stimulate

    To reinforce my audience's belief in ...
    To inspire my audience with ...
    To revitalize my audience's attitudes on ...
    To strengthen my audience's appreciation of ...
    To release into overt action my audience's existing belief that ...

4. Convince

    To get my audience to believe that ...
    To get my audience to stop believing that ...
    To change my audience's attitudes toward ...
    To persuade my audience to vote (or sign or give money or buy or other specific action) ...

MAKING THE GENERAL PURPOSE SPECIFIC

Notice again that all items in the foregoing list are incomplete statements. The final and critical task is to complete the statement of the general purpose so as to make the purpose specific. You will then have a full statement of your speech purpose—a description of the audience response you hope to get.

The value of a specific speech purpose may be illustrated by comparing speechmaking with traveling. You cannot plan a trip unless you first have a destination or itinerary; likewise, you cannot plan a speech unless you first have a specific goal. You might, of course, start a vacation trip saying, "We haven't planned anything definitely —we're just going to drive north." To say "north" is vague and general; to say "entertain" or "inform" is also vague and general.

If a traveler does not have a specific destination, he will just wander aimlessly; so will a speaker.

Stating the Specific Purpose

Make your statement of a specific purpose as specific as possible. In the following examples you will see that the first attempt to state your purpose specifically can often be improved by further effort.

General purpose: to entertain
Still too general: to amuse my audience with a talk about snoring
Better: to get my audience to laugh at some anecdotes and at some sounds of people snoring

General purpose: to inform
Still too general: to explain how to tie the fire underwriters' knot
Better: to instruct my listeners so that they will be able to tie the fire underwriters' knot

General purpose: to stimulate
Still too general: to stimulate my audience regarding the value of a college degree
Better: to strengthen my audience's belief in the value of getting a college degree

General purpose: to convince
Still too general: to convince my audience that certain classes should be dismissed during homecoming week
Better: to get my audience to sign a petition requesting dismissal of all classes on Friday and Saturday of homecoming week

Centering the Purpose on the Audience

Since the effectiveness of a speech must be measured by audience response, the statement of the speech purpose should always be audience-centered, avoiding the common dangers of being speaker-centered or subject-centered. For example, a student said that his general speech purpose was to inform, and that his specific purpose was "to explain why I believe in going to church regularly." He said he did not care whether anyone agreed with him; he just wanted to explain his ideas. Because the talk was speaker-centered, most of the class members were bored and none seemed to understand either the speaker's intention or his subject matter. However, the speaker thought his speech was effective because he had explained his own views to his own satisfaction. Consider another example. A student said that his general purpose was to convince, and that his specific

This student got a job at Sea World, helping the porpoises and seals entertain the visitors. His talks stressed little-known, attention-getting facts.
Part of the time he carried the microphone up into the audience. He said that this move stimulated more audience questions and other signs of interest.

purpose was "to prove that Alfred Korzybski's non-Aristotelian system of logic is sound." The speaker was obviously wrapped up in his subject, and had obviously spent much time in preparation. However, no one in the class was convinced—the arguments were too abstract and technical. The speaker thought it was an effective speech because, "I did prove the proposition; everything in the speech was true and well supported." The talk was not speaker-centered, but it was subject-centered—the speaker had prepared as though Korzybski were to be the judge, but Korzybski wasn't there.

The distinctions between speaker-centered or subject-centered purposes and audience-centered purposes are often delicate. Consider the following examples.

Speaker-centered: to be interesting while discussing statistics
Subject-centered: to present interesting statistical information
Audience-centered: to get my audience to show interest in the uses of statistics

Speaker-centered: to explain my definition of love
Subject-centered: to talk about the problem of defining love
Audience-centered: to get my audience to understand the differences between psychological and religious definitions of love

Speaker-centered: to give an inspirational talk on the benefits I received from membership in the Boy Scouts
Subject-centered: to praise the record of the Boy Scouts
Audience-centered: to heighten the favorable feeling which my audience holds toward the Boy Scouts

Speaker-centered: to defend my reasons for being a Republican
Subject-centered: to prove that the overall record of the Republican party is better than that of the Democratic party
Audience-centered: to get the members of my audience to decide to vote Republican in the next election

Making the Specific Purpose Concrete

The statement of speech purpose is for the guidance of the speaker; the purpose may or may not be spoken to the audience during the speech. For example, you certainly would not say to an audience, "My purpose this morning is to get you to laugh at some jokes." Nor is it likely that you would ever say, "My purpose is to make you change your minds."

The value of the speech purpose to a speaker is based on the fact that if he knows in advance the audience response he wants, he can aim everything he says toward arousing that response. A speaker is more likely to be successful if he knows what success is. In other words, speech purpose and speech effectiveness are "before and after" descriptions of audience response. Purpose is the response you hope to get; effectiveness is the response you actually get. In successful speeches the desired audience response and the actual audience response correspond.

It is easier to aim a speech at a concrete goal than at an abstract one. It is easier to judge ways and means if you can visualize the desired end, that is, if you can see and hear the desired audience response in imagination. Thus it is helpful when you can say, "I want every member of the class to contribute at least twenty-five cents to this annual drive for the Student Emergency Loan Fund," because you can visualize them digging into their pockets or purses and putting money into envelopes. It is less helpful to say, "I want the class to understand how ice cream was invented," because it is difficult to visualize anyone in the act of understanding.

You will be able to make your statement of purpose more concrete by asking yourself this significant question, "If my speech is completely successful, exactly what will my audience think, feel, or do?" The answer is the response you want to get, and to get that particular response is your speech purpose. In answering the question you should think in terms of observable behaviors.

The observable behaviors of an audience that has been successfully entertained or interested include: sitting quietly, listening attentively, perhaps smiling or laughing, asking questions afterward, or making comments such as, "I enjoyed the talk," or, "That was a fascinating subject."

The observable behaviors of an audience that has been successfully informed include: listening thoughtfully, taking notes, asking pertinent questions, and afterward talking about the subject, passing a quiz, performing an activity learned during the speech, or making comments such as, "I understand it clearly," or "I learned a great deal about the topic."

The observable behaviors of an audience that has been successfully stimulated include: listening eagerly, nodding in agreement, applauding during the speech, sometimes spontaneously saying encouraging things to the speaker ("Give it to 'em, Harry," "Right on, brother"), or spontaneously replying to rhetorical questions ("Are we downhearted?" "No!"), and afterward cheering, talking about the speech subject, performing overt acts suggested by the speaker, or making comments such as, "I believe it more strongly than ever before," or "It was deeply moving."

The observable behaviors of an audience that has been successfully convinced include: listening intently, nodding or shaking head, making facial expressions consistent with the speaker's argument, and afterward performing appropriate overt acts such as voting, signing, contributing, or making comments such as, "I agree with you now," or, "That put the problem in a new light."

If you think in terms of observable audience behaviors, you will be more likely to state your purpose specifically and concretely. Sometimes it is wise to supplement your statement of purpose by hypothesizing observable audience responses. For example, you might supplement the purpose to get your audience to believe in the principles of free trade by mentally adding, "If a show of hands were requested at the end of the talk, a majority of the class would vote favorably." An actual show of hands need not be taken. The important thing is to visualize in advance the audience response wanted, and it is possible to visualize a show of hands whereas it is difficult to visualize the behavior of believing.

As we mentioned at the beginning of this section you do not always state your purpose to the audience during a talk. For ex-

Cesar Chavez encourages his union members with a pep talk during a strike. Then he gives specific instructions on the picketing activities for that day.

ample, in a public speaking contest your underlying purpose may be to win the first prize; you are aware of this and so is the audience, but you surely would not state it during your speech. Or suppose that you are speaking to an audience that is strongly opposed to the proposition you favor. You might decide that it is impossible in one short talk to swing them completely over to your viewpoint. So your purpose might be to get them to take a step in your direction by undermining one or more of their cherished beliefs. But to say that to them would be a pretty good way to guarantee failure.

In many speeches, however, you should reveal your purpose to the listeners. Sometimes the purpose should be stated specifically, even bluntly:

TO CONVINCE

My purpose today is to ask your support in the coming election.

TO INFORM

The purpose of this lecture is to prepare you for the final examination in this course. I will explain precisely the type of examination that will be given, the materials that will be covered, and the study methods that you should use.

TO STIMULATE

The behavior of the student rooting section at last Saturday's game was a disgrace to this school. I speak for the alumni, and I do not intend to mince words—we are ashamed.

SUMMARY

The purpose of every speech should be to get an intended audience response.

Poorly chosen speech purposes mislead speakers into attempting too much, attempting too little, or attempting the wrong thing.

A single speech should have a single purpose, and everything the speaker says should be a means to that end.

The first step in determining a speech purpose is to choose one of the four general purposes: to entertain, to inform, to stimulate, or to convince. The choice among the four is influenced mostly by audience attitudes toward the topic, but other factors may also influence the decision. The second step is to state the general purpose, using one of the four terms: entertain, inform, stimulate, convince, or a synonym for one of them. The third step is to add to the statement of general purpose so as to describe the desired audience response specifically and concretely. The third step can be accomplished by asking, "If my speech is completely successful, exactly what will my audience think, feel, or do?" The answer is the response you want to get, and the response you want to get is your speech purpose.

TOPICAL PREVIEW

I You, too, should have a reservoir

II What to look for
    A Points and subpoints
    B Supporting materials
        1 Functions
        2 Forms

III How to find speech materials
    A Observation
        1 Casual observation
        2 Planned observation
    B Conversation
    C Reading
        1 Purposeful reading
        2 Use of indexes
        3 Use of general reference books
        4 Use of varied sources

IV How to record speech materials
    A Note-taking for a specific speech
    B Note-taking for future speeches

V Summary

5

Speech Materials

YOU, TOO, SHOULD HAVE A RESERVOIR

The late Adlai Stevenson, whose speeches consistently reflected a unique combination of wit, wisdom, and extraordinary mastery of the English language, is rightfully rated as one of the outstanding American speakers of modern times. Some of his presidential campaign speeches and his addresses while Ambassador to the United Nations provide models for students of speech communication. For the purposes of this chapter, however, one of Stevenson's "minor" rhetorical gems is chosen for analysis (and you will soon see why). The occasion was the World Brotherhood Dinner of the National Conference of Christians and Jews at which Stevenson introduced and made an award to Albert M. Greenfield, a real estate broker, banker, and philanthropist of Philadelphia. Stevenson spoke for approximately twelve minutes.

Stevenson opened with a *quotation* from Thornton Wilder's play "Our Town." The quotation was unusual—it was simply the address on a letter to a character mentioned in the play. The quotation was apt—it directly illustrated the theme of World Brotherhood. Then Stevenson used the "address" again, slightly abridged, to provide a surprise ending for the talk:

> Ladies and gentlemen, acting for you, I confer the World Brother-
> hood Award Citation upon Albert M. Greenfield, Sugar Loaf, Chest-
> nut Hill, Philadelphia, Pennsylvania, United States of America,
> Continent of North America, the Earth, the Solar System, the
> Universe, the mind of God.[1]

Stevenson also included three other quotations from such diverse
sources as John Donne and the Talmud. As he concluded the talk he
apparently used a *visual aid*—he must have presented some sort of
certificate or plaque to the guest of honor.

A short *anecdote* was related:

> Mr. Chairman, I have said that there is *no* flaw in the brotherhood
> title of our honored guest. I advise you now that in 1928 he was a
> delegate from Pennsylvania to the National Convention of the Re-
> publican party. I advise you further that in 1948, 1952 and 1956 he
> was a Delegate-at-large from Pennsylvania to the National Con-
> vention of the Democratic party. This is Brotherhood! And this is
> also *progress!*

The central idea of Stevenson's talk was that the dangers of nuclear warfare may force mankind to achieve what it has always
sought—world brotherhood. He developed this point by means of
explanation. Some examples:

> A very large part, I suspect, of the maturing of mankind to its
> present estate has come from adversity, or the threat of adversity.
> More frontiers of what we call progress have probably been crossed
> under the pressure of necessity than by the power of reason.

> The significance of what has happened lies not in which nation has
> first reached into outer space but in the fact that man has now
> obliterated, for better or for worse, what we used to call time and
> distance.

> What that "bleep-bleep" is saying is that now the world has no
> option, that it must turn from narrow nationalism, sectarianism,
> racialism, that the only conceivable relationship among men is one
> based on men's full respect—yes, their love, if you please—for each
> other.

Occasionally Stevenson developed his points by means of vivid
description:

> ...a science that has broken down the fences which had before
> separated the peoples of the world.

> ...until the hard steel of survival itself has been pulled against our
> too soft mouths.

> ...the one realm which knows no boundaries, no capitals, no
> foreign policy—for there are no foreigners...

[1] A. Craig Baird, ed., *Representative American Speeches: 1957–1958.* H. W. Wilson,
1958, pp. 58–63.

Several times Stevenson supported his statements by citing specific *instances*. Thus he stated that the honored guest had "taken part in the most extraordinary variety of functions ever to come to my humble attention." Then he gave instances:

> I find that he has lent his name and services (and I suspect frequently something even more tangible) to the United Fund and the Community Chest, to the Philadelphia Symphony and to the Connie Mack Golden Jubilee Committee, to the Chapel of Four Chaplains and to the Army and Navy football games.

Finally *statistics* were employed to support one of Stevenson's points:

> My research, Mr. Chairman, has gone even to statistics. I am in a position to report, what I am sure Mr. Greenfield does not himself know—except perhaps with a kind of numbness—that there is record evidence of his participation, usually as chairman, in sixty-one committees, commissions, campaigns, chambers or celebrations; and of his previous receipt of twenty-nine honorary awards.

Thus this short speech shows that Stevenson spared no effort in securing a supply, even a surplus, of suitable speech materials.

> Mr. Chairman, I have, in the discharge of my appointed duties on this occasion, made what we lawyers (you will pardon this brief "commercial") call a title search.

If such an experienced speaker as Adlai Stevenson recognized the need of a "title search" for speech materials, surely student speakers cannot afford to do less.

The most extraordinary feature of this speech, however, is that, in only twelve minutes, Stevenson used every one of the principal "forms of support" recommended for years by speech textbooks: explanation, description, anecdotes, instances, statistics, quotations, and visual aids. Probably Stevenson made no conscious effort to do this. Like all of his speeches, this one reflects habits of speech preparation built up from long practical experience. One of Stevenson's habits was the use of well-chosen and varied materials to develop and support his speech points and subpoints. He gradually accumulated a reservoir of speech materials, starting quite possibly during his student years, and he habitually drew upon this reservoir when preparing his speeches.

WHAT TO LOOK FOR

Points and Subpoints

A well-constructed speech consists of one or more speech units. As we saw in an earlier chapter, a speech unit requires a statement and its supports: the statement of a speech point (or subpoint), together with spoken or visual materials that support or develop it. The term "speech point" means a one-sentence summary of an idea. So in gathering speech materials, you look for ideas about your topic— ideas that can be put into the form of speech points. Some samples:

1. Cheating on examinations cheats the cheater.
2. Race discrimination cripples foreign policy.
3. Faith is fear turned inside out.
4. The first mark of a scholar is curiosity.
5. Space technology had added a new dimension to astronomy.

Sometimes you will come upon a single sentence that suggests a set of related points that you want for your speech. For instance, Bernard De Voto wrote in an article for *Harper's Magazine:* "The professor's function in society is to appraise, increase, and disseminate knowledge." There you have the makings of three points which might become the major framework for a speech. Or you might find helpful Clark Kerr's ironic statement of a university president's most troublesome problems—"sex for the students, athletics for the alumni, and parking for the faculty."

Usually, however, you *derive* points and subpoints, rather than quote verbatim from materials you have read or heard. Thus, you may read a magazine article that stimulates you to think of a one-sentence summary in your own words—a sentence that expresses a major point you would like to discuss in your own fashion. Or you may hear a speech with which you strongly disagree, and you are stimulated to think of a one-sentence answer. Or you draw upon your entire reservoir of past experiences and try to create at least a tentative list of points that indicates a number of things to look for.

Supporting Materials

FUNCTIONS   The bare statement of your points and subpoints is like a table of contents without the development that makes the book. You must look for materials to support each of your potential points and subpoints. Often your final choice of points will be the ones for which you have found the most adequate supporting materials. To recognize and evaluate supporting materials requires that you understand their functions. *To support (or to develop) means to clarify, reinforce, or prove a point.*

To clarify a point is to make the speaker's intended meaning clear to the audience. Suppose your point is, "Our impressions of other people often result from subliminal stimuli." Some of your listeners will not understand "subliminal stimuli." Your first job, perhaps your only job, is to clarify the meaning of your point by explaining the technical terms. More frequently, however, your point itself may require clarification, not because of technical words, but because of words that have more than one possible meaning. An example of this type of point is, "This college should adopt the honor system." What do you mean by "honor system"? Or, "Congressional investigating committees should be curbed." Exactly what committees do you mean? And precisely what do you mean by "curbed"?

To reinforce means to strengthen a point with which the audience already agrees. The point that "all of us should vote in campus elections" is clear enough, and most of your classmates would agree that the point is true. Yet a large percentage of students neglects to vote. Therefore the job is to strengthen that existing agreement. Make the point more vivid; dramatize its importance; motivate the students to turn their belief into action. You can readily think of other points that require and deserve reinforcement: "Drive safely," "Give to the Red Cross," "Be loyal to your school."

To prove means to demonstrate the probability that a statement is true. If you said, "Jim Jackson is the best qualified of the candidates for student body president," your meaning would be clear enough. If you were addressing a group of Jim Jackson's friends and supporters, you would try to reinforce the point. If the point were to be discussed before an audience who disagreed with you or were undecided, however, proof would be necessary. Any point with which the listeners are not in accord must be proved. On controversial questions, do not expect to demonstrate absolute truth; seek to establish the probability that your point is true. If your point, for example, is that "intercollegiate football is being overemphasized," you cannot show that the statement is absolutely true or absolutely false; you can only undertake to demonstrate the probability of its truth.

You will see that often a point needs to be clarified *and* reinforced, clarified *and* proved, or all three.

With a clear understanding of the functions of supporting materials, you are now prepared to look for, recognize, and evaluate the principal forms of support: explanation, description, anecdotes, instances, quotations, statistics, and audio-visual aids.

FORMS

Explanation. Explanation is most often used to clarify, sometimes to reinforce, occasionally to prove. In a talk where you plan to use a good deal of explanatory material your research should accomplish two purposes: (1) improve your own understanding of the subject; and (2) help you gear your talk to the audience's level of knowledge and experience. Explanation includes definition, analogy, classification, or analysis.

Every beginning speaker should learn to define his terms. He should learn to define not only single words but also phrases or even concepts. There are several ways of classifying types of definitions. One useful classification is this:

I. Nominal
II. Formal
III. Operational
    A. Denotative
    B. Connotative

In nominal definition you simply give a synonym such as "IQ means intelligence quotient." In a formal definition (often quoted from an authority) you first name the general class of phenomena and then give the *differentia* or details which distinguish the object or event from other members of the same class. Thus, "IQ is a measurement of intelligence which shows the numerical relationship between an individual's mental age and chronological age." In a denotative operational definition you tell the audience how the object or event acts, occurs, or is produced (often using visual or verbal examples); for example, "IQ is a numerical score which is obtained after giving a standard intelligence test." In a connotative operational definition you reveal individual attitudes toward the term being defined. For instance, "IQ is supposed to be a measure of intelligence but no one really knows whether it is valid; it is an attempt of an inexact science to become exact merely by using or misusing formulas and numbers."

College students and graduates are often called on to discuss technical subjects for audiences of laymen. In such talks special care must be taken to clarify technical words and concepts. A chemistry major gave a classroom talk on chemical warfare which was over the heads of almost all of his classmates. His reading had been from chemical journals. He would have been wise to have looked for additional materials showing how to translate technical into nontechnical language. For example, in the following quotation notice how Norman Cousins explained a technical term in plain language and with frequent references to common household chemicals and containers:

> The most revolutionary development of all in the field of chemical warfare has the code name in the United States of "GB." It is a nerve gas. It is odorless and invisible. It is easy to disseminate. It can be packaged and delivered by short-range, medium-range, or long-range missiles. It can be spread over wide areas or used in limited situations by aerosol sprays. It can even be used in tiny dispensers of the kind that carry deodorizers.
>
> GB, now being manufactured by the United States Army Chemical Corps, and, so far as is known, by other major powers, acts like a super-insecticide against human beings. Like DDT, its effect is widespread and almost instantaneous. Exposure to GB in gas form is lethal in a matter of seconds. A liquid droplet the size of a pencil dot on the skin will penetrate surface tissue and kill a man within ten to fifteen minutes.[2]

John Adams clarified a legal concept in his first speech in the Boston Massacre trials of 1770, combining definition and classification:

> The law divides homicide into three branches; the first is "justifiable," the second, "excusable," and the third, "felonious." Felonious homicide is subdivided into two branches: the first is murder, which is killing with malice aforethought; the second is manslaughter, which is killing a man on a sudden provocation. Here, gentlemen, are four sorts of homicide; and you are to consider whether all the evidence amounts to the first, second, third, or fourth of these heads....

Athelstan Spilhaus, in an address before an audience of engineers and other students specializing in oceanic sciences, provided an almost classic "exercise" in the use of definitions (seven of them) combined with classification and analysis:

> We need to move toward a better public understanding of what I've called an "ecolibrium" position—balancing the desired ecology (an harmonious pattern between organisms and their environment) with the necessary economy (the management of affairs with a view to maintaining productiveness).
>
> "Zero risk." Nonsense! There must be a realistic awareness in all activities that there is an acceptable risk and that it is not zero.
>
> "Zero effluents." Also nonsense! There must be more awareness that in the use of the components of our environment—air, land and water—there is an acceptable burden of man's wastes of the proper kind that these components can carry and that this is not zero.
>
> There must be more awareness of the fact that one proper use of air and water is to dirty it—whether we use it in the organisms that are our bodies or in the organisms we call industry. We should be aware that certainly both our own body organisms and the organisms we call industry would die under a policy of zero effluents.

---

[2] "CBR vs. Man," *Saturday Review* (July 23, 1960), pp. 9–10.

There must be awareness that air and water are commodities that we must use, clean and reuse, just as the commodity food is grown, used and regrown. We must think of the culture of our air and water—atmoculture and hydroculture, if you like—as we think of agriculture today.[3]

Brigadier General Mildred C. Bailey gave a commencement address at the University of Wisconsin, remarking in the opening, "If I, as a Brigadier General in the United States Army who happens to be a woman, seem a curiosity to you, then know that I am equally curious about you." She used explanation in the form of analysis to clarify her concept of the "generation gap":

Twentieth century man, in his genius, has developed his ability to communicate with man traveling many thousands of miles out in space. This same twentieth century man, however, finds it often difficult, if not impossible, to communicate with others in the same room. How can this be? The answer seems relatively simple. Men of space science are intensely trained to speak a common language about a mutually absorbing subject. Earthbound men, on the other hand, speak in many tongues, reflect multiple interests and a great diversity of backgrounds and culture content. Developing among them a common language and an understanding of goals is a far more complex endeavor.[4]

The importance of connotative meanings—among other things—was illustrated by Congresswoman Patsy T. Mink of Hawaii in an address before a Japanese-American citizens' organization. Blending definitions and analysis, she skillfully reinforced audience attitudes:

During the trial of Lieutenant Calley, we were told about "MGR," the "Mere Gook Rule" which was the underlying basis for Calley's mindless assertion that the slaughter of defenseless women and children, our prisoners of war, was "no big thing." The "Mere Gook Rule" holds that life is less important, less valuable to an Oriental.

Laws that protect other human beings do not apply to "gooks." One reporter noted before the verdict became known that the essence of the Calley case was to determine the validity of this rule. He described it as the "unspoken issue" at the trial.

The issue was not as unspoken as most would prefer to believe. The indictment drawn up by the Army against Lieutenant Calley stated in six separate charges that he did at My Lai murder four "Oriental human beings"... murder not less than thirty "Oriental human beings"... murder three "Oriental human beings"... murder an unknown number of "Oriental human beings" not less than seventy... and so on numbering 102. Thus, the Army did not charge him with the murder of human beings as presumably would have been the case had Caucasions been involved, but instead charged the apparently lesser offense of killing mere "Oriental human beings." [5]

[3] Delivered January 11, 1973. Reprinted by permission of Athelstan Spilhaus.

[4] Delivered May 13, 1973. Reprinted by permission of Mildred C. Bailey.

[5] Delivered November 6, 1971. Reprinted by permission of Patsy T. Mink.

Description. Description should always help to clarify, and clarification is especially useful in talking about persons, places, objects, and processes. For example, if you are giving a talk on General Douglas MacArthur, look for photographs and written descriptions of him; secure a recording of his voice; and you might even secure a firsthand description of his appearance, voice, and mannerisms from someone who had seen MacArthur in person. You would seek the same types of descriptive materials for a talk on the scenic wonders of Alaska or the workings of a deep-freeze unit. In addition to clarifying, however, description is often used to reinforce a point. For instance, if you wanted to reinforce the point that facial animation is as important for beauty as perfect features, you could describe several people—perhaps using well-known TV performers as your subjects. Description is also used to prove. For example, a man is on trial for drunken driving; the arresting officers and other witnesses testify that the defendant's breath smelled of alcohol, his speech was slurred, and he wobbled when he walked.

The most important advice for using description is to make your descriptions realistic and vivid by appealing to the senses. You want to arouse the listener's mental imagery. This advice will be progressively illustrated by the several excerpts that follow.

Arch Booth of the United States Chamber of Commerce undertook to prove his point that "Congress, too, needs an organizational overhaul." Immediately he gave a factual description of the budgetary process, followed by a descriptive analysis:

> Incredible as it may seem, at the present time neither the Congress nor any of its committees looks at the budget as a whole.
> The House Ways and Means Committee and the Senate Finance Committee decide tax policy.
> The legislative committees—such as Commerce, Agriculture, and Defense—authorize spending.
> The House and Senate Appropriations Committees recommend how much of the authorization to appropriate.
> This is a point that often confuses people. A big authorization is meaningless without an appropriation to match it. Knowing this, congressmen will often pass an outlandish authorization as a political gesture, expecting the appropriation committees to cut it down to size.
> As you can see, the process runs backwards. Congress first decides what it is going to spend, then considers whether there is enough money. A more rational approach would be to start with a list of priorities—based on what the people are willing to pay for— and then divide up the available money accordingly.
> But before that can happen, it is necessary to get the money-raisers together with the money-spenders. It is necessary to consider income and outgo at the same time. There is a committee charged with this responsibility—the Joint Committee on the Legislative Budget—but it is inactive.[6]

6 Delivered on May 11, 1973. Reprinted by permission of Arch Booth.

You will notice that the speaker does not specifically mention any of the senses although in the opening sentence the term "looks at" suggests using the sense of sight. However, his audience was the Executives' Club of Chicago, and business executives spend countless hours attending committee meetings. So perhaps the listeners did indeed "see" the congressional committees in the mind's eye, or perhaps they envisioned the process as an organization chart. It is a moot question whether Booth should have described the congressional committee procedures in more concrete words. Probably his choice was the best: He provides an excellent example of clarity and brevity in describing a rather abstract process.

The next two excerpts illustrate appeals to visual imagery. Description of something that can be seen is the most commonly useful type of sensory appeal for speakers. The excerpts further show how such descriptions can be used as direct supports to prove a controversial point or subpoint.

In the historic school segregation cases, resulting in the landmark decisions of 1954 and 1955 by the Supreme Court, the chief counsel defending the "separate but equal" doctrine, was John W. Davis, former Democratic candidate for president of the United States. His opponents had presented in the lower courts a then-novel form of evidence—testimony from social scientists who maintained that segregation produced emotional maladjustments in black schoolchildren. Davis argued that such evidence was "of slight weight" and in his rebuttal he included the following satirical description of one of the experiments:

> His investigation consisted of visits to the Scott's Branch primary and secondary school. . . . He called for the presentation to him of some sixteen pupils between the ages of six and nine years, and he applied to them what he devised and what he was pleased to call an objective test. That consisted of offering to them sixteen white and colored dolls, and inviting them to select the doll they would prefer, the doll they thought was nice, the doll that looked bad, or the doll that looked most like themselves. He ascertained that ten out of his battery of sixteen preferred the white doll. Nine thought the white doll was nice, and seven thought it looked most like themselves. Eleven said that the colored doll was bad, and one that the white doll was bad. And out of that intensive investigation and that application of that thoroughly scientific test, he deduced the sound conclusion that . . . "they have been definitely harmed in the development of their personalities."

The chief counsel for the opposing side in these hearings was Thurgood Marshall, currently Associate Justice of the Supreme Court. One of Marshall's arguments was that there were ample precedents for desegregation in various areas of American life but that for some strange reason the area of public education remained as an exception. To help prove that such segregation was illogical and unjust, Marshal movingly described the effects on school-children:

> I got the feeling on hearing the discussion yesterday that when you put a white child in a school with a whole lot of colored children, the child would fall apart or something. Everybody knows that is not true. Those same kids in Virginia and South Carolina—and I have seen them do it—they play in the streets together, they play on their farms together, they go down the road together, they separate to go to school, they come out of school and play ball together. They have to be separated in school. There is some magic to it. You can have them voting together, you can have them not restricted because of law in the houses they live in. You can have them going to the same state university and the same college, but if they go to elementary and high school, the world will fall apart.

In the two preceding examples the appeal was essentially to the sense of sight—the justices of the Court could easily visualize the white and black dolls and the behaviors of the children playing baseball or football. But mental imagery is by no means limited to the visual; some topics call for emphasis on other senses. It would be difficult to find a more instructive demonstration of how to arouse a variety of sensory images than Victor Alvin Ketcham's well-known lecture, "The Seven Doors to the Mind and How to Open Them." Here is his description of a lawyer's plea to a jury:

> You could see the dim outlines of that little country station as the train pulled in. You smell the damp of the river fog as it came up around that station and made the darkness mystifying and confusing, particularly to an old person. You could feel the sharp, icy sting of the sleet as the violence of the storm drove it into the face of the frail old lady when she stepped down from the last step of the coach and stood timidly waiting for the train to pull out. You could hear the sharp puff of the locomotive and the creaking of the old wooden coaches (he made it plain that their equipment was old and worn out) as the train pulled out and the lights from the coach windows passed along the station platform and left it in complete darkness because the railroad had not kept the light on the platform in good condition.
> Then the speaker made every person walk, in imagination, with the frail old lady, over the ice-covered, uneven boards of the old station platform. When she fell off the end, it came with a sense of personal physical pain to every person present. She fell on her face in a pile of cinders and the taste of old ashes was in the mouth and their acrid smell in the nostrils of every person present.[7]

Now go back and reread the excerpt. You can easily spot the portions of the word-picture that evoke the sensations of sight, sound, touch, smell, and taste. But you can also find the additional sensations of temperature, pain, kinesthesia, and loss of equilibrium. You should

---

[7] Willard Hayes Yeager, *Effective Speaking for Every Occasion*, Prentice-Hall, 1951, pp. 274–75. Reprinted by permission of Victor A. Ketcham, Jr.

also notice the skillful blending—almost any listener would have "a picture in his mind" of what had happened on that dark damp evening.

Anecdotes. For beginning speakers probably the most important form of support is the anecdote. It may be defined as a narrative example or story (usually brief) with a point. The anecdote is especially well adapted to the practicing of extemporaneous speaking. It is a potent technique for clarifying and reinforcing; it is sometimes an excellent way to initiate a proof. There are many kinds of anecdotes. They may be humorous, serious, or both; they may be true or imaginary; they may be straight narration or take the form of an analogy, a parable, or a fable.

In gathering materials for a particular speech, hunt for anecdotes that can be clearly related to your speech purpose, the audience, and your topic. The effectiveness of this form of support also depends on the substance of the anecdote, its relevance to the point it is intended to support, and the skill with which it is told.

The substance of an anecdote need not be dramatic or humorous if the story precisely illustrates your point. Often you can use a commonplace incident drawn from your own experience. For example, John M. Bevan opened a talk on the evaluation and improvement of current educational practices with this ordinary family incident:

> Not too long ago, my son entered my study, sat down, and began complaining about the pressures imposed by his high school schedule. "Every day it's the same five classes with one period set aside for study hall. I'm up daily at 6:30 A.M., dressed and heading out of the house by 7:30 A.M., at school and in my first class by 8:30 A.M. Then it's four classes in a row, lunch, study hall, and the final class period. School is out and an hour later the bus drops me off at the corner down the block. Shortly thereafter, it's dinner and then off to study in preparation for the next day's scheduled routine. Today my English class was assigned a creative paper that's due the day after tomorrow. Can you tell me when I'm to find the time to think, let alone create or recreate?" [8]

The preceding example might be called a one-shot anecdote—it is confined to one particular speech by one particular speaker. In contrast, American folklore includes many oft-repeated tales, perhaps fictitious, that have a timeless quality and may be used to illustrate points common to many topics. Listeners relish rehearing these stories when competently used. Lee Loevinger, speaking on the social responsibility of business and industry, provides a model example of skillfully adapting an old favorite to a new topic:

[8] Reprinted with the permission of John M. Bevan from *Vital Speeches*, XXXIX (September 15, 1973), p. 727.

This debate is reminiscent of the classical story of the traveller who saw three workmen laying bricks. He stopped and asked each of the workmen what he was doing. The first replied, "I am laying bricks." The second responded, "I am earning my living." The third answered, "I am building a cathedral." Clearly each of the answers was proper, but the frame of reference was different for each. Similarly, three businessmen might give corresponding answers. One might say, "I am manufacturing widgets." A second might say, "I am earning a profit for my stockholders." A third might say, "I am helping to build a democratic society." Each answer is correct, within its own frame of reference. However, the frame of reference of the third is the broadest for it includes the other two. This is what we mean by corporate social responsibility.[9]

Donald T. Regan, a businessman, speaking before the annual meeting of the YMCA on the relationships between "business" and "society," opened by warning his listeners that these two terms are only "convenient labels." To clarify his position that "a look behind the label can often be more informative than the label itself," he wove in this anecdote:

In this connection, you may have heard what happened shortly after Captain Cook's sailors landed for the first time on the shores of Australia. When they came back to the ship, they brought aboard with them a strange looking animal whose name they did not know. Cook sent them to ask the natives what the animal was called. Back they came with the word that "it is a kangaroo." A good number of years went by before anyone discovered what had really happened. What had happened was that Cook's sailors had pointed to the animal and asked the natives "What is it called?" The natives replied "kangaroo"—which in their language meant "What did you say?" [10]

Samuel Lefrak, addressing the Pratt Institute in Brooklyn, tackled the problem of inadequate housing in the slums and ghettos of American cities. He wanted to raise the question, "Where are we going?" Then he would give his own answer during the remainder of the speech. He raised his question by means of an anecdote:

The late Supreme Court Justice Oliver Wendell Holmes ... once found himself on a train, but he couldn't locate his ticket. While the conductor watched, smiling, Justice Holmes searched through all his pockets, without success. Of course, the conductor recognized the distinguished Justice, and so he said: "Mr. Holmes, don't worry. You don't need your ticket. You will probably find it when you get off the train, and I'm sure the Pennsylvania Railroad will trust you to mail it back later."

The Justice looked up at the conductor with some irritation and said: "My dear man, that is not the problem at all. The problem is not ... where is my ticket? The problem is ... where am I going?" [11]

[9] Delivered February 15, 1973. Reprinted by permission of Lee Loevinger.

[10] Delivered May 3, 1973. Reprinted by permission of Donald T. Regan.

[11] Delivered December 7, 1971. Reprinted by permission of Samuel Lefrak.

In this and the preceding examples the anecdotes were used to lead into, to clarify, and to reinforce the speakers' points. Additional considerations are involved when an anecdote is used to initiate proofs.

Senator Sam J. Ervin, Jr., speaking at Miami University in Ohio, on governmental invasion of privacy, sought to prove that the constitutional rights of citizens were being invaded on a massive scale. He described his personal investigations of the misuse of computerized data banks by the Census Bureau, the FBI, and other government agencies. Turning to the misuse of surveillance, he opened his proofs by telling the story of reporter Daniel Schorr. Senator Ervin devoted six or seven minutes to this story because he apparently wanted to recount in *detail* (1) what the FBI did to Schorr, (2) the various pretexts used to make it "legal," and (3) the seriousness of the damage done to Schorr. Due to the length of the anecdote elisions are made as indicated below:

> Some of you may have heard about what happened to CBS newsman, Daniel Schorr. After a series of articles critical of the Administration, Mr. Schorr woke up one morning to find himself the object of a full-scale FBI investigation. . . . Friends, acquaintances, colleagues, employers and former employers were telephoned and interviewed by FBI agents who asked about Mr. Schorr's character and patriotism, as well as his fitness for a position in the Executive Branch.
>
> . . . I sought to find out from the White House just what high-level executive position purported to justify this apparently punitive surveillance. . . . First, the White House replied that Daniel Schorr was "being considered for a job that is presently filled." A few days later . . . The White House finally lamely announced that . . . the preliminary surveillance report, which was "entirely favorable," had been "subsequently destroyed." But the damage had already been done.
>
> Daniel Schorr described the damaging effects of such surveillance on a news reporter in this way. . . . An FBI investigation is not a "routine formality." It has an impact on one's life, one's relations with employers, neighbors, and friends. . . . It has become standard humor to inquire whether I am still "in trouble with the FBI," whether it is safe to talk to me on the telephone. I am now left to ponder. . . . [Lists his professional problems.]
>
> And Daniel Schorr's case is not unique. We now have reports of extensive surveillance, wire-tapping, and even burglaries perpetrated on other reporters. [12]

Instances. Notice that Senator Ervin in the last paragraph above recognized the principal weakness of even a true and detailed anecdote as a proof, namely, that you can seldom generalize from one case since it may be exceptional or even unique. Therefore, you present the anecdote to clarify, following up with several instances or statistics to round out the proof. To illustrate the use of this se-

[12] Reprinted with the permission of Sam J. Ervin, Jr. from *Vital Speeches*, XXXIX (September 1, 1973), p. 679.

quence from anecdote to instances to statistics, here is an excerpt from Governor Ronald Reagan, addressing the California Chamber of Commerce:

> The other day I was having a meeting with some student leaders and one of them, a student body president from one of our universities, challenged me, when I was talking about some things in our younger days, that the problem was today that we no longer could understand our sons and daughters. And I tried to impress upon him that most of us knew more about being young than we did of being old. But he said, "No, it's different." He said, "You just don't understand the great change which has taken place." He said, "When you were young you didn't live in a world with instant electronic communications, nuclear power, jet travel, the magic of cybernetics, the computers that computed in seconds what it used to take men months and years to figure out." Well, that's true. We didn't have those things when we were young. We invented them! [*Applause*]
> I have already lived 10 years longer than my life expectancy when I was born. Our children don't even know the names of some of the diseases that we lived through. Diseases that had maimed and killed for centuries are now almost forgotten because of our efforts, our dollars, and our research.
> When we were born, two-thirds of the people in this country lived in substandard housing; now it's less than 10 percent. Ninety percent of all Americans when we were born lived below what is considered the poverty line; by the time it was our turn to take over and join the adult generation that had been reduced by more than half, and now in our adult lifetime we have brought that figure down to 10 percent of our citizens still below the poverty line. Let those who today cry "revolution now" take a second look and feel a little stupid—for our generation has presided over the greatest social and economic revolution the world has ever seen.[13]

In this excerpt you find Reagan using about ten instances—some are included within the anecdote when the student itemizes the things that have changed—and you also notice in the third paragraph that the instances incorporate a few statistics. The probability is that Reagan proved his point (or reinforced it) to this particular audience since most of them were middle-aged or upper-middle-aged business people.

An instance is an undetailed example, case, or fact, cited briefly. Instances may sometimes be used to clarify, but are more often used to reinforce or prove. Usually you are looking for a sequence of several instances to show generality of your point and to provide a cumulative piling-up effect. You may draw upon your past experience or current research.

Sometimes you need to look for but one instance to support a point. Clark E. Stair, of the Firestone Tire and Rubber Company, relied on a single instance to prove his point that new tires seldom cause auto accidents although poor drivers sometimes do:

[13] Delivered September 4, 1970. Reprinted by permission of Ronald W. Reagan.

At our Texas proving ground, we deliberately overload tires and otherwise abuse them until they fail. Under these severely exaggerated conditions, intentional blowouts are a daily occurrence. Yet, our safety record is outstanding. During our first fifteen years of operation, we never had a driver death or even a crippling injury.[14]

The listing of instances is often effective when you are faced with the task of clarifying the scope of a large and complex organization —and you have only a few minutes to do it. For example, Elmer B. Staats, Comptroller General of the United States, speaking at the University of South Dakota, sought to clarify the work of the General Accounting Office (GAO). He economized his time as he used two clusters of instances:

At the General Accounting Office, where we have some 3,000 auditors composed of accountants, lawyers, management specialists, statisticians, economists, engineers, systems analysts, and other disciplines, we are involved in every activity of American society.
　At some point, the long arm of the Federal Government reaches out to these activities: Our fishermen at sea, our miners under the ground, our astronauts in the heavens, our poor in the cities, our farmers on the land, our ill in the hospitals, our military forces, our embassies around the world, or our older citizens.
　Wherever the Federal Government is you can be sure that the GAO is there also, doing its part to help make all Federal activities fully accountable to the public.[15]

When reinforcing or proving a point, do not suppose that a list of instances should merely be read, recited, or rattled off in a perfunctory manner. Such a list, used imaginatively, can sometimes be made a highlight of your talk; it can be not only convincing but intriguing. Consider, for example, a portion of an address by Gerald W. Thomas on "Can the World Afford to Feed Itself?" To bring to life the many statistics required by his subject, Thomas introduced a brief discussion of one specific food product—the lowly potato. He used a cluster of historical instances:

This important food product [the potato] has shaped the lives and destiny of nations. While Idaho has become nationally known as the potato state, the potato is not native to Idaho. Neither did the "Irish potato" originate in Ireland. Rather, the wild forms of potato originated, and were first collected and cultivated, by the native Indians in the Andes Mountains of South America near Lake Titicaca. Early Spanish explorers brought the first small potatoes or "earth nuts" to Europe about 1570.
　The potato became, in time, such a popular article of the diet of the Irish that it eventually was grown almost to the exclusion of other crops. The superabundance of an easily produced food also caused a population explosion on the Island. These two factors, working together, led to the disastrous famines of 1845–1846, when a

[14] Delivered January 26, 1973. Reprinted by permission of Clark E. Stair.

[15] Delivered May 12, 1973. Reprinted by permission of Elmer B. Staats.

blight killed the potato crop. One million people in Ireland died of starvation during this "potato famine" and many migrated out of the country.

At the time the potato reached Europe the Spanish Conquistadores were intensely preoccupied with the "rape of South America." In spite of their over-riding concern for precious metals, *in all likelihood they introduced the "real" treasure to the rest of the world in the "potato"*—because, the value of the world's annual yield of potatoes—some 6.5 billion hundred weight—far exceeds the value of all the gold and silver that was ravaged from the South American Continent during the centuries of conquest.[16]

Quotations. Quotations are, of all forms of support, the most varied. This form, by its nature, can include any of the other forms; that is, instead of giving your own explanation, you can quote someone else's. Likewise you may quote someone else's description, anecdote, or instance. You may quote prose or poetry, you may quote from books, plays, speeches, almanacs, newspapers, conversations, and folk proverbs. Quotations are equally useful to clarify, reinforce, or prove.

In preparing to speak on some topics you may want to gather a few apt quotations from well-tried sources with almost universal appeal —the Bible, the Declaration of Independence, Shakespeare, Abraham Lincoln. However, the first requirement of an effective quotation is that it be directly pertinent to your point. Usually, therefore, your topic and your main points should suggest specific, and often specialized, persons or other sources.

You should be alert for quotations that are not only pertinent, but also clearly and eloquently worded. For instance, in his first inaugural address as governor of New York, Nelson A. Rockefeller used a passage that can apply equally well today.

And we know something else: we know how and why this world is divided and imperiled.

It is divided, essentially, between those who believe in the brotherhood of men under the fatherhood of God—and those who scorn this as a pious myth.

It is divided between those who believe in the dignity of free men —and those who believe in the monstrous supremacy of the totalitarian state.

It is divided between those whose most potent force is their faith in individual freedom—and those whose faith is force itself.

It is divided between those who believe in the essential equality of peoples of all nations and races and creeds—and those whose only creed is their own ruthless race for power.

When a quotation is used for proof, rather than for clarification or reinforcement, the authority of the source becomes of critical significance. The strength of an authority rests in the attitude of your

---

[16] Delivered June 27, 1973. Reprinted by permission of Gerald W. Thomas.

audience. The current TV Western hero would be a stronger authority than Einstein even on the subject of relativity—before an audience of youngsters. For older audiences, you should look for quotations from persons whom the listeners will consider expert, well qualified, and unbiased or unprejudiced. Sometimes the name of your source will suffice to establish authority; at other times part of your research will include looking up the qualifications of persons you wish to quote—consult *Who's Who* or other appropriate references.

Poetry can often be used to bring emotional or aesthetic reinforcement to a point. Joseph Richard Sizoo, in a sermon for a graduating class at George Washington University, climaxed a series of instances with a poetical quotation:

> We have changed from sailing ships to jet airliners, from hieroglyphics to electric typewriters, from clay tablets to Oxford editions, from mud huts to penthouses, but to what end? What is the good of a civilization whose art ends in comic strips, whose music ends in rock 'n' roll, whose learning ends in redback-magazine stories of smutted lives and soiled tempers coated over with psychoanalysis and tossed off as literature, whose science ends in the capacity of self-destruction? Education may rationalize life, government may nationalize life, business may mechanize life, but only religion can spiritualize life. Vachel Lindsay wrote it for us in these words,
>> Not that they starve, but starve so drearily,
>> Not that they sow, but that they never reap,
>> Not that they serve, but have no Gods to serve,
>> Not that they die, but that they die like sheep.[17]

In preparing for a speech you should gather a generous supply of quotations—more than you can use. If necessary, you should be able to cite a list of different authorities, all supporting the same point. If you are working on a controversial subject, you should collect quotations on *both* sides of the question. Studying "the other side" always helps to clarify your own thinking; quoting the opposition sometimes provides you with a needed opportunity for rebuttal; quoting them may even demonstrate that their argument condemns itself. For example, in September, 1961, President Kennedy made a clear and eloquent statement to the United Nations General Assembly:

> It is therefore our intention to challenge the Soviet Union, not to an arms race, but to a peace race—to advance with us step by step, stage by stage, until general and complete disarmament has actually been achieved. We invite them now to go beyond agreement in principle to reach agreement on actual plans.
>
> The program to be presented to this assembly—for general and complete disarmament under effective international control—moves to bridge the gap between those who insist on a gradual approach and those who talk only of the final and total achievement. It would create machinery to keep the peace as it destroys the machines of war.

[17] *Representative American Speeches: 1958–1959*, p. 167.

Next day Soviet Foreign Minister Gromyko replied to the above statement as follows:

> No one knows now what armaments and armed forces the states possess. And this is quite normal. The same situation will endure after the implementation of disarmament measures provided for in this or that stage, pending the completion of general and complete disarmament. Therefore the armament of states will continue to be unknown, but with the substantial difference that a considerable part of the armaments will have been liquidated and over this, effective control will be instituted. Upon the implementation of general and complete disarmament there will be established permanent and comprehensive control.

Gromyko's statement might be quoted for the very reason that it is not eloquent; it is not even clear; it is meaningless double talk.

In doing research for any class project be alert for brief "quotable quotes" and keep a file of them for present and future spoken and written communication needs. To suggest the possibilities:

> The difficult we do immediately; the impossible takes a little longer. (Anonymous)

> The universe seems to be nearer to a great thought than to a great machine. (Sir James Jeans)

> Woman begins by resisting a man's advances and ends by blocking his retreat. (Oscar Wilde)

> Education never ends, Watson. It is a series of lessons with the greatest for the last. (A. Conan Doyle)

> According to the laws of aerodynamics, the bumblebee cannot fly. (Anonymous)

> Whether you believe you can do a thing or not, you are right. (Henry Ford)

> With some people you spend an evening, with others you invest it. (Anonymous)

In using quotes like the above you may want to remember another one, "All epigrams are only half-truths, including this one."

Statistics.　Many speeches require the gathering of statistics—a talk on business trends or one on population growth, for instance. To find appropriate statistics you will sometimes go to special sources, such as the stock market reports or census reports. In such cases you may want to copy down long lists of figures which you can study in order to improve your own understanding of a topic, but you must also be able to condense and simplify these large amounts of numerical data before using them in the actual speech. Frequently, however, you will find books, articles, or speeches in which statistics have already been reduced to usable form.

In trying to explain the economics of inflation, you could easily lose an ordinary audience in a complex maze of statistics. To make inflation meaningful to a Chamber of Commerce audience, Addison H. Reese, a bank executive, made the problem clear in this fashion:

> By way of illustration, we traced the unhappy example of a widow who received an annual income of $10,000 in 1958. By January of 1969 the purchasing power of that income had shrunk to $8,100. This poor lady has lost consistently since then, and the $10,000 income in 1958 is now [1973] worth only $6,800.[18]

You could use the same or similar humanized example to trace the buying power of the $10,000 as each subsequent year is reached.

The energy crisis if explored in statistical detail is likely to run beyond the time limits of a classroom talk, but Carl E. Bagge, president of the National Coal Association, put one major aspect of the problem into clear perspective when he said:

> If all mankind is to queue up eventually at a kind of world fuel bank, it would be prudent to know its balance of assets and liabilities beforehand. According to a recent United Nations study of global energy resources, coal's share of total fossil fuel reserves is an overwhelming 93 percent, leaving only 4 percent for oil and 3 percent for natural gas. Further, the study estimated that, at current rates of utilization, the world by the year 2000 will have exhausted 87 percent of its oil reserves, 73 percent of its natural gas reserves—and a mere 2 percent of its coal.[19]

Pursuing the energy crisis further, let us study another good way of handling the statistics. William R. Gould, chairman of the Atomic Industrial Forum, put the perspective this way:

> Within the last three decades of this century the United States is expected to consume more energy than it has in its entire previous history!
>
> By the year 2010 A.D., less than four decades from now, we are expected to reach the last 10 percent of the earth's supply of natural gas—which is the cleanest-burning of the fossil fuels. A few decades later, we will reach the last 10 percent of petroleum.
>
> Coal, fortunately, is not expected to reach this stage until about 2300 A.D.—but its use is severely limited in many areas by air pollution problems.[20]

Of course, the chief objection to nuclear power plants is the fear that accidents would be enormously dangerous. Gould summed up his principal answer by citing a single startling statistic:

[18] Delivered January 16, 1973.

[19] Delivered May 21, 1973.

[20] Delivered April 2, 1973. Reprinted by permission of William R. Gould.

Nuclear power plants, on the record, are among the safest devices ever built by man. Not one person has even been killed, or even hurt, in a nuclear accident at a commercial power plant. And we have a combined total of more than 100 years of power reactor operation.

Frankly, I am puzzled over how we can be expected to improve on a safety record of 100 percent.

In discussing the problem of nuclear waste materials, Gould at one point converted statistics into a word picture:

If we chose to store all the wastes that would be produced by all the nuclear plants contemplated between now and the end of the century in a single warehouse, it would occupy land therein equivalent to a football field and would be approximately fifty feet high.

Of course, there are times when you cannot or do not wish to simplify and condense statistics as in the above excerpts. At such times you may well consider the possible use of graphs or similar visual aids.

Audio-visual supports. In many talks, especially when the purpose is to inform, some points can be supported best by means of audio-visual aids. For example, a complicated set of statistics might be translated into a chart, or the uses of a tape recorder might be clarified by actually operating one of the machines during the course of the speech. It is sometimes impractical or inappropriate to use visual aids, but they are so often helpful that you will want to give careful thought to them while gathering materials for almost any speech.

The list of audio-visual supports given below will suggest their great variety. Several of the listed techniques are illustrated by the photographs on page 90.

PERSONS (A speech of introduction, pages 69–71)

ANIMALS (TV talk on dog training)

CLOTHING (Talk on fashions illustrated by costumed dolls)

OBJECTS (Any TV commercial selling any object)

APPARATUS (Scientist illustrating a laboratory experiment)

MODELS (Lecture at a planetarium)

SILENT MOTION PICTURES (Football coach analyzing last week's game. Advantage of silent movies is that you can talk while they are being shown.)

SOUND MOTION PICTURES (Cheerleader analyzing last week's game. Sound as well as sight would be necessary to develop her points.)

VIDEOTAPE RECORDINGS (A speech on speechmaking)

FILM STRIPS (Talk on architecture. Still shots would be better than motion pictures.)

This student brought visual aids in the upraised package. (She got attention by delaying the revelation of what was in the box.)

An ingenious topic for a demonstration talk was "Hand Guns," which, of course, suggested the materials shown in this photo.

Careful preparation of homemade visuals, such as this cross section of the Queen Mary, will be appreciated by your classmates.

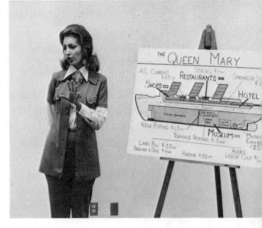

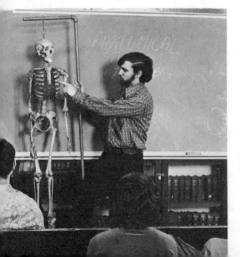

Try to imagine this talk if given by words alone and without the skeleton as a visual aid.

SLIDES (Same as film strips)

LARGE PICTURES (Talk on art with visual aids used on platform)

SMALL PICTURES (Same talk but with pictures passed around among audience)

DIAGRAMS, CHARTS, GRAPHS (Talk involving statistics or complex relationships)

MAPS (Talk in which geography is vital to the development of your ideas)

MIMEOGRAPHED OR PHOTOCOPIED MATERIALS (Talk to inform, with too many points to be remembered without written outline)

CHALKBOARD (You have seen too many examples already)

OVERHEAD PROJECTOR (See picture, page 107)

PLACARDS (Cartoons are often effective)

PHONOGRAPH RECORDS (Talk on music or the reading of poetry)

AUDIOTAPE RECORDINGS (A talk on American or British dialects)

Combined forms. This lengthy discussion of supports should not mislead you into the belief that the several forms are always clearly differentiated, or that points are usually developed by only one support. In actual practice you will find many excellent supporting materials that combine two or more of the forms here recommended. For example: Woodrow Wilson was once asked to deliver a five-minute talk, but declined on the grounds that it would require a month of preparation.

"In that case," inquired his astonished guest, "how long would it take to prepare a ten-minute talk?"

"Two weeks."

"And how long for a half-hour speech?"

"One week."

"How long for a one-hour speech?"

"Oh," said Wilson, "I can give that right now."

Now this is an anecdote, of course, but notice that it contains elements of several other forms of support: quotation, instance, explanation, statistics. You will frequently find overlapping among the six verbal forms of support. Some supports cannot be readily classified as one or another of the particular forms. Is this an anecdote or an instance? Is that an explanation or a description? Is this a quotation or a statistic? Such overlapping should not disturb you; regardless of the label, use a support if it clarifies, reinforces, or proves your point.

In actual practice you will normally expect to employ two or more supports for any point. Some of them tend to make especially good sequences. For example, an anecdote is nicely followed by instances; instances blend well into statistics; quotation teams up nicely with any of the others; explanation and description combine naturally with visual aids. Any combination of two or more forms is possible. If you want to prove a point, you might begin with explanation to make sure the audience understands the point. Next you might relate an anecdote to make the point vivid; then give instances to establish that the anecdote was not an exceptional case; next, give statistics to show proportions in terms of a whole population; and finally, quote from authorities to impress the listeners with the fact that qualified experts believe the point to be true. It all depends upon how important you think the point is and how much effort you think is required to clarify, reinforce, or prove it.

HOW TO FIND SPEECH MATERIALS

There are three principal ways of finding speech materials: observation, conversation, and reading.

Observation

From your experience as part of an audience, you know that you would much rather listen to a discussion of rattlesnakes by someone who had been bitten by one or who had witnessed the death struggle between a rattler and a king snake than by someone whose knowledge came only from books. As a listener you like materials from firsthand observation.

It should be clear by now that facts gained by direct observation are not merely permissible but vital for good speechmaking. Observation is the basis of all knowledge; it is basic to scientific method. It provides color and vitality in speech materials; it thwarts the tendency toward the bookish or the overly academic. With a little ingenuity, you can gather all sorts of excellent speech materials by observation. Here are three suggestions to get you started.

CASUAL OBSERVATION   Casual (unplanned) observation will provide you with an occasional description or anecdote if you know what to look for. For example, a student found his parked car hemmed in snugly by cars front and rear. After vainly maneuvering to get out, he went to the car in front and tried to open the door. It was locked. Then the frustrated student went berserk. He kicked the offending car furiously, apparently oblivious of the growing circle of astonished spectators. Suddenly he noticed a brick nearby. Grabbing it, he rushed back to the car and beat a window out. Hurling the brick into the car, he reached through the broken window and released the brake. This incident might be used to illustrate any number of points: campus parking problems, auto insurance, crimes of passion, temper tantrums, or emotional control.

Have you not had some dramatic experience: cyclone, tornado, earthquake, flood, fire, burglary, electrical blackout (New York City had a famous one), near-fatal accident, or the like?

Probably not a month goes by that you do not witness some incident, commonplace or unusual, that would make good speech communication material.

PLANNED OBSERVATION For example, if you were gathering materials for a speech on suburban growth, you might supplement your study of zoning maps and building codes by making a planned tour of selected construction areas—frequently using notebook and pencil (and perhaps a camera).

Planned observations are made not only through the sense of sight but through all the senses. Thus listening is a part of the method. Excellent speech materials of all types may be secured by listening to lectures or plays; to radio or television broadcasts of speeches, news comments, plays, readings; to phonograph recordings; and to sound motion pictures. And so with all the senses. You can collect material for certain speech subjects by your sense of smell, other material by your sense of taste. If you were to speak on the textures of various cloths, you would certainly make planned observations with your sense of touch.

Conversation

You can also gather good speech materials through conversations. One method is the interview. It is easy to find experts or authorities on many speech topics by scanning a list of the faculty at your institution. Experts may also by found among your local businessmen, politicians, ministers, and labor leaders. Most people are glad to help, even very important people. A university debater made a visit to Washington, D.C., where he was given cordial interviews by three senators, two cabinet officers, and the vice president of the United States. Don't become a nuisance or waste busy people's time, but don't neglect legitimate opportunities.

Sometimes interviews can provide useful local-color materials. Thus, for a classroom talk on unemployment, one student spent a night at a twenty-five-cent "flophouse," talking with his fellow guests. His speech rated a story in the campus newspaper. Good materials on unemployment might also be gathered by visiting an employment office and chatting with the applicants. There is local color everywhere if you have the eye to see it and the wit to make use of it.

Reading

Valuable as observation and conversation are, reading must, of necessity, remain the most fruitful source of research materials. Students, however, vary widely in reading ability and library skill. If you read poorly or feel lost in a big library, you should start a program of improvement at once.

PURPOSEFUL READING Much time is saved by knowing what *not* to read. Why spend several hours mechanically plodding through a book only to discover at the end that it is not what you wanted? Learn how to skim a book. Notice the title, author, and date of publication; read the table of contents; scan the index; leaf through the book and read a paragraph here and there. You can distinguish between a book likely to contain anecdotes and one likely to contain statistics. You can tell whether a book bears directly or only indirectly on the central idea of your speech. You can tell if it is too old, or poorly written. And if you seriously doubt its value to your search, put it aside, for you have many other choices.

Read slowly and critically when your purpose is to think through the subject. On the other hand, skim through materials when looking only for particular items, such as instances or statistics.

USE OF INDEXES The next step toward purposeful research is to learn to use the common library indexes. Through them you can get a perspective upon the general types and quantity of material dealing with your subject; if there is a great deal of such material, choose only the most likely references first. We shall list and describe some of these indexes here, but to give them meaning, you will have to go to your library and handle them.

To see what books a given library has that deal with your subject, consult that library's card catalogue. Although used chiefly for books, the card catalogue indexes all materials in a library. Most books have at least three cards in the catalogue, alphabetically listed under the author's name, the title of the book, and the general topic.

To find magazine articles from general and popular periodicals:
   Readers' Guide to Periodical Literature (1900–   )
For older articles of the same nature:
   Poole's Index to Periodical Literature (1802–1906)
For articles in specialized or technical journals:
   Agricultural Index
   Art Index
   Book Review Digest
   Dramatic Arts Index
   Education Index

Index Medicus
Index to Vital Speeches
Industrial Arts Index
International Index to Periodicals
Psychological Abstracts
The Public Affairs Information Service
For pamphlets:
The Vertical File Service Catalogue
For government publications:
Catalogue of the Public Documents
Monthly Catalogue of the United States Public Documents
For newspaper materials:
The New York Times Index

If you have trouble in finding or using these indexes, asks the librarian for help.

From the foregoing indexes you can secure a long list of references on almost any topic. You must learn to evaluate the references in terms of your needs. The title of an article usually gives the most direct clues, but they are frequently deceiving. If you recognize an author's name, it may help you judge. The dates of publication may be significant. Through experience you will learn what type of material to expect in various leading publications. From the data in the catalogues you can decide which books or magazines are most likely to contain the sort of materials you want.

USE OF GENERAL REFERENCE BOOKS Every library has general reference books, and many libraries place them conveniently in a section of shelves available for browsing. Spend an afternoon exploring these books. For example, suppose you are preparing a speech and would like to have a few appropriate quotations from famous people. You will find that there are books of quotations, the quotations arranged under headings by topic or by author:

Dictionary of Quotations, Evans
Familiar Quotations, Bartlett
Home Book of Quotations, Stevenson
New Cyclopedia of Practical Quotations, Hoyt
Oxford Dictionary of Quotations

You can sometimes do even better. You can find an appropriate quotation or allusion from a specific important writer by consulting a *concordance* to his works. Concordances to the Bible and the works of Shakespeare are the most commonly useful.

Speech students should be familiar with three dictionaries:
  Funk & Wagnalls, New Standard Dictionary
  Random House Dictionary of the English Language
  Webster's Third New International Dictionary
And two other wordbooks:
  Roget's International Thesaurus
  Webster's Dictionary of Synonyms
For handy reference to facts and statistics of almost every kind:
  Information Please Almanac
  New York Times Encyclopedic Almanac
  Statistical Abstract of the United States
  Statesman's Yearbook
  World Almanac and Book of Facts
For information about national and world events:
  Congressional Quarterly Weekly Report
  Facts on File
  Keesing's Contemporary Archives
For information about people:
  Current Biography
  Dictionary of American Biography
  Webster's Biographical Dictionary
  Who's Who in America; many other specialized Who's Who
  volumes
For historical facts:
  Concise Dictionary of American History
  Dictionary of Dates and Anniversaries, Collison
  Encyclopedia of American Facts and Dates, Carruth
  Encyclopedia of World History, Langer
For geographical facts:
  Columbia Lippincott Gazetteer of the World
  Webster's Geographical Dictionary
Reports of speeches in Congress, plus miscellaneous material:
  Congressional Record
For summaries of current controversial questions:
  Congressional Digest
  Reference Shelf series
For general factual materials:
  Collier's Encyclopedia
  Encyclopedia Americana
  Encyclopaedia Britannica
  World Book Encyclopedia
For oddities:
  Famous First Facts, Kane
  Guinness Book of World Records
  Things Not Generally Known, Wells
  What Happened When, Mirkin

USE OF VARIED SOURCES   Only for rare and special reasons should you ever restrict your research to the reading of a single source or author. For breadth of background, for the stimulus of reading divergent views, and for improvement in the accuracy and originality of your own thought, always read from several sources as you gather materials for your speech. One author may give you the data you need, but it takes several authors to provide you with the points of view you need if your research is to be adequate.

HOW TO RECORD SPEECH MATERIALS

Note-taking for a Specific Speech

Develop a system for keeping notes during your research on a topic, and keep all your notes in accordance with that system. Write notes on observations or conversations as soon after the event as possible, while the facts are still fresh in your mind. For notes on reading, do not pause every time you think you have something to write. That will interrupt your thought, and it may be that further on in the text the point is stated even better. Read a logical unit of material such as a section, a chapter, or even an entire short article; then pause and digest the unit in perspective; finally, if anything is worth recording make your notes. Sometimes photocopying is a timesaver.

In writing a notation, quote exactly when the materials demand absolute accuracy, when the writer has given a convenient and succinct summary of a main idea, when the writer's name will carry unusual prestige with your audience, or when he has stated a point brilliantly. Summarize in your own words when the foregoing conditions do not hold and when a lengthy block of material can and should be condensed. Note down your own reactions to the materials. Your reactions may or may not be in agreement with what you are reading. Sometimes the best use of an article is that it stimulates you to think of a rebuttal.

The following note-taking procedure is suggested:

1. Use four by six cards.
2. Record only one idea on each card. You may want to file this card later, and one card cannot be filed in two or more places.
3. On the top line write a heading for the card in capital letters. This should resemble the headline for a newspaper story and enable you to tell at a glance what is on the card.
4. On the second line write the source. For printed materials, the identification should be such that you could find the source again quickly. For sources from observation and conversation, put down whatever may have bearing on the use of the data, including the date.

5. Skip a line and then put your notation. Be extremely careful to distinguish among the three types of notations. Thus, if you are quoting directly, be sure to enclose the words in quotation marks. If you omit any words, indicate the omission by three periods separated by spaces (if the omission is at the end of a sentence, use four periods). If you insert any words, surround them with brackets (not parentheses). But never omit or insert words that would change the intent of the writer. When you are summarizing in your own words, do not use quotation marks. Your own remarks should be labeled "Comment."

Your comments may express your attitudes toward the subject matter on the card. Often, however, your comments may deal with the possible use of the materials in a speech. Some examples: "This states my central idea." "Some of these technical terms must be defined." "I could use this item in such a way as to get audience participation. Show of hands maybe?"

These suggestions are illustrated by the specimen card below.

```
"SEATTLE WHIPS WATER POLLUTION"

David Shaw, "Thanks to Jim Ellis, You Can Go Jump in the
Lake--with Pleasure," Today's Health (published by AMA),
Sept. 1973, pp. 28 ff.

     Article tells story of how one private citizen spear-
headed for 20 years civic drives against ". . . the four
horsemen of urbanization:  pollution, congestion, stagnation,
and deterioration."

     good quote:  "The city [Seattle] is 80% surrounded by
water, and, without Ellis, it might today be 80% surrounded
by the stench of stagnation and death."

     COMMENT:  Detailed answer to common question--what can
I do about ecology?  (Stress that magazine is published by
the AMA.)
```

Specimen card of notes.

Note-taking for Future Speeches

In your observation, conversation, and reading, you will continually run across materials likely to be useful to you in future talks for this class or, later on, for speeches in connection with your profession. Thus you may read a striking statement that expresses one of your most profound convictions, or you may find a delightful anecdote that you are sure could be used in many future speeches. If you fail to record these finds, you will soon forget them. The sooner you start a public speaking scrapbook, the better.

The scrapbook may be an actual scrapbook, a loose-leaf notebook, or a card file. Regardless of the form, it should be an expanding and changing record. Eventually, you will want to decide on your own set of categories to file materials, but as a beginning the following are workable:

Speech subjects and topics
Ideas for sets of main heads
Quotable quotes (see page 87)
Good words and phrases
Humorous anecdotes
Serious anecdotes
Facts and figures

A scrapbook must be a personal and individual achievement. You are the only person who can decide when to omit, when to clip and paste, when to photocopy, when to add a comment. Start the project now; it is enjoyable, and you may work on it the rest of your life.

SUMMARY

In preparing for a speech you should gather more materials than you can use in the actual speech. Your listeners should never feel that in one short talk you have exhausted your knowledge of your subject.

Research efficiency is improved when you know what types of materials to look for. Speech materials include points and subpoints, and their supports. "To support" means to clarify, reinforce, or prove a point. A practical list of verbal forms of support comprises explanation, description, anecdotes, instances, quotations, statistics. The verbal forms can be approximately matched by audio-visual aids. All the supporting materials can be used or combined in a wide variety of ways.

Three methods for finding speech materials include observation, conversation, and reading. Skill in library research will be improved if you learn to read with a purpose, use library indexes and general reference books, and read from varied sources.

For the recording of speech materials you should develop a system of taking notes on cards to be used in preparing a specific talk. You will also want to begin the compilation of your public speaker's scrapbook for possible use in future speeches.

TOPICAL PREVIEW

I   Definition of speech outlining

II Mechanics of speech outlining
    A   Detail in an outline
    B   The three major divisions
    C   The central idea
    D   Complete statements
    E   Principal, coordinate, and subordinate headings
    F   Numerals, letters, and indentations
    G   A six-step procedure for speech outlining

III Outlining the body of the speech
    A   Stating the central idea
        1   Function of the central idea
        2   Choosing and wording the central idea
        3   The central idea and the speech purpose
        4   The central idea and the audience
        5   Revising the central idea
    B   Choosing the main points
        1   Function of the main points
        2   Coordination of the main points
        3   Number of main points
        4   Using speech purpose to find the main points
        5   Stock speech designs
    C   Wording the main points
    D   Supporting the main points

IV Summary

Speech Outlining

DEFINITION OF SPEECH OUTLINING

Speech outlining is a method of putting the ideas of a speech into a condensed written form that indicates the relationships among those ideas by means of alphabetical letters, numerals, and indentations.

Thinking is the core of outlining; the outline itself is only a written record of thought. The making of a written outline assists your thinking process in several ways: (1) It helps clarify thinking by slowing you down and reminding you of idea relationships. (2) It conserves the product of thought by forcing you to record ideas before forgetting them. (3) It provides a way to test the accuracy of your thinking because you (or somebody else) can review it later on.

MECHANICS OF SPEECH OUTLINING

Detail in an Outline

Here is a stack of student speech outlines. They vary in almost all respects, including length. For brevity and stimulation of a reader's imagination, one outline entitled "Wrestling and Rassling" is a masterpiece. Here is the entire outline:

I. Wrestling takes brains.
II. Rassling takes brawn.
III. Last June in Detroit I broke my ankle.

That is condensed, all right. It tells just enough to goad the reader's curiosity—how is that last point related to the others? Such brevity in outlining is not uncommon. A substantial percentage of students think that an outline is simply a listing of three, four, or five main points. But an outline should contain more than main points—there should also be subpoints and supports.

Excessively detailed outlines, however, are as common as very brief ones. Here is just the first point from an outline for a three-minute talk:

I. In my experience last summer as a Y.M.C.A. supervisor for both boys and girls, I found that children do think and have minds of their own.
   A. "My" children were from the ages of nine to twelve.
      1. This is a dangerous age because they are preparing to enter adolescence.
   B. The real fun began when we took them to the alligator farm. The attendant guided us through the pens filled with the monsters.
      1. Billy, my most obnoxious and curious charge, disappeared.
      2. Where did I find him but in the position of almost being eaten alive.
      3. Billy was dangling from the fence of the most dangerous bull alligator's pen.
      4. I approached carefully, not wishing to scare Billy or the alligator.
      5. I said, "Billy, you shouldn't be up there. You'll get your arm eaten."
      6. Billy said, "It's my arm. If I want it eaten, I'll have it eaten."
      7. What could I do?
      8. Yes, children do have minds of their own.

The outline continues in similar style for six pages. As you see, it adds up to a script containing all the words of the speech with most of the sentences numbered and indented. Result: Too much detail destroys perspective and defeats one of the main purposes of outlining, which is condensation.

There is no hard and fast rule by which to establish the exact length of an outline. Avoid the extreme brevity of the "rassling" outline and the excessive detail of the "alligator" outline. Be guided by the general principle that an outline should contain all the ideas essential to the speech but not all, or even most, of the words. The application of this principle will become clearer as you study other aspects of outline building.

The Three Major Divisions

You have already been introduced in Chapter 3 to the fact that, of necessity, every speech has a beginning, a middle, and an end. This physical fact provides a speaker with a natural three-part sequence or thought-pattern upon which to plan a speech outline. The inexperienced speaker should use the traditional labels for the three major divisions: introduction, body, and conclusion. The three terms serve as reminders that the three parts have different logical and psychological functions, and the speaker should plan accordingly. The speaker cannot control the fact that (to the listeners) the first remarks are the beginning; the speaker can control what those first remarks will be, and he wants them to be an effective introduction to the ideas which follow. He wants to make necessity a virtue.

In a written outline the three major divisions should stand out clearly; they should be capitalized and centered but not numbered. They should not be confused as in the following student outline:

I. How would you feel if confronted by sudden death?
   A. Illustration
   B. Illustration
II. Conclusion of point
   A. How
   B. "Fear, fear itself"

Of course, the outline is too brief. A more interesting fault, however, is its confusion as to introduction, body, and conclusion. One might suspect that the rhetorical question (I) was planned as an opening designed to arouse attention, but it is not so labeled. And the use of the word *Conclusion* (II) is a further hint that the student was trying to follow the proper form. This speech may have had a good plan, but the outline conceals rather than reveals it.

The Central Idea

A well-organized talk should have a central idea to which every thought in the speech is clearly related. This central idea should be concisely stated in the outline. The importance of such a statement in clarifying the plan of a speech may be illustrated by another outline.

I. Opening sentence
II. Example of the young woman
III. The minister's troubles
IV. The story of Mark Twain
V. Closing statement

Another teaser. Apparently the student planned an opening and a conclusion—his Roman numerals *I* and *V*. Therefore *II, III,* and *IV* must be the body of the speech. But what on earth is uniting the young woman, the minister, and Mark Twain? To find out, we would have to know the central idea, which the student failed to state.

A statement of the central idea should be the first thing you write after you have written the introduction, body, and conclusion headings. The best place to write it is immediately under the word *Body.* Print a caption, *Central Idea,* at the left margin; write the statement all the way across the page.

Complete Statements

Each statement in an outline should be sufficiently complete to be clear to its intended readers. There are several types of outlines. Most common for speeches are the topical outline, the key-word outline, and the full-sentence outline. Which type should be used depends on the intended purpose and the intended reader.

The first draft of a speech outline is usually intended as a rough sketch of the over-all design. Therefore you jot down the ideas in incomplete sentences. This is called a topical outline.

At the end of the outlining process, you may want to condense the final outline into brief notes on a small card. By that time you have rehearsed the speech a number of times, and you require only a word or phrase to remind you of a given idea. Those brief notes are called a key-word outline.

In key-word outlines (and sometimes in topical outlines, too) you are using a sort of private shorthand—and only you can fully translate it. Consider, for example, the photograph of Dwight D. Eisenhower on page 52. We can actually read his card of notes. At the top is the single word GOVERNORS, printed in capital letters. The meaning was clear to Eisenhower. You and I, however, haven't the slightest notion of what he intended to say about governors. Therefore, when an outline is intended to be read by others, the customary practice is to use complete sentences. This is called the full-sentence outline.

It should be added that, even when outlining a subject for personal use only, writing the sentences in full will often help to clarify your thinking. Furthermore, you will soon forget the meaning of key words and phrases; use complete sentences when you expect to file an outline for possible future reference.

Principal, Coordinate, and Subordinate Headings

The section of the outline labeled *Body* should show the relationships of principal, coordinate, and subordinate ideas. This rule is probably the most difficult to grasp, and beginners' outlines frequently confuse such relationships badly. For example, here is an outline entitled "A Few First Aid Pointers," reproduced verbatim.

  I. Most of us are unprepared even for the smallest emergencies which might arise when living away from home.
 II. The first thing to do is call a doctor.
III. I would like to show you a few bandages which could prove handy.
    A. The bandage most often used is in the form of a triangle.
    I. It can easily be improvised.
    II. Will stay on without tape.
    III. May be folded into other forms.
    B. The way to tie these bandages is with a square knot.
    A. When people are active it is easy to trip and injure ankles.
  I. A triangle folded into a cravat makes a wonderful bandage which even allows the victim to walk.
    B. For a sprained arm or wrist there is the "sling."
    I. This is made with a plain triangle.
    C. A very useful bandage is this head bandage.
    I. It may be used to hold compresses for earaches, etc.
    I. Today everyone is beginning to realize the need for first aid training.
    A. It is now a required subject in the city schools.
    B. A working knowledge could save many lives in a real emergency.
    Note: In order to make demonstration easier I changed the order of bandages to sling, ankle, head.
    P.S. I missed the two class meetings last week because of a sprained back.

On first reading, that outline seems to be a hopeless hodgepodge. On further reflection, the student's plan can be roughly discerned. The first three items must have been meant as the introduction, the last three as the conclusion, and the other items as the body of the speech. But the form of the outline does not bring out these relationships.

In comparing two ideas, there are three logical possibilities: The first may be subordinate to the second, or the second to the first, or they may be coordinate. Any idea may be considered subordinate to another idea for any of various possible reasons: It may be a part of the principal idea (the Democratic party has two major parts: the liberal faction, and the conservative faction); or an aspect of it (the motion picture industry may be viewed from three standpoints: the financial, the artistic, and the educational); or an illustration of it (haste makes waste—for instance, . . .); or a proof of it (this proposal should be adopted for two reasons: It is needed, and it will work).

As you think about your subject, mentally juggling ideas this way and that, you should try to arrange those ideas in the form of a descending hierarchy or pyramid. At the peak is the central idea. Under this are a few main points. Under them are subpoints. At the base are facts, figures, quotations, or other forms of support. In a hierarchy of ideas each level is said to be subordinate to the level above it; the ideas within a level are described as coordinate. Putting thoughts into their proper places in a hierarchy is a measure of the accuracy of your reasoning.

Numerals, Letters, and Indentations

Relationships among items in an outline should be shown by a consistent system of numerals, letters, and indentations. In order to indicate clearly the logical relationships in the hierarchy of ideas, you should use a set of symbols corresponding with the several levels of subordinacy. The customary sequence is as follows:

I. Roman numerals
  A. Capital letters
    1. Arabic numerals
      a. Small letters
        (1) Arabic numerals in parentheses
        (a) Small letters in parentheses

When an item in an outline requires more than one line for its statement, misunderstandings of the rules for indentation often occur.

I. Short statements cause no trouble.
  A. But if a longer statement (like this one) is needed, you should *not* return all the way to the left edge of the paper—like this.
  B. Neither should you make it difficult to read the symbol by returning to a point beneath it—like this.
  C. This is the correct way. Notice that the symbol is allowed to stand out clearly.

The following model may help you to visualize all of the suggestions made in the several preceding pages, pertaining to the proper form for a speech outline:

INTRODUCTION

I. _____

II. _____

BODY

Central idea: _____

I. _____

  A. _____

  B. _____

    _____

II. _____

  A. _____

    1. _____

    2. _____

    3. _____

      _____

  B. _____

    1. _____

      _____

    2. _____

CONCLUSION

I. _____

II. _____

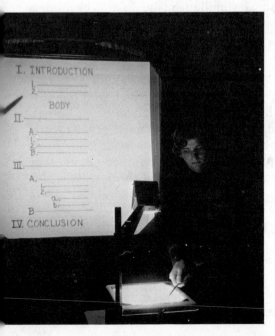

How many errors can you spot in this overhead projector shot? Compare it with the model above.

For an example of the violation of most of our suggestions about the mechanics and form of speech outlining, take another look at the weird system of captions, letters, numerals, and indentations in the outline, "A Few First Aid Pointers," page 105. For examples of proper usage, glance ahead to the sample outlines on pages 122–23, 244–45, or appendixes B and C.

A Six-step Procedure for Speech Outlining

You cannot build a speech outline without doing some hard and disciplined work. You must come to the task with proper tools and materials: You must know your audience, your subject, your purpose, and your outline mechanics.

There is no set procedure for making an outline, but each student should adopt a method and make it habitual. You may like this well-tried, six-step method:

1. State the central idea.
2. Choose the main points.
3. Support each main point.
4. Plan the conclusion.
5. Plan the introduction.
6. Test the transitions.

The foregoing procedure should be used flexibly. For example, you may find it easier to reverse the order of steps four and five. You will also find that you must work with transitions all through the outlining, especially during step three. Eventually you will be able to work on two or more steps simultaneously. In the beginning, however, master the basic sequence.

OUTLINING THE BODY OF THE SPEECH

In building a speech outline, you do not begin at the beginning; that is to say, you do not plan the introduction first. You begin by outlining the body of the speech in three steps: statement of the central idea, selection of the main points, and support for each main point. These are the first three steps in the method described above; they will be discussed in detail here. The remaining three will be discussed in Chapter 7.

Stating the Central Idea

Many students can state in a word or two their general topic for a speech, but cannot express the central idea. Before you can properly begin the construction of a speech, you must state the central idea clearly and explicitly.

The central idea may be defined as a summary of the subject matter of the whole speech. Usually it can be stated in one sentence. Occasionally two or three sentences are required. Approximate synonyms for the central idea include: the gist of the speech, the principal or key idea, the theme, the thesis or the proposition.

FUNCTION OF THE CENTRAL IDEA The central idea properly conceived and stated narrows and unifies the subject matter of the speech. Choosing and stating the central idea forces you to think through your subject, and when you think through a subject you are forced to narrow that subject and to provide yourself with a theme around which to unify a body of materials.

A speech without a carefully chosen central idea is a rambling speech—merely a series of loosely related points, connected by transitions such as "and-uh," "my next point is," or "another thing I want to discuss is . . ." The following student outline is typical:

"TARGET PRACTICE"

A. Purposes of target practice
  1. Harmony of body coordination
  2. Sense of achievement
B. Organizations representing the sport
C. Rules and method
  1. Ten commandments of safety
  2. Common sense
  3. No artificial supports
D. Positions and types of rifles
E. Target pistols versus target rifles

There are a good many things wrong with this outline besides the lack of a central idea. Many of the other weaknesses, however, stem directly from that lack. So let us analyze the outline. It is clear that the only thing that holds the points together is the fact that all of them have something to do with the subject of target practice. The points should be more closely related. It is obvious that there must be dozens, perhaps scores, of ideas on target practice. From all these possibilities, the student has chosen half a dozen. How did he happen to choose them? It would appear that he chose the first ones that came into his mind, probably rejecting those that would require research.

The outline contains several implicit central ideas. In fact, any one of the phrases A through E can be worded as a central idea in complete sentence form. Furthermore, any one of these would be enough for a short talk. For the student to attempt to cover them all means failure to achieve success with any. To put the student's faults in terms of his own topic: He used a shotgun when a rifle was required.

Now if the student had concentrated on one of the central ideas suggested above, he would have narrowed his subject. If he were actually to confine his points to one central idea, he would inevitably have a more unified speech; narrowing the subject automatically brings the points closer together.

CHOOSING AND WORDING THE CENTRAL IDEA Choosing the central idea first will guide and simplify the remaining steps. It may help if you think of the entire speech as centered on or built around the central idea. Remember, too, that the body of the speech is built specifically to support the central idea. Do not fret over trying to state it perfectly at the time, for you can revise and improve it later.

Word the central idea briefly. Its function, as we have seen, is to keep the speech unified. A lengthy statement is seldom explicit, and your statement should, above all, be explicit. The length of the speech has nothing to do with the length of the statement of the central idea. It takes more words, for example, to state the central idea of Lincoln's "Gettysburg Address" than of Conwell's "Acres of Diamonds." Lincoln's idea might be stated thus: These soldiers died in defense of the great American principle that all men are created equal, and we must dedicate ourselves to the task of justifying their sacrifice. Conwell's idea might be worded: Success and happiness are frequently found right in your own back yard. Lincoln's address took about two minutes to deliver; Conwell's about two hours.

Choose and word the central idea in terms of your specific purpose and of your audience. As you think about your general topic, ask yourself, "What can I say (narrowing subject) to get these persons (audience) to respond in this desired way (purpose)?"

The foregoing question indicates that the central idea, then, is related not merely to the subject, but also to the purpose and to the audience. The nature of these relationships will be traced in the two following sections.

THE CENTRAL IDEA AND THE SPEECH PURPOSE One of the greatest difficulties that students experience with the central idea is that they confuse it with the specific purpose. The central idea is stated in terms of the subject matter; specific purpose is stated in terms of the desired audience response. That distinction should be kept clear both in choosing and in wording the two ideas. As we said in the previous section, you choose your central idea as the best way you can think of to accomplish your purpose. To return to an earlier analogy, you aim the rifle—your speech—at the target—your speech purpose.

A few examples will illustrate the differences and resemblances among title, subject, purpose, and central idea. Notice in particular that the purposes are in terms of audience response; central ideas, in terms of subject matter.

AUDIENCE   Banquet of young people's church organization
TITLE   "A Crazy War"
SUBJECT   My experience in the army
PURPOSE   To entertain my audience with some of my experiences in the army
CENTRAL IDEA   Some of my experiences in the army were funny, some were exciting, some were sad.

AUDIENCE   High school girls
TITLE   ". . . And Eat It Too"
SUBJECT   Cake baking
PURPOSE   To explain to my audience how to bake a cake
CENTRAL IDEA   Successful cake making requires a knowledge of the proper ingredients, the process of mixing, and the techniques of oven baking.

AUDIENCE   Teachers' convention
TITLE   "Rats in a Maze"
SUBJECT   Importance of thinking
PURPOSE   To reinforce my audience's belief in themselves and their vocation
CENTRAL IDEA   We should cease paying tribute to the business tycoons or athletic heroes, and pay that tribute to our thinkers.

AUDIENCE   College speech class
TITLE   "Inventing Secrets in Order to Keep Them"
SUBJECT   Fraternities and sororities
PURPOSE   To convince my audience that national social fraternities should be abolished by this university.
CENTRAL IDEA   Fraternities on our campus do more harm than good.

THE CENTRAL IDEA AND THE AUDIENCE   The choice of central idea should be directly checked against the audience analysis. For example, in choosing and stating a central idea for the target practice speech, how would you state the central idea for an audience of college women, of college men? Despite the dominant role of the central idea in the process of building your outline, it may never be spoken to the audience. The function of the central idea is to help you think more clearly and build a unified outline of that thinking. In delivering the talk you may change the wording or leave out the statement entirely. The statement that clarifies your thinking may or may not be equally effective in influencing the listeners' thinking.

REVISING THE CENTRAL IDEA   You develop your central idea throughout the outlining process. You begin by choosing a tentative central idea, and after reasonable deliberation writing it down. As you progress through the subsequent steps of outlining, you are free at any time to go back and revise that idea.

After choosing a central idea, you may decide while outlining that it should be not merely improved but radically changed. You might, for example, have picked the central idea, "Sex education should be taught to all high school students." As you outline, your viewpoint may change, and you may decide upon another central idea such as, "Sex education should be taught to all parents." But if you do change the central idea, you immediately change the whole outline; that is, you change the entire speech.

Choosing the Main Points

FUNCTION OF THE MAIN POINTS   The function of the main points is to support the central idea. This means that if all the main points can be clarified, reinforced, or proved, then the central idea will of necessity be clarified, reinforced, or proved. Let us illustrate.

Your general purpose is to convince the audience that your central idea is true, and let us suppose that your central idea is as follows: Some type of religious education should be included in the public school curriculum. You have evolved the following tentative main points:

I. The present lack of religious education in public schools has proved detrimental in several ways to the majority of our school children.
II. The inclusion of religious education in the curriculum would eliminate or alleviate these detrimental effects.
III. A workable plan can be developed that will be fair and satisfactory to all religious denominations.

If you can prove that each of those main points is true, will the three of them suffice to prove that the central idea is true? Probably the answer is yes.

Suppose, however, that your set of main points is as follows:

I. The present lack of religious education in public schools has proved detrimental in several ways to the majority of our school children.
II. It has proved detrimental to our schoolteachers.
III. It has proved detrimental to our churches.

How about these points? Do they meet the test? Probably not. Even if you could prove all three to be true, it would not necessarily follow that your central idea is true. The trouble is that all three points aim to establish the belief that something ought to be done, but they do not establish what ought to be done. You should either narrow your specific purpose and your central idea or find a more adequate set of main points.

COORDINATION OF THE MAIN POINTS   Comparatively, main points should be of approximately equal weight or importance. In both the examples above, this test was met. However, analyze the following set:

I. The present lack of religious education in public schools has prevented most of our children from developing a working system of ethics.
II. A system of ethics, common to all denominations, could be taught without unfairness or offense to any denomination.
III. Some parents would save money.

It is obvious that the third point is not of equal weight or importance as compared with the other two. The third point should probably be omitted entirely, or demoted to a subpoint that supports a more important third point.

NUMBER OF MAIN POINTS   As a general rule the number of main points for any speech should be from one to five. The maximum should ordinarily be five because few subjects would be suitable for a single speech when more than five main headings would be logically possible without overlapping. Generally, when you think a subject requires more than five main points, you are thinking in terms of minor rather than main points. The psychological objections to more than five main points are also important. It is almost impossible for the ordinary listener to see more than five points as a related whole, and, further, few listeners are able to remember more than five points. Suppose, for example, that you hear a speech in which the speaker discusses a ten-point program for improving our state government. Could you grasp all ten points as a related program? And how many of the ten points could you name after the speech? Generations of experienced speakers have shown by their speeches that three main points are the most practical, but two, four, or five are also common. If you must have more, supplement the speech with written materials, such as pamphlets, mimeographed handouts, chalkboard lists, or the like.

To sum up, then, it is best to have a set of two to five main points of approximately equal importance, which together will suffice to support your central idea well enough to achieve your specific purpose. How will you find them? A good beginning is to review your central idea in terms of your purpose.

USING THE SPEECH PURPOSE TO FIND THE MAIN POINTS   If your general purpose is to entertain, considerable flexibility in choosing your main points is permissible. Usually all you have to do is support your central idea in the simplest sense: Amplify it or illustrate it. Careful logic is needed only in exceptional cases, which will be discussed in Chapter 12. Consider, for instance, speeches by Johnny Carson, Bill Cosby, Carol Burnett. To entertain, you ordinarily choose main points that are individually amusing or interesting or likely to get favorable attention. Often they do not have to hold together or be closely related to the main theme (as will also be discussed in Chapter 12).

If your general purpose is to inform, your main points should clarify your theme and help your listeners understand the central idea. Sometimes the central idea should be divided into constituent parts; if listeners understand each of the parts, they will understand the whole. Sometimes the central idea suggests choosing key points; if listeners understand these crucial points, they will understand the process or idea. Other methods may suggest themselves to you.

If your general purpose is to stimulate, your main points should reinforce the central idea. When you read the central idea, say to yourself, "Here is something most of my audience already believe. How can I strengthen their belief?" Sometimes this suggests proving the central idea in a way the audience has not previously considered. Sometimes it means bringing them new information, or repeating a familiar pattern with new attention-getting techniques. Whatever your method, you will look for main points of which you can say, "If I can develop these main points, I will reinforce my audience's belief in the central idea."

If your general purpose is to convince, your choice of main points is more restricted. Your central idea is normally in the form of a proposition concerning which some of your listeners are undecided or opposed. Your job is to prove the truth of the proposition to them. How can you get them to believe it? "Well," you say, "if I can show them that *this* and *this* and *this* are all true, they will have to believe *that* is true." It sometimes helps to think of the main points as the reasons for believing the central idea.

Thus by reviewing your central idea in terms of your general purpose, you may find a set of main points suited to your needs. However, beginning speakers often draw a blank because they are not sure of what they are looking for. This difficulty can be met by becoming familiar with some of the many stock sets of main heads.

STOCK SPEECH DESIGNS There are many logical and psychological speech patterns that have universal value and convenience; most of them have been used over and over again by speakers and writers down through the centuries. Here is a list of some of these stock designs.

1. Past, present, future (or other time sequence)
2. Local, state, national, international (or other space sequence)
3. Cause, effect
4. Need, desirability, practicality, alternatives
5. Problem-solution
6. Who, what, why, when, how, where
7. Advantages, disadvantages
8. Attention, need, satisfaction, visualization, action
9. Theory, practice
10. Physical, mental, emotional, spiritual
11. Heredity, environment
12. Thinking, feeling, doing
13. Structure, function
14. Political, economic, social
15. Resemblances, differences
16. Background, characteristics, accomplishments
17. Stop, look, listen (or other slogan)
18. Symptoms, prevention, cure
19. Extended analogy
20. Partitioning a quotation
21. ABC's (or other letter combination)
22. Spelling a key word

Some of these patterns will be more fully described in the next two sections. A few reflect such fundamental logical or psychological relationships that they will be discussed in detail in later chapters. The list is not exhaustive; as you read it you may be reminded of a few patterns of your own.

Fitting stock designs to subject matter. In using the check list to help you choose a set of main points you must, of course, adapt a given basic design to your particular subject matter. First, you may increase or reduce the number of points in a given design. Thus for item 1 (past, present, future) you could use any two of the three; or you could expand the number of points by subdividing past into ancient and medieval. For item 6 (who, what, why, when, how, where) you might choose any number of the six points.

Second, you can change the sequence of any item. Item 3 could be developed from effect to cause, rather than from cause to effect.

Third, you can expand and adapt the wording. Do not say, "My first point is the problem"; state in your own words what the problem is. In phrasing points, you may follow the idea pattern suggested by the key words without necessarily using the words themselves. Sometimes you may use synonyms—instead of "problem" say "difficulty," "trouble," or "the mess we're in." Sometimes the idea pattern may best be implied rather than stated directly. For example, the "Gettysburg Address" has three main divisions in accordance with item 1 of our list. However, Lincoln did not bluntly say, "First, I shall talk about the past; then about the present; etc." He did it this way:

PAST: "Fourscore and seven years *ago* . . ."
PRESENT: "*Now* we are engaged in a . . ."
FUTURE: ". . . dedicated to the great task remaining *before* us . . ."

Having given the foregoing general suggestions for finding main points from one or more stock patterns, we turn now to some examples of exactly how this might be done for specific subjects. *Use of stock designs.* Check list item 6 (who, what . . .) is one of the most useful, especially when your general purpose is to inform. Many good combinations are possible from among the six possible headings. Thus if you were speaking against a proposed amendment to the state constitution on the grounds that the proposal is being presented to the people under false colors, your main points could be these:

I. *Who* is really behind this measure
II. *What* the proposal actually means
III. *Why* the proposal is being presented

If you are trying to explain a thing or process, the following main ideas serve equally well for an explanation of anything from a washing machine to a philosophy of life.

I. *What* it is
II. *How* it works
III. *Who* can use it

You will notice as you study the items various other useful combinations that can be drawn from the six key words: who, what, why, when, how, where.

Assume that you want to speak in favor of a plan for relieving campus parking congestion. Several of the check list items might be suitable: note in particular items 4, 5, 8, and 18. With item 5 (problem-solution) the simplest design would be to develop just two main points:

I. We have a serious problem of campus parking.
II. Solution X will solve that problem.

But perhaps a variation upon the basic design is desirable. Suppose there have been two leading proposals. You might then try:

I. We have a serious problem of campus parking.
II. Solution Y is inadequate.
III. Solution X will solve the problem.

Other elaborations of the same basic design could be suggested by changing circumstances. Here is another possibility:

I. We have a serious problem of campus parking.
II. Several alternative solutions have been proposed.
III. Each proposal can be tested by certain criteria.
IV. Solution X emerges as our best available solution.

By now it is clear how you can use the check list to suggest sets of main points, and to suggest how you can adapt items on the check list to a central idea. The last four items of the list, however, may require additional clarification.

Extended analogy means that your main points are derived from an analogy that extends throughout the speech. An analogy is a comparison, more detailed than a simile, showing resemblances between two apparently dissimilar things. Thus if a commencement speaker compares life to a ship's voyage, his main points might develop from:

I. Weighing anchor
II. Steering a straight course
III. Riding out the storms
IV. Coming safely to harbor

Partitioning a quotation means that you secure your main points by dividing a quotation into its several parts. Many provocative quotations lend themselves to this treatment. One speaker discussed the subject, "Putting Faith to Work," before a church group. He quoted Admiral Hart, "Dear God, give us strength to accept the things that cannot be changed. Give us courage to change the things that can and should be changed. And give us wisdom to distinguish one from the other." The speaker then used the three sentences in this quotation as the three main points of the talk.

Item 21 (ABC's) of the check list has been used by innumerable popular lecturers. Someone entitling his speech, "The ABC's of Democracy," chooses three key words beginning with A, B, and C respectively, and builds each main point around the key word. He chooses, for example, ability, bravery, and cooperation. Another common variation is to choose a set of key words, all beginning with the same letter. Ross Smyth used this design in a Rotary Club talk on international government; early in the speech he provided this preview of his main points:

> Is it not then possible to have world peace and justice through a system of world law within a generation? Or are the problems too great? It seems that the greatest problems of mankind are Peace, Pollution, Poverty and Population—the four P's. Let us look briefly at each.

Closely related to the above items is item 22 (spelling a key word, having each letter of the word stand for a main point). There is an old story, however, about an alumnus who was speaking on "The Meaning of Yale." After a lengthy introductory section he came to his first main point, "Y stands for youthful spirit," and discussed this point for twenty minutes. The second point was, "A stands for achievement." That took twenty minutes more. In the midst of "L stands for loyalty," a bored listener remarked, "I'm glad this isn't the Massachusetts Institute of Technology."

Wording the Main Points

In general, the main points should be worded (1) to make them clear and easy to remember; (2) to show that the points are interrelated parts of a total pattern; and (3) to motivate the listeners to want to respond in the fashion sought. Usually the main points should be restated one or more times during a speech in order to increase clarity, vividness, or persuasiveness.

To illustrate imaginative use of the language in stating and restating main points, we will analyze an address by Walter B. Wriston delivered before the Regional Plan Association (RPA). He introduced his central idea and main points thus:

> All of you familiar with RPA's "Choices for '76" are well aware that metropolitan New York now consists of over 1,600 distinct and separate kinds of political units. Each of them, as Bob Wood, former undersecretary of HUD, has noted, has its own power to raise and spend the public treasure. Each operates in a jurisdiction determined more by chance than by design.

Such Balkanization, with its premium on dissent and discord, has produced an excess of Utopian solutions—all the way from giving New York back to the Indians to making it the fifty-first state.

The sheer size of metropolitan New York itself and the scope of its problems, from crime and corruption to poverty and pollution, have also produced a high tide of political rhetoric. The trouble is that many people, with the noblest intentions, have concentrated on symptoms of the sickness afflicting this city while overlooking the underlying cause. Reduced to its simplest terms, the great problem of New York City is that we no longer enjoy majority rule. The political system has evolved to a point where the smallest pockets of dissent are in a position to frustrate the will of the majority, not just for days or for weeks but for years.[1]

You will note that Wriston is using an adaptation of the "Problem-solution" design. He has characterized the problem by the terms "Balkanization" and "smallest pockets of dissent"; he has characterized the solution by "enjoy majority rule" and "the will of the majority."

During the remainder of the speech he restates his two main points in different ways: (1) the problem—"powerlessness of the powerful," "strident demands of the stubborn few," "tyranny of a privileged minority," "cater to individual dissent," "unbridled individualism," "bedlam," "fragmentation," "protest group for every cause," "multitudes of one-issue blocs," "bureaucratic maze," "political labyrinth," and "decentralized inefficiency"; (2) the solution—"give the city back to its people," "authentic power," "a melting pot," "sense of unity," "the will of the majority," and "dissent of the majority." The closing sentence of the speech: "The people who bestow power have every right to demand that this power be used to serve the broad needs of the city as a whole, and that the desires of the many not be held hostage to the dissent of the few."

Restatement of points in the same words is sometimes more effective than varied vocabulary. Thus to achieve emphasis you may say, "My final point is that we have no alternative. I repeat, ladies and gentlemen, we have no alternative." Or verbatim repetitions may be scattered throughout the speech in the manner of a slogan. You have read Antony's speech from *Julius Caesar* and have relished the repetitions of "Brutus says he was ambitious" and "Brutus is an honorable man."

You will want to develop discrimination in choosing when and how to restate your points to avoid monotony. Do not restate every point just for the sake of restating. Even so, the power of restatement is indicated by national advertisers who repeat slogans on television and radio *ad nauseam*, and find repetition effective for their purposes.

[1] Delivered April 5, 1973. Reprinted by permission of Walter B. Wriston.

Supporting the Main Points

You now have a central idea and a set of main points; together they provide you with your overall speech plan. Of course, they are not a speech; they are only part of the framework, and the main points have yet to be developed. Think about each main point and about your audience. Ask yourself "Will this sentence make my idea and its implications clear to my audience?" If not, what should you do to clarify it? "Will this sentence express something they already believe?" If so, what should you do to give it new life and intensify the belief? If they do not believe, what should you do to make them believe?

In looking for answers to these questions, we return to familiar territory. In Chapter 3 we defined a *speech unit* (statement, support, and transitions)—the basic concept of all speech organization. The concept was illustrated by the one-unit talk on "there is no use trying to please everybody," supported by the Aesop fable. This simplified example contained all the basic elements of speech construction. You now realize that longer and more complicated speeches involve the following elaborations of those elements:

1. Subpoints (as well as a main point)
2. Several main points (instead of one)
3. Several supports (instead of one)
4. Several forms of support (instead of anecdote only)
5. More numerous, subtler, more complex transitions

To prepare you for these elaborations, in Chapter 5 we defined and illustrated the functions of supporting materials (to clarify, reinforce, or prove). We said that a main point often requires two or more subpoints to support it. The job of choosing subpoints is logically the same as the job of choosing main points as described in the preceding section. You will notice that subpoints are to a main point what main points are to the central idea. The same logic is repeated again when a point or subpoint is clarified, reinforced or proved by means of explanation, description, anecdotes, instances, quotations, statistics, or audio-visual aids. Returning to the analogy between the structure of a speech and a pyramid: Each level or "layer" supports the level to which it is subordinant.

Let us apply these principles by doing some outlining. Study the student outline on the next page with the instructor's critical comments in longhand. You will see that many aspects of this outline deserve commendation. The use of numerals, letters, and indentations is satisfactory; the general effect is orderly; the number of main points and subpoints is proper; parallel wording has been used

How do main points make an overall pattern?

Title and Subject: "Labor Unions" *What is speech purpose?*

Body

Not really a main point

I.   Labor has arrived at a democratic means of dealing with management.

   A.   Instead of violence, we have negotiation.

   B.   Instead of mass killing, we have mass strikes.

Supports overlap. - all seem to support a single point.

II.   How do labor unions accomplish their purpose?

   A.   Collective bargaining.

   B.   Not just one man strikes, all the workers strike.

III.   Unions have promoted general welfare.

Not really in sequence with points I and II

   A.   Workers can afford to educate themselves as well as their children.

   B.   Keep up demand, which in turn maintains production.

for *I.A* and *I.B*. However, the outline can be improved—not made perfect, but improved.

Three major criticisms can be made: (1) The specific purpose and central idea are not clear. (2) There is overlapping among the statements. (3) The subpoints are not supported.

The purpose is not clear—is the student trying to inform or to convince? It would be difficult to summarize the whole outline into a clear-cut statement of central idea. To form a basis for improving the outline, let us suppose the attitudes of the audience are either undecided or unfavorable toward labor unions. The purpose might then be to convince the audience that they should approve of labor unions. Now we want a central idea that will summarize the evidence necessary to support that purpose. A choice might be: Labor unions have promoted the general welfare of the United States.

This brings us to the main points. The student's three main points do not hang together; they fail to form an overall related pattern. The second main heading is in the form of a question, but questions are transitions, not main points. The subpoints overlap. Notice that *I.A* is to all effects the same as *II.A*; likewise *I.B* and *II.B*. Why not combine *I* and *II* entirely? How do *I* and *II* compare with *III*? The first two deal with labor union methods, while the third deals with labor union results. Therefore two main heads are all we need. Can these two main heads be worded so that they will adequately support the central idea? Here is one possibility:

I. The methods of labor unions have become more peaceful and orderly.
II. The results of labor unions have benefited the whole country.

The two main points are in balance; the wording is fairly satisfactory; and surely if both can be proved the central idea is true.

Now to develop the first main point. We want subpoints that will prove that the point is true. The student's outline suggested two methods employed by the labor unions: strikes and collective bargaining. History suggests that both methods have been used with increasing effectiveness, moderation, and wisdom, and therefore perhaps the following subpoints can be sustained.

A. The method of strikes has become less disruptive.
B. The method of collective bargaining has become stronger.

Now we must support both *A* and *B*. To prove that strikes have become less disruptive, we can show that strikes have become less destructive (the student's outline referred to a change from mass killing). We perhaps can also show that strikes are becoming less numerous. Both these points require direct support—instances, statistics, quotations.

Now we want to develop the second main point: results. Results of strikes and collective bargaining are said to promote the general welfare. A support for this point is suggested by the customary divisions of labor, management, and public.

A. Labor has benefited.
B. Management has benefited.
C. The public has benefited.

If all three of these are true, then *II* is true, but all three points require direct support.

Very well, let us put the whole thing together and see how the outline looks.

BODY

Central idea: Labor unions have promoted the general welfare of the United States.
I. The methods of labor unions have become more peaceful and orderly.
   A. Strikes have become less disruptive.
      1. Strikes have become less destructive.

a. *True anecdote:* Early mass killings
b. *True anecdote:* Recent orderly procedure
2. Strikes have become less frequent.
a. Statistics showing decline
b. Quotation from labor authority
B. The method of collective bargaining has become stronger.
1. Collective bargaining has become more widespread.
a. Quotation re early lack of bargaining
b. Instances of recent successful bargainings
2. Collective bargaining has become more efficient.
a. Explanation of how efficiency improves with practice
b. Description of current practices
II. The results of labor union activities have benefited the whole country.
A. Labor has benefited.
1. Statistics on better hours
2. Statistics on better pay
3. Description of improved working conditions
B. Management has benefited.
1. Quotation on increased productivity of workers
2. Statistics on increased demand for products through increased buying power of workers
C. The public has benefited.
1. Explanation of educational programs of unions
2. Statistics on higher standard of American living

This revised outline is not a finished product. However, it shows how the student's original outline may be improved. In particular it shows how points and subpoints can be supported in terms of the purpose, the central idea, and the audience.

Let us do some more practice outlining. Get a pencil and some paper so that this time you can take a more active part. Suppose that you are to talk to a college group that is not a speech class. Let us choose as your subject "The Values of Speech Training," since by now you probably have quite a few ideas about it. Your purpose is to convince your audience that every student should have some speech training.

Now what might be an adequate central idea? Think about your audience and your speech purpose, and write down at least one possible central idea. Because the audience is a college group you might think of something like, "Speech training will help broaden and integrate your entire program of college course work." But think again. You are talking to students, not to faculty. Reread the statement carefully. Can you prove that it is probably true? Does it apply to *every* college student? Most students might agree that speech courses would "help," but they might mentally add "only a little bit." So you must look further for a central idea. What are some educational needs common to all students? Well, one universal need is preparation for democratic citizenship. Does that provide a clue? Very well, continue the thought process until you are able to write down a satisfactory central idea.

Next you need a set of main points. Perhaps you have already solved this problem in the course of your thinking about a central idea. If so, write down the gist of the main points. If not, the list of stock designs on page 115 may help you. How about an adaptation of item 14 in that list? Put the key words on paper; let them stimulate your thinking:

I. Political (This ties up with democracy and citizenship.)
II. Economic (Almost everybody must be prepared to earn a living.)
III. Social (We all want to be able to get along with other people.)

In choosing and wording the central idea and the main points you should be influenced at all times by the kind and amount of available supporting material. At the present moment you are trying to outline a talk to convince, and the ultimate task of your supporting materials is to prove your points. Do you have or can you get appropriate instances, statistics, and authorities? What else do you need? Do you need some anecdotes or visual aids to enliven the talk?

Go ahead with your thinking until you have completed a rough outline for the body of this talk. Then turn to Appendix B. Here you will find a sample student outline for a speech on "The Values of Speech Training." As you compare your ideas with his, you may evolve a third plan that will be the best of all.

You will notice, of course, that the outline in the appendix presents not only the body of the speech but also includes the introduction, conclusion, and important transitions. These three steps in speech construction will be discussed in the next chapter.

SUMMARY

Speech outlining is a method for putting the ideas of a speech into a condensed written form that indicates the relationships among those ideas by means of letters, numerals, and indentations.

Thinking is the core of outlining. The outline itself simply records some of the thinking process. However, an understanding of the mechanics of outlining and a systematic procedure for building an outline will often assist you during the thinking process.

Important suggestions on outline mechanics include the following: (1) In a speech outline the words *Introduction, Body,* and *Conclusion* should be capitalized and centered but not numbered. (2)

The central idea of the speech should be written immediately below *Body*. (3) Each statement in an outline should be sufficiently complete to be clear to its intended readers. (4) The section of the outline labeled *Body* should show the relationships of principal, coordinate, and subordinate ideas. (5) Relationships among items in an outline should be shown by a consistent system of numerals, letters, and indentations.

A definite but flexible procedure for building an outline follows: (1) State the central idea. (2) Choose the main points. (3) Support each main point. (4) Plan the conclusion. (5) Plan the introduction. (6) Test the transitions.

The central idea is a brief summary of the subject matter of the whole speech. The central idea should be chosen and worded with both the purpose and the audience in mind. By thus summarizing in advance the subject matter of a proposed speech, the speech materials are narrowed and unified.

An outline should contain from one to five main points. Taken together, the main points should suffice to support the central idea. Main points may simply represent a speaker's idea of the natural divisions of his subject. However, the choice of main points is usually assisted by studying a list of stock designs. The main points should be worded so as to show the total pattern, to make the points easy to remember, and to motivate the listeners.

A main point is usually supported by two or more subpoints, which in turn are supported by explanation, description, anecdotes, and so forth. As usual, the supporting materials should clarify, reinforce, or prove the point to which they are subordinate.

TOPICAL PREVIEW

I Planning the conclusion
   A Undesirable conclusions
   B Desirable conclusions
   C Writing out conclusions

II Planning the introduction
   A Purposes of the introduction
      1 Arousing favorable attention
      2 Promoting friendliness and respect
      3 Leading into the subject
   B Undesirable introductions
   C Desirable introductions
   D Writing out introductions

III Testing transitions
   A Functions of transitions
   B Wording of transitions

IV Summary

7
Conclusions,
roductions, and Transitions

Your introduction may determine the attitude with which the audience will listen to the rest of your talk, or perhaps whether they will listen at all. Your transitions may determine whether the audience will follow your train of thought during the body of the speech. Your conclusion may determine what their final attitude will be. Usually your first and last words will be the easiest for the audience to remember.

PLANNING THE CONCLUSION

The purpose of the conclusion is to bring the entire speech into focus on the central idea. All that you have said—points, subpoints, supports—should be pulled together in the conclusion so as to hit with combined impact. The conclusion should give the speech a "rounded off" effect, and give the listeners a sense of completeness.

In order to accomplish its purpose the conclusion must be carefully planned and carefully phrased. Effective conclusions seldom are improvised during the delivery of the speech, and they rarely arise from the inspiration of the moment. Failure to understand the purpose of the conclusion or failure to plan properly causes speakers to fade in the homestretch.

Undesirable Conclusions

a. The abrupt conclusion.   Audiences like to feel that a talk is rounded off at the end. They dislike a speaker who completes his discussion of the last subpoint of his outline and then abruptly sits down. The effect is even worse if he pauses and says, "Well, I guess that's about all I have to say . . ." A well-planned conclusion may seem abrupt, however, if the speaker has failed to warn his audience that his conclusion is under way. The speaker should let his audience know when he starts his conclusion by implication, by change in mood or manner, or by using a transition such as "in conclusion" or "finally."

b. The multiple conclusion.   Audiences also dislike speakers who string several conclusions together like sausages. The audience becomes increasingly exasperated as the speaker builds up to what seems to be the final sentence—then goes on to another final thought —and then to another—and another.

c. The apologetic conclusion.   A speech should end on a positive note. Do not spoil your talk by ending lamely with, "I'm afraid I haven't clarified the electoral college system very well but I just thought that maybe . . ." Or, "I don't want to bore you with further details, but there is one final point that ought . . ."

d. The tacked on conclusion.   Some speeches have an unfortunate break in logic or psychology between body and conclusion. A conclusion should spring from the body of the speech. A speaker should not think of introduction, body, and conclusion as three separate entities, but as interwoven parts of the whole. The progression from body to conclusion should sound natural and inevitable.

e. The anticlimactic conclusion.   Some speeches seem to build up to an awful letdown. After a forceful and slashing attack on the evils of some existing situation, the speaker ends merely by proclaiming that something should be done or that there ought to be a law against it. Then there is the speech that starts strongly and gradually runs out of gas, the conclusion sputtering slowly to a stop.

f. The indecisive conclusion.   A more subtle weakness exists in the conclusion that leaves a first impression of adequacy but a second impression of doubt in the listeners' minds. Just what *is* the main point of the speech or the exact response expected? If the speaker seems uncertain, the listeners will also seem uncertain.

Successful conclusion: The speaker called for a show of hands, and he got almost unanimous response.

Desirable Conclusions

Three types of conclusions will serve most purposes: (1) a summary that swiftly recalls the main points of the speech; (2) an appeal that identifies your speech with the desires and aspirations of your audience; (3) a call for action that enlists audience support for your proposal. These ways of concluding may be used singly or in combination. Their effectiveness is often enhanced by the following rhetorical devices:

1. Enumeration	6. Rhetorical question
2. Restatement	7. Epigram
3. Allusion	8. Prophesy
4. Quotation	9. Personal reference
5. Climactic anecdote	10. Challenge

Let us study a few examples.

A student gave a classroom talk on superstitions, including "knock on wood," tracing them back to their ancient origins. She concluded by restating her main point and then using an effective nonverbal stimulus:

> We are not only the products of the physical inheritance of our ancestors but we continue to perpetuate the remnants of their superstitions.
> "Knock on wood" [She raps her knuckles on the rostrum.] and hope that we all do well in this course.

Arthur R. Taylor, President of Columbia Broadcasting System, participated in a symposium at Amherst College on "What's Worth Doing?" He discussed career opportunities in American business corporations, ending with a summary and an appeal to student aspirations. His last sentence was a carefully understated call for action:

> In sum, ladies and gentlemen, life with the American corporation need not be drab, uninteresting or require excessive compromise. There is—and increasingly will be—room for personal independence, for those who serve individual goals and those who wish to serve higher goals. Corporate careers can, indeed, be an exciting and fulfilling road for the pursuit of those goals because, first, the American corporation is one of the few machines capable of chipping away at our mutual problems; second, the corporation allows young men and women to express their individuality, to speak their minds, to have a "piece of the action." The successful corporation wants the outspoken, the creative, the questioning individual who seeks new ways of doing things. I'm very hopeful for the future and perhaps there are some here who would join that hopefulness.[1]

Vernon E. Jordan, Jr., Executive Director of the Urban League, addressed the annual AFL–CIO Convention in support of several joint-actions between his organization and theirs. He brought his entire speech into focus by means of an apt quotation from a founding father of the labor movement:

> Many years ago, Samuel Gompers was asked: "What does Labor want?" "What does Labor want?", he replied. "We want more schoolhouses and less jails; more books and less arsenals; more learning and less vice; more leisure and less greed; more justice and less revenge; in fact, more of the opportunities to cultivate our better natures, to make manhood more noble, womanhood more beautiful, and childhood more happy and bright."
> And that, my brothers and sisters of the great American labor movement, is what black people want![2]

[1] Delivered January 18, 1973. Reprinted by permission of Arthur R. Taylor.

[2] Delivered November 22, 1971. Reprinted by permission of Vernon E. Jordan, Jr.

Don Paarlberg, an economist in the U.S. Department of Agriculture, addressing the National Milk Producers Federation, opened with a rhetorical question, "Are the family farms going to survive, or will they be swallowed up by huge corporate farms?" He analyzed this question in a rather lengthy, detailed, well-organized, sometimes technical speech. In his brief conclusion he summarized and challenged them to reach a decision:

> For most American agriculture, the family farm can continue to be the major organizational form:
>
> > If it is permitted the flexibility that will allow the efficient use of modern technology and management.
> > If it is provided with good research, education, and credit.
> > If it makes wise use of the principles of cooperation.
> > If it continues to enjoy the good will of the public.
>
> All these things are possible if we decide we want it that way.[3]

President John F. Kennedy's 1961 Inaugural Address was justly acclaimed by leaders of both major political parties. His conclusion brought the whole speech into focus; it combined emotional appeal with a call for action; restatement and epigrams were effectively used:

> And so, my fellow Americans: ask not what your country can do for you—ask what you can do for your country.
>
> My fellow citizens of the world: ask not what America will do for you, but what together we can do for the freedom of man.
>
> Finally, whether you are citizens of America or citizens of the world, ask of us here the same high standards of strength and sacrifice which we will ask of you. With a good conscience our only sure reward, with history the final judge of our deeds, let us go forth to lead the land we love, asking His blessing and His help, but knowing that here on earth God's work must truly be our own.

Clarence Darrow was the most famous defense attorney of the first half of this century. During his long career he took part in many important cases, and he delivered many memorable pleas to juries. One of the most dramatic of his courtroom speeches was given in 1912 when Darrow was accused of trying to bribe jurors in a labor case; Darrow spoke in his own defense. After carefully and logically analyzing the evidence in order to show that the charges were a frame-up, he concluded with an emotional plea which put a call for action into the form of a prophecy:

> There are people who would destroy me. There are people who would lift up their hands to crush me down. I have enemies powerful and strong. There are honest men who misunderstand me and doubt me; and still I have lived a long time on earth, and I have

---

[3] Delivered November 30, 1971. Reprinted by permission of Don Paarlberg.

friends—I have friends in my old home who have gathered around to tell you as best they could of the life I have lived. I have friends who have come to me here to help me in my sore distress. I have friends throughout the length and breadth of the land, and these are the poor and the weak and the helpless, to whose cause I have given voice. If you should convict me, there will be people to applaud the act. But if in your judgment and your wisdom and your humanity, you believe me innocent, and return a verdict of Not Guilty in this case, I know that from thousands and tens of thousands and yea, perhaps millions of the weak and the poor and the helpless throughout the world, will come thanks to this jury for saving my liberty and my name.[4]

The emotional impact of Darrow's plea was reported by Weinberg:

All through the trial, it was the feeling that jurors number seven and number eleven were against Darrow. But when the accused attorney concluded his speech, the two men were openly weeping, as was everybody else in the courtroom including the judge.[5]

Conclusions vary greatly in length. Sometimes a whole speech can be focused by a single concluding sentence, but sometimes many sentences are required. However, the conclusion should rarely run more than 5 percent of the length of a speech.

Writing Out Conclusions

After planning a conclusion, a speaker has considerable freedom in the form he uses to outline it. Parts or even all of the conclusion should sometimes be written out, especially when quotations, epigrams, or key words and phrases are to be used. Freedom of form is needed because the job of focusing final attention on the central idea differs from the job of developing the central idea in the body of the speech.

Once you have your conclusion prepared, you are ready to build the final part of the outline—the part you might have supposed should be done first.

PLANNING THE INTRODUCTION

By this time you undoubtedly have deduced why we have delayed consideration of the speech introduction. The reason, of course, is

---

[4] Arthur Weinberg, ed., *Attorney for the Damned*, Simon and Schuster, 1957, p. 530.

[5] *Attorney for the Damned*, p. 531.

obvious. You cannot plan an introduction until you know what you want to introduce.

The opening words of a talk are often the most important. The very fact that they are heard first gives them psychological significance. If you fail to secure the listeners' attention at the beginning of a speech, you make it harder to secure later on. And, of course, if you entirely fail to arouse their interest, you might as well not give the talk. Furthermore, if you should antagonize the listeners at the start, you create mental resistance that is difficult to overcome. And if you begin by confusing your audience, you will have trouble in correcting your mistake when you try to reexplain what you meant to say.

Purposes of the Introduction

The purposes of a speech introduction are three: to arouse favorable attention, to promote friendliness and respect, to lead into the subject.

1. AROUSING FAVORABLE ATTENTION   Once in a while your listeners know beforehand what your subject is to be and arrive eager to hear what you have to say. They lean forward with attention as you start to talk. But that is only once in a long while. Usually if they lean forward it is because they are tired and want to stretch, or because they are nearsighted. They expect you to make the subject interesting. The listeners' attention is on a variety of other matters: that cute blonde in the third row, that overhead light that keeps flickering, that dental appointment tomorrow, that tight left shoe, and so forth. So you must devise a way to overcome inertia and distractions.

If you walked to the rostrum and fired a shotgun, you would get attention all right. But that attention would probably hurt your subsequent speech rather than help it. You must not only attract attention; you must attract favorable attention.

Getting favorable attention is the first concern of any speaker. Once captured, it must be held during the rest of the talk. In fact, the psychology of attention is so basic to speech communication that we shall not only discuss it in this chapter but later devote an entire chapter to it.

2. PROMOTING FRIENDLINESS AND RESPECT   The aim of your opening remarks is higher than merely to get attention; you must also promote good will toward yourself as a person. In this class you can initially count on a sympathetic and friendly attitude. You

can reinforce that favorable attitude early in each classroom talk by showing that you have chosen your topic with them in mind, that you have tried to prepare thoroughly, and that you are aware of the fact that this class is a unique community with many shared concerns. You will certainly not command respect by attempting to get by with only glibness and a flashy smile. One student was overheard describing a classmate, "You open the front door and look into the backyard."

The job of establishing rapport when you speak before groups of strangers will be discussed in Chapter 11.

3. LEADING INTO THE SUBJECT   Yet a third aim must be achieved during the beginning of your speech. You must lead into your subject, and just getting into it any way is not sufficient. What is the best way to approach the subject in order to accomplish the speech purpose?

Again audience analysis must be considered. What is their predominant attitude toward your subject? Are they already in favor of it? If they are, you may want to jump into the body of the speech directly. But if they are undecided, you may want to approach your subject more gradually. Are they opposed? If so, you may want to establish a common ground before getting into the body of the speech. If they are indifferent, you may want to approach your subject through its most entertaining aspects.

At this time you also must consider when and how to state your central idea to the audience. On pages 108–12 we discussed the fact that the time, place, and wording of the central idea should first assist your thinking as you plan the outline, and that later adaptations might be made in terms of the audience. Now ask yourself when and in what words the central idea should be stated.

Should the central idea be stated in its normal place, at the beginning of the body of the speech? Usually this is the best place for several reasons: It satisfies the listeners' desire to know what the speech is about; it prepares the listeners for what is to follow; it helps the listeners grasp the speech as a unified whole. However, these reasons are sometimes outweighed by others. If you anticipate opposition attitudes, it is best to delay revealing your central idea or purpose until later in the speech. If you tell them the point early they may close their minds at once. Likewise, if your purpose is to entertain or stimulate, it is sometimes wise to build a speech on suspense, delaying the revelation of the point until the very end. On the other hand, there are rare occasions when you may want to state the central idea earlier than usual, perhaps as the first words of the speech, in order to get attention. Weigh the alternatives and decide where to state the central idea.

Undesirable Introductions

a. The "hem-and-haw" introduction. Nobody is favorably impressed by the speaker who, from lack of either preparation or of confidence, starts off in a hesitant, faltering manner. "This is—uh—a good time to begin—uh—thinking about—I mean preparing for—the—uh—final examinations. Well—uh—I thought I might sort of discuss them." The opening should be definitely planned. Sometimes it may even be wise to memorize the first sentence or two.

b. The apologetic introduction. Start positively. You should be modest, of course, but do not apologize for your presence by either words or manner. "I couldn't think of a topic today so I . . ." "Public speaking is not in my line, and I don't know why . . ." "I'm afraid all of you know more about this subject than I do, and I don't suppose you'd be much interested in . . ."

c. The trite introduction. Your classmates have a right to expect a little more originality than "My topic for today is 'Inflation.' This is a very important matter to each and every one of us. All of us become concerned when our pocketbooks are affected. And today inflation casts its ominous shadow throughout the land. The time for action has come. We now stand at an economic crossroads." Also avoid too many trite phrases so often heard when speakers begin a speech: "It is a pleasure and a privilege," "Throughout the history of mankind," "I am reminded of the story of," "I view with alarm," and so on.

d. The pedantic introduction. Lectures by professors are too often models of poor communication. Avoid the jargon of your major field when talking to people outside of that field. Even professors and graduate students of speech communication are guilty of atrocities: "The study of communicative dysfunctions involves the establishment of the symptomatology and etiology in a given case before making a determination of the therapeutic strategies that can be appropriately programed and operationalized." Since you are exposed so frequently to college lectures and textbooks, you will probably agree with this comment by a fellow sufferer, "Just because you can't see the bottom, doesn't mean that the waters run deep—perhaps they're only muddy."

e. The misleading introduction. There is always a speaker who thinks he must begin by telling a joke. He is likely to pick one because he thinks it is funny, not because it leads into his subject. Perhaps it goes something like this: "My father used to tell of a man who was about to be hanged, and was asked if he had any last words. 'Well,' he replied, 'all I can say is—this has certainly been a lesson to me.' "

The audience laughs—politely or loudly, depending upon how well the joke was told. But what does the speaker say next? Suppose he says: "I don't know whether this talk will be a lesson to anyone or not. Probably it will be a lesson for me. In any event, I'm going to discuss today why the United States should have a new major political party."

What is your reaction? Irritated, aren't you? The joke was misleading because it did not really lead into the proposed subject. Only a tortured transition made it connect with the subject at all (although a good transition might have saved it). Jokes, however, are not the only type of misleading opening; any other opening device can be similarly misused.

Desirable Introductions

Keeping in mind the foregoing functions of a speech introduction, let us list the most frequently successful ways of opening a talk:

1. Reference to previous speaker or chairman
2. Reference to occasion
3. Honest compliment to audience
4. Appropriate joke or other humor
5. Unison audience reaction: singing, applause, show of hands
6. Statement of central idea or main points
7. Startling statement
8. Quotation
9. Illustrative anecdote
10. Development of common ground
11. Rhetorical question
12. Personal reference
13. Reference to recent event
14. Visual aids
15. Definition of terms.

The introduction may consist of just one of the above ingredients; more often, however, it consists of a combination of two or more. When a combination is attempted, the ingredients should usually be blended rather than simply strung in sequence.

You might assume that the ideal opening would consist of three ingredients: one to get attention, one to promote good will, and the other to lead into the subject. That is a perfectly good possibility. However, a single ingredient may simultaneously accomplish any two or all three of the functions. For example, an illustrative anecdote might be found that would command favorable attention, establish your pleasantness, fairness, cooperativeness, and insight, and at the same time lead naturally and effectively into the body of the speech. Such a multiple-purpose ingredient is not always easy to think of but is worth the try.

Next let us analyze some actual speech openings in light of our previous discussion.

A student majoring in forestry introduced a classroom speech by handing out envelopes in which there were leaves from trees. After everyone had taken the leaves from the envelopes, felt them, and smelled them, he said, "My subject today is 'Poison Oak!'"

He certainly got attention: first, through curiosity aroused by the visual aids; second, through a startling statement. But he continued:

> Before anyone faints, let me state that those leaves you have in your hands are *not* poison oak. In this box [showing the leaves] you can see the real thing.
>
> You will notice that your leaves are quite similar to these, however. And so today I want to explain how you can identify poison oak by its foliage.

The speaker shows friendliness and good will as he opens an all-day workshop on Indian affairs, bringing together representatives from government, university, and Indian tribes.

He made sure that the initial attention would be favorable, and then led directly into his subject. The introduction also promoted friendliness and respect toward the speaker because his listeners thought the introduction intelligent, clever, and amusing, and because they respected the care and preparation the introduction showed. The same effects were achieved in a different fashion by another student in a classroom talk on "Beer." He opened thus:

> Last week I visited the 32nd street market and did some research. I watched the different shopping behaviors of dozens of customers who were buying liquor, wine, and beer. I was surprised when the manager proudly told me that his market does the largest business in alcoholic drinks in California and almost the largest of any store west of the Mississippi. He also confirmed what my eyes were telling me—the most popular beverage was beer. Of course, I bought a six pack so that I could do some homework. Next day I went to the library to look into the history of beer. And Tuesday I took a field trip to watch a brewery plant in operation. The more involved I became, the more enthusiastic I became. Today I'm assuming that all of you drink beer. In moderation, of course! I hope to increase your enjoyment of beer by showing the ancient history of this boon to mankind, and by briefly describing the modern mass production of it.

Carl L. Gay, a student at Washington State University, was invited to address the 50th Annual Washington State Forestry Conference in late 1971. He opened with a succinct resume of the recent events that highlighted the campus uprisings of the late 1960's, the climax of violence, and the sudden change to nonviolence. This led him swiftly into the body of his talk dealing with the current and future concerns of young Americans:

> Seven years ago, when I was still a budding teenager, Mario Savio, wearing a sheepskin jacket and hair that was by today's standard short, inaugurated the free speech movement by leading 800 University of California at Berkeley students into Sproul Hall to be arrested. For the six years that followed, America was at war with her students. The battlegrounds and strategies by now are familiar to us all: campus sit-ins, teach-ins, strikes, and confrontation with police who "saw campuses only through the tinted visors of riot helmet." Many viewed it as a revolutionary threat to the security of our nation. Many thought it would lead to the revolutionary change our country needed. Whatever it was, it appeared to climax in the spring of last year. The rocks and bricks, the rifles and billy clubs appeared to be laid down. When the new school year began, a year ago September, an apprehensive nation breathed a sigh of relief.[6]

Warren E. Burger, Chief Justice of the Supreme Court, began a speech for the American Law Institute, by reference to the occasion, a brief quotation, and a statement of his central theme:

[6] Delivered November 5, 1971. Reprinted by permission of Carl L. Gay.

Forty-one years ago last week, the Institute met in Washington—probably in this very room—when the Mayflower [Hotel] was new and sparkling. Now the Mayflower has taken on the air of grace and patina that I like to think comes with age, but the problems you and I are concerned about are very much the same. I was in Law School when Chief Justice Hughes welcomed the members of the Institute that spring morning of 1931 when he spoke of the growing burdens on the Federal Courts, the need for more judges, and for better methods. He expressed his concern in terms of "the ultimate goal that ever recedes—even as we advance and press on."

Today I welcome you at a time when that "ultimate goal" Hughes spoke of seems to have receded even farther from our grasp than ever before.[7]

Thomas J. Watson, Jr., Chairman of the Board of International Business Machines Corporation, a prestigious industrialist and advocate of free enterprise, addressed the Mayo Foundation. He used the problem-solution design for organizing his speech which called for a new form of national health insurance. He opened his talk with startling statements which did double duty because they commenced his development of the "problem" portion of the speech design. The startling statements were in the form of a rhetorical question:

Let me start by asking a question that this great medical center brings to mind: How would you like to live in a country which—according to the figures available in the United Nations—during the past two decades has dropped from seventh in the world to sixteenth in the prevention of infant mortality; has dropped in female life expectancy from sixth to eighth; has dropped in male life expectancy from tenth to twenty-fourth; and which has bought itself this unenviable trend by spending more of its gross national product for medical care—$1 out of every $14—than any other country on the face of the earth?

You know the country I am talking about: Our own USA, the home of the free, the home of the brave, and the home of a decrepit, inefficient, high-priced system of medical care.[8]

A. Bruce Johnson, an economist, talking on inflation before the American Institute of Chemical Engineers, sought to establish a friendly and informal approach to his economically nontechnical discussion. He quoted and paraphrased a humorous Art Buchwald column, leading by natural stages into his own definition and analysis of inflation:

In his syndicated column Art Buchwald once asked his readers, "Where does the word inflation come from?" Answer: In 1887 there was a bar and grill owner in San Francisco named George Inflation. One day he failed to receive a shipment of booze from the East. Since the demand for booze was great, George Inflation decided to charge 15 cents for a shot of whiskey, instead of the standard 10

---

[7] Delivered May 16, 1972.

[8] Delivered November 19, 1970. Reprinted by permission of Thomas J. Watson, Jr.

cents. He also made the shot glass smaller. This did not stop his customers from buying booze, so he raised the price to 20 cents, then 25 cents. The other bars in San Francisco raised their prices accordingly and when their customers complained the other bar and grill owners would say, "Blame it on Inflation." Thus inflation soon became a part of the English language.

Buchwald's second question was, "Why is everyone so fascinated by inflation?" Answer: Because there are so many things that you can do with it. You can hold it; you can turn it around; you can spiral it; you can send it sky high; you can let it get out of hand; you can try to curb it; restrain it; stop it; and during feeding hours, you can go to the bank and watch it eat up your savings.[9]

The above excerpt may be contrasted with the typical trite student example on the same subject, page 135; this type of opening humor may be contrasted with the hackneyed, "I am reminded of the joke about the two traveling salesmen."

Paul MacKendrick, a professor at the University of Wisconsin, spoke on "The Relevancy of History" as guest speaker at Vanderbilt University. He opened with an illustrative anecdote, the climax of which may have surprised many of his listeners. The story obviously led into his subject matter and central idea:

> Once upon a time, when the world was young, a man with a high forehead and a grave, bearded face, an aristocrat whom democrats delighted to honor, stood before his fellow-citizens, in the fairest suburb of the city, and, on a painful occasion, delivered the most eloquent praise of democracy ever uttered. They were involved in a war, which he and they saw as a war between democracy and totalitarianism, and he was speaking over the first dead who had fallen in that war. He told his listeners that their democracy was worth dying for, but far more worth living for, because it was a democracy: a society in which careers were open to talent, where men pursued wisdom without dilettantism, enjoyed equal rights under law, practiced a generous foreign policy, knew what reverence was, saw to it that power rested with the majority and not with the few, loved beauty, enjoyed a high standard of living, rejoiced in an open city without purges or military secrets, participated universally in decision-making, and lived in a spirit of tolerance.
>
> Two years later, the speaker was dead; twenty-seven years later the democracy lay prostrate and defeated before its totalitarian enemy. It seems not entirely irrelevant to ask why.
>
> The time was 431 years before the birth of Christ, the eloquent speaker was Pericles, the city was Athens, the enemy was Sparta.[10]

In a short talk the introduction may require but a sentence. As an approximation, one can say that the average length for an introduction should seldom take more than 10 percent of the total time

[9] Delivered in April 1973. Reprinted by permission of A. Bruce Johnson.

[10] Delivered November 10, 1971.

of the speech. But fluctuations are wide. It is conceivable that under unusual circumstances an introduction should comprise over half the speech. Length should be determined by the three functions of a speech opening. What do you need to do in order to accomplish the three functions?

Writing Out Introductions

Writing down the outline of your planned introduction, like writing down the conclusion, is subject to most flexible rules. This is true because the job of getting attention, promoting friendliness and respect, and leading into the subject, is quite different from the job of supporting the central idea. Unlike the body of the speech, for example, the introduction does not necessarily require the use of speech units with strict regard to point and support. So the ideas for the introduction may simply be listed. Likewise, unlike the body, the materials for the introduction need not necessarily be severely condensed; some or all of the introduction may be written verbatim to insure a smooth and positive start.

We now come to the final step in building an outline—and sometimes the most intellectually demanding.

TESTING TRANSITIONS

Functions of Transitions

Transitions show the logical or psychological relationships among the divisions of your outline. During the construction of a speech outline, attempts to state transitions between points help the speaker test the strength of the structure of the outline. For example, a point, subpoints, and supports in correct outline form look all right on paper. Try rehearsing that section aloud. If you have trouble connecting adjoining items or holding the several items coherently together, that is a hint that something is wrong. Perhaps one item does not belong, or the sequence should be altered, or the section should be reworded.

During the delivery of the talk the function of your transitions is to show the listeners how each point fits into the scheme of the speech. Sometimes, especially with minor items, the relationships are so plain that the audience is bound to grasp them; stating them only belabors the obvious and bores people. Most of the time, however, speakers err in the opposite direction; they lack enough transitional statements. The relationship among points is clearer to the speaker than to the listeners. In the first place, the speaker can see the points, all labeled and indented, as he reads his outline. The listener can only hear them—he cannot pause to think about the relationship involved or go back and relisten; he must perceive the relationship instantaneously. In the second place, the speaker has been through the mental processes of preparing the speech and may forget that what seems clear to him now was not clear earlier. The listener has no such advantage; he is thinking through the speech for the first and only time. Therefore transition statements should be scattered liberally throughout the speech, constantly telling the audience why B follows A, and C follows B.

Therefore the stating of transitions fulfills two functions: During the building of the outline, it helps to test the speaker's logic; and during the speech delivery, it helps to show the audience what the speaker's logic is.

Wording of Transitions

If you have carried out the process thus far described in this chapter, you have before you what appears to be a completed speech outline. You have an introduction, a body, a conclusion, and a central idea. The body of the outline has its main points, subpoints, and supports. You have made mental transitions throughout the outlining process, for the outlining process is a thinking process. But silently thinking that two points are related is easier than expressing that relationship aloud. The final test of your important transitions is wording them aloud. This task can be broken down into four steps and undertaken in the following order:

1. Getting from introduction to body of speech
2. Getting from body to conclusion
3. Getting from a point to a coordinate point
4. Getting from a point to a support

1. TRANSITIONS BETWEEN INTRODUCTION AND BODY   The transition from introduction to body is usually the most critical transition in the entire speech because it involves your central idea which, as we have seen, is the keystone of the speech. We have also previously pointed out that the important decision is whether or not to state that central idea here, postpone stating it, or state it earlier. The central idea is most commonly placed between the introduction and the body of the speech. In order to set up a hypothesis to illustrate the use of transitions at this place in the outline, let X be the last item of introduction, Y be the central idea, and Z be the first main point of

speech body. The first function of the transitions is to get from X to Y, and from Y to Z. But we may want to accomplish more than this one function. For example, we may want to show the overall relationships among X, Y, and Z, or we may want to include a preview of all the main points. There are two types of transitions to fulfill the two functions. *Connective* transitions show the relationship between two adjoining points; *perspective* transitions show the relationships among several items.

Both connective and perspective transitions can be achieved in various ways:

1. Connective words and phrases
2. Rhetorical questions
3. Repetitions
4. Perspectives centered about first, second, third
5. Perspectives centered about speaker, audience, occasion

These are not the only ways to effect transitions, but they will suffice most of the time. We will next show how transitions are effected in actual practice.

For illustrative purposes we will set up a hypothetical section of a speech outline. Our hypothetical case will, of course, require the three ingredients X, Y, and Z.

X (last item of introduction): Anecdote about a friend, Helen Jane, who wasted endless hours, curtailed her recreations, reduced her grades, and almost developed an inferiority complex—all because of slow and inefficient reading habits. Assume the anecdote ends with Helen Jane saying, "And you may be just as inefficient in your reading as I was!"

Y (central idea): Modern psychology has developed scientific methods by which you and I can learn to read better and faster.

Z (first main point of speech body): Make an accurate test of your present reading rate.

The foregoing wording, beginning with the last sentence of X, will be retained, as we now apply our five kinds of transitions.

a. Connective words and phrases.
    "... And you may be just as inefficient in your reading as I was!"
    However, modern psychology has developed scientific methods
        by which you and I can learn to read better and faster.
    Therefore, make an accurate test of your present reading rate.

Those two transition words are helpful but leave something to be desired. Perhaps you can think of substitute words or phrases that would be improvements. The main trouble, however, is that connective words and phrases are better adapted to minor transitions. At best in this example, they will only connect X with Y, and then Y with Z. They cannot show interrelations among all three, or give broad perspective, or make the central idea stand out prominently.

b. Rhetorical questions.

"... And you may be just as inefficient in your reading as I was!"
I wonder if we are? And, if we are, must we suffer the same tragic consequences as Helen Jane suffered?
Modern psychology has developed scientific methods by which you and I can learn to read better and faster.
How, then, can I get started? How can I begin to improve?
Make an accurate test of your present reading rate.

You will note that this is better, and perhaps good enough. However, rhetorical questions sometimes have to be supplemented by other methods if perspective is desired.

c. Repetition.

"... And you may be just as inefficient in your reading as I was!"
Yes, you may be inefficient in your reading but modern psychology has developed scientific methods by which you and I learn to read better and faster.
These scientific methods begin when you make an accurate test of your present reading rate.

Repetition is similar in the scope of its usefulness to rhetorical questions: more flexible than simple connectives, but still mostly limited to two-point transitions.

d. Perspectives—"first, second, third."

"... And you may be just as inefficient in your reading as I was!"
Well, in that case we have available a step-by-step solution for the problem. Modern psychology has developed scientific methods by which you and I can learn to read better and faster.
There are four major steps in carrying out these methods. I shall describe all four. Let us begin with the first step—make an accurate test of your present reading rate.

It can be seen that this type of transition gives broader perspective than the previous types. A particular advantage is that it carries through the entire set of main points. For example, a little later on, you can say, "Having described the first step, we may now proceed to the second step." However, listeners may get a bit tired of "first," "second," and "third." To offset this, you can often use synonyms for these words: *the beginning of the process is, the origin of the inquiry is, the starting point of this series is,* and others.

e. Perspectives—"speaker, audience, occasion."

"... And you may be just as inefficient in your reading as I was!" *Helen Jane might have added, "you and thousands of others." And because this problem is so serious, I want to describe for you this morning how* modern psychology has developed scientific methods by which you and I can learn to read better and faster.

To make this description vivid, I would like to take you now on an imaginary trip through a reading clinic. So get ready for the clinicians to make an accurate test of your present reading rate.

Twice in the above passage *I* (the speaker) was related to *you* (the audience) as well as to *this morning* and *now* (the occasion). Synonyms, of course, should often be used for all three terms. This kind of transition provides the broadest perspective and also serves to emphasize the statement of the central idea.

2. TRANSITIONS BETWEEN BODY AND CONCLUSION   The transition from body to conclusion is usually easier to handle than transition from introduction to body. It can often be done with a word or phrase, although a sentence or several sentences may occasionally be justified.

Among the common words used for transition between body and conclusion are *finally, lastly,* and *summarizing.* Among the common phrases are *in conclusion, last of all, to sum up, to recapitulate,* and *in closing.* Rhetorical questions, such as, "And what are we to conclude from all these facts?" are often useful.

A transition may be stated in figurative language to lend color: "As we have followed this long train of evidence, we have been led inevitably to the lair of the true criminal in the house of juvenile delinquency."

3. TRANSITIONS BETWEEN COORDINATE POINTS   On the main points in the body of the speech rests the fate of your central idea of your speech purpose. You want the audience to grasp those points, and you want the audience to know at any given time which one you are talking about. This means that you should make it clear when you are finishing one main point and starting the next. The same thing is true when you are handling a series of coordinate subpoints.

Most of the ways of transition already treated can be used between coordinate points. Here are some sample possibilities:

Now having described my first reason, I would like to discuss the second.

You have before you the crux of our problem. What is to be our solution?

But all that is past. Let us look at the present.

This brings us to the fourth and final stage.

Before you are the sinister results. Next we must unearth the causes.

We have just visited the East, the South, and the Middle West. Our next stop is in the Far West.

4. TRANSITIONS BETWEEN POINT AND SUPPORT The speaker must make clear the relationship between each point and its supports. However, the job is fundamentally the same as making major relationships clear, though on a smaller scale. Transitional devices need be less elaborate, and more frequent use can be made of repetitions, questions, and connective phrases. Here are some common ones:

For example	What does this (term) mean?
For instance	Let me explain
This is illustrated by	Likewise
Accordingly	Not only . . . but also
Therefore	But even more important
According to	Now let us turn to
On the other hand	Approaching it from another angle
As I previously pointed out	What are the proofs?

Minor transitions are seldom written into the outline. Major transitions or exceptionally difficult ones should be inserted at the proper point in parentheses. To prevent confusion, they may further be labeled "transition" instead of given a letter or numeral.

SUMMARY

The purpose of the conclusion is to focus the speech. You should avoid multiple conclusions, and conclusions that are abrupt, apologetic, tacked on, anticlimactic, or indecisive. Three useful ways of concluding a speech include summary, emotional appeal, and call for action. Any of the foregoing three ways may be improved by enumeration, restatement, quotation, anecdote, rhetorical question, epigram, prophecy, or personal reference.

The purposes of the introduction are three: to arouse favorable attention, to promote friendliness and respect, and to lead into the subject. You should avoid introductions that hem and haw, and those that are apologetic, trite, pedantic, or misleading. There are many useful ways of opening a talk, such as reference to previous speaker or chairman, appropriate humor, quotation, and rhetorical question.

Transitions show the relationships among the items of your outline. Testing the transitions means testing both your thinking process and your ability to make your thinking process clear to the audience. A good test of transitions is made when you put them into spoken words. You should test the transitions between all major parts of your outline.

Ralph Nader here reveals a blend of the three "V's" of effective speech delivery—visual, vocal, and verbal.

Speech Delivery

three

TOPICAL PREVIEW

I Importance of nonverbal communication

II Personal inventory
    A The distracting stage
    B The neutral stage
    C The awkward stage
    D The skillful stage

III A planned program

IV A program for practice
    A Skillful habits
        1 Posture
        2 Platform movements
        3 Conventional gestures
        4 Characteristics of effective gestures
        5 Handling notes
        6 Handling visual aids
    B Spontaneity of gesture and movement

V Summary

8

Visual Communication

IMPORTANCE OF NONVERBAL COMMUNICATION

Your next classroom talk will begin before you utter a word. The talk will begin when you rise and walk to the front of the room. The *first* impressions your audience get will be visual ones: your appearance, your dress, your walk, and your posture just before speaking. *During* the talk your audience will get visual, vocal, and verbal signs and symbols. The three sets of impressions will either be supplementary or contradictory; and if they contradict, the visual will usually prevail. The *final* impressions will be visual: After you have said the last word, you walk back to your seat.

Nonverbal communication, especially the visual (there are various other kinds), has received increasing attention from scientists in recent years, and their research has revealed that these nonverbal signs and symbols are more pervasive and significant than was previously suspected. Your verbal and vocal communication with other people can be turned on and off, but your silent nonverbal communication is continuous and is harder to control. In any social situation you can stop talking but you cannot make yourself invisible. Even a poker face is a type of facial expression, not an absence of it. Likewise, your dress, posture, head movements, incipient gestures, unconscious body shifts, and tiny visible mannerisms are continuously broadcasting silent stimuli to other people. In comparison with this nonstop nonverbal transmission of signs and symbols, your verbal behaviors may be viewed as occasional interruptions.

An instructive half-hour can be spent in watching a TV talk show with the audio turned off. You probably cannot make much sense out of what they are saying unless you are skilled in lipreading. But make notes on all the ideas that are communicated to you by the video alone. Do not take for granted the stage sets and props; if they were not there you would certainly notice the difference. Observe everything systematically and jot down plenty of notes. The chances are that you will be surprised at how much you have absorbed and what kinds of messages you have received. You may even find that you rather strongly like or dislike one of the participants—all based on visual cues only.

Thus bodily action is no mere decoration of the speech; it is an integral part of it and is woven into the whole communication fabric. Furthermore, it is one important part where a little of the right kind of practice can produce big dividends in a hurry.

To get those dividends: first make an inventory of your assets and liabilities in regard to appearance and bodily action; second, plan a program for self-improvement; third, put the program into practice, in class and out.

PERSONAL INVENTORY

In trying to see yourself as others see you, objectivity is essential. Your instructor, and perhaps others, can help you make an accurate self-appraisal. If you have the chance to study yourself in motion pictures or videotape recordings or candid camera shots, you can see yourself more objectively; you certainly can by studying yourself in a mirror.

It will be useful to estimate the stage of the learning process where you now stand. We suggest four stages, arranged in progressive sequence: (1) the distracting stage, (2) the neutral stage, (3) the awkward stage, and (4) the skillful stage. Not all of your appearance and bodily action are likely to fall into just one of the four categories. You may find that you are in the distracting stage on posture, neutral on platform movement, awkward in gesture, and skillful on facial expression; or any other combination. Since all of your qualities are likely to be within one of these categories, let us examine them in some detail.

The student warily eyes the audience from behind the false protection of the rostrum.
His posture stiffens as he begins inching into the open.
Posture "at attention." He must practice loosening up his whole body and gesturing wholeheartedly.
Finally, he is in the open but still tense—gesture is limp, elbows are clamped to his sides.

The Distracting Stage

In the distracting stage your appearance and bodily actions actually decrease your effectiveness as a speaker. If you succeed, it is in spite of your appearance and bodily actions. If you are in this stage, you may note the following in the mirror:

DRESS   Careless or sloppy; overdone; inappropriate for the occasion
POSTURE   Weight on one foot, hip thrown out prominently; straddle; feet together ("at attention"); teetering; swaying
PLATFORM MOVEMENT   Motionless throughout talk; pacing; jiggling; awkwardness; scraping of feet when walking
BASIC HAND POSITIONS   Hidden behind back; clasped in front of stomach; rammed into pockets; rubbed together; held tensely at sides
GESTURES   Incomplete or incipient; limp; same gesture all the time; too many gestures; fiddling with pencil, notes, jewelry
FACIAL EXPRESSION   Unchanging; inappropriate to the thought; overdone; mannerisms, such as blinking the eyes or smacking the lips
DIRECTNESS   Eyes notebound; looking at floor, ceiling, out the window; faraway look; eyes constantly shifting

The Neutral Stage

In the neutral stage your appearance and bodily movement neither significantly help nor significantly hinder your speaking effectiveness. On the basis of our check list, we might describe the neutral stage as follows:

DRESS   Drab
POSTURE   Not very good but not bad enough to distract
PLATFORM MOVEMENT   Occasional unplanned changes of position
BASIC HAND POSITIONS   Usually with hands lightly clasped behind back or lightly resting on speaking stand
GESTURES   None, or perhaps an occasional movement of head
FACIAL EXPRESSION   A little
DIRECTNESS   Looking at audience about half the time; looking at notes too often

The Awkward Stage

You reach the awkward stage when you have begun practicing to improve and are still so conscious of your appearance or bodily actions that your appearance is stiff and your actions jerky.

The student bravely moves away from the furniture, and makes the first attempts to gesture with her whole body. Some awkwardness is perfectly normal and will soon disappear with further practice.

If you are in this stage, your posture may be right but you neither feel nor look comfortable. If you change platform position, the change seems mechanical rather than spontaneous. If you try to keep your arms relaxed at your sides, you find them straying to some other position, and you will suddenly and guiltily jerk them back. If you practice a certain gesture, you make it jerkily, or overdo it, or time it badly. Sometimes you even look at your own gesture instead of at the audience. If you practice to get more facial animation, you seem at times to be making faces. Such ineptitudes are a part of a natural, and usually necessary, awkward stage. In general, they mean that you have not practiced long enough to integrate a given position, movement, or gesture into an all-in-one-piece habit.

The Skillful Stage

In the skillful stage your appearance and bodily action increase your communicative effectiveness. Now in the mirror you see:

DRESS   Neat; well groomed; attractive

POSTURE   Alert and yet at ease

PLATFORM MOVEMENT   Inconspicuous; helps punctuate thought; adapted to situation, occasion, and speech content

BASIC HAND POSITIONS   Usually hanging relaxed at the sides; occasionally lightly clasped behind back, one at side with other bent at elbow; one or both resting lightly on speaking stand

GESTURES Spontaneous in number and variety; habitual in execution; appropriate to occasion, content, and speaker's personality; expressive

FACIAL EXPRESSION Animated; communicative

DIRECTNESS Looking at audience most of time; looking at all the audience; actually seeing the audience

A PLANNED PROGRAM

Do not suppose, however, that there is only one correct way of doing everything in the skillful stage. Your program should be tailor-made for you only, and should differ from that of everyone else in the class. Do not look for a cut and dried formula. You may develop a gesture that is highly effective when you use it, but that might appear ludicrous if any of your classmates tried it. If you study six excellent public speakers, you will find six entirely different behavior patterns. They will all be different, yet all effective. This is certainly fortunate—what a dreary world it would be if all speakers looked, stood, moved, and gestured alike!

In manner as well as appearance men and women should be different on the platform. For example, most men can occasionally clench a fist and even pound the table for emphasis; but what woman can use these gestures effectively? In general, women's gestures should be graceful and subtle. At one of the national political conventions, viewed by millions on television, a prominent woman speaker harshly reprimanded the delegates for noisiness and poor attention. This restored order but briefly. She then refused the help of the chairman and insisted on wielding the oversized gavel herself in a manner which, as one newspaperman put it, "resembled a railroad workman driving a spike." She would have been far more effective had she been gracious rather than hard-boiled, and had she asked the chairman to handle the gavel rather than pound it herself.

Dress and grooming should be appropriate to the occasion and therefore inconspicuous so as not to distract from the speech itself. Campus fashions are always casual, and for a classroom talk you should usually follow the prevailing campus styles. It would be noticeable if you dressed more formally on the days you are scheduled to speak. Even in the classroom, however, the current mode becomes distracting if carried to extreme—there is a difference between casual and sloppy. A man will irritate his listeners if he appears before the class needing a shave or his beard trimmed, or if he extends his hands only to reveal dirty fingernails. Women are usually more careful of their grooming than men, but they sometimes overdo a style or fad in dress or hairstyling or makeup.

Dressing appropriately for a classroom talk is an altogether different problem from dressing for off-campus groups. Perhaps now, certainly in your near future, you will be asked to speak before nonstudent groups. You may need to remind yourself that fashions you take for granted in daily university life, may be viewed with amusement or alarm by other groups in the community. So we return to the principle that, as a speaker, you want the group to pay attention to what you have to say, rather than to what you are wearing.

Perhaps a word should be added for both sexes about physical endowments. Think over a list of your favorite public speakers. Are all of them beautiful or handsome? Are any of them downright homely? You will soon realize that facial animation is more important than perfect features or a cover-girl complexion, that good posture and bodily movement are worth more than an athletic build or an attractive figure, that directness and sincerity are more valuable than good looks.

Next let us consider planning the improvement of posture and basic hand positions. Check yourself with a large mirror; do not assume a special pose, but stand as you habitually do. Start talking aloud as though you were before the class. Is the general effect satisfactory? If so, you can forget about posture, arms, and hands. If not, make a note to work out better habits.

Continue your practice speech before the mirror. Try changing position and observe how you walk. Do you need more practice on moving about? Try a few gestures. Do the gestures feel natural? Do they look all right? Perhaps your walking and gesturing should be let alone; perhaps one or both should be noted as requiring some work.

Finally, check your habitual facial animation and directness before the mirror. Does your facial expression help express your changing thoughts and moods? And what has been your experience when speaking before the class—do you usually maintain eye contact with members of the audience? Do you look at your notes too often? Again you must decide whether or not to add to your proposed program.

In making the foregoing evaluations, do not be hypercritical. At the same time do not be complacent; try to be honest and objective. If in doubt, consult your instructor.

In planning your program, it is wise to recognize that you cannot do everything at once. Lay out the program in sequence, planning to master one thing and make it habitual before going ahead to the next one.

This student is rapidly emerging from the awkward stage of half-hearted gestures. Notice the vigor suggested by the blurred hand. He shows the potential for bodily eloquence.

A PROGRAM FOR PRACTICE

You now have before you a concrete program for improving your appearance and bodily actions. You should even have an approximate time schedule for the semester for getting the job done. You are wondering now how to get it done.

The job divides itself into two major parts: (1) practicing in private to establish a set of skillful mechanical habits; (2) using those habits spontaneously while giving a speech. Practice produces habit, and habit makes it possible for the speaker to produce easily and naturally the gesture his inner impulse requires.

The establishment of mechanical habits is the basis for spontaneity on the platform. If a speaker feels the urge to gesture, but has no particular habits of gesture, he is likely to saw the air meaninglessly or merely twitch the hands. If that same speaker has developed a set of habitual gestures, he will gesture skillfully and unconsciously at the proper moment.

Skillful Habits

Making or breaking action habits in speech is practically the same as in any other mechanical skill—driving a golf ball, fingering a flute, riding a bicycle. One is tempted to say that the three big rules are practice, more practice, and still more practice. But more is involved: As in golf, you must practice the right things and in the right way.

1. POSTURE   To improve your habitual posture, you should begin by standing in front of a large mirror and experimenting. The object is to find a posture that looks natural, alert, and yet at ease. The exact positions of the feet, trunk, shoulders, arms, and head depend on height, weight, and build. Work out a trial posture and check it with your instructor. Once you have determined your own best posture, practice it frequently and with exactness in front of a mirror. Practice it throughout the day—sit right and stand right wherever you are. Your speech class is only a convenient checking-up point in this schedule. At first, the new posture may feel unnatural and awkward because it differs from your old posture. If you stick to your guns, gradually you will find that you can maintain the new posture with less and less attention. There comes a time when you are pleasantly surprised to discover that you have been maintaining the proper posture for the past half hour or longer *without having consciously thought about it*. When this happens, your job is done. The new posture has become a habit. The tables have been turned—now the *old* way feels unnatural or awkward!

2. PLATFORM MOVEMENTS Practice walking about the platform before a mirror. Experiment. Try moving forward, backward, to the left, and to the right. Try moving a short distance and a longer distance. Start with the foot that is already closer to the point to which you plan to go; when moving to the left, start with the left foot; when moving to the right, start with the right foot. Study the angle of the feet—are you turning the toes in, or splaying them out? What length of stride looks best? Talk, and try to synchronize your movements with what you say. Move sidewise to indicate transition to a new idea, forward to emphasize a point, backward to begin a new one. In such fashion, decide on the most effective set of movements. Then practice them as often as possible alone.

The same procedure applies to your basic hand and arm positions. Let your arms hang relaxed at your sides. Do not get the elbows too tight to the body. At first, your hands may seem like two huge hams, hanging conspicuously. Eventually the new position becomes comfortable and natural.

3. CONVENTIONAL GESTURES Gestures should be worked out one at a time. Your program should provide for developing a wide repertory, giving you eventually maximum variety. There are, however, seven gestures that have acquired almost universal meanings. These are often called the conventional gestures, and they afford a good starting list for practice.

a. Giving and receiving. This gesture is accomplished by extending either or both hands with fingers separated and palms toward the audience. You can produce the gesture by handing an imaginary cake of soap to somebody, or by extending your hand as though to receive a packet of matches. As you practice it, use first one hand, then the other, then both together. Do not clamp the elbows into your sides. Keep the thumbs well out.

b. Rejecting. The hand or hands are extended, usually with a sweeping motion, palms turned down and away from the speaker. You can approximate the effect by preventing an imaginary kitten from leaping into your lap.

c. Nodding and shaking head. Try these common gestures with varying degrees of vigor. Be careful in nodding the head to avoid bowing the trunk.

d. Dividing Extend the hand, with fingers closed, and make a chopping motion or move the hand from side to side. You will approximate the gesture if you bring your hand down on a table and say, "On this side put the books; on that side, the papers."

e. Pointing. In public speaking it is not impolite to point the index finger to locate or identify something. Thus you point as you say, "That chart pictures the problem."

f. Clenching fist. This gesture is most useful when reinforcing an idea, to indicate power or determination. The gesture usually looks best if the row of knuckles is parallel with the speaker's shoulder, and the wrist slightly bent. The gesture is appropriate when exclaiming, for example, "We will *never* give up!"

g. Restraining. The hand is extended at about shoulder height, palm facing outward and downward. This is the gesture you use when saying, for example, "Now, take it easy. Just wait a minute. We're coming to that."

You should be able to use any of these gestures in several effective ways. Perhaps one or two are not suited to your style and should be avoided entirely. The job is for you to work out as many of them as possible until you can use them effectively. Then practice your way of making them until the execution becomes routine. Most can be practiced in conversation. All can be practiced in speech class.

After the conventional gestures have been mastered, you can experiment to create others that will become standard in your own speaking although perhaps rare in the speaking of other people.

4. CHARACTERISTICS OF EFFECTIVE GESTURES
There are certain criteria by which to judge and perfect any set of gestures. Observe your own and practice to acquire the desirable characteristics.

a. Strength. Unless you are ridiculing or showing what not to do, avoid flabby or listless gestures. Every gesture requires decisiveness or vigor to make it look real and alive. The exact amount of vigor required must be determined by experiment, in terms of the mood felt and the thought spoken.

b. Carry-through. The importance of carry-through is well illustrated in sports—pitching a baseball, putting the shot, stroking a tennis ball. Each gesture should be made completely and wholeheartedly. Some gestures are made with the hand only, some with the hand and the arm, but vigorous gestures are made with the whole body. If you are going to point to a flag on the side of the platform, do not make a weak, halfhearted motion with the hand and wrist; it is you who are pointing, not just your finger; the whole body should point to that flag.

c. **Proper timing.** If your gestures fall just a little behind the words to be emphasized, the effect is awkward or even humorous. The effect is almost as bad when the gesture comes noticeably too soon. The gesture should be made at the precise time the stressed word is spoken, or just slightly before. Acquiring the knack of precise timing requires much practice. Invent short statements, appropriate to each gesture, and practice to get your words and movements coordinated.

5. HANDLING NOTES   The question is often asked, "Is it permissible to use notes?" Yes. But don't overdo it, and learn to use notes skillfully. During the semester, both in practicing alone and in speaking before the class, develop a definite habit system with regard to notes. For example, put your notes on cards, as already recommended, and develop a personal system for writing them so that you can tell where you are at a glance. When you are on the platform, it should not be necessary to study your notes as though you were seeing them for the first time.

When you are introduced, come to the platform with the notes in your pocket or carry them inconspicuously in your hand. During your opening remarks, take the cards from your pocket and place them on the stand in a casual way so the audience will scarcely know you have done it.

Develop the knack of glancing at the notes when changing your position around the speaker's stand. Experienced speakers can do this many times during a speech; yet the audience never realizes that there are any notes at all.

In introducing an important quotation, or statistics, or a list of facts, utilize your notes deliberately and conspicuously. This technique makes the materials stand out from the rest of the speech, makes them seem more important, and gives the audience the feeling that absolute accuracy is guaranteed.

For most short talks, however, it is more effective to use no notes. You will not need them if you have a proper outline and have rehearsed adequately. However, if it will give you confidence, you can carry them in your pocket as insurance against an emergency. If you need the notes, take them out unhurriedly as though you had planned to all the time.

6. HANDLING VISUAL AIDS   You must also develop habits for the effective handling of visual aids. This requires advance planning and practice in just when to introduce them, how to handle them, how long to display them, and how to dispose of them. For example, suppose you were going to use a chart. You would not display the chart at the very beginning of your talk unless you planned to discuss it immediately. Usually you do not allow the audience to see the chart until you come to the point which the chart illustrates. Then you must be sure that the chart is clearly visible to the entire group. If it is large enough, you might hang it on the wall; otherwise, you might hold it up close to the front row, or even walk from one edge of the audience to another, giving everyone a chance for a close look. If the chart is hanging on the wall, avoid the temptation to turn your back on the audience and address your remarks to the chart, and avoid the danger of putting yourself between the chart and the audience. Usually it is best to stand to one side of the chart and use a pointer. When you have completed your references to a visual aid, you should usually remove it from view; otherwise it may distract from your discussion of subsequent points.

In a sense, of course, you are your own principal visual aid; you cannot expect a chart or an object to do all your work for you. Generally the effectiveness of the audio-visual support will be largely determined by your words and movements in relation to it. Charles F. Brannan used a visual aid when he addressed the National Farm Institute:

> At my request a bushel of corn has been placed on the platform. If you will assume that this bushel of corn is the first extra bushel beyond our assumed domestic need, beyond export requirements, and beyond even the safe reserves required to protect the nation against crop failure or other emergency, then it is a symbol of our major national farm problem. It is the extra bushel. It is the bushel for which . . .[1]

Obviously, the effectiveness of Brannan's visual support depended largely on his platform positions in relation to the bushel of corn, his gestures toward it, the emphasis he gave to key words such as "*this* bushel."

Spontaneity of Gesture and Movement

As we pointed out earlier in this chapter, skillful mechanical habits should be the servants of your thoughts and feelings. The urge to stand alertly, the urge to move about or gesture, the urge to smile or frown, the urge to look your listener in the eye—all should arise from your thoughts and feelings. Spontaneity comes from within. You will find that the spontaneous impulse to use bodily action comes naturally to you. Just follow the impulse.

If at first you find it difficult to let yourself go, here are three suggestions to help to get you started:

---

[1] A. Craig Baird, ed., *Representative American Speeches: 1949–1950,* H. W. Wilson, 1950, pp. 204–05. Reprinted by permission of Charles F. Brannan.

The skillful stage: This student gestures spontaneously and forcefully. He uses his

1. In planning the content of a speech, provide some ideas that will *require* you to move about or use your hands. For example, include something that requires writing on the blackboard, handling a book, or demonstrating a visual aid.

2. Provide a few spots where you are to describe something that involves size, height, shape, position, or movement. Any one of them will strongly suggest the use of descriptive gestures. Thus the table was "this wide," the youngster was "so tall," the urn was "shaped like this," the two groups were lined up with "one of them over there" and the other "here."

3. Provide yourself with a chance to mimic some person. Act out his mannerisms, imitate his gestures. He walked with a peculiar limp "like this"; he had a habit of twirling a pen in his fingers "like this."

In using any of the foregoing suggestions, never try to remember particular gestures that you may have used during practice, but do remind yourself that you are going to use some movements or gestures. Once you break the ice, the release of inner impulses into bodily communication will come easily. Eventually all your bodily actions while speaking will be in response to your thought and feeling, and the actions will be carried through skillfully and automatically. Thus you are in the midst of a speech; you are not consciously thinking of your delivery at all, but you feel an urge to emphasize a point and simultaneously you do it by some means, often involving bodily movement. You do *not* think, "Now I shall raise my right arm, clench my fist, and shake it on such-and-such word"; rather you *feel* that what you are about to say should be made emphatic, and so you do clench your fist, and you do it exactly

whole body and gives an all-in-one-piece effect.

in the way that you have made habitual by privately practicing. Then clenched fist and strong statement blend into each other so naturally that neither you nor your audience is aware of the gesture as such.

When you have restudied the above advice and put it into class-room practice, you will resolve the apparent paradox that sponta-neity of bodily action during a talk is based upon previous private practice of the mechanics of gestures.

SUMMARY

Bodily communication includes dress and grooming, posture, plat-form movements, gestures, facial expression, and eye contact with the audience. The visible elements of speech are not mere decora-tions but are integral parts of effective communication.

Take a personal inventory of your use of the visible means of communication, plan a program for self-improvement, and put your program into practice.

In taking personal inventory you should consider four stages of the learning process: the distracting stage, the neutral stage, the awkward stage, and the skillful stage.

Your problem should be tailor-made for you, and should differ from that of everyone else in the class.

Putting your program into practice may be divided into two main jobs: (1) practicing in private to establish a set of skillful mechanical habits; (2) using those habits spontaneously while giving a speech.

TOPICAL PREVIEW

I "Mend your speech a little"

II Voice production
    A Respiration
    B Phonation
    C Resonation
    D Articulation

III Voice and articulation inventory
    A Audibility
    B Accuracy
    C Meaningfulness
    D Pleasantness

IV Determination of potential vocal ability

V The program in practice
    A Audibility exercises
    B Articulation exercises
    C Exercises for meaningfulness
        1 Analysis of vocal monotony
        2 Sensitivity to meaning
        3 Developing vocal variety

VI Summary

Vocal Communication

"MEND YOUR SPEECH A LITTLE" (KING LEAR)

Charles Laughton is justly regarded as one of the foremost actors and public readers of his generation.[1] But what about his voice? You will probably agree that nature did not bless Laughton with a particularly good voice. Probably half of your friends have better natural voices than Laughton. He has made the most of what he has. Making the most of the voice you have will be the theme of this chapter.

In this text the emphasis must of necessity be on voice improvement, not on speech correction. If your instructor suspects you have an organic defect in your vocal mechanism, he will recommend medical advice and the help of a speech pathologist. If you have vocal defects symptomatic of fundamental emotional or mental disturbances, he will refer you to a speech or psychology clinic. If you have long-standing habits of faulty production of certain sounds, or if you have a marked foreign dialect, he will refer you to a speech clinic. If you need work on changing your basic pitch or vocal quality, he will refer you to an expert tutor. In short, voice

---

[1] Hear one of his phonograph albums, such as *The Story-Teller* (Capitol, TBO 1650) or *Charles Laughton Reading from the Bible* (Decca, DL 8031).

deficiencies that require long periods of treatment with individual guidance throughout cannot be handled in this text. Here you will have plenty to do learning how to make freer and better use of the voice you already have.

Voice improvement requires five steps: (1) studying the basic process of voice production, (2) making a personal inventory, (3) determining your potential, (4) planning a program, and (5) practicing the program.

VOICE PRODUCTION

The speech process is so complicated that even experts are uncertain about many of the details. Had nature devised a mechanism solely for the production of speech, a much simpler instrument could have sufficed. As it is, all the organs used in speech also serve other, and often more primary, biological functions. As Gray and Wise have said:

> Indeed, the opportunities for maladjustment of so many reflex arcs governing so many muscles performing so intricate a process, are so infinitely numerous that the marvel is not that we sometimes speak faultily but that we speak at all. The vital, life-sustaining functions of breathing and taking food are more comprehensible, because the reflex arcs connected with them are natively established; but the function of speech, being in a sense overlaid or superimposed upon the musculature of these primitive functions and being forced to use borrowed mechanisms, represent acquired or learned adjustments, adaptations, and coordinations nothing short of miraculous.[2]

You will realize, therefore, that the story of voice production must here be simplified and confined to essential details. With that thought in mind, we may conveniently divide speaking into four major processes: (1) respiration, (2) phonation, (3) resonation, and (4) articulation. The following discussion will be clearer if you refer to the accompanying diagrams frequently.

Respiration

The *torso* (trunk of the body) contains two major cavities: the upper, called the *thorax* (chest cavity), and the lower, called the *abdomen*. The two are separated by a sheet of muscle and tendon called the *diaphragm*, which thus becomes the floor for the thorax

---

[2] Giles Wilkeson Gray and Claude Merton Wise, *The Bases of Speech*, Harper, 1959, p. 234.

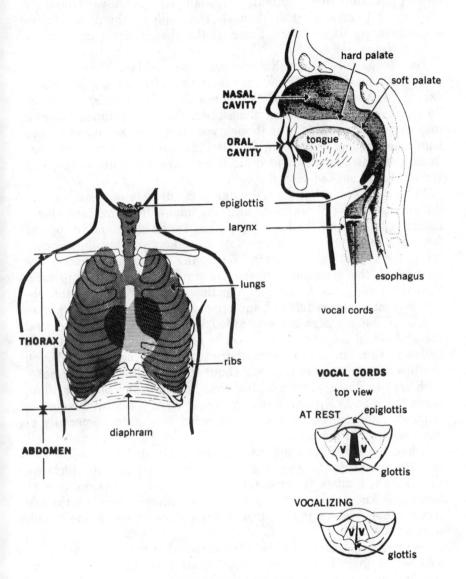

THE SPEECH ORGANS

and the ceiling for the abdomen. The thorax contains the *lungs* and heart; the abdomen contains the stomach, intestines, liver, and kidneys. The walls of the thorax consist of muscles and bones. The bones are the *ribs, vertebrae* (backbone), *scapulae* (shoulder blades), and *clavicles* (collarbones). The walls of the abdomen, to a much larger degree than those of the thorax, are composed of muscle tissue.

The lungs are cone-shaped and sponge-like. They contain practically no muscle tissue, and their role in breathing is passive except for the elasticity of the tissue. In other words, the lungs do not expand and contract themselves during breathing. Instead, they are acted upon. It is as though you took a large sponge in your hands and squeezed, forcing the air out. Then if you relaxed your fingers, the elasticity would bring the sponge back into shape, and air would be sucked into the cells.

The lungs are acted upon by three major sets of muscles: the diaphragm, the rib muscles, and the abdominal muscles. Their action is to squeeze the lungs by pulling in the sides and lifting the floor of the thorax during *exhalation,* and by putting the process into reverse during *inhalation.* When the abdominal muscles are contracted, the abdominal organs are pressed inward and upward, thus decreasing the volume of the thoracic cavity. When the abdominal muscles are relaxed, the opposite effect occurs. The movements of the rib cage are controlled by both the rib muscles and the abdominal muscles. The action is like that of an old-fashioned bellows. You can approximate the effect of this action by placing the tips of your fingers together about a foot in front of your nose, with elbows down; then, keeping your fingers in the same position, move the elbows up and down. You will soon see how this action expands and contracts the space between your arms, especially at the lower end of the cone.

When the lungs are squeezed, the air is forced from the air sacs out through a tributary system of air vessels, the last of which are the *bronchial tubes* (anyone who has suffered the discomforts of bronchitis knows about them), which lead directly into the *trachea* (wind pipe). Thence the column of air escapes through the mouth or nose.

The beginning student should remember that frequent inhalations are better than fewer very deep inhalations. In exhalation the speaker should learn to control the abdominal muscles. He should be able to start or stop the exhalation at will, suddenly or gradually, strongly or gently. Finally, he should learn to control his breathing with the torso muscles rather than with the muscles of the neck and jaw.

Phonation

At the upper end of the trachea, the *larynx* (voice box or Adam's apple) is suspended by muscles which can move the larynx upward and downward. The larynx is constructed of a number of cartilages. Inside, attached to the cartilages, are the *vocal cords,* which are not in the least like cords or strings but rather like folds, or curtains, or lips. The vocal cords consist of bands of relatively thick muscle tissue, bordered along the inside edges by a thin white membrane. The opening between the vocal cords is called the *glottis.*

When the voice is used, compressed air from the lungs strikes the vocal cords; the cords are set into vibration; the vibration of the cords sets the surrounding air to vibrating; and the air in vibration is the sound. (The action by which this is done may be compared with that of the lips when one is playing a trumpet.) The vibrations thus produced may be measured in two ways. The amplitude of the sound waves is a measure of the loudness or intensity of the sound. The frequency (or number of waves per second) is a measure of the pitch.

Going up and down the scale in pitch is a function primarily of the vocal cords. However, the individual muscles that move the cords closer together or farther apart are not subject to conscious control. They can be controlled only as a group, and indirectly. You hear the pitch of your own voice, and wishing to change it, you unconsciously change the position of the cords. Thus development of nice discriminations in pitch is more a matter of ear training than of vocal-cord training. Loudness or intensity is partly a function of the vocal cords and partly a function of breathing. When you exhale air forcefully, you cause the vocal cords to vibrate at larger amplitudes that produce louder sounds.

Many people when speaking in public suffer tension in the muscles of the neck and throat. This results in voice fatigue, strain, and other undesirable effects. The goal is to have a relaxed and "open" throat.

Resonation

If the process of voice production could be confined to respiration and phonation only, the effect would be somewhat comparable to playing the mouthpiece removed from a horn—you could produce sound and vary its duration and pitch, and to a limited extent vary its loudness, but it would be a thin and squeaky sound. The process by which sounds are amplified and modified is called resonation.

The first group of organs used for voice resonation are cavities, the most important of which are the *pharynx* (throat), the *oral cavity* (mouth), and the *nasal cavities* (nose). Sound waves are amplified by being reflected from the surfaces of the cavities, roughly in the manner of a megaphone. At the same time the sounds are modified by changing the shape and size of the throat and mouth, and by permitting or preventing the escape of air through the nasal cavities. These changes produce the different vowel sounds.

Resonation also involves the tissues of the upper part of the body, especially the bones of the head and chest, which amplify and modify tones by acting as sounding boards. However, the effects of these sounding-board tissues are of much less importance than the effects of the cavities.

The total process of resonation not only amplifies the voice and gives vowels their different sounds, but also provides the richness, or mellowness, usually termed voice quality. Because the bodily structures of human beings are all different and because individuals differ in making the innumerable small adjustments of the many organs during speech, no two voices are ever exactly alike. The term *quality* is used to describe that characteristic which distinguishes one voice from another when both voices are approximately alike in the pitch, duration, and loudness of vowel sounds.

Practical application of the preceding discussion to your own speaking voice indicates that three main aspects are involved in resonation: loudness, production of vowel sounds, and vocal quality. Faulty resonation accounts for such difficulties as a weak or thin voice, errors in vowel sounds, or such unpleasant voice qualities as nasality or stridency.

Articulation

Speaking requires one more process. You must further modify sounds to produce the consonants, and you must join vowel and consonantal sounds together (or separate them) to produce complete utterances. These tasks are performed chiefly by the *lips, tongue, teeth, hard palate, velum* (soft palate), and *jaw*. In general, the consonants are produced by blocking the column of vibrating air in various ways. For example, you may completely block the flow of air with your lips for a moment and then release it, creating a small explosion which becomes *p* or *b*. Or you may partially block the stream of air by placing the lower lip close to the upper teeth, and the friction that results by forcing the air through this narrow opening becomes *f* or *v*. The practical application of this final process to your own speaking determines the clearness and accuracy of your articulation and pronunciation.

You learned to talk when you were a child, but would you reveal good or poor speech habits if you were observed by experts through this one-way glass?

VOICE AND ARTICULATION INVENTORY

With the facts of the preceding section in mind, you will be better prepared to evaluate your own voice. You will need further assistance, however, which your instructor will provide. He will give you a systematic appraisal; in doing so he may use some kind of printed or mimeographed form. One useful voice and articulation criticism form is presented on page 376 of the Appendix. Regardless of what form sheet is used, your instructor will record his impressions of your voice as compared with certain standard criteria. The criteria may be stated in various ways, but they can usually be classified into four major categories: audibility, accuracy, meaningfulness, and pleasantness.

Audibility

Audibility is a matter of degree. It may be that your natural voice is so soft that your listeners must constantly strain to hear you. Or your audibility may be spotty; listeners may be able to catch most of what you say, but be forced to guess at the gaps in terms of the context. Or perhaps your voice is audible during the first and middle parts of statements but trails away or dies out on the endings. You may be audible in some situations but not in others—you may or may not adjust effectively to size of room or audience, to acoustics, to competing noises. Even under difficult conditions, you should remember that too loud a voice is often as objectionable as too soft a voice—most people dislike being bellowed at.

Accuracy

There are two kinds of vocal accuracy: accuracy of articulation and accuracy of pronunciation. If your listeners do not know whether you said "none" or "one," your articulation is inaccurate; if you say something that sounds like "known" for "none," your pronunciation is inaccurate. The first is a problem of distinctness; the second of correctness. In practice the two problems often overlap.

Articulation is the process of forming, joining, and separating speech sounds. You should carry out this process with enough accuracy to be easily understood and yet not sound overprecise. In evaluating your own speaking habits, you may find that you already speak with reasonable distinctness, adequate for most of your needs. More likely, however, you can stand improvement.

Pronunciation involves the sounds you make and the syllables you accent, rather than how distinctly you make them. As you know, standards for pronunciation vary among regions of the country, and you probably use the accent of the region in which you grew up. In the United States there are three major accents: general American, Eastern, and Southern, with local versions within each of the three. Furthermore, the preferred pronunciation of many words is in constant flux. Any rule for choosing an overall standard, therefore, must be flexible. Normally, that pronunciation is best that attracts the least attention. This usually means avoiding localisms, avoiding imitations of an accent different from your accustomed one, and adopting the current pronunciations used by educated people of the region in which you live.

Perhaps the most common faults of articulation and pronunciation are due to general slovenliness or "lip laziness." Ask yourself how often during face-to-face or telephone conversations your listeners ask you to repeat what you have just said. It is but small exaggeration to report that college students will say,

> Lives of great men all remind us
> We can make our lives sublime,

with such laziness of the articulators as to sound like,

> Liza greatmun awe remindus
> Weaken maycar liza blime.

Sometimes the articulatory fault lies in one or more specific consonant sounds. Those which give the most trouble are *s, r, ng, th, l, z, sh, j,* and *ch.*

You may habitually make one or more of the following five types of errors in pronunciation:

1. *Sound substitutions:* tremenjous for tremendous; jist for just.
2. *Sound reversals:* childern for children; calvary for cavalry.
3. *Sound additions:* athuletes for athletes; warsh for wash.
4. *Sound omissions:* pitcher for picture; pome for poem.
5. *Misplaced stress:* compar'able for com'parable; superflu'ous for super'fluous.

All of us, of course, make occasional mistakes in trying to pronounce controversial or unfamiliar words, such as "camellia" or "culinary." Such mistakes should be distinguished from those due to sloppiness and carelessness, such as "git," "ketch," "strenth," "jist," "kin," "exscape," "instid," "liberry," and "wunst." As already mentioned, it is equally undesirable to go to the other extreme and become so precise as to sound affected.

Meaningfulness

At this point in your inventory, the question arises: How much meaning do you convey with your voice? Suppose for example, that in the transcript of a trial one of the witnesses answered, "Oh, yes." How would you know what meaning the witness intended to convey without having heard him say it? "Oh, yes," can be spoken in many different ways, each with a different meaning; you can even make it mean "no." In other words, variations in loudness, inflection, pitch, and rate produce meaningfulness in a speaking voice. So the question may be restated: Are you using all the variety your voice is capable of? And is your voice capable of a sufficient range of variety—that is, is it flexible?

Variety is most needed in rate, loudness, and pitch. If you lack such variety the result is monotony, probably the most common fault of beginning speakers. Monotony of rate is characterized by an unchanging beat, monotony of loudness by sameness, and monotony of pitch by the repetition of the same note or pattern of notes.

Pleasantness

It is difficult to get a reliable judgment of the pleasantness or unpleasantness of your own voice from friends and relatives; they are so accustomed to it that their reaction to it is different from that of strangers. However, you will find it instructive to secure reactions from your classmates to see how much agreement they show in trying to describe your vocal quality. Do they tend to use adjectives with a pleasant connotation, such as mellow, resonant, soft, musical, interesting, or forceful? Or do they use adjectives with an unpleasant connotation, such as nasal, breathy, harsh, strident, fuzzy, grating, whining, or thin?

Suppose that you have now secured ratings of your audibility, accuracy, meaningfulness, and pleasantness from your classmates and instructor. These evaluations will not help you unless you can hear yourself as they do. To hear yourself objectively a tape recorder is almost indispensable. In recording your voice it is wise to try several kinds of speaking: conversation, an extemporaneous speech, reading from prose and poetry. It is also helpful to record in cooperation with somebody else—to provide for side-by-side comparisons and contrasts. The first time you hear your own voice played back, you will probably exclaim in confusion, "That's not me!" Your confusion will result from the fact that it is physically impossible for you to hear yourself during ordinary speech as others hear you. They hear only one set of vibrations, the external, while you hear these plus the internal vibrations. So you have to get used to this new voice. There is the advantage that you can rather easily listen to your recorded speech as though it were the voice of a third person coming in on the radio, and appraise it objectively. If you tuned in on that voice, would you stay tuned, or turn the dial?

DETERMINATION OF POTENTIAL VOCAL ABILITY

Once you have evaluated your voice, you must try to imagine its future potential. It will be difficult for you to imagine the full possibilities until you learn to listen critically to conversations, speeches, radio, television, and especially to phonograph or tape-recordings.

Listen to the best two or three conversationalists you know, paying critical attention to the ways they use their voices. On what points are they strongest? Who are the two or three best speakers in your class? Next time they speak, listen attentively to their voices. What are their strongest points? Attend a meeting where an effective speaker is taking part. How about his audibility, accuracy, meaningfulness, pleasantness of voice? Listen to radio and television. Choose several speakers who are acknowledged as good. Listen to their voices. Notice details of their articulation and pronunciation, their variations in quality, pitch, rate, and loudness.

Are these speakers effective in spite of, or because of, voice and articulation?

Phonograph and tape-recordings have the advantage that they can be replayed for careful listening and can be compared almost directly with recordings of your own voice. Allowances must be made, however, in terms of each speaker's purpose as compared with your own purposes. A good idea of your own potential can be secured by speaking a given piece, recording it, playing it back, then playing the same piece as spoken by a professional on a phonograph record. The immediate contrast between what you were able to put into the reading and what the professional put into it will reveal vocal possibilities that will surprise you.

Many excellent spoken recordings may be found at your library or record shop. A challenging example of vocal variety is provided by Orson Welles' *No Man Is an Island* (Decca, DL 9060). Welles reads eight selections from famous speeches, Pericles to Zola. The differences among these readings are so marked that you can easily imagine that you have listened to eight different men.

A few phonograph records of speaking voices were produced in the early years of the industry; in recent times, however, the number, variety, and availability of spoken records have increased many-fold. A new dimension has been added to literature, drama, and history as well as to the field of speech. The voices of great teachers, readers, and actors can be heard and studied in your own living room; authentic sounds of history in the making can also be heard there. In your speech course you should become well acquainted with this new kind of literature, and simultaneously you will be rewarded with many ideas about what can be done with the speaking voice. You will be better able to set goals for your own voice improvement when you can literally hear those goals. You do not have to develop the voice of a Charlton Heston or an Ingrid Bergman. Even if you could, it might not be worth your time. Exercise discretion and build a practical program for yourself, setting your goals in a proper perspective.

THE PROGRAM IN PRACTICE

Audibility Exercises

If your voice is always audible, you need read this section only for an understanding of how the voice functions. If your voice is weak, do not be unduly alarmed. So much speaking is done through radio, television, or public address systems that a weak voice is not an insurmountable handicap. But if you do not speak audibly, you should find the principal cause, then practice to eliminate it.

1. The cause may possibly be faulty breathing. Some years ago this was considered almost the only cause. Recent research, however, casts much doubt on the matter. Some people, in fact, use less breath on loud sounds than on quiet ones. If your instructor finds that a fundamental change in breathing habits is indicated, however, many exercises are needed, with guided practice over a relatively long period of time. You will need a clinician to do the guiding.

2. The cause may be simply a lack of energy, coupled with a failure to realize that you have fallen into the habit of speaking inaudibly. The obvious advice to speak louder is the principal treatment. To break the habit you must deliberately and systematically practice talking louder. Practice in daily conversations, using a friend as a checker; in your class talks use your instructor as critic. Remember that breaking this habit, like breaking other habits, will take time and constant reminders.

3. The cause may be a failure to adapt your voice to groups or rooms of different sizes. If so, find an unused classroom and ask a friend to be your audience.

    a. Stand at the front of the room with your friend only two feet away. Talk for a while, asking your friend to check for appropriate loudness.

    b. Have your friend sit in one of the front rows. Repeat the foregoing.

    c. Have your friend move several rows further away and repeat.

    d. Have him go to the back row and repeat again.

Be careful that you do not simply raise the pitch, becoming shrill; be careful also that you do not become *too* loud. Now this whole procedure can be best practiced in class talks or in any other audience situation by remembering the rule: *Talk to the back row.* To check on yourself, have someone sit in the back row with instructions to signal if you speak too softly or too loudly.

4. The cause may be the habit of dropping or swallowing the endings of sentences. If your voice is adequately loud on the first and middle parts of sentences, you can easily hold up the end, too. Practice the same procedure as in item 2 above, but concentrate on sentence endings.

5. You may not open your mouth wide enough. Find out whether or not you do by sitting alone with a small mirror in your lap and talking in your normal way. Occasionally, glance at the mirror, catching yourself off guard, and watch for the amount of space between your upper and lower teeth, and for the amount of variation in this space on different sounds. You may be surprised at the small amount of space and of jaw movement. To eliminate this

fault, exaggerate your jaw movements while reading aloud or talking. Ask your instructor to indicate the right amount and then get the feel of it. You will find at first that the right amount will feel as though it is too much; but before long it will feel perfectly natural. Attention to articulation exercises, soon to be discussed, is also helpful in solving this problem.

6. Inaudibility may be caused by habitually speaking below your natural key. Men sometimes get into this habit because they think a lower pitch sounds more masculine; women sometimes think a low, husky voice is glamorous. Get a competent critic to assist you, and then practice reading a passage several times, raising the overall pitch level slightly for each reading until you have established the best combination of pitch and audibility. Practice at this pitch level in conversations as well as in class speeches.

7. Remember that some people's voices are naturally soft or light. Those people should not try for additional loudness by strain and struggle. Sometimes it is better to let the loudness alone and compensate for lack of it by developing exceptionally clear articulation. Your attendance at plays has doubtlessly demonstrated that even a whisper, properly articulated, can be heard throughout a large theater.

Articulation Exercises

There are approximately fifteen vowel sounds, nine diphthongs, and twenty-five consonant sounds in the English language. We say approximately, because some people do not make fine discriminations between vowels, and actually use fewer sounds than other people do. We stress sounds because there is a vast difference between them and written symbols. For example, many people think there are just five vowel sounds corresponding to the five symbols a, e, i, o, and u. A moment's reflection will show that the one symbol a represents several different sounds (e.g., abate, bat, ball, bah). One way of studying the relationships between the written and the oral is to use the phonetic alphabet—a system of written symbols in which there is a one-to-one relationship between symbols and sounds. Obviously the twenty-six letters of the ordinary alphabet had to be supplemented by the invention of additional symbols.

Following is a list of the principal sounds used in the United States from the International Phonetic Alphabet (IPA). In each item notice (1) the usual written symbol, (2) the phonetic symbol in brackets, and (3) a sample word.

CONSONANTS

1. p, [p], papa
2. b, [b], baby
3. k, [k], kick
4. g, [g], gag
5. t, [t], tat
6. d, [d], dad
7. l, [l], lull
8. r, [r], rare
9. m, [m], mum
10. n, [n], none
11. ng, [ŋ], ringing
12. y, [j], yes
13. wh, [hw], what
14. w, [w], wow
15. th, [ð], this
16. th, [θ], think
17. h, [h], hah
18. f, [f], fife
19. v, [v], vivid
20. j, [dʒ], Georgia
21. ch, [tʃ], church
22. zh, [ʒ], measure
23. sh, [ʃ], shush
24. z, [z], zeals
25. s, [s], sass

VOWELS

26. oo, [u], rule
27. oo, [ʊ], wool
28. o, [ɔ], law
29. a, [a], calm
30. a, [æ], cat
31. e, [ɛ], pet
32. i, [ɪ], pit
33. ee, [i], see
34. a, [ə], above
35. u, [ʌ], up

DIPHTHONGS

36. a, [eɪ], date
37. o, [ou], crow
38. u, [ju], you
39. ou, [aʊ], out
40. i, [aɪ], pipe
41. oi, [ɔɪ], oil

If you are told you are producing a certain sound inaccurately but cannot hear the fault, or cannot correct it even when trying, you should consult with your instructor. At the same time, you may consult a book in which every sound is separately considered, its production described in detail, and special exercises suggested. Two such books are: Grant Fairbanks, *Voice and Articulation Drillbook,* Harper, 1960; John A. Grasham and Glenn G. Gooder, *Improving Your Speech,* Harcourt Brace Jovanovich, 1960.

Articulatory errors that you can hear, when they are called to your attention, and that you can correct, when you try, are the kind that will be handled in this text. They are the most common,

This student practices acticulatory exercises at home. She experiments with consonantal sounds to coordinate the audio-visual-kinesthetic sensations.

and are due to carelessness, lack of attention or effort, "lip laziness," imitation of poor models, or talking too fast. The result may be either a general slovenliness or merely an indistinctness on certain sounds.

1. An excellent exercise for general slovenliness of articulation is whispering. This adaptable exercise can be practiced in many ways. For example, get the cooperation of a friend and find an unoccupied room. Have the friend sit about fifteen feet away. Then converse with him entirely in a whisper. Do not allow any voice to creep into the whisper—just use the breath. Keep trying until your friend can understand you. You will soon discover the purpose of this exercise: When you try to communicate by whispers, you are forced to pay attention to the formation of all sounds, and to put more energy into forming them; thus you get the feel of what you should be doing during ordinary talking. An added advantage of the whispering exercise is that it can easily be transferred from practice sessions to your actual class speeches—during a speech you can deliberately reduce your loudness to a point where your voice becomes a semiwhisper.

2. If your trouble is with specific sounds, and you can hear the errors, the following exercise can be recommended. Make a list of the sounds that are troublesome and then make a list of words and phrases that include these sounds. Look for words where the sound is the initial one, other words where the sound occurs within the word (the medial position), and still other words in which the sound is the final or terminal one. Show this list to your instructor for verification. Now sit down alone somewhere and practice, preferably with a voice recorder. A hand mirror, especially of the magni-

fying type, will also be of assistance. Begin practicing the list, producing the sounds the wrong way and the right way in alternation. Study and compare with three purposes in mind: first, watch the positions of the jaw, lips, and tongue; second, listen to the difference in the sounds; third, feel (with your eyes shut) the differences in the positions of the jaw, lips, tongue, and soft palate.

This audio-visual-kinesthetic method of practicing is being used at home by the student in the pictures on the preceding pages. In this session she analyzes the positioning of the articulators (especially tongue, lips, and teeth) in relation to two common sound substitutions—w for r (wait for rate) and th for s (thaw for saw). If you practice these four sounds as she is doing, you will quickly gain new insight into the mechanics of consonantal sound production, and you should be able to figure out which sound she is practicing in each of the pictures. If you want to increase the level of difficulty on th for s, you can tackle sentences such as, "The sea ceaseth and sufficeth us." For w and r, try "The little red wagon runs wild." Notice in the first three pictures that the student uses an ordinary inexpensive cassette recorder with a directional microphone (on the side table); she avoids the common beginner's mistake of holding the mike too close to her mouth. In the fourth picture, she tries out a borrowed miniature battery-powered recorder; it is small enough to be carried in a pocket or purse, yet it contains a cartridge with forty-four minutes of tape. With or without such equipment, however, you can profitably practice coordinating the audio-visual-kinesthetic sensations.

When you get the proper sound associated with the proper feel, your problem is half solved. Now you must transfer this practice into ordinary speech. This can be done by conscious effort, possibly with the aid of a critic at first. Your aim is to make the sound the correct way often enough to start the formation of a new habit.

3. Inaccuracy may lie not so much in the production of specific sounds as in joining and separating them during conversation. Thus, you may be guilty of the following:

"Whirl ut gitcha?"
"I'm gonna gitcha drink."
"You dint gimme whatcha promised."
"Chowt! Yawlmos gotcher self run over!"

In working on such slovenly speech habits, use a combination of exercises 1 and 2 described above; but do not overdo them. Avoid sounding overprecise and pedantic. Notice that many adjoining sounds are normally blended or assimilated. For example, read the following sentence slowly and precisely, "He was satisfied because he had done the assignment." Now read it at your normal rate, stressing the words "satisfied" and "done." Notice the natural blending and assimilation of some of the first and last sounds of adjoining words. Thus your goal is to produce separate sounds clearly enough to be distinct, but at the same time not to sound like a school child reciting a piece.

4. For careless and sloppy mispronunciation of common words, like "jist," "git," "kin," "whur," and "ketch," no special exercises are needed. Probably, when reading aloud for others or simply being careful, you pronounce such words perfectly well. The task, therefore, is to introduce new habits into your daily talking. This, curiously enough, is not easy. Take one or two words to begin with and resolve to practice them all week. Approach this practice both positively and negatively.

The positive approach is to remind yourself every hour to introduce these words into conversations. When you are talking with someone about the next game, deliberately say, "I *just* hope that Bill Banowsky *gets* a chance to *catch* a couple of passes." Or, "I *just* can't wait to *get* to the game." And so on. These words are so common that it is easy to put them into your talking without distorting the flow of thought. You must, however, use them frequently and correctly in actual speech.

The negative approach is to stop yourself, go back and repeat the word, "That *jis'* gives me . . . I mean, that *just.* . . ." This method can be reinforced by a helper, such as your roommate. Make a bargain with him that every time he catches you mispronouncing the words being practiced, you pay a fine—and he gets the money!

As soon as you have formed new habits on the two or three chosen words, you are ready to choose two or three more. Even if you correct your pronunciation of only a few common words, you will be rewarded by a noticeable rise in the whole cultural level of your speech.

Exercises for Meaningfulness

1. ANALYSIS OF VOCAL MONOTONY Suppose your inventory lists your voice as monotonous. Perhaps the rate or loudness of your speech does not vary, or your pitch is a monotone. These faults can rarely be ascribed to organic defects; the cause is more likely to be emotional. Perhaps you are tied up by stage fright; or maybe you simply have not learned to relax. Or the faults may be a manifestation of your whole personality—to put it brutally, maybe your voice is uninteresting only because you haven't taken the trouble to make yourself an interesting person. Maybe you have not learned to sense the full meanings of what you read or think about; maybe your voice is not flexible enough to express the meanings you intend; or perhaps you simply have never tried.

Regardless of its cause, monotony is a voice problem especially well adapted to treatment in this course. If you follow the other suggestions in this text, *every class speech you give should mark an improvement in meaningfulness.* Our entire subject involves the communication of meanings. And everything you learn and apply—audience awareness, good choice of subject, definite speaking purpose, efficient research, clear organization, rehearsal of language and body action, emotional adjustment—all contribute toward meaningful talking.

2. SENSITIVITY TO MEANING Often the first job in learning to communicate meanings is to become more sensitive to them. A good way to start is to restudy some old familiar literature—things you learned in childhood and have heard so often that they now have almost no meaning for you. The game is to give them a meaning, or a new meaning, or several meanings. Read over Lincoln's "Gettysburg Address," which you probably know by heart, and think about it. Can you detect Lincoln's basic organizational plan? Can you read the speech so that the implications as well as the actual statements become significant? How many different meanings can you draw from that famous closing phrase, ". . . that government of the people, by the people, and for the people shall not perish from the earth"? Stress different words; each stress will suggest a new meaning. Then practice in the same way on such pieces as the Pledge of Allegiance or the Twenty-third Psalm.

3. DEVELOPING VOCAL VARIETY

a. Rate. The simplest way to achieve more vocal variety is by learning to change pace. Learn deliberately to slow down or speed up your rate, depending on the thought and mood of the content. A slow rate helps convey the suggestion of thoughtfulness, deliberation, or sadness. A fast rate is appropriate for joy, excitement, and descriptions of things in motion.

You probably think of rate as number of words per minute. But rate can be altered in either of two ways: You can change the duration of a given sound, or you can change the length and number of pauses. You will need practice to sense the difference between the two ways.

A completely mechanical exercise to make you aware of rate changes, both in duration and pauses, is counting, or reciting the alphabet at different rates. Thus:

O-o-o-one,   Tw-o-o-o,   T-h-r-r-e-e-e-e-e
O-o-o-one,   Tw-o-o-o,   T-h-r-r-e-e-e-e
One,   Two,   Three

One,   Two,   Three
OneTwoThree   (And other variations)

Next, choose literary passages that vary widely in mood and thought, and that obviously demand different reading rates. For a slow rate, try the Lord's Prayer; for a fast rate, Lanier's "Song of the Chattahoochee." Count the words and time yourself to become aware of how much you are varying your rate of reading. Slow them down or speed them up by changes in both duration and pauses.

b. Phrasing.   Pauses are oral punctuation, which differs radically from the written variety. In general, the two main purposes of pauses are to enhance your meaning and to permit you to breathe. The principal rules can be listed:

1. Pause at logical places.
2. Pause frequently.
3. Adjust length of pauses to the meaning.
4. Inhale often, and inhale during meaningful pauses.

Practice these rules by reading passages aloud, marking them for different possible phrasings. In marking them, a single diagonal (/) can indicate a pause of ordinary duration, while a double diagonal (//) can indicate a longer or dramatic pause.

Following is an example of too many pauses, most of them at illogical points, and several of them too long:

The first // reason / we worry // is this: We // worry because we / like to. / Yes, that's // what I / said: because we like // to.

A better phrasing for the same sentences would be:

The first reason we worry / is this: / We worry because we like to. / Yes, / that's what I said: / because we like to.

Another acceptable phrasing, more dramatically done:

The first reason we worry / is this: // We worry because we like to. // Yes, / that's what I said: // because we like to.

You can invent or find many other passages of varying lengths, which you can practice and mark in a similar fashion. You will become aware of the crucial effect of any pause upon the meaningfulness of a statement. You will note particularly how a dramatic pause emphasizes the word immediately before or after that pause.

While practicing the relation of pauses to meaning, you can also study your breathing. Synchronize your breathing with meaningful pauses. Ordinarily, this does not present much of a problem because the number of pauses required for proper meaningfulness far outnumbers the times it is necessary to inhale. Just remember that there is no advantage in taking very deep breaths. If you learn to pause often enough for proper meaning, and if you inhale as often as you want to during such pauses, you will have no difficulty. The chief virtue of practice is to verify that fact.

c. Loudness.   It is easy to produce variety by experimenting with various degrees of loudness. Try going from a whisper to a roar and from a roar to a whisper. Try a gradual crescendo or diminuendo; then try stressing a word or phrase by suddenly increasing or decreasing its loudness. Again, a good mechanical exercise is counting aloud, trying out the variations of loudness just described. Also, find some selections of various types that suggest opportunities for loudness variation. Let yourself go when reading them— don't be afraid to shout.

d. Pitch.   The subtlest but best road to variety is by varying your pitch. This can be done gradually (a glide) or suddenly (a step). A rise in pitch usually conveys a question: Is that you? A drop in pitch usually suggests finality: This is the end. A combined rise and fall indicates doubt: I am not sure. Possible pitch variations are infinite.

Here is a good mechanical exercise to develop flexibility and range. Start counting at your lowest comfortable pitch level; gradually move up the scale until you hit the highest pitch possible without cracking; then go back down the scale gradually until you reach your lowest note again. The same exercise can be done by talking up and down the musical scale. You can speak do, re, mi, as a singer sings them. In these exercises, you can ascertain your range by finding your lowest and highest notes on a piano. Talking the scale while playing the notes on the piano is also a helpful exercise. Finally, find selections that call for obvious pitch differences. For example, the remarks of a child would require high pitch; those of a ghost, very low pitch. Try for extremes just to see what your voice can do.

e. Combined variations.   A final suggestion for practice in vocal variety is to compose or to find materials in which changes in rate, loudness, and pitch can be practiced all together. An excellent example is Edgar Allan Poe's "The Bells." The ideas, emotions, and choice of words all combine to make this poem a challenging voice exercise. Stanza 1 describes sleigh bells and calls for a rapid rate, little loudness, mostly high pitch, and an overall tinkling effect. Stanza 2 describes wedding bells and calls for a medium rate, medium loudness, varied pitch, and a resonant or mellow effect. Stanza 3 describes fire bells and calls for a very fast rate, extreme loudness, mostly high pitch, and a harsh or strident general effect. Stanza 4 describes funeral bells and calls for a very slow rate, medium loudness, mostly low pitch, and a ghostlike or hollow effect. At the end of each stanza you will find the word "bells" repeated many times. These repetitions provide an opportunity to imitate the kinds of bells described by the poet. There is sufficient thought and emotion in the poem to permit penetration into the mood of each stanza and communication of the mood of each.

SUMMARY

Your goal is not to change your voice, but to make the most of what you have. Voice improvement requires five steps: (1) understanding how the speaking voice is produced, (2) making a voice and articulation inventory, (3) determining your potential, (4) planning a program, and (5) practicing the program.

To understand how the speaking voice is produced, you must understand the processes of respiration, phonation, resonation, and articulation.

In making a personal voice and articulation inventory, you must evaluate your speaking in terms of acceptable standards. An acceptable speaking voice is audible, accurate, meaningful, and pleasant.

You can help determine your vocal potential by listening critically to conversations, platform speeches, radio, television, and phonograph or tape-recordings.

A personal program for voice improvement should first include a list of faults that can be rather quickly eliminated. The ultimate goal should be fitted to your future proposed vocation.

There are many exercises for voice improvement that can be practiced with or without your instructor's help. Practice sessions are often most successful when a tape recorder is used. The purpose of all voice and articulation exercises is to make your speaking more communicative.

TOPICAL PREVIEW

I   What's in a name?

II   Words as symbols

III   Characteristics of effective language
    A   Clarity
        1   Meaningful words
        2   Simple words
        3   Precise words
        4   Correct usage
    B   Interest
        1   Concrete words
        2   Figurative words
        3   Sentence variety
    C   Propriety
        1   Slang
        2   Profanity
        3   Obscenity

IV   Language and the occasion
    A   Extemporaneous speeches
    B   Impromptu speeches
    C   Written speeches
    D   Memorized speeches

V   Summary

10
Verbal Communication

WHAT'S IN A NAME?

When a football coach is planning a new play he usually gets a pencil and paper and starts drawing diagrams. He represents each player by an x or an o, and shows their movements by arrows. The convenience of this method of planning is at once apparent: Instead of moving 200-pound players from here to there on the gridiron, the coach moves symbols—letters that stand for the players—on a sheet of paper. While drawing the diagrams the coach murmurs to himself, "So we put the tight end there and the tackle there. No, wait a minute. That won't do. The tackle goes here." Thus he manipulates mental symbols, language symbols, to test the play in thought before trying it in an actual game.

Next day the coach shows his squad the new play. Again he presents a diagram, this time on a chalkboard. Again he accompanies the drawing with language symbols, this time spoken aloud. In addition to thinking, the coach is now communicating by both written and spoken symbols.

The above example illustrates the three most common forms of language symbols: the mental (from electrochemical impulses), the written (by light waves), and the spoken (by sound waves). Consider the concept symbolized by the word *football*. You can think it, read it, write it, hear it, or say it. Whichever you do, the word itself is a symbol, and the symbol stands for the same thing, whether it is thought, read, written, heard, or said.

But how does it happen that a certain word becomes the symbol for a particular object or event? A word acquires a meaning through arbitrary agreement and repeated usage, as briefly indicated in Chapter 1. Pigs are not called pigs because they are such dirty creatures, nor was the name assigned by editors of a dictionary. A number of English-speaking people began to refer to this animal by the symbol *pig*, and proceeded to use the word with that intended meaning or denotation. Other people agreed upon other symbols: the French agreed upon *cochon;* the German, *Schwein;* the Italian, *porco;* the Spanish, *cochino.* Dictionaries record such agreements after they are in widespread use.

In the original denotation, *pig* would be reported in the dictionary as "a domesticated animal with a long, broad snout and a thick, fat body covered with coarse bristles; a young hog." However, a word often gains additional denotations as people associate it with their personal experience. Thus, one or more individuals watch these animals as they are wallowing in mud, and associate *pig* with the concept *dirty.* Similarly, people see the animal eating from a trough, and associate *pig* with *greedy* or *gluttonous.* If someone says, "The man eats like a pig," or "Policemen are pigs," and if the usage becomes widespread, then connotations become denotations and eventually are recorded as such in dictionaries. In this manner words may accumulate a variety of denotative meanings. Dictionaries, for example, further report that pig can mean "meat from a pig; pork," "an oblong casting of iron or other metal," "an earthenware vessel; crock," "hot water vessel," or "an immoral woman."

The word pig has relatively few denotations in comparison with many other words. Opening at random a large unabridged dictionary, one finds that approximately two columns of fine print are required for definitions of *law* and on the next page another two columns are devoted to an astonishing variety of denotations of *lay.* The student of speech communication can spend an instructive hour leafing through a dictionary, pausing occasionally to study words that have especially lengthy lists of denotative meanings.

Now we come to a basic but often overlooked fact—agreements about word meanings are only approximations. The same word can never mean exactly the same thing to any two people. For example, the words *Los Angeles* are commonly accepted to symbolize a large city in California. But what about the full and exact meaning? A New England student's experience with the symbol *Los Angeles* comes from talk he has heard, books he has read, and movies he has seen; therefore the name may suggest to him all-year tans (from swimming pools in every back yard), Disneyland, and glamorous movie stars dining in plush restaurants. But to a student who has lived in Los Angeles most of his life, the associations would be more likely to include smog, endless miles of suburbs, and traffic which sometimes races madly, sometimes inches maddeningly, on the freeways. Thus, to the sometimes surprising number of denotations listed in a dictionary, you must add the infinitely longer list of connotations.

Exact communication in either speech or writing is impossible, even in science and mathematics. Scientific vocabularies are created in an effort to approach complete accuracy, but even technical terms have different meanings for different scientists. For example, the leukemia specialist's associations with the word *leukemia* are different from those of a general practitioner who may never have treated a case.

Spoken ideas are not transferred directly into the listener's mind, but must be translated by the listener. Thus the speaker tries to find words that will arouse thoughts and feelings similar to those he is trying to communicate. The arousal of thoughts and feelings and the active role of listeners are charmingly illustrated by the story of the minister who always said the right thing upon first seeing a new baby. Proud parents remarked that the minister noticed the things that made their baby different from, and better than, any other baby in the town. When a friend complimented him upon his tact, the minister confessed that he always said the same thing. "Well," he would declare beamingly, "This *is* a baby!"

You will see that the advice to make your language clear is easier to give and accept than to put into practice. Nevertheless, the job of communicating is not a hopeless one. An understanding of the nature of our language, its limitations, its confusions, and its dangers, is the first major step toward improving your own word accuracy. Do not suppose that the meaning of a word is self-evident, or that a word has only one meaning, or that the same word means the same thing to different people.

WORDS AS SYMBOLS

A word is only a symbol for something, yet we constantly behave as though the word were the thing itself. For example, when someone vividly describes cutting a lemon and biting into a slice, your mouth may water as though you were biting into an actual lemon. People can be made to laugh, weep, tremble, or become violently ill—all by means of words alone. So many people react so violently to the number thirteen that in some office buildings and hotels the floor above the twelfth is called fourteen to avoid having a "thirteenth floor." A label—*socialistic, communistic*—can defeat a proposed new law. "Sticks and stones may break my bones, but names will never hurt me!" simply isn't true. Names are words, and words are symbols. And wars are fought for symbols. Said Byron:

Religion—freedom—vengeance—what you will,
A word's enough to raise mankind to kill.

When we have learned to treat words only as symbols, realizing that the meaning is not in the word but in us, we will be less gullible as listeners and more accurate as speakers.

We must learn to look beyond the symbols to the things symbolized. Shall we support a proposed policy because it is called "the American way"? Precisely what do the proponents mean by the American way? Exactly what is the proposal? Does the proposal *actually* correspond with our definition of the American way? Such questions will help get at the meaning beyond the symbols. When preparing your own speeches remember that your words should be firmly rooted in meaning, for beautiful words won't clarify ideas that aren't there. Begin with an analysis of your ideas to clarify what you want to say—what facts or opinions, what thoughts or feelings. Then only are you ready to consider possible choices of symbols.

Help your listener do his share of the job. You cannot explain anything to your listener; he explains it to himself. You cannot tell him a story; he tells himself the story. You cannot talk him into your point of view; he talks himself into it. Your job is to use words that will arouse in the listener a process of thought or feeling; once begun, the listener will carry the process through to a conclusion. You hope you have stimulated him so that his eventual conclusion will agree with your own; but you cannot do his thinking for him, nor should you want to. It is similar to shopping for clothing. We resent high-pressure sales talks; we want to examine the clothing and sell it to ourselves. If the clothing is good, the salesman needn't worry. Likewise, in speaking, if the ideas are sound we should need only to present them; the listener will sell himself.

How can you improve the accuracy of communication through language? Employ the suggestions we have just discussed: (1) treat words only as symbols; (2) look beyond the symbols to the things symbolized; and (3) help the listener do his share of the job.

You can take stock of your present ability to arouse thought in your listeners. Soon after your next class speech ask several classmates to give a brief summary of your talk. You may be surprised at the results. Perhaps you will find yourself silently exclaiming, "But I didn't say *that!*" Or, "Is that all you got out of it?" Or, "But you missed the whole point." However, you may get a summary that carries your point further or states it better than you did! Whatever the result, this sort of checking will teach you that your goal is to get across the gist of your main point.

CHARACTERISTICS OF EFFECTIVE LANGUAGE

Clarity

Always remember your "ignorant" audience. You have thought about or experienced the ideas to be presented in your speech; your listeners will be ignorant of what you intend to say. Your first task, therefore, is to choose words that will make your ideas as clear as possible to them. You do not expect them to get exactly the same meaning from your words as you get, but you do expect them to understand your main ideas. You can reduce the possibility of misinterpretation among your hearers by stating your points carefully, restating them in different words, and supporting them. You may then approach the goal suggested by Quintilian, "Not that language may be understood, but that it cannot be misunderstood."

1. MEANINGFUL WORDS   To say, "Use meaningful words," may strike you as unnecessary advice. "I do use meaningful words," you insist. Yes, but in addition, what percentage of meaningless words do you use? Have you any pet words or phrases which you constantly inject into your speaking? Here are some common examples:

well	more or less
see?	like
I mean	in other words
see what I mean?	really
and-uh	in my opinion
as a matter of fact	it seems to me

The exasperation this habit produces can be sensed by supposing that Lincoln had said at Gettysburg, "Fourscore and seven years ago—see?—our fathers brought forth on this continent—see?—a new nation—get what I mean?" Your instructor will tell you if you have such language mannerisms. Pet words and phrases can be eliminated if you practice listening for them and heading them off.

The overuse of trite expressions will also boost your percentage of meaningless words. Old familiar sayings can be packed with meaning if used in proper contexts, but constant reliance upon hackneyed terms should be avoided. Listen for them when you practice your speech. Better just say *white* rather than *white as snow; I was lucky* rather than *I had a stroke of luck; last* or *final* rather than *last but not least.*

Most beginning speakers can improve their oral styles by reducing their use of adverbs and adjectives. When you use a modifier in practice speech or in writing, try striking out the word—you will be surprised how often the omission improves clarity and interest.

Perhaps the worst offender is the word *very*. You may find yourself relying upon *very* every time you want added emphasis, but usually you get the opposite effect. Winston Churchill has provided many memorable examples of word economy. Read aloud his tribute to the Royal Air Force, "Never in the field of human conflict was so much owed by so many to so few." Now try adding modifiers and see what happens! For example, "Never in the [broad and vast] field of human [military] conflict was so [very] much [legitimately] owed by so [very] many to so [very] few." Inserting *any* of the bracketed words reduces the punch.

Mark Twain reported about one modifier-filled paragraph (in "A Double-Barrelled Detective Story"): "It was a joke ... not a vestige of sense in any detail of it." The whole incident was fictitious, yet he alleged to fool nearly everyone who read the paragraph. Haven't you often listened to people who talk on and on saying nothing? In the following passage search for the meaning. Look for the facts; evaluate the thought:

> If you want my opinion and you can take it or leave it for whatever it is worth, I'd say that I, for one, would like to give a vote of thanks to the state of Wisconsin for having the good sense and the sound judgment with reference to the real underlying problems which confront this whole country today—the good judgment, I say, to elect to the United States Senate a man who is unafraid to undertake a task for which men, and women, too, have been persecuted in the past, just the same as they are today, and will be tomorrow.

Words should symbolize facts and reasoning; a surplus of empty words can reflect a shortage of ideas.

2. SIMPLE WORDS   The genius of great speakers lies not in their ability to use long words or unusual words, but in their ability to put simple words together in meaning-packed combinations. Lincoln said, "You can fool all of the people some of the time, and some of the people all of the time, but you can't fool all of the people all of the time." Note that Lincoln said *fool*, not *mislead* or *deceive*, and certainly not *victimize* or *outmaneuver*. He said *all*, not *the totality*, *the aggregate*, or *one hundred percent*. He said *people*, not *populace*, *multitude*, or *general public*. All of Lincoln's speeches are models of simplicity. The "Gettysburg Address" has 265 words; of these, 195 are one-syllable words. Try to imagine him saying:

> Eight and seven-tenths decades ago the pioneer workingmen in this continental area implemented a new group based on an ideology of free boundaries and initial conditions of equality.

For effective usage listen again to Winston Churchill:

I have nothing to offer but blood, toil, tears and sweat.

We shall fight on the beaches, we shall fight on the landing grounds, we shall fight in the fields and in the streets, we shall fight in the hills; we shall never surrender.

If the British Empire and its Commonwealth last for a thousand years, men will still say, "This was their finest hour."

Or study the simplicity of Franklin Roosevelt's language:

The only thing we have to fear is fear itself.

The test of our progress is not whether we add more to the abundance of those who have much; it is whether we provide enough for those who have too little.

More than an end to war, we want an end to the beginnings of all wars.

Don't be misled into using big words and stilted phrases; don't be "overwhelmed by the magnitude of the occasion."

Take a few lines from a speech full of big words, and see if you can state the same thoughts in short plain words. Make a game of it; word games are fun. You take the first big word in the speech and ask what it means; then you look for a small word that means the same thing. You may need a bit of time to get just the right word at first, but the time is well spent. You will soon find that a real need for big words is rare. In fact, you can spoil a speech with high-flown prose—the "grand style" has long been out of date. As a rule short words give a thought more punch. So chop the big words out of the speech, and watch how well short words fill the gaps. Of course, short words will not do the job all of the time. You may want to say, "All the words in the last twelve lines have but one—*syllable!*"

3. PRECISE WORDS Some of us are so word-lazy we expect too much from a few overworked expressions. For example, *cute* may be used to describe anything from a baby to a house; *beautiful* may be expected to communicate our feelings about a sunset, girl friend, golf shot, rug, painting, song, or race horse. What word could replace *cute* or *beautiful* in each of these instances? What word would be precise?

You cannot increase your working vocabulary without effort. You should study your dictionary and a wordbook such as *Roget's Thesaurus*. This type of study provides you with alternatives for expressing almost any meaning. For example, there are probably over 200 variations on the word *said*, of which these are a few:

replied	asked
thought aloud	implored
drawled	denied

added	shouted
agreed	protested
bellowed	snorted
went on	murmured
declared	muttered

Rudolf Flesch believes that the "lack of well-used verbs is the main trouble with modern English writing." We might say the same for speaking.

It is necessary, therefore, not only to develop a list of alternative words, but also to be able to choose the precise one. A nice choice among several shadings of meaning can help clarify your idea. A wrong choice can be ridiculous—for instance, that by the chairman introducing one of the first women to be elected to the United States Senate. Intending to say that the speaker was justly famous, the chairman blurted, "I now present one of the most *notorious* women in this nation."

You can find words that come close to expressing not only the thing itself, but also your degrees of approval or disapproval. An exercise in such nuances is the "I, you, he" game. Here are some examples:

I am thrifty; you are stingy; he's a miser.
I am slender; you are thin; she is skinny.
I'm a statesman; you're a politician; he's a rabble-rouser.
I agree; you must admit; he's forced to confess.
I'm well read; you're studious; he's a bookworm.
I'm in love; you're infatuated; she's boy crazy.
I'm a liberal; you're a radical; he's a communist.

Try inventing some yourself, noticing the insinuation of approval or disapproval.

To illustrate further the importance of nuances of meaning, let us suppose that a Senator has made a statement that differs from his previous position. Here are some ways of describing his behavior:

The Senator is now forced to confess . . .
He finally admits that . . .
He concedes that . . .
He acknowledges that . . .
He gladly agrees that . . .

The Senator may also: conform, accord, harmonize, assent, assert, consent, subscribe, affirm, declare, avow, announce, take back, pretend, boast, say, remark, comment, eat crow, or promote bipartisan unity.

Another technique for getting precision in meaning is to define important terms for your audience. Most of the commonly accepted meanings of words are listed in a good general dictionary, but sometimes a dictionary definition of a word or phrase is inadequate. You must then compose your own definition or seek one in the appropriate literature. For example, Justice Oliver Wendell Holmes defined a difficult concept in these words:

> If there is any principle of the Constitution that more imperatively calls for attachment than any other it is the principle of free thought —not free thought for those who agree with us but freedom for the thought that we hate.

4. CORRECT USAGE You have been practicing language usage most of your life; you began studying it during your elementary school years. By this time you should have an adequate awareness of ordinary grammatical usages, but you have probably acquired a few bad habits. In this course, therefore, attention will be confined to eliminating habitual errors. A single habitual mistake (such as saying *them* for *those*) not only detracts from your meaning, but also stamps you as uneducated and lowers you in the esteem of your listeners.

Check yourself against this list:

SOMETIMES ACCEPTABLE	USUALLY PREFERRED
he laid down to nap	he lay down to nap, he napped
sit it on the desk	set (put, place) it on the desk
I expect you found it	I suppose you found it
try and be there	try to be there
choose between the three	choose between the two, choose among the three (or more)
between each inning	between the innings
the reason is because	the reason is that
it looks like we'll win	it looks as if we'll win, we'll probably win
he is dark complected	he is dark complexioned, he has a dark complexion
which do you like best, *a* or *b*?	which do you like better, *a* or *b*?, which do you like best, *a*, *b*, or *c*?
it's me	it is I

When you practice your speech you should decide whether a generally correct form will be correct in that speech situation.

In finding and correcting your own weaknesses in grammatical usages an English handbook is essential. Some standard references are H. W. Fowler, *A Dictionary of Modern English Usage* (Oxford);

Porter Perrin, *Writer's Guide and Index to English* (Scott, Foresman); and John C. Hodges, Mary E. Whitten, *Harbrace College Handbook* (Harcourt Brace Jovanovich).

Interest

Anything that makes language clear is also likely to make it interesting. Language that is sparklingly clear will catch attention. However, language may be adequately clear, yet dull. Clarity is basic but not enough; on it you must build interest. Concrete words, vivid words, and varied sentence structures help make your language interesting.

1. CONCRETE WORDS   Abstractions are necessary and desirable in speech because they are often the quickest way of saying something. Usually your points and subpoints will be stated in abstract words. To say that a plan has all the strengths while avoiding the weaknesses of the present system is highly abstract. We do not know what the plan is, what the present system is, or the strengths and weaknesses of either. But most of a speech is spent in supporting the points and subpoints, and supports should be worded concretely. The substance of almost any good 5,000-word speech can be told in less than 50 words; the other 4,950 words are devoted almost entirely to concrete details. Abstract statements can summarize or generalize your ideas, but concrete details are necessary to relate your ideas to your listeners' experience. You want to guide the listeners' thinking, but it takes only a little abstraction to put an audience to sleep.

There are degrees of abstractness or concreteness. Thus the word *all* is highly abstract—you cannot visualize *all,* nor feel it, nor taste it, nor hear it. *All living things* is only slightly less abstract. By degrees we can become concrete: *all animals, all cats, all Persian cats, several Persian cats, six Persian cats, a yellow Persian cat.* And perhaps finally: "The yellow Persian cat crouched behind the peach tree and fixed unblinking eyes on the sparrow."

Practice using specific and concrete words. Consider "automobile." Was it a Mustang, Mazda, VW, or Rolls Royce? Was it a truck, a station wagon, or a camper? You say, "He drove it down the street." Can you be more specific? Did the car creep, roar, race, rattle, or whiz? Was it a street, road, alley, lane, or freeway? "The race car shot through the alley like a bullet through the bore of a rifle."

2. FIGURATIVE WORDS   When Winston Churchill wanted to refer to the fact that America had just entered World War II, he did not prosaically state, "The United States has declared war." He used figurative words: "The United States ... has drawn the sword for Freedom, and cast away the scabbard."

Figures of speech are based on the principle of showing resemblances between apparently dissimilar things. A simile is a comparison, generally introduced by *like, as,* or *as if.* A metaphor is the calling of one thing by the name of another. For example, Shelley's "Ode to the West Wind" opens with a metaphor in the first line, and introduces a simile in the third line:

> O Wild West Wind, thou breath of Autumn's being,
> Thou from whose unseen presence the leaves dead
> Are driven, like ghosts from an enchanter fleeing,

Figures of speech make language vivid and colorful. In 1931, on his ninetieth birthday, Justice Oliver Wendell Holmes in a radio address used this figurative analogy:

> The riders in a race do not stop short when they reach the goal. There is a little finishing canter before coming to a standstill. There is time to hear the kind voice of friends and say to oneself, "The work is done." But just as one says that, the answer comes, "The race is over, but the work never is done while the power to work remains." The canter that brings you to a standstill need not be only coming to rest. It cannot be, while you still live. For to live is to function. That is all there is in living.

Daniel Webster gave us many examples of figurative language:

> Knowledge, in truth, is the great sun in the firmament. Life and power are scattered with all its beams.

> He smote the rock of the national resources, and abundant streams of revenue gushed forth. He touched the dead corpse of Public Credit, and it sprung upon its feet.

In his famous speech at the Democratic National Convention of 1896, William Jennings Bryan used vivid figures of speech, such as:

> The humblest citizen of all the land, when clad in the armor of a righteous cause, is stronger than all the hosts of Error.

> You shall not press down upon the brow of labor this crown of thorns, you shall not crucify mankind upon a cross of gold.

Figurative language can, of course, be overdone or poorly done. Mixed metaphors can be ludicrous: "The American space avalanche has racked up a tidal wave of achievements." But when used with discretion, figures of speech are (to use a metaphor) the salt and pepper in the food for thought that you offer your listeners. For example, Norman Topping used the following vivid sentence in addressing a university gathering, "Without a faculty devoted to excellence, a university's buildings would echo with questions unanswered and with answers never questioned." [1]

3. SENTENCE VARIETY   The interest value of your language is also heightened by sentence variety. You should use long sentences and short ones; loose sentences (in which the sentence is grammatically complete before the end) and periodic ones (in which the sentence is not grammatically complete until the end). You should use rhetorical questions often, dialogue, exclamations, and imperatives occasionally, and incomplete sentences rarely.

Let us analyze sentence variety in a passage from Winston Churchill's address to Congress on December 26, 1941. The passage begins with a lengthy sentence of loose construction, in which the main clause and essential meaning occur at the beginning of the sentence. The second sentence is also long but is periodic, for the main clause and the meaning are not complete until the end of the sentence. Then to give contrast to the two long sentences, Churchill has a brief simple statement, "They have certainly embarked upon a very considerable undertaking." Then come two long periodic sentences, holding us in suspense and building toward a magnificent climax. The brief sentence that follows hits like a hammer, and might be classified either as a rhetorical question or an exclamation: "What kind of people do they think we are?" The climax of the passage comes with the powerful rhetorical question, "Is it possible . . . ?"

> We know that for many years past the policy of Japan has been dominated by secret societies of subaltern and junior officers of the Army and Navy who have enforced their will upon successive Japanese cabinets and parliaments by the assassination of any Japanese statesman who opposed or who did not sufficiently further their aggressive policy. It may be that these societies, dazzled and dizzy with their own schemes of aggression and the prospect of early victories, have forced their country, against its better judgment, into war. They have certainly embarked upon a very considerable undertaking; for, after the outrages they have committed upon us at Pearl Harbor, in the Pacific islands, in the Philippines, in Malaya, and the Dutch East Indies, they must now know that the stakes for which they have decided to play are mortal. When we consider the resources of the United States and the British Empire, compared to those of Japan, when we remember those of China, which has so long and valiantly withstood invasion, and when also we observe the Russian menace which hangs over Japan, it becomes still more difficult to reconcile Japanese action with prudence, or even with sanity. What kind of people do they think we are? Is it possible they do not realize that we shall never cease to persevere against them until they have been taught a lesson which they and the world will never forget?

[1] Reprinted by special permission of Norman Topping.

Propriety

Your language may be both clear and interesting, yet your speech will be damaged if it is perceived by listeners as irritating or offensive. Sometimes slang raises the issue of propriety; profanity and obscenity always do.

1. SLANG Slang has a long and honorable history, well recorded in scholarly literature which offers such tidbits as that the word *nice* (e.g., "We had a nice trip.") originated about 1765 and at first was pure slang. Likewise, such useful words as *strenuous, spurious, puffy,* and *clumsy* were coined as slang about 1600 and condemned by purists (including Ben Jonson) as uncouth and vulgar. Shakespeare adopted and immortalized some of the slang of his day, usually because it met genuine vocabulary needs, for example, *hubbub, fireworks, foppish, fretful,* and *sportive.* Jumping to more recent vocabulary needs, what would you call a racketeer if there were no word *racketeer?* Or what else would you suggest instead of *jeep?*

Of course, only a small percentage of slang comprises neologisms (new words) or fills genuine vocabulary gaps. Usually current slang consists of assigning new meanings to standard words or phrases: *groovy, hung up, with it, freak out, corny, up tight.* Most of it is ephemeral—popular today, old fashioned tomorrow. Even so, good slang provides temporary variety, color, humor, and sometimes a form of social commentary.

Some of the best American slang comes from the college campus. But most slang soon dies because of mediocre or inferior quality, as well as overuse. Therefore, in classroom talks you should use slang with discrimination. And slang, even more than standard language, becomes monotonous or irritating when used too frequently. You must also remind yourself that campus slang may be meaningless to off-campus groups. When you do use slang, do not apologize by saying, "If you'll pardon a colloquial expression . . ."

2. PROFANITY Probably almost all of us use profanity on certain occasions. If you hit your thumb with a hammer, you may exclaim *damn* rather than *doggone.* Some public speakers use profanity occasionally because of conversational habit, or because they think it is forceful or earthy. For instance, in the nationally televised Senate Watergate Hearings, John N. Mitchell, former Attorney General, sprinkled a few *hell's* and *damn's* into his testimony. The questions raised were whether he needed these words, and whether the use of them added to or detracted from or had no effect on his defense of his actions. The answers would depend upon each viewer's perceptions of the context, including Mitchell's reputation as a salty character. The same criteria should be applied to yourself. If you use profanity in a speech, intentionally or unintentionally, the usage will be evaluated in the context of your temperament or personality, your subject matter, your speech purpose, your audience, and the occasion. Your experience as a listener tells you that the number of contexts in which profanity is acceptable is severely limited. When in doubt, do not use it.

3. OBSCENITY Acceptable public contexts for obscenity are close to zero. Nevertheless, during the late 1960's certain speakers at student protest rallies deliberately used obscenities as a cheap way to get audience attention. The tactic boomeranged against both the speaker and his cause; before long, repetition destroyed even the shock effect. Do not confuse public with private conversation.

LANGUAGE AND THE OCCASION

Speech delivery may be classified into four types; extemporaneous, impromptu, reading from manuscript, and memorized. In the long run you will want to master all four styles. In this text, however, emphasis will be placed on the extemporaneous speech because it is the most widely useful, and because it is basic to the proper practice of the other three. It develops the fluency needed for impromptu talks and the communicativeness needed for speaking either from manuscript or from memory.

Extemporaneous Speeches

In Chapter 3 we presented a method of practicing aloud for an extemporaneous (that is, nonmemorized) talk. We assume that you have been using that method in preparing your class talks up to now. You have discovered that you can get your ideas worded without memorization, though perhaps clumsily at first. By repeatedly talking through each speech outline, (1) you clarify your thinking, (2) you choose words listeners will like, and (3) you gain fluency.

When you first talk through an outline, you are likely to find that you take too much time, that you are wordy and rambling. Why is it that on this first run-through your statement of point is usually confused, and even your telling of a simple story is hard to follow? Because your thinking is confused and hard to follow. Why is it that your choice of words gets better after several trials? Because your thinking has improved. In short, as you rehearse ideas extemporaneously, you literally think aloud; and as you word ideas differently, you are clarifying your thoughts. When you praise a classmate for being able to think on his feet, what are you praising? Not his ability to stand before the group and silently ponder! You are praising his ability to talk without having memorized the words.

Although wordiness is the most common difficulty, a groping for words is sometimes encountered. Thus, after stating your idea, "In choosing anecdotes for a speech, be sure that each has but one apparent point," you can think of no more to say. What is the trouble? Again, it is your thinking. You have an idea but you have not thought it through; you have not developed it. So practice aloud. Try stating the thought in different ways. Presently the implications of your idea begin to take shape; by talking about it, you clarify your thinking.

In practicing your talks aloud, you have undoubtedly noticed that you can listen to yourself even when concentrating on the thought to be expressed. More than that, you can listen for one thing at a time, even while all the other necessary speech activities are proceeding. You are analyzing your thought and thus clarifying it, but more is needed: You must also choose words that will communicate your thinking to the prospective listeners. The words that best clarify your own thinking may or may not be the right words for the audience. Therefore you should practice with your prospective audience consciously in mind, varying your choice of words from trial to trial to suit your listeners.

Do not imagine that at this time you are expected to produce polished and memorable phrases. Churchill's prose took years to develop. Your present goal is to learn to use words that are direct, personal, concrete, and immediately clear to your audience.

To show that effective extemporaneous language need not be exalted, consider an excerpt from the verbatim transcription of a talk, given without notes, before a convention of the Chamber of Commerce of the United States by Clarence B. Randall, then president of the Inland Steel Company.

> You're perfectly certain that the proposed tax bill is wrong. Do you know why?
>
> Supposing somebody walked up and said, "All right, wise guy, you write the tax bill!"
>
> Can you write a tax bill for the United States? I don't mean in detail.
>
> Have you got an idea of where the revenue should come from to support our debt?
>
> We've got the debt; there's no doubt about that. You think it ought to be paid off. Have you got a clear idea of where the money should come from?
>
> Well, you know you shouldn't pay it, but are you clear as to who should pay it? Is it fair to yell about controls and false economy in high places if you haven't thought through, yourself, what is the sound tax basis?

> You start talking to your employees—they'll ask you some questions on that.
> No good talking to them until you've got an answer.
> I don't care whether you've got the right answer or not, as long as it's your answer; as long as it's held with integrity; as long as you can talk about it with your voice down and be pleasant.[2]

This is not elegant language. It illustrates that effective extemporaneous phraseology need not be fancy or oratorical. Study the quotation again and note some of the characteristics. Most of the sentences are short, but they are varied in structure. There are rhetorical questions, dialogue, repetitions, and an incomplete sentence. All words are simple and familiar without being trite. Adjectives and adverbs are conspicuously few; verbs and nouns do most of the work. There are many contractions, and other conversational informalities include a "well," and the frequent use of "got." There are a few colloquial words: "supposing," "yell," "no good talking"; a touch of slang, "wise guy"; and an occasional awkward combination, such as "come from to." But the total effect with the use of "I," "we," and "you" is that of direct communication.

Furthermore, the experienced speaker will be able to sprinkle his speech with an occasional neat, vivid, or brilliant expression. For example, at another time in the speech just cited, Randall said:

> If you ask me, in one sentence, to express the present American foreign policy, I would say, we propose to fight half of the world; feed the other half; and have business as usual at home. And that can't be done.[3]

Impromptu Speeches

An impromptu speech is one given without previous specific preparation. It should not be confused with the extemporaneous, which, as we have seen, is carefully prepared in thought and flexibly prepared in language.

Most daily conversations, interviews, and group discussions are impromptu and do not trouble us greatly. However, occasionally you may attend a meeting and be called upon unexpectedly to "say a few words." The possibility of such emergencies worries most students.

You can often anticipate situations in which you might be called upon, and so be prepared. In fact, many a brilliant impromptu talk has been carefully planned in such fashion.

[2] A. Craig Baird, ed., *Representative American Speeches: 1951–1952*, H. W. Wilson, 1952, p. 118. Reprinted by permission of The *Atlantic Monthly* Co.
[3] *Representative American Speeches*, p. 117.

If you are caught, search for an idea, not for words. If you can think of a point and supports, the language will take care of itself. An appropriate main point is likely to be given to you ready-made by the previous speaker or the nature of the occasion. The first step is to think of one or more supports quickly. The best bet usually is to try for an anecdote, because words flow most easily when you are narrating a story. Another good technique is to look about quickly for something that can be adapted as a visual aid: a glass of water, a salt shaker, or a newspaper.

Generally the easiest way to start is by reference to the situation or to something just said. Weave this reference into the statement of your main point. Support it with an anecdote and visual aid, or other form of support if you have thought of any. Then restate your main point and sit down.

This formula is based on the assumption that you have been applying the extemporaneous method of speech practice, through which you become accustomed to constructing speech units, acquire a supply of generally useful supports, and develop fluency. These are the skills that come to your rescue.

Written Speeches

There are circumstances where reading from manuscript is appropriate or required, as in the case where the speaker's words may reflect the official policy of a business or even a nation. Properly done, the manuscript speech has the advantage of precision of thought and language. But if improperly done, the manuscript speech can be especially dull and uncommunicative. There are two special considerations in this style of speaking. First, the written language must lend itself to oral style. Second, the speaker must follow the written page while maintaining a communicative bond with the audience.

When given the opportunity to prepare a manuscript speech, beginners often make the mistake of composing an essay rather than a speech. Speech is a transitory thing. Listeners cannot go back and "reread" (that is, "relisten to") something they missed or did not understand. Materials delivered orally have to be immediately understood as they are delivered; otherwise they are lost. In a sense, oral language must have "instant intelligibility." The best approach in writing your first manuscript speeches is to "talk out" the sentences and passages as you translate your thoughts into language. Some speech writers actually compose initial drafts of manuscript speeches by dictating their ideas to a tape recorder. When the first written version is composed from the recording, the material usually maintains a degree of its oral quality.

Many manuscript speeches, however, are composed by someone other than the speaker—perhaps a great speech of the past, or a speech composed by a regular speechwriter. Many times works of prose and poetry are a good subject for oral interpretation. In any of these cases, the speaker's main task is to deliver the material in a meaningful manner to an audience. Since the rise of radio and television, there has been an increased awareness of the problems of communicative reading. Many colleges and universities offer full length courses in the subject. At first, reading from manuscript may seem to be a comparatively easy task—that is, until you try it. In too many cases, manuscript readers are only *readers*, not speakers. Think about the characteristics of visual and vocal communication discussed in Chapters 8 and 9. Much of the effectiveness of oral communication comes from its special dimensions of voice and action. If these are not used to good advantage, oral communication loses many of its special qualities. This is the main problem in reading from manuscript. Speakers become so attached to their manuscripts that they forget these special assets of oral communication, and in the process they lose their communicative bond with the audience. The object in communicative reading or the oral interpretation of literature is to give the listener more meaning than he could gain by reading the material silently.

If the work is not your own manuscript, the first step is to insure that you thoroughly understand every aspect of the material. Try not only to get the main ideas, but also, in the case of a speech, to interpret the author's speech purpose. Be prepared to think in terms of this purpose as you deliver the material.

The next step is to practice reading the manuscript aloud. When possible it is helpful to type the manuscript with triple spaces between the lines. Become thoroughly familiar with it. You can invent your own system for marking words to be emphasized and places to pause. Practice delivering the material until you are able to look up frequently from the manuscript at your audience. On key words and phrases it is especially desirable to look away from your manuscript and at your audience. Think the thoughts as you read. If there is no need to remain completely within the manuscript, there is nothing wrong with delivering a portion of it extemporaneously. Introductions, transitions, anecdotes, and conclusions lend themselves well to this treatment. The objective is to get something of the extemporaneous spirit into your whole mood and manner.

When you are not reading your own manuscripts, you can benefit by reading aloud from the great speeches of the past and from other types of literature. Oral interpretation of literature is especially helpful in gaining a good sense of meaningfulness in vocal communication. The practice will not only improve your delivery and add to your storehouse of speech ideas, but will measurably increase your vocabulary. In experimental research, James Young found that students experience the largest vocabulary gain in oral reading when compared with silent reading or simply hearing the material.[4] Therefore, if you want to build your vocabulary, read aloud regularly from good literature. Practice reading naturally, conversationally, meaningfully, or perhaps just for fun.

Memorized Speeches

In a beginning speech class the best advice on the memorization of speeches is: Avoid it.

SUMMARY

Words are symbols, and are the chief tools of thought and of communication. We must constantly look beyond the symbol, however, to find its meaning; and we must constantly remember that ideas are not transferred to our listeners, but aroused in them.

Effective language should be clear, interesting, and appropriate. Clarity is enhanced by using meaningful words, simple words, precise words, and correct English usage. Interest value is enhanced by using concrete words, figurative words, and variety in sentence structure. Propriety is guarded by using slang in a discriminative manner, profanity rarely, and obscenity never.

From the standpoint of language, there are four types of speech preparation and delivery: extemporaneous, impromptu, written, and memorized. In this text, the extemporaneous will be emphasized because it is the most widely useful, and because it is basic to the other three.

---

[4] James Douglas Young, "An Experimental Comparison of Vocabulary Growth by Means of Oral Reading, Silent Reading, and Listening," unpublished doctoral dissertation, University of Southern California, 1951.

Audience responses may range from silent agreement to thunderous "V for victory" response to cheerleaders' urging.

Audience Responses

TOPICAL PREVIEW

I "Things are different"

II Necessary audience information
    A The occasion
    B Common traits and interests
    C Attitudes toward your topic
    D Attitudes toward you

III How to gather information about an audience
    A Observation
    B Inquiry

IV Use of audience analysis data
    A Finding common ground
    B Slanting the subject
    C Selecting supports
    D Adapting the language
    E Preventing blunders
    F Adjusting vocal and visual delivery

V The unexpected

VI Summary

Audience Analysis

"THINGS ARE DIFFERENT"

A college debate team and its coach were invited to present an open forum program before a steelworkers' union. Four of the students gave prepared speeches; half a dozen other students joined the audience.

There were about a hundred union members, all big burly fellows, some with handlebar mustaches, all dressed in their Sunday best. During the speeches the audience was extraordinarily attentive; some of the men leaned forward in their chairs or nodded their heads vigorously from time to time. When the forum period came, however, the students in the audience were forced to do most of the talking.

After the meeting the coach told the union president that the response during the forum had been disappointingly small. "I'm surprised to hear you say that," said the president, "it was the best I've ever heard them do—when English was being spoken. Of course, when our *Polish* organizer is in charge, things are different!"

This anecdote illustrates that what the speaker intends to transmit may not coincide at all with what the listener receives. Apparently the students did communicate something—but something completely different from what they intended. The intended program became a shambles at the decoding stage. It made little difference whether the students had spent hours of research on the subject, gathered imposing quantities of data, indulged in brilliant reasoning, or clothed ideas in rich and accurate language—all these were canceled by the single fact that these steelworkers did not understand much English.

The debaters had prepared themselves almost entirely in terms of their subject matter. They had only a vague and stereotyped notion of a labor union meeting, much less of differences between such meetings. If the coach or any of the students had spent even a few minutes telephoning, they could easily have found out about the language problem. Then, an entirely different type of program would have been planned—something more useful to all concerned.

Scarcely ever can you afford the luxury of preparing a speech entirely in terms of yourself. You must also prepare in terms of your specific audience and the available means of bridging the gap between you and them. Therefore, the usual first step in efficient speech preparation is getting acquainted in advance with your prospective listeners.

NECESSARY AUDIENCE INFORMATION

"Getting acquainted in advance with your prospective listeners" means gathering information about them which is likely to be useful in planning your speech. More specifically, you will want information regarding:

1. The nature of the occasion
2. Common traits and interests
3. Attitudes toward your topic
4. Attitudes toward you

Each of these four major headings may be subdivided into detailed questions. You will then have a check list to stimulate and guide your inquiries about any group.

The Occasion

1. *Date and hour:* Anything unusual about the date—holiday, anniversary, or such? Anything unusual about the hour? Time limits for your speech?
2. *Attendance:* Size of audience? Is attendance required or voluntary?
3. *Place of meeting:* Outdoors or indoors? Shape and size of room or auditorium? What kind of seating arrangements? Speaker's platform? Lectern or table? Any stage props—water pitcher, flag, map,

gavel, chalkboard? Any room decorations? What kind of lighting? Heating and ventilation? Any acoustical problems—dead spots, echoes, public address system, competing noises? Are there facilities for showing slides or motion pictures?

4. *Type of meeting:* Regular or special? Who is sponsoring the meeting? What is the purpose of the meeting? What is likely to be the general atmosphere, or mood, or tone?
5. *Type of program:* Who planned the program? Is there a printed program? What will precede and follow your talk—other speakers, music, refreshments, an open forum?

Common Traits and Interests

1. *Age:* children, adolescents, young adults, middle-aged adults, senior citizens, mixed
1. *Sex:* all men, mostly men, all women, mostly women, approximately equal
3. *Race:* black, white, oriental, foreign born, mixed; language problems
4. *Family status:* single, married, parents, children
5. *Economic status:* wealthy, well-to-do, middle bracket, poor, destitute, mixed
6. *Educational status:* elementary school, high school, college, mixed
7. *Community:* farm, small town, small city, big city, mixed
8. *Occupation:* big business, small business, professional, trade, housewives, students, retired
9. *Religion:* Protestants, Catholics, Jews, other denominations, freethinkers; regular members, occasional attendance, seldom or never attend; mixed
10. *Politics:* Republican—liberal or conservative; Democrat—liberal or conservative; independent; radical; third party; mixed
11. *Memberships:* lodges, fraternities or sororities, clubs, labor unions
12. *Entertainments:* favorite radio-TV programs, movies, dancing, athletic events, hobbies, games
13. *Sources of information:* books, magazines, newspapers, lectures, acknowledged authorities

Attitudes Toward Your Topic

1. *Favorable:* strongly or moderately
2. *Opposed:* strongly or moderately
3. *Undecided:* passively neutral or actively conflicting
4. *Indifferent:* uninformed or simply uninterested

Religious audiences vary greatly. Here a preacher exhorts his followers during the "Jesus Movement." His second audience—the bystanders—are somewhat less ecstatic.

Attitudes Toward You

1. In what respects are you like or unlike most of your audience (see list of traits and interests above: age, sex, race)?
2. Will the audience know about these resemblances and differences?
3. What are your personal reasons for speaking here?
4. Will the audience know these reasons?
5. How many in the audience are personally acquainted with you?
6. Will most of the audience be favorably inclined toward you personally, or will they be prejudiced against you?
   a. Will your appearance be a help or handicap?
   b. Will your voice be a help or handicap?
   c. Will your personality and usual speaking style be helps or handicaps?
   d. Will your reputation, rank, or title be a help or handicap?

You will not need to know all the foregoing details about every audience in order to prepare adequately. For any one audience, however, particular items will be important. The value of the check list is to help you spot the significant items for any particular audience.

Usually the most significant facts to know about the occasion are the size of the audience and the type of meeting. Is it a group of a

Here another group has gathered for religious worship. Contrast both speaker and audience behaviors with the preceding picture.

dozen or of a thousand? Is it an informal get-together or a solemn ceremonial?

Usually the most significant facts to know about the audience are their age and sex. Is it a group of children or retired oldsters? Is it a men's club or a women's club?

Usually the most significant things to know about their attitudes toward your topic are whether they are already interested, and, if your topic is controversial, whether they are in general for or against your position.

Usually the most significant thing to know about their attitudes toward you is whether they will have any reason to react in advance either favorably or unfavorably.

HOW TO GATHER INFORMATION ABOUT AN AUDIENCE

Observation

Observation and inquiry are the basic methods for getting advance information about your audience. You will frequently find that you can figure out the answers quickly and easily because of previous knowledge of the group. When you speak before audiences with which you are familiar, such as your club or fraternity, or any group you have addressed previously, you should have on hand most of the information you need. Let us imagine, however, that you are asked to speak for the first time at a meeting of the Interfraternity Mothers' Club. You can get most of the information you need simply by analyzing the nature of the club. The audience will be all women; you can guess their average age; and you know their family status. Obviously you would need only a little supplementary information—about the date, hour, place, and size of your audience—most of which you could probably get from the person who invited you to speak.

It is unlikely that you will ever be asked to speak before a group completely outside of your previous experience. However, the less you know about a given group, the more important it becomes to study it in advance. The task is usually easier than it appears.

Inquiry

The first thing to do, as we have just seen, is to question whoever invites you to speak. Then consider ways of getting additional information. If it is an organized group, try to attend one of its meetings and take notes from direct observation, supplementing them by chatting with the members. If direct observation is impossible, you must depend on inquiry. If you have friends who are members of the group or who have spoken before the group, call on them. It is usually proper to request information from the officers of the group whether you know them personally or not. Whatever the circumstances, you can either interview in person, or telephone, or write letters.

Sometimes you can secure audience information from publications. Most large organizations publish their own newspapers or magazines; small organizations often send out mimeographed newsletters or the like. For example, suppose you were going to speak to a group of people connected with the Santa Fe Railway. This company publishes monthly the *Santa Fe Magazine,* and a recent copy of the magazine would be a mine of information about the specialized activities and interests of employees of Santa Fe.

Useful information about many audiences can be gathered by studying public-opinion polls. These surveys are published regularly and cover a wide variety of topics. Often they are reported in terms of particular segments of the population. Thus on a given question the poll may contrast the views of businessmen and labor, men and women, Democrats and Republicans, or students and nonstudents.

USE OF AUDIENCE ANALYSIS DATA

Having gathered some information about your audience, you next naturally ask, "What do I do with it?" The answer is that you use it to adapt your material and presentation to the audience. Note that you are adapting to the audience, not surrendering to it. You need not and should not compromise your conscience.

You have seen in previous chapters that all the steps in speech preparation should be influenced by your knowledge of your prospective audience. For example, you will recall from Chapter 4 that the most important criterion in determining speech purpose is the attitude of listeners toward your topic. At all times during your speech preparation you should try to put yourself in your listeners' place, seeing and hearing the future speech through their eyes and ears. You should pay special attention to five specific methods of audience adaptation: finding common ground, slanting the subject, selecting supports, adapting the language, preventing blunders, and adjusting vocal and visual delivery.

Finding Common Ground

You begin by trying to find common ground. You look for areas of likeness or agreement which already exist or can be established between you and your audience with regard to your speech purpose. Ideally you want to create feelings of mutual identification with regard to both you and your speech purpose. Consider the following illustration.

During an important political campaign the two major candidates were invited to speak to student convocations on the campus of a large university. The first candidate arrived to find an audience of some five thousand students and faculty. Placards were waving, and students led small cheering sections prior to the speech. During the open forum period a student leader posed the question, "How, sir, can a student best prepare himself for political life and public office?" The candidate replied that he favored a broad preparation in the humanities rather than a specialization in political science. The answer elicited a mixed response: There was a clearly audible but confused murmur of many subdued voices. The probable reason for this reaction was that the university had a nationally famous political science department and equally famous schools of international relations and of public administration.

Two weeks later the second candidate spoke to approximately the same audience. He climaxed his first few sentences with the admission, "But perhaps I am not properly qualified—I majored in political science." Order was restored after at least two minutes of applause.

Let us analyze this example. Obviously the second candidate had secured a report of the earlier meeting and had taken the time from a strenuous schedule to study the report so that he could establish common ground with this particular audience. One might well say that the prolonged applause showed appreciation of the subtle compliment from the candidate. A deeper analysis would show that the candidate identified himself with the special traits and interests of this audience. But even more important, he simultaneously got his audience to identify themselves with him. He was off to a strong start. This initial mutual identification was on a purely personal level, but it eased his remaining task, which was to establish common ground regarding his speech subject and purpose. How, then, does a speaker interrelate these two areas of common ground, the "person-to-person" with the "idea-to-idea"? Consider another example.

On radio and television the problem of finding common ground becomes acute; anyone may tune in. In an effort to make his speech palatable for everyone, the speaker may become insipid. On the other hand, he may prepare for a particular segment of the potential listening audience, and say to himself about the others, "Good riddance. Let 'em turn the dial." The ability to find common ground, even on radio, was one of Franklin Roosevelt's achievements. During the tense months before Pearl Harbor, he addressed the nation as follows:

> My Friends: This is not a fireside chat on war. It is a talk on national security; because the nub of the whole purpose of your President is to keep you now, and your children later, and your grandchildren much later, out of a last-ditch war for the preservation of American independence and all of the things that American independence means to you and to me and to ours.
>
> Tonight, in the presence of a world crisis, my mind goes back eight years ago to a night in the midst of a domestic crisis. It was a time when the wheels of American industry were grinding to a full stop, when the whole banking system of our country had ceased to function.
>
> I well remember that while I sat in my study in the White House, preparing to talk with the people of the United States, I had before my eyes the picture of all those Americans with whom I was talking. I saw the workmen in the mills, the mines, the factories; the girl behind the counter, the small shopkeeper; the farmer doing his spring plowing; the widows and the old men wondering about their life's savings.
>
> I tried to convey to the great mass of American people what the banking crisis meant to them in their daily lives. Tonight, I want to do the same thing, with the same people, in this new crisis which faces America. We met the issue of 1933 with courage and realism. We face this new crisis—this new threat to the security of our nation—with the same courage and realism.

This example, like the previous one, illustrates speaker-audience identification. The Roosevelt example, however, goes beyond person-to-person identification. It shows how a speaker can get his listeners to identify themselves with his subject and purpose.

Slanting the Subject

Assume that you want to uphold the advantages of small colleges over large universities. You could prepare the talk without any particular audience in mind; that, however, would be a mistake because the speech would then consist entirely of ideas that you think are important. Your ideas about small and large colleges would be persuasive only if you happened to share a similar background and viewpoint with most of your auditors. But the arguments that convince you will not necessarily be the best arguments for someone else. What attitudes will most of your listeners have toward the topic? Perhaps the majority already favor small colleges, or perhaps the majority favor large universities. The whole slant of your subject should be drastically influenced by your knowledge of the audience's attitudes toward your topic.

Let us see how audience slanting works by studying an actual speech. Samuel R. Spencer, Jr., President of Davidson College, North Carolina, delivered a commencement address at neighboring Erskine College, South Carolina. Unlike most commencement speakers, Spencer courageously chose to advocate his views on a controversial problem—school desegregation. Dramatizing his topic was the fact that Erskine was graduating its first black student.

Analyzing this audience, we may note a few highlights: (1) the overwhelming majority were southerners, mostly from the immediate area; (2) probably a majority were students and their young friends and relatives; but (3) a substantial number would be the parents and other older relatives; (4) since Erskine is a Protestant denominational school we may deduce that a majority of the listeners were Protestant church members; and (5) the majority would be whites. Spencer realized that audience attitudes would be split with regard to desegregation—during the address he put it this way:

> But what shook most of the South to the roots was the 1954 Court decision. For seventeen years we have been wrestling with its consequences. It must be admitted that many of us have interpreted the Court's "deliberate speed" mandate with an emphasis on the adjective rather than the noun.[1]

Knowing that he would encounter opposing attitudes from some, Spencer wisely approached his thesis gradually. He opened the address by establishing common ground on a person-to-person basis:

[1] Waldo W. Braden, ed., *Representative American Speeches: 1971–1972*, H. W. Wilson, 1972, pp. 172–181. Reprinted by permission of Samuel R. Spencer, Jr.

Erskine is a brier patch for me. More than a half century ago, my father also stood in or near this spot and received an Erskine diploma. My mother's father was an Erskine graduate of a generation before that. The red clay of the South Carolina Piedmont was my native landscape, and Winthrop graduates in South Carolina red brick schoolhouses nurtured me through the elementary and high school years. The majority of you are South Carolinians, and even those who were outlanders four years ago now have, as a result of your stay at Erskine, a stake in what happens to this state and region. Consequently, I speak to you of the class of 1971 as South Carolinian to South Carolinians, Southerner to Southerners, American to Americans.

Soon he introduced his topic by asking the class a question:

What do you think will be the most important continuing problem on which you will have to make decisions as a citizen during the next twenty years? Depending on your interests and points of view, you could legitimately name a number of things—ecology and the environment, war, space exploration, inflation and the economy, public health and welfare. But if the question were broadened to ask for a list of such questions, there is one which I believe almost all of you would include. At least I hope that you would include it, for to me it will undoubtedly be the matter with which all of us will have to continue to wrestle—that of public education.

As a former professor of history, Spencer would be expected to review historical highlights of the problem—and he did. Recognizing students' desires for relevancy to current problems, he did not belabor the history, and he soon stressed the "emergence of new and progressive southern leadership" by listing seven current governors of southern states. He revealed his central idea by quoting from one of them, "The time for racial discrimination is over." And he told the class, "Under such circumstances I think we have to take the long view rather than the short. It is obvious also that we must deal with conditions as they are, not as we might like them to be." The entire address had a southern slant, emphasized by occasional contrasts with the other regions, as for example:

Meanwhile the problem of the black minority, once considered "peculiar" to the South, has become a national rather than a regional one. Half of the black citizens of this country now live outside the South; one third of them are now concentrated in fifteen cities. Our good fortune lies not in the fact that others are also having to take hold of such thorny questions as racial balance, busing, protests, proportional representation, and the like. Rather, it lies in the fact that the South will solve its educational problems, and be done with them while the rest of the country is still in the throes of the struggle.

The title of Spencer's address was "A Call for New Missionaries," and during his historical review he had discussed the educational missionaries who had invaded from the North during the Reconstruction period. This theme was picked up in the closing words:

The chances are that you do not know where you will be, either literally or figuratively, ten or fifteen years from now. But when the call comes to you in some nameless town or city, as it surely will, to participate, to help, to give your time and your money and your effort on behalf of educating those who come after you, don't pretend that you are hard of hearing. Don't try to hide. You will be wanted and needed. If I may suggest a response, the best one I know is from the Scripture: "Here am I, Lord, send me."

Looking back, you will see that Spencer slanted his entire address in terms of his audience analysis, and you will see the important difference between adapting to, not catering to, an audience.

Selecting Supports

Another common method of audience adaptation is through the selection of supporting materials. For any one point there are likely to be several explanations, any one of which adequately develops the point. The type of audience may help you choose the explanation to employ: Pick the one that would be most likely to connect with the listeners' experience. The same principle applies to all the other forms of support. Take quotations, for instance: Assuming you had a choice, the Secretary of Commerce would be a better person to quote for a businessmen's meeting than a poet; the reverse would be true of a literary club meeting.

James Conant, while president of Harvard, used the following anecdote in an address before the American Chemical Society to support his point that the recent growth of the chemical profession "has been one of the amazing social phenomena of our times."

When this country entered World War I it so happened that a leading professor of chemistry was a relative of the then Secretary of War. Taking advantage of that fact he called on him in the first week after war was declared to offer on behalf of the American chemists the services of the profession to aid in the war effort. The Secretary said he would look into the matter and asked his caller to return a day later. When he did so the Secretary of War thanked him once again for his offer of assistance, asked him to transmit the thanks to his fellow chemists, but said it would be unnecessary to accept the proffered assistance because on looking into the matter he found the War Department had a chemist.[2]

Dr. John A. Schindler, a physician, spoke before a Farm and Home Week audience about illnesses resulting from mental and emotional causes. Dr. Schindler discussed three types of poorly adjusted people. He illustrated his characterization of the first group, "grumpy" people, with the following anecdote.

[2] A. Craig Baird, ed., *Representative American Speeches: 1951–1952*, H. W. Wilson, 1952, pp. 138–39. Reprinted by permission of James B. Conant.

I have a friend who illustrates that group. He has a farm, a beautiful farm, and a couple of years ago in our country we had a wonderful crop of oats. I drove past his farm one week early in July and I saw this field of oats and I thought to myself, "This ought to make Sam happy." Now, I had inquired among his relatives and friends as to whether they had ever heard Sam say a happy, pleasant word. None of them ever had, excepting his wife, who thought that he had the first year they were married, but that was so long ago that she wasn't sure. So I drove into Sam's yard and saw Sam, and I said, "Sam, that's a wonderful field of oats," and Sam came back with this, "Yes, but the wind will blow it down before I get it cut." But I watched this field. He got it cut all right, he got it threshed, and I know he got a good price for it—'twas the year before last.

Well, I saw him one day and I thought, "Now I've got Sam where he just can't get out of this!" So I said, "Sam, how did the oats turn out?" And he said, "Oh, it was a good crop, and I guess the price was all right, but you know a crop of oats like that sure takes a lot out of the soil." Some time later in October—it was a beautiful October—on a nice, warm afternoon, I saw him on the street and I said, "Sam, it's a wonderful day, isn't it?" I said it real enthusiastically, to try to make it contagious. But not Sam, he didn't catch. He just said, "Yes, but when we get it, we'll get it hard." [3]

Both the foregoing anecdotes are good ones; both support a point. But Conant's was chosen because it would appeal particularly to chemists; Schindler's because it would strike a responsive chord among farmers. If the speakers and audiences had been reversed, Conant could have illustrated the recent sudden increase in the importance of chemistry by telling an anecdote about a farmer, perhaps showing the recent improvements in insecticides. Schindler could have illustrated that some people always see the darkest side of things by telling the story of an overpessimistic chemist. Thus we can see how supports can be adapted to a particular audience.

Adapting the Language

It is important to modify the language in terms of the audience. Let us consider other parts of the speech by Dr. Schindler from which we have just quoted an anecdote. Here was a physician addressing a Farm and Home Week audience on a medical subject. He could have put the entire talk in medical terminology, but he never forgot that he was addressing laymen and referred only briefly to technical terms: "The name that it used to go by is psychoneurosis. The name that it has now is *psychosomatic illness.*" Most of the time Dr. Schindler used words like "cares, difficulties, and troubles," and those three words were made even more effective when he said, "Now the thing that brings on this illness is this layer of c.d.t." He used *c.d.t.* to stand for cares, difficulties, and troubles; thus tying in

[3] William Hayes Yeager, *Effective Speaking for Every Occasion,* Prentice-Hall, 1951, pp. 238–39. Reprinted by permission of Dr. John A. Schindler.

with the common farm and home term *DDT*. After discussing causes, Dr. Schindler discussed cures, but he did not say "proper therapeutic measures"; he discussed "how to get over it." His first suggestion for curing the disease was, "Stop looking for a knock in your human motor." In all probability if Dr. Schindler were discussing the same subject before a medical convention, his choice of words would be strikingly different.

Preventing Blunders

Information about your audience not only helps you decide what to say, it also warns you of what not to say. Information about race, religion, and politics is especially valuable in saving you from blundering.

A single intemperate word or phrase can wreck the effectiveness of an otherwise excellent presentation. During the Senate Watergate Hearings, attorney John J. Wilson, representing two of the most important witnesses, gave aggressive, knowledgeable, and effective assistance to his clients during several days of testimony. This highly favorable public impression was severely damaged during a recess when he expressed displeasure to newsmen regarding Senator Daniel K. Inouye, referring to him as "that little Jap." Public protest was prompt—thousands of telegrams, phone calls, letters, and editorials demanded an apology. Inouye's service on the committee was praised, and the fact was stressed that this senator was an authentic American war hero who had lost an arm in his country's service. Wilson then made matters worse by saying, "I would not object to being called 'a little American.' " Replied one letter-to-the-editor, "I will call him a little American—a *very* little American." Wilson's *faux pas* should remind you that derogatory epithets are always dangerous and sometimes disasterous. You should avoid such terms as wop, kike, nigger, whitey, and the like.

Religion is another touchy area. There are occasions when a friendly, good-natured exchange of humor about Catholics, Jews, and Protestants is appreciated by all the hearers—as President John F. Kennedy demonstrated. But few of us have the "JFK touch." In groups of mixed religions it is usually wise to avoid reference to any specific denomination or to any controversial religious belief; religion should be brought into the talk only when absolutely necessary for the development of the subject, and references should be planned so as to touch upon beliefs common to all the denominations in the audience. If you are preparing to talk before a group of one faith, it is obviously wise to become familiar with its special customs and beliefs. For audiences with strong religious convictions, many appropriate speech materials are available: Biblical allusions and

During college years, your most typical audiences are class meetings. But after graduation (or sooner), they become a-typical (unless you become a teacher).

stories, quotations from church publications and from outstanding religious leaders, religious poems and hymns.

Politics is another topic where audience analysis is of special importance. If you are actively involved in campus or community politics, you may be serving on a committee of your chosen party, and you may attend some of the rallies. Obviously anything you might say at such meetings would be inappropriate and probably counterproductive if spoken at a rally of an opposition party. Our political mores are such that we expect partisan statements and overstatements when a one-party group gets together. This tolerant attitude was delightfully epitomized by President John F. Kennedy at one of his TV press conferences when a reporter mentioned that the Republican National Committee had recently adopted a resolution condemning current Democratic policies, and the newsman inquired, "Do you have any comment?" Kennedy suddenly grinned and said, "I'm sure the vote was—uh—unanimous." Ordinarily, however, you talk to groups (such as your speech class) where political affiliations are mixed. Here our mores are such that vigorous partisan statements or overstatements are likely to be perceived as insults by

Young Democrats at a national political convention—most of them are students or recent graduates. Only yesterday their audience behaviors were like those in the preceding picture.

the opposing party, bad judgment by independents, embarrassment by your own party.

Age and educational level of an audience can also mislead a speaker into blunders—nobody likes to be underestimated. You should avoid talking down to any audience (children included); it is usually better to say, "as we all know," than, "let me now explain this to you."

Adjusting Vocal and Visual Delivery

Queen Victoria is said to have complained that she disliked conferences with Gladstone because "he always addresses me as though I were a public meeting." The great statesman should have analyzed his audience.

The size of an audience should suggest a variety of possible adaptations of your visual and vocal delivery. If it is a small group you might well plan a direct conversational approach, informal but lively. You might increase your effectiveness by bringing the audience into the speech through some form of group discussion. You certainly would plan to avoid a Gladstonian style.

Many factors determined through audience analysis can help you in planning and practicing bodily action. Thus for small intimate groups the lift of an eyebrow can be an effective gesture; for a somewhat larger audience a shrug of the shoulders might be a better choice. For a large crowd in an auditorium, however, the foregoing gestures might not be visible beyond the first few rows of seats—therefore a sweep of the hands and arms might be required if you want to communicate by gesture.

Likewise, aspects of your vocal delivery such as loudness and rate should be adjusted to such audience data as size of group, type of meeting place, general mood or atmosphere of the occasion, presence or absence of some type of public address equipment.

THE UNEXPECTED

Sometimes, of course, it is impossible to get advance information about an audience; or the information you do get turns out to be wrong. For example, a speaker traveled to a nearby town to discuss "Television and Your Child" before a parent-teacher association. Much of his material was for parents only, but when he arrived at the meeting he found that over one third of his auditors were between the ages of two and nine! It was not until later that the speaker discovered that there was an important bowling tournament that night, that all the fathers had gone to the tournament, and that the mothers had had to bring their children to the PTA meeting or else stay home. No one could have foreseen the situation. Confronted with the unexpected, the speaker could only make some last minute changes and revise his speech as he went along.

Audience analysis is a ticklish business; audience data are usually incomplete and often misleading. Should we, therefore, discard audience analysis entirely? Not at all.

There are several reasons for this statement. In the first place, the alternative is weak. If you do not plan, you depend on chance. This means that if your speech happens to suit your audience, it is only by accident. Because so many variables are involved, the probability of success by accident is small. As baseball managers say, it is better to "play the percentages." In the second place, when you have analyzed your audience and make a mistake, you have a better chance of spotting the error early in the speech and salvaging something by impromptu alterations. If you have not analyzed your audience and make a mistake, you can scarcely have any insight into the situation at all, and the mistake is likely to become a complete disaster. In the third place, you cannot learn from your accidental mistakes since you do not even know what goes wrong or why; every time, however, that you try to analyze an audience and misjudge, you learn a lesson and eliminate future mistakes. Finally, if you proceed by the method of chance you never get any better. The planner improves with practice. Even experienced speakers will occasionally misjudge an audience, but such misevaluations are rare.

In general, then, analyze every audience in advance and plan your speech accordingly. You will make mistakes, yes, but they will be beneficial mistakes. Such miscalculations in the future will not throw you off balance because you will have developed the healthy attitude of expecting the unexpected.

SUMMARY

Audience response is always the test of speaking effectiveness. You can increase your chances of securing favorable audience response by analyzing each audience in advance. There are three main problems: what to look for, how to gather it, and how to use it.

Advance information about an audience is gathered from observation and inquiry.

The principal types of needed data include the nature of the occasion, common traits and interests, attitudes toward your topic, and attitudes toward you.

In general every detail of speech preparation should be adapted to the audience. More specifically, adaptation means finding common ground, slanting the subject, selecting the supports, modifying the language, preventing blunders, and adjusting vocal and visual delivery.

Despite advance analysis and planning, the audience may not turn out as expected. Therefore it is wise to expect the unexpected, and to make adjustments when needed just before or during the delivery of a talk.

Adapting to your audience does not mean surrendering to it. In general, audience adaptation means the establishment of a feeling of speaker-audience identification. This means, of course, that the speaker should identify himself with his listeners. More important, however, are the audience attitudes. The listeners should have a sense of identification with the speaker: The people who comprise the audience should have a feeling that the speaker and his ideas are of the people, by the people, and for the people. You must become not a speaker, but a spokesman. You cannot achieve this goal by accident. That is why you must learn how to analyze your audience, and to adapt to it.

TOPICAL PREVIEW

Gaining Audience Attention

ATTENTION!

When the sergeant bellows, "Ten-hut!" the private snaps to attention, freezes in position, and listens for the next command. When the radio or television announcer says, "Your attention please; we interrupt this program to bring you a special news bulletin," you sit up in your chair, lean forward a bit, forget other matters for the moment, readying yourself to hear the bulletin. When the quarterback barks a signal in a football game, each player becomes a picture of attention. His posture proclaims his concentration on the ball and the opposing players. He neither hears the great roar from the crowd nor sees the hundreds of objects and movements actually within his vision. These examples indicate that attention involves observable postural adjustments and inner adjustments, by which a person heightens his response to a given stimulus while reducing his response to competing stimuli.

Elwood Kretsinger invented an electronic device, popularly dubbed the wiggle meter, by which the physical movements of an audience can be measured and recorded. Experiments with the wiggle meter have shown that when an audience is listening to non-humorous speech materials the amount of movement in the audience varies inversely with the amount of attention or interest. When the average person listens to interesting materials, he sits quietly. When bored, he writhes, looks around the room, confers with his neighbors, yawns, stretches, or fidgets.

Not only can we measure the physical manifestations of attention, but we also know something about attention as a mental phenomenon. Are you aware at this instant of the number at the bottom of this page? Probably not. Nevertheless, it has been in your field of vision as long as the page has. Furthermore, you cannot, even if you try, keep your attention centered on that number for very long. You attend to the number a while; then your attention shifts to something else; then you return to the number again until your attention again wanders. As the physics majors put it: Attention is AC rather than DC; that is, attention fluctuates.

Getting attention is a means to an end in any type of communication. The successful speaker must not only catch attention at the beginning of his speech, but he must also attempt to maintain it throughout his talk. If your purpose is to entertain, the attention step is both a means and an end. But in speeches to inform, stimulate, or convince, attention is a necessary preparatory step to understanding, to a reinforcement of attitudes, or to a change of attitudes.

WHAT MAKES A SPEECH DULL?

A teacher of speech communication must, by reason of his profession, listen to an extraordinary number of speeches. One teacher kept tabs and discovered that he had heard approximately 2,500 speeches one particular year—most of them by beginners, of course. Only a few speeches were genuinely interesting; most were so-so; many were so abysmally boring that only grim determination prevented the teacher from falling asleep. You have heard many boring speeches, too. What makes speeches dull?

When listening to a national political convention, our attention begins to lag when the speaker launches into his "I give you a man who . . ." and inevitably concludes with ". . . the next President of the United States. . . ." But politicians have no monopoly on the use of these hackneyed ideas and phrases:

"It is a pleasure and a privilege . . ."
"I am reminded of a story."
"There is just one thought I want to leave with you today."
"So let's get down to brass tacks."
". . . and stay on the beam . . ."
"Let's show our metal."
"And never say die."

This vigorous speaker wants to get audience response. To see what response he got, turn to the next page.

"This is no panacea."
"But just plain common sense . . ."
"So let's put our shoulders to the wheel."
". . . and give it all we've got."

Each of us is bound to use some trite materials like the foregoing. Used in a new context, however, a platitude can be interesting; used only occasionally, trite words or ideas may do little harm, but used throughout a speech, triteness will bore an audience into complete inattention.

Too frequent use of abstract words is also likely to produce a dull speech. The speech employing too many abstract words usually deals only with theory. Its points and subpoints are likely to be supported almost entirely by explanations, lacking instances, anecdotes, and descriptions. Examples of speech so abstract as to be not merely dull but almost meaningless are sometimes found in high places. An official of the National Production Authority in a talk on material allocations said:

> We are peaking our program philosophically but it is naive to assume the allotment program is an equity program unless the allotments are so abysmally low that they permit the agency to relax and allow market determination as a percentage of base period sidetracking military return with adjustments. This is based on use levels proportionately and is in the market test sense. We now have a quantitative framework with marginal qualitative allocations to formalize the procedure for further refining and implementing of our objectives.[1]

[1] *Los Angeles Times*, April 13, 1951.

Skillful delivery does not offset dull ideas and trite language.

Then there is the pedantic speech, an exercise in minutiae. College professors are sometimes guilty of this when they maintain that if they have something to say, it is up to the student, however bored he may be, to get it. Legal language, which attempts to account for every loophole, is frequently boring and pedantic. Read this portion of a legal decision, being sure to pay careful attention:

> We hold that paragragh number 3, in its language and in its coordinate contextual position and relationship, was of such ambiguity or doubtfulness, on what the parties had intended it to connote, and to provide safeguard for between them, as not to be required facially to be viewed as having had a meaningless significance, such as appellants contended, and that a court was accordingly entitled to seek light and explanation from the extrinsic manifestations of intentions ... etc. (etc. for 129 more words until the end of the first sentence).[2]

Some speeches are dull because the speaker's ideas seem to stand still; they do not march. Other speeches are dull because the personality of the speaker is colorless. Still others kill audience interest because of the speaker's monotonous voice. Likewise, dullness can result from monotony of bodily action; the speaker who paces steadily back and forth on the platform will hypnotize his listeners into a coma just as readily as the speaker who stands like a post. Finally, speeches may be dull because they are too long. Mark Twain is credited with a story about an overlong sermon. At the end of twenty minutes he was so favorably impressed he decided to put in five dollars when the offering was taken. Twenty minutes later, he de-

[2] *The New Yorker* (December 15, 1956), p. 164.

cided that two dollars would suffice. After another twenty minutes, the proposed contribution shrank to one dollar. When eventually the sermon ended, Mark Twain awoke from a doze and placed a dime on the plate.

WHAT MAKES A SPEECH INTERESTING?

Adaptation of Material to the Audience

An artist, a farmer, and a realtor stood looking at a hillside. What did they see?

"See those lights and shadows!" exclaimed the artist.

"Hm. Looks like the topsoil's washed away," murmured the farmer.

"That'll subdivide into fifty lots," said the realtor. "Wonder what's the owner's price?"

All three were looking at the same hill but each paid attention to a different aspect, each in terms of his personal interests.

Naturally this same phenomenon is true of an audience. That presentation of idea or choice of words will be most interesting which most nearly corresponds with audience interests. Thus presentation of ideas and language should be modified in light of the audience analysis in order to get and hold attention.

Factors of Attention

Experimental research and practical speaking experience show that there are several factors of attention that influence the intensity of a listener's interest. These include:

1. Significance
2. Humor
3. Uniqueness or familiarity
4. Problems
5. Concreteness
6. Antagonism
7. Variation

1. SIGNIFICANCE   In general, a detail is considered significant by your listener when it affects *him*. His attention to your talk may be lagging—mention his name, or any of his special interests, and his attention will snap back to your speech immediately. But what are his interests? For any audience, most of those interests will be variations on a few basic themes. The basic needs and wants of human beings have been classified by many scholars in several fields of study. A

list for the public speaker was provided by A. E. Phillips in his *Effective Speaking* (Newton, 1938), a pioneering work, first published in 1908, which has had great influence on modern speech education. Phillips listed seven impelling motives of human behavior: self-preservation, property, power, reputation, affections, sentiments, and tastes. How can you apply this list to the preparation of an actual talk?

Consider the first basic interest: self-preservation. Whatever affects the health or safety of your listener is likely to capture his attention. Ralph Nader has demonstrated this principle by his numerous effective talks on the daily dangers confronting consumers. The chemistry major who talked on the dangers of certain widely advertised drug compounds made the dangers real, and he got attention, as did the student who advocated regular checkups on vital automobile parts. A premedical student got attention by discussing his classmates' chances of becoming victims in a future polio epidemic. A speech on the Pure Food and Drug Act, on household accidents, or on the local water supply can be made to appeal to the instinct of self-preservation.

Any of the other impelling motives can be similarly treated. Your listener will pay attention if you can show him how to make money, get elected, be applauded, make friends, feel patriotic, or indulge a favorite hobby.

2. HUMOR   The most widely used method of getting audience attention is humor. Psychologists have offered many theories as to what makes things funny. Most of the theories assume that humor is based on *incongruity* coupled with *a sense of well-being.* A sense of humor, therefore, is sometimes defined approximately as a sense of proportion.

Incongruity means that some element of a situation is inharmonious, out of step, unexpected. Thus, in planning how to use a given bit of humor ask yourself, "What is incongruous here?" Then plan how to present the material to emphasize the incongruity, and possibly to exploit the unexpected.

For telling humorous anecdotes, special study should be given to the question of timing. The proper placement and duration of a pause can make or break the success of most oral humor. The incongruity and unexpectedness are usually heightened by a pause just before the punch line. Study the timing of Bill Cosby in his monologues—pauses are not too long, not too short, not too soon, not too late. Also, when you get a laugh from your audience, wait until the laughter subsides somewhat before going on with your talk.

Facial expression and attention to inflection of key words are two other delivery techniques of special importance. Some famous hu-

When you tell an anecdote, live it! This student counselor shows how it's done as he responds to an interviewer from the campus newspaper.

morists use a deadpan or slightly surprised expression when the audience laughs; others prefer laughing with the audience. Some of Johnny Carson's humor is wordless—his reactions to a guest's remarks may be portrayed entirely by facial expressions as he looks at the guest and then at the audience. Just the right inflection of a key word or phrase sometimes makes the joke. It has been said that Jack Benny received more genuine laughs from a single "Well?" than other humorists from a whole program.

A speaker must be extremely wary of using humor based on race, religion, or sex; a joke, even if sidesplitting, does not get favorable attention if it is offensive. Neither should he use humor that is unrelated to the speech subject, because the object of speech humor is not simply to get the listeners' attention, but to get their favorable attention, and to get it focused on an idea. Just telling a funny story is not enough; the audience's appreciation of humor is doubled when they recognize its pertinence to the point being discussed.

Some writers warn against using old jokes, but even old jokes have their value. If the humor is relevant and well told, familiarity apparently does not diminish the listeners' enjoyment. As a matter of fact, it is hard to conceive of a truly new joke. Adlai Stevenson made good use of this old joke during a campaign talk in Albuquerque:

> Somebody has been asking me how I was feeling and it reminded me of a story of a man who was shot in the back by Indians in an attack on a wagon train out in this country in the early days. Some time later some troopers came along and found the poor man unconscious with three arrows between his shoulder blades. They revived him with whisky, and when he could whisper they asked if it hurt awfully, and he said, "It sure does, especially when I laugh." [3]

The effectiveness of the story lies both in the way Stevenson told it and in the fact that it makes a point. When you have a good anecdote, do not drag it in by the heels. Plan the transition into it carefully. Stevenson should have avoided the hackneyed "I am reminded of the story of a . . ." Word the transitions with originality. If you begin with an anecdote, do not introduce it with either praise or apology. In other words, *do not* start off like this, "Mr. Chairman, Ladies and Gentlemen: The other day I ran across what I thought was a pretty good story; at any rate, I hope you will think so. . . ." Instead, start by going right into the story: "A traveler in the Ozarks noticed a picturesque old native sitting on the porch of a dilapidated cabin. The traveler stopped and to get a conversation going, inquired, "Have you lived here all your life?" Pausing briefly in his whittling, the oldtimer replied, "Not yit."

Once the anecdote is under way, *live it:* show how the characters felt; tell it with animation. Use dialog and act it out when appropriate, but avoid using dialect with which you are not familiar. Decide in advance whether or not the anecdote should be related briefly, building up quickly and getting the point across before the audience has time to do more than get the general effect; or whether to build up slowly, giving them a chance to savor all the details. Plan it and tell it so as to build up to the climax. Do not backtrack; never use an unnecessary detail or elaborate any detail unless elaboration is necessary. If names, places, or times are part of the anecdote, make them specific and believable. For example, avoid calling all child characters "Little Johnny"; use some specific name such as "George" or "Ernest" or "Conrad." Plan your story so as to avoid anticlimax; a good suggestion is to plan the ending first and then build up to it. If the anecdote is properly told, its point should be clear to the audience. If you do state the point of the anecdote, state it only for emphasis.

Some students report, often with justification, that they cannot tell a joke without killing it. However, there are probably types of humor that they can present effectively, and they should seek them. In fact, all speakers are wise to experiment with a variety of kinds and styles of humor. In addition to anecdotes, there are puns, paradox, satire, understatement, overstatement, limericks, irony, and exaggeration.

[3] *New York Times*, September 12, 1952.

At a banquet honoring Senator George Smathers of Florida, the puckish humor of John F. Kennedy took the form of a series of quotations from the guest of honor—perhaps invented, certainly a bit exaggerated:

> Senator Smathers has been one of my most valuable counselors at crucial moments. In 1952 when I was thinking of running for the United States Senate, I went to Senator Smathers and said, "George, what do you think?" He said, "Don't do it, can't win, bad year." [That was the year Mr. Kennedy won his Senate seat.]
> In 1956, I didn't know whether I should run for vice president or not so I said, "George, what do you think?" And Senator Smathers replied, "It's your chance!" So I ran and lost.
> In 1960 I was wondering whether I ought to run in the West Virginia primary, but the Senator said, "Don't do it. That state you can't possibly carry." [He did.]
> And actually, the only time I really got nervous about the whole matter of Los Angeles was just before the balloting and George came up and said, "I think it looks pretty good for you."

Limericks or other humorous verse can sometimes be woven in effectively, especially if wording or meter provide unexpected effects. Satire, irony, and ridicule must be used with discretion. It is almost always safe to make fun of yourself. For example, "The chairman said that my colleague and I were noted for our wit. The implication is unfortunately just. There are two of us; and two half-wits add up to one wit." Other persons can be teased provided the teasing is done with obvious good nature. Will Rogers backed Ogden Mills for Congress because he owned a silk hat and because "he is the only candidate for Congress who can go into a Fifth Avenue home without delivering something." Finally, you can make fun of other persons or things when you are sure the audience is opposed to those persons or things. For example, see how Governor Dewey treated the Democrats' income tax forms:

> But even the experts can't advise how to do business under the New Deal, because they can't understand the laws themselves. I have here a dozen examples. Just listen to this little gem for Section 23 (P) of the present tax laws about contributions to employees' pension plans. It says "they shall not be deductible under Subsection (A) but shall be deductible, if deductible under Subsection (A) without regard to this subsection, but only to the following extent...." From here on it gets technical! [4]

A final suggestion: Test your proposed humor aloud; some humor reads well but tells poorly, or vice versa. For speech purposes, humor should usually provide opportunities for verbal play, vocal play, meaningful pauses, facial expressions, pantomime, or other oral devices.

[4] New York Times, October 4, 1944.

3. UNIQUENESS OR FAMILIARITY People are attracted by the unique. They are interested by things unusually big or small, heavy or light, expensive or cheap. A speaker discussing the advantages of microfilming business papers got attention when he said, "A stack of papers twice as high as this building when microfilmed can be stored in a single drawer of an ordinary filing cabinet." A striking statement gets attention—"Yesterday I held a million dollars of United States currency in my hands!" Travel talks about strange sights or strange customs get and hold attention. Unusual personal experiences arouse interest. If you have faced an aroused grizzly bear, you may be sure the experience will serve you well in a speech. Odd facts of all sorts interest people.

But don't go overboard. Anything too unusual defeats its purpose. A physical education instructor, giving a talk before a high school, decided to get attention by casually undressing himself during the first part of the talk. Once it was revealed that he had a gym suit under his regular clothes, he proceeded to do some calisthenics. The shock of his "strip tease" had been so great, however, that it blotted out everything else in the speech.

Anything completely removed from the listeners' previous experience is meaningless. For example, suppose you were a chess enthusiast and wanted to explain an unusual move to people who did not play chess. If you said, "So I moved the queen's bishop to king's rook three as a gambit!" it would be as though you had spoken to them in a strange language. The unusual, therefore, has meaning only if the speaker relates it to the familiar.

In the right context, the familiar belief or sentiment can capture attention. If you eloquently utter a truth deeply felt by your audience, they will pay attention.

Here we have a speaker's dilemma: if his materials are too unusual they become bizarre, meaningless, or distracting; if too familiar, they become trite. Triteness is an elusive quality. We have heard the parables of Jesus dozens of times, yet we do not consider them trite. One kind of material might seem trite in a sociology lecture; the same material in a sermon might seem almost startling. A patriotic speech given during peacetime might seem a series of tiresome platitudes; the same speech given during a war crisis might bring the audience to its feet cheering. Triteness, then, is a matter of judgment and context. To define it would require qualifications, such as: Triteness is saying the same old thing, in the same old way, by the wrong speaker, at the wrong time, before the wrong audience. The solution for the dilemma is to find a good combination of the unusual and the familiar. Two practical formulas are to give an old idea a novel twist and to present a new idea in familiar terms.

4. PROBLEMS

A powerful way to capture attention is by posing a problem for the audience to solve with you. If the following story catches and holds your attention, you will have an illustration of how suspense and curiosity operate.

> A loud-talking and inquisitive American businessman was riding a train when an Englishman with only one leg entered the car using a crutch.
>
> "I see you were in the war," remarked the businessman after a brief pause.
>
> "No, I was not in the service."
>
> "These traffic accidents get worse every year."
>
> "No, sir, I was never in a wreck of any kind."
>
> "Surgical operation, maybe?"
>
> "No."
>
> So the American finally asked point-blank how he had lost the leg.
>
> "I will tell you only on one condition," replied the Englishman, "that you will promise not to ask another question."
>
> "I promise."
>
> The Englishman nodded pleasantly.
>
> "It was *bit* off," he said.

You can often organize your whole speech in terms of a problem solution. If you can begin by presenting the problem vividly, in terms of your listeners' experience, and in such a way that it appears difficult to solve, you will have attention. Your audience will be waiting to see if you can solve it or exactly how you will solve it. If you handle your materials skillfully, the audience will try to beat you to the solution. The audience competes with you just as the reader of a detective story competes with the author.

A speaker gave a series of talks on techniques for dealing with people before groups of factory foremen and supervisors. The following sequence worked best:

1. Relate in detail an actual case.
2. Ask, "If you had been that supervisor, what would you have done?"
3. Analyze the elements of the problem.
4. Reject several possible but inferior solutions.
5. Present the recommended solution.

For example, the speaker would begin by relating the case of Joe who had been with his company for over a year and had been considered a good worker. Occasionally, however, Joe was surly for no apparent reason. One morning he arrived late, walked into his department, threw his coat on the floor, and went to his machine to start working. The supervisor came over and said, "Joe, you're sup-

Buckminster Fuller addresses a student audience and commands concentrated attention. Compare this sequence with that on pages 231–32.

posed to hang your coat on the hooks. You know that." Then in front of all the other workmen, Joe said loudly, "If you want it hung up, hang it up yourself." The speaker would ask, "If you were that supervisor, what would you do?" The audience might suggest various answers, such as:

Hang up the coat yourself.
Command Joe to hang it up.
Ask another worker to hang it up.
Tell Joe he is fired.
Ask Joe to come to your office for a talk.
Call for the superintendent.
Pretend the whole incident is a joke.

By the time several possible solutions were written on a chalkboard, the case would be dramatized into a puzzle, and the attention of the audience would be aroused by the desire to find out what the best solution should be. (Incidentally, what do you think is the best solution?)

5. CONCRETENESS   Ideas as well as language can be either concrete or abstract or a mixture. In fact, you can express a concrete idea in abstract words, or vice versa. Just now we are primarily concerned with concrete ideas. For instance, if you were discussing excessive administrative overhead costs, you might draw upon a bit of German folklore:

> At a state banquet given by Frederick the Great to his courtiers and noblemen, the monarch asked those present to explain why his revenues continued to diminish despite increased taxes. An old General dryly remarked, "I will show Your Majesty what happens to the money." Procuring a piece of ice he lifted it high for inspection; then he passed it to his neighbor and requested that it be passed from hand to hand to the King. By the time it reached Frederick it was about the size of a pea.

The term "excessive administrative overhead" is an abstraction; you cannot visualize an abstraction, cannot see it, hear it, touch it, or smell it. However, you can visualize passing a piece of ice from hand to hand. By analogy you can associate an abstract idea with a more attention-getting concrete idea.

Concrete ideas often include the visualization of movement, and movement gets attention. Newspaper offices often have big plate glass windows through which one can see the giant printing presses. When the presses are still, nobody does more than glance at them absentmindedly. But when the presses are operating, it is difficult to pass the place without stopping for a look. The same irresistible urge collects crowds of sidewalk superintendents to watch the excavating for a new high-rise building. Our attention is attracted by movement or activity. The speaker should try to put some of his ideas in the form of illustrations in which movement can be visualized. When presented in such form, the idea itself seems to move.

6. ANTAGONISM A dogfight draws a crowd. A conflict gets attention. A speaker can also introduce the element of conflict into his talk.

Describe a conflict—a football game, a prize fight, a race, a military battle. Mental conflicts may be equally interesting—the conflict between good and evil, perhaps, as in the story of Dr. Jekyll and Mr. Hyde. Attack policies or ideas. The most attention-getting moments of a campaign speech are likely to be when the speaker is lambasting the opposition. Deliberately antagonize an audience. A speaker was asked, for example, to discuss Americanism before a meeting of the American Legion. His speech could have been banal, but he began by stating that he proposed to give the arguments in favor of communism. He did so amid increasing tension. When he suddenly changed his mood and manner and said, "Now we're going to answer those arguments," the Legion cheered madly and followed the rest of the speech with blow-by-blow relish. But do not congratulate yourself on holding audience attention by antagonizing everyone from beginning to end of your speech. Thus, a young faculty member speaking to a convocation on Parents' Day ticked off a list of students' problems, tracing each fault back to home upbringing, and ending with these words, "So let's face it—*you blew it!*" Nor should you stoop to attracting audience attention by the cheap device of dropping in an occasional obscenity. Your communication goal is not to get attention at any cost but to get *favorable* attention directed not to you but to your message.

7. VARIATION A speech should be planned to provide variety in its details, both of content and delivery. The serious should alternate with the humorous; the humor should be of different types; the unusual and the familiar should be combined; and the rate of delivery, the pitch, and the volume should vary. As was pointed out early in this chapter, human attention constantly fluctuates. During a talk you must catch the listeners' attention again and again. Variety does that for you.

Variety of detail does not mean that the overall effect must become disorganized. Hold a dime in your palm and try to concentrate your attention on it. You can pay attention to the whole dime only briefly —your attention fluctuates. You find yourself attending to details: the date, the motto, portions of the presidential face. Your attention has fluctuated, but all within the pattern of a dime. The same thing happens during a speech. Audience attention also fluctuates, but if the speaker is skillful he provides diversity within unity; he controls the fluctuations, leading his audience from item to item, holding them from start to finish.

ATTENTION-GETTING IN THE SPEECH TO ENTERTAIN

When your purpose is to entertain, favorable attention becomes the end itself and not just a means. Interest is not only the first requirement but almost the only one.

The most common speech given primarily to entertain is the after-dinner speech. However, this type of talk can be appropriate at any meeting, especially at social gatherings where good fellowship and recreation prevail. Many clubs have the custom of holding occasional meetings for entertainment only, or of devoting part of every meeting to fun alone. But banquets provide the most common occasion for talks to entertain.

Humor is the trademark of most entertaining talks, but there are many exceptions. Tales of adventure, travel, or mystery can be highly entertaining without relying on humor. In a predominantly humorous speech, humor is often enhanced by having an underlying theme of serious thought or sentiment. The great comedian Charlie Chaplin was a master of emotional rebound—making us laugh all the harder by alternating the humorous and the sentimental. Talks to entertain, however, should make use of all the factors of attention, not of humor alone.

Delivery

Variety is the keynote for entertaining talks. Entertaining talks usually provide opportunity for voice and language variety by way of mimicry, exaggeration, dialog, dialect, and special sound effects.

A variety of bodily actions can be used: unusual facial expressions, impressions, impersonations, pantomimes, incongruous postures or gestures. Use of visual aids is sometimes helpful.

The total effect of the speaker's personality should be friendly, direct, lively, and good natured. The prevailing tone should be optimistic. Variety of delivery, however, does not mean that the speaker should be constantly in motion. A speaker can be downright dramatic by standing motionless—if his motionlessness contrasts with previous action or corresponds with the thought being expressed. Likewise, attention may be gained by silence or by a quiet voice. You can build down to a climax as well as build up to one.

You do not have to be funny or lively to be entertaining; you can be serious and deeply moving, yet hold the listeners spellbound.

Organization

Sometimes all that is required is to string together a series of stories on a thread of free association. Monologues by popular TV comedians, such as Bob Hope or Dick Cavett, provide ready examples.

1. SIMPLE THEME WITH ILLUSTRATIONS A step beyond the string-of-beads plan for a speech is the simple theme with illustrations. However, the theme with illustrations is still extremely loose in organization, and the logic need not be tight. The speaker chooses a central idea (as recommended in Chapter 6) and lists a few main points, but his emphasis is on finding a way to weave in attention-getting supporting materials. The organization usually consists of one or more loosely constructed speech units. In humorous talks logic may even be reversed—a point may be "proved" by obviously false logic.

Consider an example of a simple theme with illustrations. One student decided to give a classroom talk about the humorous side of his army experiences. He might simply have chosen five minutes' worth of his funniest experiences and strung them out like beads. Instead, he chose a simple theme: Getting into the army and getting into college are very much the same. He picked three main points:

1. They have similar entrance requirements.
2. Both develop the skill of standing in line.
3. Both involve about a ton of paper work.

He developed the first main point by anecdotes about the physical examinations and a comparison of a school board with a draft board. This framework provided an ample opportunity for using many attention-getting devices.

2. REGULAR OUTLINE WITH STRESS ON ATTENTION The third type of organization for speeches to entertain may be called the regular speech outline with special emphasis on the factors of attention. By regular we mean the process covered in Chapter 6. Here is an outline for a talk to entertain entitled "How to Worry Successfully."

INTRODUCTION
 I. Most of the things we worry about are absurd, and we know it.
   Anecdote: The horse in the bathtub

II. Worrying does no good, and we know it.
   Explanation: How to worry about the nuclear bomb
      Transition: Nevertheless, we go right on worrying. And since we insist on doing it . . .

Central Idea: My thesis today is: Let's make a good job of it. Let's have the biggest and best collection of worries in town!
Transition: I can help you achieve all this. I shall present a specific and practical program. And the first step in this program is . . .
   I. Try to live in the future.
      A. Worry is always about the future.
         1. *Explanation:* The past doesn't exist; the present is a fleeting moment; only the future can actually be worried about.
         2. *Quotation:* Mark Twain, "I'm an old man and have known many troubles—most of which never happened."
      B. Worry always takes place in the imagination.
         1. *Explanation:* It's all mental and about the future.
         2. *Anecdote:* The elderly couple who made and lost a fortune by imaginary speculation on the stock market.
   II. Enjoy your worrying.
      A. *Explanation:* Main cause—people worry because they want to.
      B. *Instance:* Girl who worries after lovers' quarrel—more fun when he comes back.
      C. *Instance:* Mother who worries to get attention and control the family: "You know how I worry."
      D. *Instance:* Lady who brags, "I'm the best little worrier you ever saw."
   III. Avoid making decisions.
      A. *Description:* Man afraid to decide for fear decision will be wrong.
      B. *Anecdote:* Mule who starved to death between two haystacks.
         Transition: By this time you should clearly understand how to worry successfully.

Summary: You must try to live in the future—not just plan for it but live in it. You must learn to enjoy your worries—revel in them, boast about them, feel sorry for yourself. You must avoid making decisions—and if you do make one, go back and reconsider. Follow this program and you, too, can have bigger and better worries. But if you fail to follow it, you'll scarcely be able to worry at all.

In analyzing the outline you will notice that all seven of the factors of attention described in this chapter have been employed.

a. Significance. The subject of worry is vital to almost all adult audiences even though they may not admit it. They came to enjoy the talk but have a sneaking hunch that maybe it will actually help them.

b. Humor. The speech is liberally sprinkled with humor of several types. There is incongruity all the way through.

c. Uniqueness and familiarity. This is the principal attention-getter. The entire speech illustrates the use of an old idea with a novel twist.

d. Problems. Curiosity is aroused when the title is first announced. After the central idea is stated suspense is maintained by not revealing in advance all the steps in the program—the listener is encouraged to wonder what the next point will be. As the talk progresses, the audience discovers the reverse logic being used; most of them begin the game of translating it into positive terms.

e. Concreteness. There is little theorizing. All the explanations are kept brief and are illustrated by anecdote or instance. Notice, for example, the definition of worry in connection with the anecdote of the mule between the haystacks.

f. Antagonism. Worry is defined as an unresolved inner conflict, and the element of struggle is developed in several supports, especially the anecdote about the old couple buying imaginary stocks and bonds.

g. Variation. All the factors of attention are used, and all the forms of support, except statistics.

ATTENTION-GETTING IN OTHER SPEECHES

Getting attention is a means to an end in speeches to inform, stimulate, or convince. The better you control the audience's attention, the better your chances of getting information across, reinforcing existing beliefs, or building new beliefs. According to some psychologists, beliefs and attitudes are shaped by whatever dominates our attention most often and most fully.

In speaking to inform, stimulate, or convince, make your supports do double duty. When you choose an anecdote, instance, or quotation, give it a double test. (1) Does it clarify, reinforce, or prove your point? (2) Does it contain one or more of the factors for catching attention? Remember especially the principle of diversity within unity. Plan the framework of your ideas and then fill out the details with a variety of forms of support and delivery.

Thus in speeches to inform, stimulate, or convince, attention plays a supporting role. However, the role is vital—you cannot inform, stimulate, or convince your audience if they are not paying attention. Capturing and holding interest is a prerequisite to any further audience response.

SUMMARY

In speeches to inform, stimulate, and convince, catching and holding audience attention is the first requirement; in speeches to entertain it is almost the only requirement because dullness defeats everything else a speaker attempts to do.

Speeches are dull when language and ideas are trite, abstract, or pedantic; when the sequence of ideas doesn't march; when the speaker's personality is colorless; when voice and bodily movement are monotonous; or when speeches are too long. Speeches are interesting when they are adapted to the audience, and when they apply the factors of attention, such as significance, humor, uniqueness or familiarity, problems, concreteness, antagonism, and variation.

Speeches to entertain should include a maximum variety of delivery and appropriate speech organization, as well as constant use of the attention-controlling factors. The organization of entertaining speeches may be simply a string-of-beads plan, or a simple theme with illustrations, or a regular outline with stress on the attention values.

TOPICAL PREVIEW

Gaining Audience Understanding

PERSON-TO-PERSON

Whether your audience is one person or many, the basics of informative speaking are the same. During your early years, you may have found that one particular relative or older friend was especially good at answering your questions about the how's and why's of things. What made that person especially helpful? Vice versa, one of your friends may say, "You're an economics major. Will you explain to me what a 'Dow Jones average' really means?" What should you do (and avoid) in order to help your friend to understand Dow Jones? You can experiment with the suggestions in this chapter by analyzing these person-to-person, teaching-learning experiences. Then you turn from one-to-one situations and apply the same principles in one-to-many communications.

OCCASIONS FOR INFORMATIVE SPEAKING

Here is a representative list of speaking situations where the purpose is predominantly to inform:

Class lectures
Student recitations or class reports
Adult education lectures
Announcements
Instructions or directions
Book or play reviews
Committee reports
Chalk talks
Industrial training lectures
Scientific reports
Demonstration talks

You have been on the receiving end of many such talks, especially class lectures. You have doubtless complained about some of them. It is a sad truth that college lectures are often notable only as models of what every speaker should avoid. Listed here are some common complaints about informative speeches.

COMMON COMPLAINTS ABOUT INFORMATIVE SPEECHES

It was dry. "That man can dive deeper and come up drier than anyone I've ever heard."

It was over the listeners' heads. "It was too deep for me. Half the time I didn't even know what he was talking about."

It had too many facts. "After ten minutes I surrendered. How does he expect us to remember all those facts?"

It was too technical. "You should have heard the two-dollar words. What did he think we were? Experts?"

Gregor Piatigorsky, renowned cellist, here gives person-to-person instruction. He uses multiple techniques, such as tell, show, listen, criticize, and demonstrate.

It was too theoretical. "He's the *vaguest* guy. He never said anything you could get hold of."

He talked too fast. "What a machine gun! I was trying to take notes. Every time I wrote down a point, I missed the next one."

He read too much. "Honest, it got so all I could do was count the pages."

He was too aloof, or *colorless,* or *passive.* "First I wondered if he was mad about something. Pretty soon I wondered if he was human. Finally I wondered if he was alive."

THE PLAN OF THE INFORMATIVE SPEECH

The frequency of such complaints can be cut down if the informative speech is properly planned in advance. The recommended six-step procedures for preparing and outlining should be followed, but additional suggestions regarding some of the steps will be helpful in preparing and delivering an informative speech.

Audience Interest in the Subject

In planning a talk to inform, the analysis of the audience usually centers on their probable attitudes toward the topic. A good way to begin the analysis is to find out if they are already interested in the topic, for you should know to what extent the topic is likely to carry itself and to what extent you must hunt for special methods to make it interesting. For example, it would be safe to suppose that women would be interested in hearing a talk on current fashions, as it would be just as safe to suppose that men would not be interested. But how about a talk on the history of the World Series? Pretty obvious.

Audience Knowledge of the Subject

You cannot inform your audience that two plus two equals four—they already know that. To inform implies that the information given is new to them. You cannot inform your audience that "the framble issifies and solarates twice a week"—that is new to them but they would not understand it. You cannot inform your audience merely by reading a long list of statistics. The data may be new and understood at the moment they are given, but you have not informed unless the listener can remember either the statistics or what the statistics were supposed to show.

Three convenient tests of the success of a speech to inform are: (1) How much information was new to the audience? (2) How much information did they understand? (3) How much information will they remember?

You have to estimate in advance what your listeners already know about your topic. It is crucial to success that this estimate be approximately accurate. If you underestimate the audience's background, they will consider your information stale; if you overestimate, they will not be able to understand you. Suppose, for example, you planned to talk about the slide rule. Imagine a class comprising mostly liberal arts majors, and then imagine a class of engineering students. An explanation of the slide rule that would be simple enough for the first group would be boring to the second, and if the talk presented information new to the engineers, it would be meaningless to the liberal arts students.

The danger of overestimating the amount of new material to include is greater than the danger of underestimating it. The speaker must avoid the temptation to show off his knowledge. He must remember that it takes more words to present a .fact in speech than it does in writing. He must not be misled into thinking that college lectures are standards for informative speaking. Whether or not notes will be taken is of particular importance in determining the amount of material to be given. If note-taking is appropriate or required, as in a classroom lecture, much more information can be included. If note-taking is inappropriate or an unaccustomed task, as in most nonclassroom speeches, the amount of factual material must be reduced accordingly.

Audience Prejudices Toward the Subject

On some topics, even though your purpose is to inform, allowance must be made for audience prejudices for or against that topic. If the newspapers, for instance, have been headlining the heroic battle of a captain to save his storm-battered ship, audiences would be favorably inclined toward the captain, eager to learn more facts about him. On the other hand, prejudice against a subject such as communism may be so strong that there may be emotional resistance against even an impartial history or explanation. Therefore the speaker cannot suppose that a fact is a fact to all audiences. Evolution, for example, is not accepted as a fact by fundamentalists. The speaker must anticipate whether the listeners' attitudes will be receptive, resistant, conflicting, or apathetic toward even unbiased facts.

Use of Learning Aids

When you undertake to build the outline of an informative talk, you should modify the six steps in outlining (central idea, main points, supports, conclusion, introduction, transitions) in terms of what we may call aids to learning. The following aids to learning are of special importance.

1. AUDIENCE ATTENTION   Psychological research has demonstrated that the more interestingly the information is presented, the more easily it will be learned. This takes us back to the preceding chapter where we discussed audience attention both as an end in itself and as a means to an end. When the end is to inform, the factors of interest become the means to that end.

Some informative speakers seem to take the attitude that they are casting pearls before swine. "It's my job to give this important information," they say, "and it's the listeners' job to get it. If they're too stupid or lazy to get it, so much the worse for them. I refuse to sugarcoat my profound learning." Surely anyone who professes to teach must assume greater responsibility than that; for the speaker has an obligation not merely to his subject but to his audience as well. Therefore the materials should be reasonably interesting as well as accurate. Soundness need not be sacrificed. If the speaker is willing to work hard, accuracy, clarity, and interest can be combined.

The speaker should introduce his subject with materials that contain one or more of the factors of attention. Then he should outline the proposed subject matter, and look it over with an awareness of the tendency of human attention to fluctuate. He should counteract this tendency by choosing a few critical spots, well spaced throughout the speech, where he should insert other attention-getting materials.

2. AUDIENCE MOTIVATION   The problem of catching and holding attention is closely allied to what is probably the most important aspect of informative speaking, stimulating the audience's wish to be informed. Experienced teachers often suspect that they do not so much teach as motivate their students to learn. The success of any

Students in an innovative "urban semester" class are highly motivated by the emphasis on field study. When they meet to exchange experiences, they give more than half of the professor's "lecture" for him.

informative talk depends on the speaker's ability to arouse his audience's wish for the information he is giving them.

In delivering an informative talk, do not simply introduce the subject and proceed to develop the main points. As early as possible in your speech try to establish in the audience a want or need to know more about your subject. Then, from time to time during the remainder of the talk, use techniques that will revive this want. There are many ways to do this.

a. Penalty.   The importance of motivation as an aid to learning is epitomized by the Air Force practice in teaching the men how to pack a parachute: Each man must pack his own! This example illustrates the technique of motivation by the threat of penalty. If you can show that failure to learn what you present will result in a penalty, you have provided motivation to learn. There are many ways to appeal to penalty motivation. For instance, say or imply, "If you don't learn this . . .

"You will flunk this course.
"You will be out of date in your conversation.
"You will endanger your health.
"You will lose money.
"You will disappoint your friends or relatives.
"People will make fun of you."

b. Reward.   Reward is usually a better type of motivation than penalty because most people respond more willingly to promises than threats. Suppose you are an art student and want to give a talk on color combinations. You might motivate the listeners to learn about the subject if you put your central idea something like this, "Knowledge of color combinations will make you better dressed and better looking." The variety of possible rewards for learning is suggested by the following list. Say or imply, "If you learn about this . . .

"You will improve your grade in this course.
"You will win a prize.
"You may save your life or someone else's.
"You will make more money.
"You will become a leader.
"You will be more popular.
"You will be healthier.
"You will increase your enjoyments."

Promise of reward and threat of penalty can often be combined. The traditional schoolroom device for providing motivation is the grading system. If you learn, you are rewarded by higher grades and honors; if you do not learn, you are penalized with lower grades and failure to be promoted. A fundamental complaint about the grading system is that it is artificial, extraneous to the materials to be learned. Nevertheless, the grading system has increased learning for most students. Psychologists have found that a student's learning has been increased merely by telling him whether he is right or wrong when he is answering a list of questions. Most of us would probably agree, however, that motivation is more desirable when it is an integral part of the subject matter to be learned. A talk on some aspect of traffic laws, driving, or care of an automobile can readily be motivated, for example, with promises of both rewards and penalties.

Motivation to learn about the duties of the United Nations Security Council could not so easily be provided by punishments and rewards. But there are other means of motivation.

c. Curiosity. Another way of motivating an audience to learn is by arousing and satisfying curiosity. When a topic is skillfully presented, the audience may be attracted simply to learn for learning's sake. One of the best ways to arouse curiosity is by introducing a question or series of questions into the early part of the talk. For example, a science major opened a classroom talk with these words:

> How hot is the sun? How heavy is it? What are sunspots? How old is the sun? Does the sun really burn? These are some of the questions people have asked me many times. We will answer these questions today.

As we mentioned earlier, you may have to contend with prejudice or resistance to learning. One way of handling this problem is by a tactful and indirect approach. For example, suppose you wanted to explain the nature of communism. You might say, "One of the major purposes of the extensive diplomatic missions to Russia and China by the United States is to broaden our knowledge of how communism works in practice. These missions have unearthed some interesting facts . . ." Then by means of an explanation of the missions' work you could discuss the nature of communism, probably with audience approbation instead of antagonism. A stronger strategy is to turn the motivation around. To refer to the previous example, an informative talk on communism could be motivated by saying, "Ignorance of the Russian system is dangerous to world peace; knowledge of their system will help us to maintain peaceful coexistence." You might go on to say, "We will study communism, not necessarily because we admire it or because we wish to adopt it, but because unless we understand what it is and why it exists we cannot successfully meet its proponents in the field of world diplomacy." In this fashion you might persuade your hearers to want to study communism, even though they are prejudiced against it, by arousing their curiosity as to what it really is.

3. PRESENTATION OF THE UNKNOWN IN TERMS OF THE KNOWN

We learn by experience. Some learning is by direct sensory experience. You learn about colors by seeing them; you learn something about bells by hearing them; you learn one thing about electricity by touching a live wire. On the other hand, some learning is by vicarious experience. You learn about the Civil War by reading history books, by looking at Brady's famed photographs, by hearing stories passed down in your family from an ancestor soldier. Taken together, direct and vicarious experiences constitute your personal stock of information.

New information is given meaning in terms of the information we already have. We use the known to reveal the unknown. For example, if you mentioned the null hypothesis to an audience with little background in statistics, you would receive only blank stares. The audience may never have experienced the phrase before. Suppose you tried to explain the hypothesis by saying, "The null hypothesis assumes that the differences between two sets of data have occurred by chance." Again, no learning would occur, for the audience would understand the individual words, but the total would still be meaningless to them. But if you began by explaining chance in terms of flipping a coin, learning would commence, for you would have established a relationship with the audience's experience. You could further explain and demonstrate with an actual coin that the chances of getting heads twice in two flips are only one out of three, and so on. Furthermore, the chances of flipping ten heads consecutively are mathematically remote. You could have each of two members of the audience flip a coin ten times and record the results. Then you could explain that the best guess would be five heads and five tails by each participant, and that neither set of results should be very far from that guess. In this fashion you could continue your speech with a better hope of clarifying the null hypothesis to the audience.

If you want to explain the energy and heat of the sun to an audience of laymen, there is no use in talking about 3.8×10^{33} ergs per second unless you can first relate ergs and powers of ten to the past experiences of the audience. Nor would true learning result from telling them that the sun's surface is probably 6,000 degrees centigrade in temperature. To make the extreme temperature meaningful, state how much hotter 6,000 degrees is than a red-hot stove or the heat required to melt steel. But to state that the sun is too hot to burn would give you no familiar basis to work from; therefore you could not relate that amazing statement to a layman's past experience.

The need to relate information to the listeners' own experience is not confined to technical subjects; it applies to all new materials. The point was wonderfully illustrated by a little boy in Sunday school when the teacher was trying to explain that Moses was "filled with the spirit of the Lord." She asked if the children knew what this meant. Kenneth thought he knew: "He was like Charlie Updale. Charlie's our cheerleader. He's full of school spirit!" The Sunday school teacher may well have noticed that Kenneth's learning justified the teaching methods of Jesus, who so often put his moral principles into parables, saying that the principle "may be likened unto...." He presented the unknown in terms of the known.

4. DEMONSTRATION   Telling is often not enough to insure learning. If someone were to try to tell you with words alone how to tie a dry fly, the process would probably sound like one of the most complex invented by man. However, if he supplemented the telling by showing you the actual materials and demonstrating the process, you would realize that the task is simple.

Armed services training programs and psychological research have highlighted the fact that for certain types of materials the learning process can be tremendously accelerated by use of visual aids or demonstration. Of course, visual aids are effective in talks where the purpose is to entertain, stimulate, or convince. Their most important value, however, is in their contribution to informative talks. It is wise, therefore, to review your outline from the standpoint of the possible use of visual aids. To refresh your memory for

Professor Janet Bolton, lecturing on oral interpretation of literature, often reads passages to demonstrate such interpretation; she encourages immediate questions or comments from students.

details of such possibilities, review pages 89–91. Remember, however, that visual aids should be appropriate to the subject—they should not be used just for the sake of using them.

Organization of the Informative Speech

Suppose you were going to memorize these two word lists:

bumper	spygt
headlights	goober
hood	bixet
motor	rokotinget
windshield	wuzzi
wheel	jafe
seats	taba geetis
brake	loors

There are the same number of words and letters in both lists. Nevertheless, you can readily see that it would be much easier to learn the left list than the right. The reason is that the left list is a meaningful group—all the words have meaning because they are parts of a car; the right list has only nonsense words with no unifying theme or principle.

We have all had the experience of studying a problem or a set of materials or a sequence, of reaching a stalemate, and then suddenly of finding that the whole thing clicks into place. This suggests another useful method in planning a speech to inform. Present a meaningful group of details and at the proper moment reveal the principle that relates those details to one another and makes them a pattern. The moment the listener grasps this unifying principle the details all seem to fall into their proper places, and the listener has learned.

1. INTRODUCTION Since the most frequent criticism of informative talks is that they are too dry, the speaker should open with an attention-getting idea in order to head off an initial response of resignation to boredom. If possible choose an opening attention-getter that also leads into the subject.

The attitude of the audience toward the speaker is also important. If the listeners get the idea that the speaker is poorly qualified to speak on the subject, resistance to learning is created. It may be necessary directly or indirectly to establish your right to speak on the chosen subject.

In leading into the topic, the question of motivation should be carefully considered. At the earliest feasible time you should try to show why the audience wants or needs the information about to be given. Usually this material can best be included in the introduction; sometimes it becomes part of the speech body.

For some subjects, especially technical ones, learning requires that one or more terms be defined before getting into the body of the material. Definitions are a commonly used technique for leading into the subject.

In talks to inform, more than in other types, it is wise to give a preview of the main points. A preview provides the audience with a framework or pattern which, as we have just seen, helps them understand the details. The preview usually comes as part of the transition between introduction and body.

2. BODY When a central idea for the informative talk has been chosen, two principles of learning should be held in mind. First, can you present the idea so that the audience will be eager to learn about it? Second, can you develop the idea so that it will take on an easily seen and easily remembered pattern? Choose your main points to form that pattern and phrase them so that the pattern is evident. Parallel phrasing will help, and so will careful progress from the known to the unknown, or a plain arrangement in time or space.

If you will refer back to the list of stock designs on page 115, you will find that the following item numbers are often adaptable to informative speeches: 1, 2, 3, 6, 9, 11, 12, 13, 15, and 19. Of these the time-sequence and space-sequence items are especially useful. The time sequence can provide designs of considerable variety. You can present your points as past, present, future, or subdivisions within one of the three. You can use units of time of any appropriate dimension, ranging from seconds to eons. You can describe a process by time stages from beginning to end, or present historical or biographical materials in chronological order. Your points can move either forward or backward in time.

The space sequence is even more flexible. Depending on the sub-

This student conducts a campus tour on Visitor's Day. She organizes her materials in spatial sequence. The buildings, landmarks, exhibits, and campus maps provide visual aids.

ject matter, you can have your points move from east to west, north to south, outside to inside, left to right, top to bottom, front to rear, corner to corner, clockwise around a circle, zone to zone, city to city, or nation to nation. You can explain the plan of a new campus building by a sequence of points moving from basement to top floor; or describe a battle by moving from one flank to the other along the battle line. The clarity of a space sequence can frequently be increased by maps or diagrams.

The transitions within the speech body are especially important in talks to inform. Transitions indicate how the details belong to the overall pattern and tell the listener just where you are in the progress of your talk. To be safe, make your transitions obvious; a liberal use of numerals often helps. For example, "Having described the engineering and the tooling, we now come to the third stage in aircraft manufacture, the fabrication of parts." If you do not have a clear transition, you may be talking about fabrication while half the audience thinks you are still talking about tooling.

ROLE OF INFORMATION IN OTHER SPEECHES

Thus far in this chapter we have centered on the problem of preparing primarily informative speeches. But when other purposes are foremost, giving information becomes a means rather than the end itself.

It is a truism that in trying to convince people of something, it is always necessary to give information in order to prove the arguments. In trying to reinforce attitudes, it is necessary to introduce new facts or opinions as part of the reinforcement process. Even in talks to entertain, as we saw in the last chapter, new materials are essential in getting and holding attention.

Thus presenting new information is a basic process in all public speaking. The suggestions in this chapter apply to the whole talk when the purpose is to inform; they apply to the informational parts of every other type of speech.

SUMMARY

Three tests of the effectiveness of a speech to inform are: How much information was new to the audience, how much was understood, and how much was remembered.

Effectiveness can be increased and common complaints about speeches to inform can be decreased if the speaker plans, not only in terms of the subject, but also in terms of the audience and of psychological aids to learning.

In adapting an informative talk to an audience, the speaker should consider the listeners' interest, knowledge, and prejudice in relation to the subject matter.

In planning a speech to inform, five aids to learning should be remembered. (1) Learning is aided when materials are presented in attention-getting ways. (2) Learning is aided when the learner is properly motivated. Motivation means that the listener is made to want to learn, usually through threat of penalty, promise of reward, or arousal of intellectual curiosity. (3) Learning is aided when the unknown is presented in terms of the known. (4) Learning is aided when telling is supplemented by showing and demonstrating. (5) Learning is aided when materials are presented in meaningful patterns.

TOPICAL PREVIEW

I   Definition of attitude

II   Outlining the speech to reinforce attitudes
    A   The central idea
    B   Main points and subpoints
    C   Supports

III   Occasions for talks to reinforce attitudes
    A   Introductions
    B   Welcomes
        1   Introduction
        2   Body
        3   Conclusion
    C   Presentations
        1   Introduction
        2   Body
        3   Conclusion
    D   Responses
        1   Introduction
        2   Body
        3   Conclusion

IV   Role of reinforcing attitudes in other speeches

V   Summary

Reinforcing Audience Attitudes

DEFINITION OF ATTITUDE

An attitude may be defined as a predisposition to respond to a given stimulus in one way rather than another. Let us illustrate.

When the starter for a women's swimming race (photo on next page), tells the competitors to "Get set," you can see that each girl becomes, almost literally, a picture of an attitude. The "predisposition" is shown by the crouched, forward-leaning posture, the whipcord muscles tensing, the sucking in of air, the eyes focusing on a chosen spot of water, the intense facial expressions. In addition there are internal responses of the muscles, nervous tissues, and glands that we cannot see. All these behaviors express readiness to respond to the sound of the starter's gun. Theoretically any of the girls might respond in any of a thousand ways. For instance, one girl might stand up and exclaim, "What the devil was that?" But actually she will respond by diving into the pool and swimming rapidly down a marked lane. All of her training has predisposed her "to respond to a given stimulus in one way rather than another."

But what about ordinary attitudes toward innumerable personal or social problems? The kinds of attitudes with which speakers have

Compare these swimmers' observable behavior with the definition of an attitude given on preceding page.

to deal? A friend inquires, "What's Paul's attitude toward gambling?" You reply, "He's bitterly opposed to it." Reflection will reveal that Paul's attitude is the same in all fundamental respects as that of the runner. Paul has a predisposition to respond to a given stimulus. What stimulus? Probably almost anything that pertains to gambling: the sight of playing cards or dice, a newspaper story, somebody's remarks about the odds on a prize fight. Such a stimulus will touch off a characteristic response in Paul. He will sense antagonistic thoughts and emotions welling up; he may frown, walk away, give a bit of a sermon on the evils of gambling, write a letter to his newspaper or congressman. He will respond in some such accustomed way rather than by paying no attention, being amused, praising the practice of gambling, or asking for more dope on the fourth at Santa Anita. Paul's response is thus predetermined by his attitude.

Assume that you have an audience of people with attitudes similar to Paul's, that you approve of their attitudes, and that you want to give a speech to reinforce their attitudes. You should begin by choosing a central idea adapted to the purpose, audience, and subject.

OUTLINING THE SPEECH TO REINFORCE ATTITUDES

The Central Idea

Usually the central idea in speeches to reinforce attitudes is a strong statement of praise or condemnation. If you and your audience are opposed to gambling, your central idea might be a statement praising a law or proposed law to limit some type of gambling, or praising the antigambling program of the audience, or condemning the laxity of law enforcement against gambling in a particular community, or condemning the operations of a nearby race track. Just what you would praise or condemn would depend on the audience and occasion.

Let us take another example. What is your attitude toward George Meany, president of the AFL-CIO? If you admire him and are to speak to an audience of union members, your central idea might be, "George Meany has contributed mightily to the industrial progress of America." But if you detest him and are to speak before members of management, your central idea might be almost the reverse. If your ideas and those of your audience are different, your speech purpose will not be to reinforce attitudes. Reinforcement is appropriate only when speaker and audience are like-minded.

Main Points and Subpoints

The basic speech design, of course, comprises a logical pattern. Furthermore, the logic should relate the design to the central idea. In speeches to inform or convince we think of this logic as carrying the audience along toward comprehension or conviction. When we want to reinforce a belief, however, the reasoning comes after the fact; we do not try to instruct or prove, but to justify. Therefore the logic in speeches to stimulate is a form of rationalization. This fact suggests two possible methods.

The first method is to restate for the audience the reasons that led them to their belief. The second is to give them a new set of reasons for the same old belief. In giving the old reasons, it is usually best to state them in vivid though familiar words. They should strike a cherished and familiar chord; the listeners should nod and say to themselves, "That's right," or even break into spontaneous applause.

In giving new reasons, a good method is to give the familiar a novel twist; the listener's reaction should be, "Say! That's good. I must remember that."

Giving old ideas a novel twist is illustrated by Bruce Barton's oft-quoted speech, "Which Knew Not Joseph." This speech was delivered before an audience of public-relations executives, and the opening point was as follows:

> There are two stories—and neither is new—which I desire to tell you, because they have a direct application to everyone's business. The first concerns a member of my profession, an advertising man, who was in the employ of a circus. It was his function to precede the circus into various communities, distribute tickets to the editor, put up on the barns pictures of the bearded lady and the man-eating snakes, and finally to get in touch with the proprietor of some store and persuade him to purchase the space on either side of the elephant for his advertisement in the parade.
>
> Coming one day to a crossroads town, our friend found that there was only one store. The proprietor did not receive him enthusiastically. "Why should I advertise?" he demanded. "I have been here for twenty years. There isn't a man, woman or child around these parts that doesn't know where I am and what I sell." The advertising man answered very promptly (because in our business if we hesitate we are lost), and he said to the proprietor, pointing across the street, "What is that building over there?" The proprietor answered, "That is the Methodist Episcopal Church." The advertising man said, "How long has that been there?" The proprietor said, "Oh, I don't know; seventy-five years probably." "And yet," exclaimed the advertising man, "they ring the church bell every Sunday morning."[1]

Thus Barton took the old idea of the necessity of repeating advertisements, and gave it an unusual slant. Apply this principle of combining the familiar with the novel to our list of stock designs, page 115; you will note that several of them will probably be especially effective for talks to reinforce attitudes, for example, numbers 6, 16, 17, 19, 20, 21, 22.

The phrasing of points in talks to reinforce requires care. The words should be colorful, impressive, and impelling. The audience expects you to tell them what they want to hear but to say it better than they can; to tell them, in Alexander Pope's words, "What oft was thought, but ne'er so well exprest." This fact partly explains the long life of most of our universal quotations, such as sayings of Ben Franklin or memorable passages from Lincoln. It is often effective to include superlatives: the first or last, the best or worst, the greatest or least, the only, the impossible.

---

[1] Homer D. Lindgren, ed., *Modern Speeches*, F. S. Crofts, 1926, pp. 406–07. Reprinted by permission of Bruce Barton.

Supports

When the supports are used to reinforce a point they do not have to clarify or prove the point, but only illustrate it, elaborate it, strengthen it, make it more real. Therefore supports should be chosen and worded so as to revive memories and traditions, touch upon aspirations and ideals, or appeal to the sentiments. Supports should be worded vividly and colorfully. Presentation can often be dramatic and forceful; too much restraint in wording and delivery may diminish the effectiveness of supports to reinforce existing beliefs.

The anecdote is the most fruitful source of support to reinforce attitudes. A story of the suffering and heroism of a crippled child, for example, will reinforce the layman's attitude toward the March of Dimes more than any scientific exposition or significant table of statistics.

Russell Conwell's lecture "Acres of Diamonds" is one of the most famous American speeches with the purpose to reinforce attitudes; the supports are mostly anecdotes. Here is an example of one of Conwell's stories:

> There was a man living in Pennsylvania, not unlike some Pennsylvanians you have seen, who owned a farm, and he did with that farm just what I should do with a farm if I owned one in Pennsylvania—he sold it. But before he sold it he decided to secure employment collecting coal oil for his cousin, who was in the business in Canada, where they first discovered oil on this continent. They dipped it from the running streams at that early time. So this Pennsylvania farmer wrote to his cousin asking for employment.
>
> .   .   .
>
> His cousin answered, "All right, come on."
> So he sold his farm, according to the county record, for $833. . . . He had scarcely gone from that place before the man who purchased the spot went out to arrange for the watering of the cattle. He found the previous owner had gone out years before and put a plank across the brook back of the barn, edgewise into the surface of the water just a few inches. The purpose of that plank at that sharp angle across the brook was to throw over to the other bank a dreadful-looking scum through which the cattle would not put their noses. But with that plank there to throw it over to one side, the cattle would drink below, and thus that man who had gone to Canada had been himself damming back for twenty-three years a flood of coal oil which the state geologists of Pennsylvania declared to us ... four years ago ... to be worth to our state a thousand millions of dollars. The man who owned that territory on which the city of Titusville now stands, and those Pleasantville valleys ... sold the whole of it for $833.[2]

2 Russell H. Conwell, *Acres of Diamonds*, Harper, 1915, pp. 10–12.

The second most fruitful source for reinforcing supports is quotations. When the purpose is to stimulate, quote well-tried authorities, acknowledged leaders, and heroes—the Bible, Washington, and Lincoln among others. Look also for appropriate quotations from poetry and drama, Kipling and Shakespeare, for instance.

Cumulated instances are often effective in reinforcing attitudes. They gain power when comparison or contrast is utilized. Wendell Phillips was a master of this technique, and in his eulogy of Daniel O'Connell he said:

> I remember the solemnity of Webster, the grace of Everett, the rhetoric of Choate; I know the eloquence that lay hid in the iron logic of Calhoun; I have melted beneath the magnetism of Sergeant S. Prentiss of Mississippi, who wielded a power few men ever had ... But I think all of them together never surpassed, and no one of them ever equalled O'Connell.

Explanation, statistics, and visual aids can be used effectively when the main purpose is to reinforce, but they are not so frequently useful as the other forms of support. Explanations should be succinct. Statistics should be simplified and clearly appropriate to the purpose. A college speaker made appropriate use of statistics in a talk condemning our public schools for failure to teach responsible citizenship. He composed a questionnaire, which he administered to a large number of high school students. Questions included items such as, "Who is the representative in Congress from your district?" Simple percentages showing the pupils' ignorance on this and other questions were cited to reinforce an idea that his audience already believed. Visual aids can occasionally be utilized. For example, in a

Billy Graham bases points on texts from the Bible; most of his sermons clearly illustrate reinforcing attitudes.

talk to reinforce attitudes toward safe driving, the speaker might show enlarged photographs of a few gruesome smashups.

Returning to more typical materials in speeches to stimulate, consider a classic of American speeches, Senator George Graham Vest's brief "Tribute to the Dog." Notice how Senator Vest reinforced the favorable attitude that most people have about dogs.

> The one absolutely unselfish friend that man can have in this selfish world, the one that never deserts him, the one that never proves ungrateful or treacherous is his dog. A man's dog stands by him in prosperity and in poverty, in health and sickness. He will sleep on the cold ground, where the wintry winds blow and the snow drives fiercely, if only he may be near his master's side. He will kiss the hand that has no food to offer; he will lick the wounds and sores that come in encounters with the roughness of the world. He guards the sleep of his pauper master as if he were a prince. When all other friends desert, he remains. When riches take wings, and reputation falls to pieces, he is as constant in his love as the sun in its journey through the heavens.
>
> If fortune drives the master forth an outcast in the world, friendless and homeless, the faithful dog asks no higher privilege than that of accompanying him, to guard him against danger, to fight against his enemies. And when the last scene of all comes, and death takes his master in its embrace and his body is laid away in the cold ground, no matter if all other friends pursue their way, there by the graveside will the noble dog be found, his head between his paws, his eyes sad, but open in alert watchfulness, faithful and true even in death.[3]

OCCASIONS FOR TALKS TO REINFORCE ATTITUDES

There are numerous speaking occasions where it is appropriate and desirable to reinforce attitudes:

Keynote speeches for conventions	Reunions
Commencement addresses	Good-will talks
Eulogies	Political party rallies
Commemorations	Sermons

Pep talks as at salesmen's meetings, football rallies

There are also speeches for special occasions where the purpose is almost always to reinforce attitudes. They are called special simply

---

[3] Lewis Copeland, ed., *The World's Great Speeches*, Garden City, 1942, p. 651.

because the situations require variations from the standard speech designs. Basic types of speeches for special occasions include:

Speeches of introduction Responses
Welcomes Presentations
Farewells Acceptances

Introductions

In introducing a speaker your overall job is to set the right tone, direct favorable attention toward the speaker, and increase the audience's desire to hear him. This should be accomplished with a minimum of words. The better known the speaker, the shorter the introduction. For example, there is the oft-quoted speech of introduction by Shailer Mathews for Woodrow Wilson: "Ladies and gentlemen: the President."

You should have more information about your speaker than you will actually use in the introduction; you should be in a position to choose from available details those that will best impress the audience and relate the speaker to the occasion. It is worthwhile to consult the speaker beforehand in order to determine the best approach. For example, a speech teacher was asked by two fraternities to speak at their initiation banquets, which were held a week apart. At the first of the banquets the toastmaster introduced him as a professor of speech. The effect of his introduction was to prepare the minds of the audience for a classroom lecture or for a professional orator, and to direct their attention toward the expected finesse of gesture, voice, and language rather than toward the ideas to be discussed. Thus warned, the speaker tactfully advised the toastmaster prior to the second banquet. As a result he was introduced as a member of the faculty who had been active for many years in fraternity work. The second introduction produced favorable and appropriate attention.

Naturally in building favorable attention you say only complimentary things about the speaker. But do not overcompliment or fawn on the speaker, and do not put him on the spot with too much praise. You have doubtless heard introductions that gave the speaker a build-up that no human could live up to.

It is your duty to announce the speaker's topic, but resist the temptation to make a speech about it yourself. On too many occasions the chairman has made a longer speech about the speaker's subject than the speaker himself had prepared. Of course, it is usually desirable to comment briefly on the significance of the topic or to express curiosity about it, but do not try to steal the speaker's thunder.

Speeches of introduction often comprise a wooden listing of vital statistics or professional accomplishments, which the audience may scarcely bother to hear. Try to humanize your remarks and present the speaker as a real person. Give the listener the impression that he is meeting the speaker on an individual and friendly basis.

Sometimes the design of your remarks will require mentioning the speaker's name early. Generally, however, it is more effective to build to a climax by saving the name until the very end of the introduction. When you do give the name, be sure to articulate it with special care.

As you mention the speaker's name in closing your introduction, turn toward him and smile. Step back from the speaker's stand or the center of the stage but remain standing until the speaker has reached his place. It is often wise to lead the applause as he is approaching the stand. Avoid sitting directly behind the speaker during his talk. If possible, place your chair far to one side of the platform or sit in the front row with the rest of the audience. If you must remain in plain view on the platform, discipline yourself to look attentive and appreciative during the speech. Avoid distracting movements and facial expressions.

When the speaker has finished and is returning to his chair, you should lead the applause as you walk back to the rostrum. Sometimes a brief, sincere expression of the audience's appreciation is in order, but usually the chairman's approval can best be expressed by facial expression and general manner.

A different procedure is required when you have to introduce a succeeding speaker. Then you may properly refer to one of the previous speaker's ideas as a transition into your introduction of the next speaker or topic. When several speakers are to be introduced, it becomes the chairman's duty to weld them together into a unified program rather than to give the impression of a series of unrelated speeches.

Welcomes

The general effect of a speech of welcome should be to make the visiting person or group feel wanted and at home. The welcomer's mood and manner should be cordial, cheerful, and sincere. Tact, taste, and ingenuity are essential. The welcoming talk should be brief—one or two minutes will usually suffice.

1. INTRODUCTION   The opening should touch at once on the welcoming theme. The welcome may take the form of a direct statement

or may be presented in the form of a quotation or short anecdote. If you are representing a group in extending the welcome, be sure to say so: "On behalf of the university . . ."; or, "I know that I speak for every member of this audience when I say . . ."

2. BODY   You have three things to talk about in the body of the welcoming speech: the person or organization being welcomed, the hosts, and occasion. You should praise all three by describing the achievements of the guests, giving useful information about the hosts, and enhancing the importance of the occasion.

3. CONCLUSION   Restate the welcome in the conclusion. If the guests are gathered for a conference or a convention, predict or wish them success in their deliberations.

Presentations

There are two principal types of presentations: gifts and awards. The presentation of a gift usually represents a special occasion, such as the presentation of a gift to a retiring employee, or to a colleague whom you are honoring, or to an elderly couple on their golden wedding anniversary. The presentation of awards is usually an annual event such as a competition. The formality of the talk should be regulated by the occasion, and the talk should be brief: one to five minutes.

1. INTRODUCTION   The introduction may be confined to a single sentence of greeting, or to a statement of the speaker's purpose. For some awards a brief review of the history or nature of the award may be needed.

2. BODY   In the body of a speech of presentation you may have to talk about the recipient and the gift or award, and sometimes the occasion or the losers. Which of these to emphasize most depends on the situation. In presenting a gift to a colleague in celebration of his twenty-five years of service, for instance, almost the entire talk should be devoted to the recipient—his achievements, abilities, and character. However, in presenting the prizes to winners of an intercollegiate debate tournament, little need be said about the winners; most of the remarks should center upon the awards and the occasion, with suitable praise for the losers.

In praising the winner or recipient, do not overdo your praise—the poor fellow has to respond. If the occasion permits, the compliments to the recipient should be tempered with humor. In discussing the gift or award, do not neglect to consider its possible symbolic value.

3. CONCLUSION The entire talk should be planned so that the actual presentation of the gift will come as a natural climax. The final words may be those of congratulation.

Responses

In responding to introductions, welcomes, or presentations the keynote is tact, for the situation in itself creates a difficult dilemma. If the speaker pooh-poohs the praise in the introduction as inaccurate, undeserved, or overdone, he will be insulting the chairman and possibly the whole audience. If he seriously accepts the praise as no more than his just deserts, he brands himself as an egotist. If he attempts to compromise between these extremes, he is in danger of sounding coy or ludicrous. Therefore ways and means must be found to respond with tact, modesty, and gratitude.

1. INTRODUCTION Almost always the first sentence must express the sincere personal feelings of the speaker about the praise or the award. These may be feelings of happiness, embarrassment, or confusion. The emotional content rather than the exact wording is the important thing.

Sometimes it is appropriate to relieve the situation with a quick humorous thrust, as when Harry Emerson Fosdick said, "Flattery won't hurt you if you don't inhale," or when Ernest Holmes suddenly broke the tension by referring to the introduction with a twinkle, "Of course all of it was true."

The person who has received an award or who has been welcomed as a guest may be expected to give a full-length speech. If so, his response to the chairman may become the introduction of the speech proper. There are two speeches, of which the response is the first.

2. BODY In a response, the most successful plan usually is to reply to praise with praise. You can praise the person, or the organization, or the spirit of the welcome; or you can praise the gift or award, indicating its merit and appropriateness; or with grace you can frequently share the credit for winning the award by praise of your colleagues and coworkers.

3. CONCLUSION Restate your appreciation of the honor conferred. This is one speech where you can meaningfully make your last words, "I thank you."

ROLE OF REINFORCING ATTITUDES IN
OTHER SPEECHES

In this chapter we have been concerned with talks in which the predominant purpose is to stimulate—to reinforce existing attitudes. However, reinforcing attitudes is a basic speech method and should inhere in any talk, no matter what the purpose. When reinforcing attitudes is not an end in itself, it is usually a means to the other speech purposes.

Let us illustrate how reinforcing attitudes is a basic means in talks to entertain, inform, and convince. When the main purpose is to entertain, the reinforcement of existing attitudes or beliefs may be an excellent technique for arousing or holding favorable attention—you will recall that the familiar is one of the factors of getting attention. In talks to inform you will also recall that one basic means is to clarify the new in comparison with the known. Thus the reinforcement of what the listeners already know is frequently a useful technique for adding to their knowledge. The next chapter will show that in attempting to build or change attitudes, one of the fundamental devices is the reinforcement of existing attitudes before relating them to the new attitude that the speaker wants to build. Once again it is a matter of distinguishing between ends and means. Reinforcing attitudes may often be an end in itself. When it is not, it becomes a means rather than an end.

SUMMARY

An attitude is a predisposition to respond to a given stimulus in a given way. A speaker often has to reinforce existing audience attitudes.

The central idea in speeches to reinforce attitudes is usually a statement of a belief that you and all or most of your audience accept, and that you will usually develop by praising or condemning. The main points and subpoints should be chosen, not to instruct or prove, but to justify the central idea. The most useful forms of support in talks to reinforce attitudes are usually anecdotes and quotations. Supports should revive memories and traditions, touch upon aspirations or ideals, or make a sentimental appeal.

Ordinary speaking occasions where reinforcement of attitudes is appropriate are numerous, and they include keynote speeches, commencement addresses, reunions, and pep talks.

Special speaking occasions where reinforcement of attitudes is appropriate include introductions, welcomes, farewells, responses, presentations, and acceptances. In speeches for special occasions a few variations from standard speech designs are needed.

When the general purpose is to stimulate, the reinforcing of attitudes is an end in itself; when the purpose is to entertain, inform, or convince, the reinforcing of attitudes is a means to the end.

TOPICAL PREVIEW

I Democracy in action

II The meaning of "convince"

III Logic versus psychology

IV Logical validity
   A Evidence
      1 Kinds of evidence
      2 Tests of authority
   B Reasoning
      1 Inductive reasoning
      2 Deductive reasoning
      3 Reasoning by analogy
      4 Causal reasoning

V Psychological validity
   A Drives
   B Motives
   C Attitudes
      1 Attitudes toward the topic
      2 Attitudes toward related topics
      3 Attitudes toward the speaker

VI Outlining the speech to build attitudes
   A The design
      1 The design for direct argument
      2 The design for indirect argument
   B Supports
   C The introduction
   D The conclusion

VII Summary

15

Building Audience Attitudes

DEMOCRACY IN ACTION

In 1973, in the midst of her antiwar activities, actress Jane Fonda accepted the invitation of a student organization to express her views at an open meeting on the campus of the University of Southern California. About four thousand students exercised the right "to peaceably assemble." Some came to applaud, some to heckle, and the majority to see what would happen. Highlights of what happened are told pictorially on the next two pages.

During the opening portion of Miss Fonda's remarks, the audience was attentive and relatively quiet (first and second pictures). Soon however the audience began to respond, pro and con, more vigorously. An organized group of opponents hanged her in effigy and heckled loudly (third and fourth pictures). Miss Fonda sought to answer her opponents (fifth picture). The most conspicuous member of the crowd was a local politician who mounted the "scaffold" and repeatedly tried to shout down the speaker with the aid of a bullhorn (sixth picture). Meanwhile Miss Fonda's supporters heckled the hecklers. After almost an hour the meeting became so noisy that Miss Fonda began leading the singing of "The Star Spangled Banner"—a symbolic behavior that united the factions; the non-verbal signs of approval (clenched fists, "V" signs, hands over

Jane Fonda begins her speech at a campus meeting.

Students are interested and relatively quiet.

Soon, however, an opposition student organization hangs her in effigy.

And heckles loudly.

Miss Fonda fights back.

A local politician assumes leadership of the loyal opposition.

Miss Fonda concludes the meeting by leading the singing of the national anthem.

heart) are seen in the final photo. After the national anthem the crowd peaceably disassembled.

For the student of speech communication the most instructive aspect of this and similar campus meetings is found by analyzing the attitudes that the four thousand students brought with them and what happened to those attitudes during and after the meeting. There were two groups of students who brought along strong convictions representing opposite extremes toward the then current policies and developments in Southeast Asia. Certainly neither of these groups changed the beliefs of the other, except to antagonize and make those opposing attitudes stronger. The majority of the students' attitudes fell between the extremes. This middle group were undecided or "leaning"; almost all of them were attentive and concerned. Our question is, "Did the verbal or other symbolic behaviors during the meeting change the attitudes of this majority group?" The answer is, "Probably not." Confusion and an exchange of slogans is not likely to change very many minds. Of course, many students enjoyed exercizing freedom of speech, even though this often meant that a dozen or more people were simultaneously shouting differing responses at the top of their lungs. Furthermore, the whole event stimulated interest, and new attitudes were probably built when students rehashed the meeting and the issues in small groups of two or three or four. This type of aftermath is so important in the building of new attitudes that one wonders why so many speakers seem to overlook it when planning speeches intended to persuade.

THE MEANING OF "CONVINCE"

To convince means to build an audience attitude.

In your everyday life you have frequently known people who think that to convince means to have an argument with somebody. And having an argument seems to mean proving that the other fellow's ideas are ridiculous. "I tried to get him to listen to reason," for instance, implies that you are reasonable while he is not. No wonder so many attempts to convince end with one contestant angrily declaring, "I don't care what you say, I still believe I'm right!"

Many people think that the speaker alone is active in convincing and the listener is merely a passive recipient. But check your own experience as a listener. Have you ever said, "My mind was changed for me"? Probably not, but you have said, "I changed my mind." Have you ever changed your mind on an important issue after listening to a persuasive speech? If so, which of the following statements comes closest to expressing your feelings after the speech?

He convinced me that . . .
After hearing him I was convinced that . . .
After thinking it over I became convinced that . . .
After talking it over with some of my friends, I became
    convinced that . . .

The chances are that you "became" convinced. It is even accurate to say, as we have previously seen, that a speaker never convinces anybody—the listener must convince himself. The speaker provides a stimulus, but nothing happens unless the listener responds. The speaker can set the conviction process in motion, but the listener must carry the process through. And he often does this after, rather than during, the speech.

LOGIC VERSUS PSYCHOLOGY

The ordinary American listener is often accused of responding mostly to so-called appeals to emotion. Perhaps we contrast emotional appeals with appeals to reason, but to do so is misleading.

Many people believe that speeches or sections of speeches are either logical or emotional, and that as you increase the proportion of one, you decrease the proportion of the other. Furthermore, many people believe that they can readily tell whether a speech is logical or emotional. As mentioned in Chapter 1, the foregoing popular beliefs were tested experimentally by Randall Ruechelle.[1] He asked a large number of listeners and readers to evaluate many speeches, rating the speeches in terms of degrees of logical and emotional appeal. The agreement among the judgments was scarcely greater than would have occurred if the respondents had flipped coins. It is fair to say that the concept of appeals to reason vs. appeals to emotion can be misleading in studying persuasive speaking.

However, the widespread confusion between logic and emotion should not obscure the fact that an important distinction should be made between logic and psychology. Every speech can be evaluated by the question, "Is it logically sound?" as it can also be evaluated by asking, "Is it psychologically sound?" The logical test is used impersonally to judge the speaker's reasoning. The psychological test is used personally to estimate audience response. Both of these ways of judging a speech can be applied to the same materials.

---

[1] Randall C. Ruechelle, "An Experimental Study of Audience Recognition of Emotional and Intellectual Appeals in Persuasion," *Speech Monographs*, Vol. XXV (March 1958).

Perhaps the relationship between logic and psychology may be clarified by comparing a speech to a glass of orange juice. The food values of the orange juice are like the logical values of the speech. Food values such as vitamins, calories, and minerals are impersonal; they remain the same even though nobody drinks the orange juice. Chemical tests will reveal their presence. However, if someone drinks the orange juice, he evaluates it by its flavor. Reaction to flavor is a personal thing, and may vary among different people. Better flavor does not imply lower food value, for a certain brand of orange juice might be low on both, another brand high on one and low on the other, and a third high on both. The flavor of the drink, then, resembles the psychological values of the speech. Likewise, the logical and psychological soundness of a speech cannot be considered simply on an either-or basis. Orange juice commits no sin by having a pleasing flavor; neither does a speech. Buyers of orange juice should be concerned with both food value and flavor; they want an orange juice that is both nutritious and flavorful. The speech audience asks whether the thought in a speech is logically sound and whether the speech affects them personally. When a speech is successful, the audience should answer yes to both questions.

Especially when the speech purpose is to build audience attitudes the materials in the speech should be evaluated both logically and psychologically. This double test should be applied to the introduction, body, and conclusion, as well as to the central idea, main points, subpoints, supports, and transitions. The entire speech should be logically and psychologically valid.

LOGICAL VALIDITY

None of your listeners will change his mind if he thinks your ideas are illogical. You may go through a sophisticated stage of life, during which you think that people are irrational, that they would not recognize good logic if they heard it, and that they can be moved only by emotion. If you do think this way, you had better not let your listeners know that you do! Your listeners, like you, think they make their decisions on logical grounds. Be sure that your ideas will withstand the impersonal tests of logic.

In a talk to convince, the central idea is usually stated in the form of a proposition. The main points, subpoints, and supports should all prove the proposition. Logical support of a proposition can be considered under two headings: evidence and reasoning.

The annual Moot Court competition of students at USC School of Law.

The logical validity of their arguments is severely tested by the panel comprising United States Supreme Court Justice Potter Stewart, California Supreme Court Justice Donald Wright, and United States Circuit Court Judge Walter Ely.

Evidence

Evidence is anything known to be true. Reasoning is the process of drawing inferences from evidence. Therefore you begin with evidence and end with a conclusion. Reasoning is the process by which you get from the one to the other. For example, the house next door has been vacant and for sale. You observe one day that the realtor's sign has been removed, and that a stranger is mowing and watering the lawn. A neighbor tells you she saw the same stranger looking at the property last week. Now you have three pieces of evidence. First, you infer that the probable reason for the removal of the sign is that the house is no longer for sale. Second, you infer that the probable cause of the stranger's visit last week was to view the property for the purpose of deciding to buy. Third, you infer that his care of the lawn probably means he is getting ready to move in. You reach the conclusion that the stranger has bought the house.

The conclusion reached in the illustration may seem obvious and inevitable. But suppose the realtor's sign had not been removed at all, but had merely been shifted from the lawn to the porch, where you could not see it. Suppose the neighbor had been mistaken and had seen someone else visit the house last week. And suppose the stranger was a gardener who had been hired to keep the lawn attractive pending a sale. It is clear therefore that the soundness of your conclusion depends on the truth of the evidence and the validity of your inferences.

1. KINDS OF EVIDENCE   Evidence may be classified in several ways. One useful way is to distinguish between facts and opinions. Facts can be defined as objects or events directly verifiable by the senses; that is, you must directly observe them. An opinion, on the other hand, is a fact that is reported by language. The key difference, therefore, lies in the human element. Whenever a direct observation becomes a report of something, some degree of interpretation necessarily takes place; hence it is always to some degree an opinion.[2]

Factual evidence is uncommon in public speeches; it is mostly confined to visual aids. If you show the audience an oil painting, you are presenting factual evidence; if you describe it for them, you

---

[2] There are, of course, many definitions of these terms as, for example, the legal, philosophical, or psychological. However, the present definition is basic to human communication; for further discussion see: F. S .C. Northrop, *The Logic of Sciences and the Humanities* (Macmillan, 1949), pp. 39 ff.

are presenting testimonial evidence. Avoiding unnecessary subtleties, however, we can include as facts the recalling of matters that
the listener has directly experienced in his past. If you say that the
city hall is white and the listener has himself seen the city hall, it is
sensible to consider the evidence as fact, even though it is only a
statement and the actual city hall is not in the immediate view of
the audience.

All evidence, however, has its hazards, even direct sensory evidence. The magician presents direct sensory evidence, yet the whole
audience is fooled. Several witnesses see the same accident, yet
give contradictory testimony in court. Probably the chief reason for
differences is that we tend to observe what we expect or want
rather than what *is*. A professor, for example, noticed a student
walking down the hall in the direction of his office. He quietly fell
in step just behind her. Reaching the office door, the student
knocked. "Come in," said the professor. She opened the door and
was nonplused to find an empty room. She had heard what she
expected to hear.

Most evidence in speeches is opinion, that is, testimonial evidence,
either the testimony of the speaker or of someone quoted by the
speaker. Of course, all testimonial evidence should be traceable to
someone's actual observation. However, there is bound to be some
difference between an observed fact and a reported fact, as the
report of anything observed will be colored by the observer. Two
people might observe a goldfish swimming in a bowl. The observed
facts would be the same, but their two reports of what they saw
would be different. And if the goldfish were also able to submit a
report. . . .

The hazards of testimonial evidence are greater than those of
factual evidence because people differ not only in what they
perceive, but even more in what they remember and in the ways
they narrate it. The unreliability of memories was known even
before Freud came along with his theories of how we tend to forget
the unpleasant. The confusion that often results when several people
try to tell about the same idea was discussed in Chapter 10 in
connection with the difficulties of language.

In fact, the hazards of evidence are theoretically so numerous and
so great that it is somewhat surprising to find how well people get
along in actual practice. We get along because, consciously or unconsciously, most of us apply a few tests to the validity or truth of
the evidence we hear. When a speaker undertakes to influence other
people's attitudes, it is his obligation to test the truth of his proposed
evidence systematically and rigorously. It is also to his advantage
to do so.

2. TESTS OF AUTHORITY Since most public speaking evidence is testimonial, the qualifications of the authorities used in a speech become of critical importance. An authority is the person or persons responsible for the truth of a given piece of evidence. Sometimes a speaker himself is the authority; frequently, however, a speaker quotes somebody else. The qualifications of authorities can be tested by applying these three questions:

1. Is the authority competent?
2. Is the authority biased?
3. Is the evidence of the authority consistent?

a. Competence. The competence of an authority must, of course, be evaluated in the light of the particular evidence for which he is responsible. For example, we should immediately ask if this particular evidence requires an expert. If you were giving a speech on cancer research, for example, and you wanted to introduce evidence on the efficacy of radiology treatments, a layman's opinion would not be competent, nor even the testimony of a general practitioner. The authority should be a specialist. In the same speech, however, if you wanted to introduce evidence showing the devastating effects of cancer on a victim's relatives, the testimony of an unskilled laborer impoverished by his wife's illness would be competent.

In a speech on cancer research, if you are a college student, you have to rely on other authorities for most of your evidence. It would be unnecessary and impractical, however, for you to document every fact and opinion in the talk. You, the speaker, can be responsible for the truth of some of your evidence. In general, you can be responsible for evidence that conforms closely with general public knowledge and human experience. For example, you might say, "More than a third of a million people die of cancer each year in the United States," or, "Cancer strikes on an average in one of every two homes." Probably most listeners would consider you competent to report such evidence without explaining the exact source of the figures, for it is widely known that cancer takes a staggering toll.

b. Bias. The question of bias is the second test of an authority. You can usually classify available authorities as probably biased in favor of or against your subject, or as probably unbiased. An authority who is prejudiced in favor of your proposal should be used with caution. It is better for you to eliminate a dubious authority than to have your audience reject him. The probability of truth is increased not only when an authority is unbiased, but also when an authority testifies *against* his apparent prejudices. For example, suppose you were discussing the proposition, "Should Musicians Be Unionized?" The national president of the American Federation of Musicians would quite naturally be biased in favor of unionization. To quote him on that side of the question would carry little weight. However, if an accurate quotation from him against some aspect of unionization could be found, the qualification of the authority would be high. Meanwhile, evidence from the United States Bureau of Labor Statistics would probably be considered an unbiased source.

c. Consistency. The third test is consistency. Is the authority consistent with himself? Is he consistent with other authorities? Is he consistent with ordinary human experience? If a senator's statement of yesterday contradicts a statement he made last year, or contradicts his voting record on relevant bills, his qualifications as an authority are impaired. When a fact or opinion seems to contradict common knowledge, the authority must be scrutinized carefully—if you do not do it, your audience will.

On most controversial subjects, however, well-known leaders and even unbiased experts are likely to contradict one another. In a sense that is what makes a subject controversial. When authorities disagree, the issue must be settled by weighing comparative probabilities and making choices. Of two sets of evidence, which is more extensive, more pertinent, more reliable? In answering such questions, both the speaker and the listeners will be assisted by applying the tests of competency, bias, and consistency.

Reasoning

The logical validity of a proposition involves the speaker's reasoning as well as his evidence. The ability to reason accurately from the evidence is probably the most important single characteristic of an effective speaker.

Psychologists are not unanimous in their definitions of reasoning. One definition is that reasoning is mental experiment in which symbols are substituted for real objects or events. An example from Galileo is often cited to illustrate the definition. In Galileo's day it was thought that a heavier object would fall faster than a lighter one. Galileo reflected that if two bricks of equal size and weight were dropped side by side, they should fall at the same velocity. If they were attached together, doubling their weight, should the two bricks fall twice as fast? Galileo reasoned no. Then he experimented by dropping objects from the tower of Pisa, and found that attached bricks fell at the same velocity as separate ones. His mental experiments were verified.

Reasoning has also been described as the detection of relationships. In the example of Galileo the reasoning could be called a symbolic comparison of probable relationships between weight and velocity.

1. INDUCTIVE REASONING   Inductive reasoning is usually defined as the thought process in which reasoning moves from the specific to the general. If the evidence indicates that this case, this case, and this case are true, you reason that in consequence a general principle is true. However, the validity of inductive reasoning requires checking. For example, since Washington, Adams, Jefferson, Madison, and every other president of the United States were all men, you can reason inductively that all our presidents have been men. However, you cannot conclude that American presidents must be men or that all of them in the future will be men. If many municipally owned electrical companies charge lower rates than many privately owned companies, you can reason inductively that municipally owned companies on the average charge lower rates than privately owned companies. But can you conclude that all municipally owned plants are cheaper than all privately owned ones? Or that cheapness of rates is not offset by differences in quality of service, or taxes?

2. DEDUCTIVE REASONING   Deductive reasoning is defined as a thought process in which reasoning moves from the general to the specific. If one general principle is true of certain instances, that general principle must apply to similar instances. Aristotle invented the syllogism to express and to test the deductive type of reasoning. A syllogism contains three terms: the major premise, the minor premise, and the conclusion. A standard example:

All men are mortal (major premise).
Socrates is a man (minor premise).
Therefore, Socrates is mortal (conclusion).

For two thousand years the syllogism dominated logic, but in recent years it has been subjected to criticism. In light of modern criticism of the syllogism it seems fair to say that a mastery of the syllogism is unnecessary for beginning students of speech. Instead, in practice two tests can be applied. First, if you introduce a general principle, is it actually true or accepted as true? Second, is your specific case relevant to the general principle? The answers to both questions are matters of common sense.

3. REASONING BY ANALOGY Analogy is a thought process in which reasoning moves from the specific to the specific, or from the general to the general, by comparing or contrasting two items or concepts. The conclusion depends on whether the resemblances outweigh the differences, or the reverse. There are two types of analogies. First there is the literal analogy. You compare the municipal services, say, of city X, which adopted a city manager plan of government, with those of city Y, which did not. This may be used as a proof, the validity of which will depend on whether X and Y are sufficiently similar in all relevant respects. Second, there is the figurative analogy. A student speaker condemned modern advertising on the ground that it reveals only one side of the story, and illustrated his point by holding up a wooden box, which he praised in advertising lingo. Having "sold" the box, the speaker turned it around so that the audience could see that the back of the box had been crushed. Another student who spoke immediately afterward, gave a rebuttal: "Advertisers must sell more than one piece of merchandise. Suppose you had bought this box. After finding the broken side, would you ever buy another one? Not from *this* advertiser!" Thus the second student turned the analogy around by pointing out a difference that the first speaker had failed to see. Figurative analogies are almost always open to such attacks and should usually be used only to illustrate, not to prove.

4. CAUSAL REASONING Causal reasoning is similar to analogy in that the thought process moves from the specific to the specific, or from the general to the general. You reason from cause to effect when you say, "If this law is passed, taxes will rise." You reason from effect to cause when you say, "Where there's smoke, there's fire." Probably the most common abuse of causal reasoning is the fallacy known as *post hoc, ergo propter hoc* (after this, therefore because of this). Just because one thing follows another does not necessarily mean that the first causes the second. Superstitions, for example, illustrate the *post hoc* error: A black cat crosses your path and an hour later you break your wrist watch; *ergo*, the black cat was the cause of your bad luck.

The foregoing kinds of reasoning can be used by the student either while planning the structure of a speech or while testing the validity of the first draft of the outline. In planning or testing the logic of a speech, pay particular attention to the transitions. Transitions show relationships and, as we have seen, relationships are the heart of reasoning.

PSYCHOLOGICAL VALIDITY

Your evidence and reasoning may be sound, yet you may put your audience to sleep, or antagonize them. To build a new audience attitude you must relate your evidence and reasoning to the listeners' drives, motives, or existing attitudes.

Mild emotions, such as moods and feelings, are always with us— they are part of being alive. Occasionally our moods or feelings flare up into anger, fear, grief, or joy. If emotions do not become too intense, they may reinforce our beliefs and actions. But intense emotions disorganize our behavior, and are likely to boomerang against a speaker who plays upon them. For example, during World War II a speaker appealing for blood donations illustrated his talk with films showing closeups (with sound) of rough surgery being performed near a battle front. The films aroused intense emotions. Some members of the audience turned their eyes and held their ears, some were nauseated, two or three fainted. The result was that these intense emotions prevented many of the listeners from giving blood.

Intense audience emotions are difficult to arouse, unnecessary, undesirable, and sometimes disastrous in speeches to build attitudes. Milder emotions are usually helpful, but should be considered by-products by a speaker. Ordinary audience emotions will take care of themselves if the speaker can relate his proposal to drives, motives, and existing attitudes.

Drives

Drives set people in motion. Consider the hunger drive. When you need food, the internal stimuli of hunger drive you to action. If you were hungry in a completely strange environment, you would be driven to indulge in random exploratory activity until food was found.

There are, however, only a few drives. Psychologists have not agreed on the exact number, but following is a generally accepted list of basic drives: hunger, thirst, sex, fatigue, sleepiness, exploration, visceral tensions (as of bladder or bowels), and internal reactions to pain, heat, and cold. Drives are about the same for everyone. They are a common denominator of human behavior.

We learn through drives to satisfy our most basic needs, because drives determine the direction of hundreds of attitudes and habits. For example, imagine that somehow all your drives were suddenly reversed. Instead of approaching food, you would avoid it; instead of avoiding hot objects, you would seize them; and instead of withdrawing from approaching traffic, you would step in front of it. What would happen? You would soon be dead.

In times of distress or disaster, demagogues and other public speakers can appeal directly to drives, since when in distress we drop our civilized trappings and react more obviously in direct response to our drives. Witness, for example, the lying, fighting, and cheating in connection with food rationing during World War II; or the stampedes that occur in buildings that catch on fire; or the riots in communities stricken by famine or drought.

In normal times, however, the influence of drives is only indirectly observable, and appeals to drives should be made only indirectly by public speakers. For instance, members of an ordinary audience are seldom starving through an inability to secure food, so a direct appeal to the hunger drive by a speaker would usually be absurd. However, a speech favoring a new irrigation dam might indirectly appeal to audience drives because of the promise of avoiding future possible food shortages or floor disasters. Therefore an understanding of our biological drives is important to the speaker, because drives are the foundation upon which we build, through learning, a vast structure of motives and attitudes.

Motives

Motives may be described as learned responses by which drives are likely to be satisfied. Making money, for example, is a motive. We learn during childhood that money can be used to satisfy the hunger drive, among others. Therefore, we work eight hours a day, motivated mainly by the desire to make money.

Motives are learned, but people vary in their learning capacities and opportunities. Because motives are learned and because each drive may be satisfied in many different ways, each individual acquires numerous motives. Because people are different and their environments are different, motives vary from one person to another and from one social grouping to another. Despite the fact that motives vary greatly among individuals, a basic list of motives common in our society follows.

1. To make money
2. To be healthy
3. To avoid danger
4. To be attractive to the opposite sex
5. To get married
6. To beget and rear children

7. To care for one's parents
8. To have friends and companions
9. To enjoy physical comforts
10. To gain social approval
11. To conform to customs and traditions
12. To have personal freedom
13. To maintain self-respect
14. To have a clear conscience and peace of mind
15. To satisfy curiosity
16. To have adventures
17. To compete successfully against other people
18. To help other people
19. To have a worthwhile religion
20. To achieve ideals

The foregoing list or a similar one is essential in planning a talk to build attitudes. Decide upon the attitude you want to encourage in your listeners, and ask yourself, "Will my proposal make or save money for my audience? Will it keep them healthy? Will it protect them from danger?" And proceed to work through the list of motives. Unless the answer is "yes" on one or more of these questions, you might as well not give the talk.

The use of the list of motives just given requires judgment on the speaker's part. The list does not include all possible motives, and some of the motives listed overlap or fuse. Furthermore, one motive may move one person but not another. In planning a talk, however, the speaker must consider how to relate his proposition, his points, and his supports to motives existing in his particular audience on this particular subject at this particular time and occasion.

Attitudes

Having considered motives, you should make the next step in planning and testing the psychological strength of your speech to relate your proposal to particular audience attitudes. Three types of attitudes should be studied: attitudes toward your topic, toward related topics, and toward you.

1. ATTITUDES TOWARD THE TOPIC   When your purpose is to build new audience attitudes, it is important to estimate the probable attitudes toward your topic before the speech is given. Ideally you would give your audience an attitude test when preparing your speech, and each member would mark a ballot such as this:

I favor the proposal	strongly	☐
	moderately	☐
	mildly	☐
I am undecided		☐
I oppose the proposal	mildly	☐
	moderately	☐
	strongly	☐

Of course, a direct administration of ballots to a prospective audience is seldom practical. Sometimes, however, you can estimate the attitudes by sounding out several representative members of the audience beforehand. If direct inquiry is impractical, estimate the probable distribution of attitudes from indirect evidence, such as common traits and interests. Who are these people: Catholics, Republicans, Boy Scouts, war veterans, college students, blacks, home owners, Rotarians, unionists, farmers, or members of the Benevolent and Protective Order of Elks? A good guess can be made of the attitudes of almost any group on almost any speech proposal.[3]

Having estimated existing audience attitudes toward your proposal, if you and some of the audience are at odds, consider how to change their attitudes. Ideally you would supplement your pre-speech attitude test with a postspeech test using a ballot such as this:

I favor the proposal	more than before	☐
	about the same	☐
	less than before	☐
I am undecided		☐
I oppose the proposal	less than before	☐
	about the same	☐
	more than before	☐

Let us reiterate that pre- and post-tests need not actually be given in order to apply the principle. You can imagine that the ballots were given. The advantage of ballots, real or imaginary, is that you can see them or visualize them, and by making the principle specific and concrete you can understand the process of building attitudes.

[3] See Chapter 11.

By contrast, you may have only a vague abstract idea if you think in general of the process of building attitudes, because there are usually no observable behaviors when a person is changing his mind or being convinced. As we have shown, then, when your purpose is to convince, you first state your purpose in terms of building attitudes, and then visualize that purpose in terms of shifts of opinion.

2. ATTITUDES TOWARD RELATED TOPICS The audience's attitudes toward related topics are as important as their attitudes toward your particular proposal. New attitudes are never built in a vacuum; they are built upon or added to old attitudes. Suppose your listener already holds beliefs A, B, and C. You try to get him to agree that if (or since) A, B, and C are true, therefore D (proposed new belief) must also be true. Or likewise, if (or since) A, B, and C are not true, therefore (negatively) D must be true.

The role of attitudes toward related topics is especially crucial when the attitude toward your proposal is undecided. On important controversial questions, "undecided" almost always means "conflicting," for the listener has one or more related attitudes predisposing him in favor of your proposition and one or more pulling him in another direction, in a sort of internal tug of war. For example, according to leading pollsters, a significant and sometimes decisive percentage of voters remains undecided up until the last week or two of a presidential campaign. For most of them this does not mean that they are neutral or that they are apathetic. It means that they are torn between conflicting attitudes. Thus a voter may dislike a candidate but approve of his proposed policies; or vice versa. The voter may favor the foreign policies of a candidate but dislike his domestic policies; or vice versa. The voter may like both candidates but is fearful of the top advisors surrounding both. Thus you can see that indecision is likely to be an active, dynamic, and even painful state. Furthermore, it is not enough merely to say, "He is undecided because of a conflict in his attitudes." The additional question is, "*What* attitudes?" If you can figure those out, you are well on your way to planning the best psychological approach.

When, however, your audience consists mainly of opposed, rather than undecided, listeners, your vital need becomes finding an opening wedge. Related attitudes can provide that wedge. Your listener, for example, may strongly oppose socialized medicine and vehemently denounce mixing politics with medical care. But wait a moment! What are his attitudes toward the work of the Public Health Service? Toward county nurses? Toward the nearby state hospital? Toward the city's department of sanitation? These and other agencies provide samples of government-controlled medical care. Since he is likely to approve of some of these, you can use that approval as an opening wedge against his initial resistance to your argument.

3. ATTITUDES TOWARD THE SPEAKER The check list (on page 214) of possible attitudes toward a speaker is of particular importance when his purpose is to convince. In a nutshell the issue is: Will you as a person arouse approval or resistance in your listeners? Approval may be defined as an attitude of a listener that predisposes him to accept almost anything the speaker says. Resistance is the predisposition to reject. A speaker's prestige or credibility actually derives from an attitude within the listener.

The speaker provides the stimulus that sets the audience attitudes into operation. The stimulus may be any known aspect of the speaker: his physique, voice, dress, reputation, age, sex, or race. Approval or resistance involves a dynamic relationship between listener and speaker. For example, your age may be a source of approval with a younger audience, or a source of resistance with an older group. If you are a college student twenty years old, you may be looked up to as an authority by high school students of fifteen, but you may be regarded as a young whippersnapper by businessmen of fifty. Increase or decrease the speaker's age, or the audience's age, and the attitudes of approval or resistance will probably vary accordingly.

OUTLINING THE SPEECH TO BUILD ATTITUDES

Planning and testing your speech in terms of logical and psychological validity does not mean that you should abandon the six-step procedure for outlining.[4] In speeches to build attitudes, however, as you follow the six steps, you should test your outline in two ways: (1) *Analyze* the points, supports, and transitions from the standpoints of evidence and reasoning; and (2) *adapt* the points, supports, and transitions to the drives, motives, and existing attitudes of the particular audience. During the remainder of this chapter we shall see how the principles of logical and psychological validity can be applied to speech organization.

[4] See Chapters 6 and 7.

The Design

You begin the organization of your speech by choosing the central idea and main points. Two approaches to the choice of central idea and main points in speeches to convince will be called the direct and indirect approaches. The *direct* approach may be characterized as follows:

1. You state the attitude you favor early in the talk.
2. You preview your reasons.
3. You prove your contentions forthrightly by evidence and reasoning.
4. You rely on support featuring expert authorities and statistics.
5. Your delivery is straight from the shoulder and forceful.

The *indirect* approach has been described by Benjamin Franklin:

> The way to convince another is to state your case moderately and accurately. Then scratch your head, or shake it a little and say that is the way it seems to you, but that of course you may be mistaken about it; which causes your listener to receive what you have to say, and as like as not, turn about and try to convince you of it, since you are in doubt. But if you go at him in a tone of positiveness and arrogance you only make an opponent of him.

Contrast the indirect approach with the direct. Which is better? It depends on your audience and your subject. In some circumstances the direct approach may be received as arrogant, as Franklin suggests, but under other circumstances the indirect approach may be condemned as pussyfooting or dodging the issue.

It is well to follow the rule that to argue directly with an opponent not only fails to convince him, but usually antagonizes him. However, you may be willing to antagonize your opponents in order to influence third parties. That is, the direct approach may be preferable when most of your listeners are undecided, while only a few are opposed. You sacrifice a few votes in order to gain many.

On the whole, however, the indirect approach recommended by Benjamin Franklin is more frequently useful than direct argument. The indirect approach is suggested for speeches in which you are talking to people whose attitudes you seek to change. Indirect arguments for such audiences are your only hope. Check your own experience against this assertion. Can you recollect any "knock-'em-down and drag-'em-out" argument with anybody in which you actually conceded that you were wrong and shifted over to your opponent's point of view? More likely you got angry and defended your original position, right or wrong.

Between these two extremes are many choices, combining in varying degrees the direct and indirect approaches. A study of the transcripts of the Kennedy-Nixon debates of 1960 shows a combination of approaches. Because of the debate situation they were forced to use direct arguments with each other, but when they addressed the voter public both Kennedy and Nixon tended to use more moderate appeals. Both candidates realized the risk in antagonizing undecided voters.

1. THE DESIGN FOR DIRECT ARGUMENT One useful method for building a direct argument is by applying an appropriate stock speech design. As suggested in Chapter 6, a stock speech design is a pattern of points that is applicable to many different subjects. A direct argument either for or against many proposals can often be adapted from a stock design that has four key words: need, desirability, practicality, and alternatives. This design implies a comparison between the speaker's proposal and the *status quo*—the existing system or attitude. One way of elaborating this design is as follows:

I.   Is there a need for a change?
    A.   Are there existing or threatened evils?
    B.   Are these evils due to the present system?
II. Is the proposed change desirable?
    A.   Will it eliminate or alleviate the evils?
    B.   Will it provide additional advantages?
    C.   Will it avoid new or greater evils?
III. Is the proposal practical?
    A.   Can it be satisfactorily financed and administered?
    B.   Will it satisfy interest groups involved?
    C.   Have similar systems succeeded in the past?
IV. Is the proposal better than possible alternatives?
    A.   Is it more desirable?
    B.   Is it more practical?

The foregoing design can help you build a direct argument that is both logically and psychologically sound. The first step in using the design is to apply logical analysis to the proposal. If you are proposing that the United States should adopt a policy of free trade, you begin by analyzing the present tariff policy or *status quo*, asking yourself if there is a need for a change from the present policy. You jot down a list of evils or dangers resulting from the tariff policy. These are your potential subpoints under "need." The analysis is of the subject matter without reference to any particular audience. Using the stock design to guide your thinking, you continue to analyze tariffs and free trade until you have gone through the entire list of questions. The list protects you against the danger of overlooking any important logical points. In fact, you are likely to conclude your analysis by finding that you have listed too many points and subpoints for a single speech.

The second step in using the stock design is to adapt it psychologically to your particular audience. From the list of possible points and subpoints just compiled, choose some and word them in terms of audience drives, motives, and existing attitudes. For instance, you would hardly say to an audience, "The lack of adequate traffic supervision on our main highway has introduced many existing and threatened evils." You would translate the point into audience language, and "existing evils" would become, "At least one auto accident has occurred on our main highway since we began our meeting an hour ago." And "threatened evils" would become, "When you next take your family for a drive on our main highway, you may become one of the twenty-five people a day who...."

In the foregoing fashion you plan a design that meets the impersonal tests of logic, and you then translate it into points and language that will be interesting, clear, and impelling. Review these points early in your speech so your listeners will be able to see the whole pattern and feel that it is a logical one. They can then follow you step by step as you develop each argument.

2. THE DESIGN FOR INDIRECT ARGUMENT   One of the most useful stock designs for an indirect argument is that of problem-solution. One way of elaborating this design is as follows:

I. Analysis of problem
    A. Is there a serious problem?
    B. What is the nature of the problem?
    C. What are its causes?
    D. What are the obstacles to its solution?
II. Finding a solution
    A. What are the possible solutions?
    B. By what criteria should solutions be evaluated?
    C. How do the several possible solutions compare in terms of these criteria?
    D. What should be the final choice?

Notice that this design applies regardless of whether you plan to speak for or against a given proposal, and that you can use the design in the same way described for direct argument—that is, analyze and adapt. Analyze in terms of subject matter; then translate into terms of audience motivation.

The problem-solution design leads to a speech outline that will give you at least a fighting chance to change an opponent's mind. You begin with what John Dewey has called "a felt need," which occurs when some drive or motive has been thwarted. You help the listener analyze this thwarting and help him to review the ways of satisfying his thwarted drives. Then you suggest criteria drawn from his existing knowledge and beliefs, and help him apply these criteria to two or more of the possible solutions. If you are successful, the listener will himself have built a new attitude that will replace his former one.

SUPPORTS

After choosing main points and subpoints in accordance with the designs suggested for direct and indirect argument, supports for the points must be found.

The bare statement of a point is rarely enough to insure that all the listeners will understand clearly and accurately. They may read in a meaning different from what you intend. Therefore it is sometimes necessary to clarify a point as a preliminary to proving it.

As it has already been pointed out, an indispensable technique in attitude-building is the establishment of relationships between old and proposed new attitudes. It is often wise to reinforce an existing attitude before going on to relate it to the new proposal.

However, the characteristic role of the supports in talks to convince is to prove. You can employ explanation, description, and anecdotes to prove, but more frequently you need instances, statistics, and quotations. Logically, those supports are chosen that best fit this formula: If these supports are true, therefore, the point must be true. Psychologically, those supports are chosen that relate most closely to the listeners' existing knowledge and beliefs.

Suppose, for example, that you are planning a talk favoring national health insurance and that one of your main points is that our present system of medical care is financially unfair. You might begin the support with a brief explanation to clarify the phrase "present system of medical care." Then you might give a description of a person's reactions to the receipt of a devastating doctor bill, in order to reinforce the audience's unfavorable attitude toward anything that is unfair. Next you might relate an anecdote that would reinforce the distaste for anything unfair, and in addition begin the proof by establishing at least one case of unfairness in paying the doctor bills. "But this is not an *exceptional* case," you would say by way of introducing a series of brief instances that are definitely intended as proof of unfairness. "In fact," you continue, "this sort of unfairness is typical of our whole nation. Just look at these statistics that were recently compiled by such-and-such highly reliable agency." The statistics, of course, are also cited as proof. "Finally," you say, "let me quote Dr. Richard Ek," and you establish Dr. Richard Ek as qualified and unbiased, quoting him as saying that the present system is financially unfair. The quotation concludes your proof.

If the anecdote, the instances, the statistics, and the quotation are all true, it follows that the point must be true. However, some listeners may not be convinced of the soundness of your argument, for supports prove the point *only for the listeners who think so.*

What makes them think so? Relationship to their own previous experiences. That is why anecdotes are so often accepted as proof. Logically, an anecdote is poor proof. But it is easier to relate anecdotes than statistics, for example, to the listeners' past experience. Choose your proofs logically but also choose them psychologically. Look for supports that will be "true" to the listeners' experience.

For an example of an effective attempt to tie a point of view to the listeners' experience, study the following opening of an address by Oscar Ewing, a Federal Security Administrator who was in favor of national health insurance. This speech, on a problem that has continued in the public eye for many years, was broadcast over a national hookup to a large and heterogeneous audience.

> Good evening. I want to talk to you tonight, not about the nation's health, but about your own health. Suppose that tomorrow morning, you should become suddenly ill—seriously ill. Suppose you found that you needed an operation, with special medical care, and all kinds of x-rays and drugs. Suppose you had to stop working for some months while you went through your operation and your convalescence. Suppose the doctor's bill, the hospital bill, and bills for special laboratory services and medicines, added up to hundreds of dollars—maybe even thousands. Would you be able to afford it?
>
> If you are like most other people in this country, I can tell you the answer just as quickly as you would tell it to me if I were sitting there in the room beside you. The answer, for most of us, is one word: No.
>
> Most of us are neither very rich nor very poor. People who are very rich don't need to worry about their medical bills, any more than they need to worry about whatever other bills they run up. On the other hand, people who are very poor do generally get medical treatment in the United States, because we have charity care which does make doctors and hospitals available to the real needy. But, if you are like the majority of Americans, you are somewhere between those two extremes. You've got a job. You've got your self-respect. And you like to stand on your own two feet. But you're not made of money; and when sickness strikes, when you wake up one morning with acute appendicitis, or when your old folks get sick, or when your child comes home from school restless and feverish, you have two worries—your first worry is that they should get the best treatment in town; and your second worry is how you're going to pay for it.

If you have ever been lying in a hospital bed after an operation worrying about where the money to pay the bills would come from, you know what I mean. If you have had to go to a loan company and borrow money to pay a hospital bill, you know what I mean. If you have ever received a note from your child's school, telling you that your little boy or your little girl needs adenoids or tonsils out, and wondered how you'd pay for it, you know what I mean. If your wife has noticed a lump in her breast, but puts off going to the doctor because of the cost, you'll know—and she'll know—what I mean.[5]

Notice that Mr. Ewing's hypothetical anecdote and descriptions provided excellent probability that many listeners would find similarities to their own personal experiences. Also notice that in less than three minutes Mr. Ewing touched on at least seven motives. Can you spot them?

The Introduction

The importance of the opening portion of a talk to build attitudes is illustrated by your own experiences in listening to other people. Suppose you are opposed to national health insurance and a public speaker is trying to persuade you to change your mind. His chances for success are likely to be made or broken within the first minutes of his talk. If the opening is dull, your mind will wander to other matters, and he will be defeated by competing stimuli. If you feel a personal dislike for the speaker, you will actively resist accepting his ideas—"I wouldn't like him even if he was good." If you decide that the speaker is poorly informed or biased on the subject of health insurance, you set up a mental barrier against what he is about to say. If the opening words are, "I intend to speak tonight in favor of socialized medicine," the speaker puts you on guard, in the position of being his opponent, and you immediately set out to find rebuttals to all his coming arguments.

On the other hand, if the opening is interesting, if the speaker is likable and has prestige, and if he begins with some aspect of the subject with which you can agree, then he may be able to get you to change your attitude toward his proposal. For an example of an effective introduction in a talk to build attitudes we may refer back to Mr. Oscar Ewing's remarks just quoted. All three functions of a good opening were fulfilled.

Study especially how he led into his subject. Mr. Ewing was defending the then-unpopular side of a controversial question, so he sought to begin on common ground—a most important fact to remember about introductions to talks to convince.[6] Mr. Ewing did

---

[5] Harold F. Harding, ed., *The Age of Danger: Major Speeches on American Problems,* Random House, 1952, pp. 350–51. Reprinted by permission of Oscar Ewing.
[6] For a discussion of the common-ground principle, see Chapter 11.

not mention the words "national health insurance" nor directly touch on anything with which most listeners could disagree. Could you raise several hundreds or even thousands of dollars right now? Of course you couldn't. If you were sick, would you worry about the doctor bill? Of course you would. Do you want to protect the health of your children, that of the old folks, and of your wife? Of course you do.

The Conclusion

Mr. Ewing brought his entire speech into focus when he concluded with two rhetorical questions and a restatement of his central idea:

> What would health insurance mean to you? It would mean that, when someone asks you, as I ask you, "Can you get all the medical care you and your family really need?" you could answer with confidence and relief, "Yes, under national health insurance I can."

The most common way of closing an attitude-building talk is a summary, followed by a restatement of the belief you have tried to establish. However, you may be trying not only to build an attitude, but also to release the attitude. If so, additional processes and techniques must be considered. These additional considerations may influence the whole structure of the speech; they drastically influence the speech conclusion.

SUMMARY

To convince means to build audience attitudes. Fundamentally, listeners must always build their own attitudes; however, a speaker can provide the audience with reasons and motives for building an attitude.

In a speech to build attitudes the materials should be evaluated from both the logical and the psychological points of view. The logical is in terms of the subject matter; the psychological is in terms of audience response. Each speech or part of a speech should be judged from both points of view, not from the either-or point of view.

Logical validity involves evidence and reasoning. Evidence is anything which can be found to be true by the senses; reasoning is the process of drawing inferences from evidence. The major types of evidence are facts and opinions. The major types of reasoning are inductive, deductive, causal, and reasoning by analogy.

Psychological validity involves drives, motives, and existing audience attitudes. The speaker should avoid confusing *emotion* with *motivation.* Existing attitudes include attitudes toward your topic, toward related topics, and toward you.

In outlining talks to build attitudes there are two basic designs, the indirect and the direct. The indirect design is usually better when talking with persons whose attitudes are opposed to yours. The direct design is usually better when arguing before persons whose attitudes are neutral or undecided. A basic suggestion is to look for common ground.

TOPICAL PREVIEW

16
Releasing Audience Attitudes

"LET'S ALL SING!"

In 1928, a psychology student attended a revival meeting led by Aimee Semple McPherson, a world-famous woman evangelist who founded her own church and attracted many thousands of converts. The psychology student went to study crowd behavior, and later wrote a paper detailing his observations.

One had to go early to get a seat, although the auditorium accommodated several thousand persons. While the congregation waited for the services to begin, they were entertained by music from a pipe organ, orchestra, choir, and male quartet. The quartet sang a number making fun of the devil, which had the crowd laughing heartily. Time passed swiftly.

Then came Aimee Semple McPherson. A spotlight followed her from the side entrance as she walked smiling to the center of the stage—a strikingly handsome woman, tall, well proportioned, and with auburn hair. She wore a long, flowing white gown. Her first words were, "Let's all sing!"

All sang. She led them. Most of the songs were lively. In one song she had all the men whistle the chorus; in another she had the whole audience clap hands to emphasize the tempo. In between the hymns she talked *with*—not *at*—the people. "How many of you folks are

Evangelist Aimee Semple McPherson was a master of the art of releasing audience attitudes. Her techniques to stimulate an audience and get overt response from them are worth studying.

visiting here in California?" she asked. "Stand up so we can welcome you." Many people stood and smiled while others applauded. She asked other questions to be answered by raising hands or standing. One that probably had special significance for the corps of ushers and other assistants was, "How many of you are visiting our church for the first time? Stand up and let us welcome you here!" After a while it seemed natural and easy to raise hands, or stand up, or participate in other active ways.

Then came the sermon. She had a husky, appealing voice and a dramatic manner. The sermon was sprinkled with vivid illustrations. She stressed again and again that you must repent and be saved. She stressed the dangers of waiting too long—you might be stricken by an auto accident on your way home this very night!

Then came the conclusion. "All those who love Jesus," she commanded, "stand up." Everybody stood. Then she said something the psychology student did not quite comprehend. He was thinking about it when most of the congregation suddenly sat down—apparently the regular members had understood the statement. Those left standing were prospective converts, and she was now pleading directly with the prospects to come to the altar. The student sat down. Meanwhile, many people were making their way down the aisles. The congregation began to sing some old revival hymns, such as "Almost Persuaded."

Aimee Semple McPherson concentrated on the group kneeling at the rail. Many people repented that night; many rose from their knees rejoicing; many joined the church. The meeting illustrated with almost brutal simplicity the mechanics of releasing audience attitudes.

RELEASING ATTITUDES

Let us think of attitudes in terms of stimulus and response. Any act by a speaker or listener can be described as a stimulus or response or both. Generally, however, the voice, language, and bodily actions of a speaker are considered stimuli, while the thoughts, emotions, and overt acts of the listeners are considered responses. As we have seen, communication is a two-way process, and stimuli and responses are reciprocal. Thus the speaker tells a joke (stimulus), and the audience laughs (response). But the audience laughter is also a stimulus. It stimulates the speaker, and members of the audience, by laughing, stimulate one another.

As we have recently learned, some stimuli are internal (hunger), and others are external (sight of food). Stimuli are also classed as directly sensory (sound of crashing thunder), and as symbolic (sound of spoken words).

Responses may also be classified as internal or external, directly sensory or symbolic. In addition, responses may be described as preparatory (watering of mouth) or consummatory (eating food). Applying this classification to attitudes, you will see that your attitude toward Russia is predominantly internal, symbolic, and preparatory. By contrast, the act of casting a vote in an election is external, directly sensory, and consummatory.

An attitude is a response; your attitude toward Russia is a response to various stimuli. An attitude is also a predisposition to further response; your attitude toward Russia will influence the way you vote on certain issues. Furthermore, the attitude itself may be considered a preparatory response; what you do as a result of an attitude may be called the consummatory response. Diagrammatically the sequence is like this:

A. *Stimulus*

↓

B. *Preparatory response*

↕

C. *Stimulus*

↓

D. *Consummatory response*

Let us put the foregoing sequence into the form of a concrete illustration. To eliminate subtleties suppose we utilize a common type of radio-TV program.

A. *Stimulus:* Pleasant sights and sounds, such as dancing and music, together with words of praise for the name of a product

B. *Preparatory response:* A favorable attitude toward the product —a predisposition to respond to a stimulus in one way rather than another, in other words, a predisposition to buy the product

C. *Stimulus:* "Go to your telephone *now* and call 534–2311. We will send you a Deluxe vacuum cleaner absolutely *free* for ten days. And if you are among the first twenty-five to call we will. . . ."

D. *Consummatory response:* You call 534–2311.

Relation to Speech Purposes

Some writers consider the release of attitudes as a fifth major speech purpose: to actuate. However, the arousal of overt actions as a response to a speech may be a part of the purpose in any talk: laughter or applause (to entertain); actual performance of a manual skill or passing a written examination (to inform); voting, signing, or buying (to convince or stimulate). In fact, it would be difficult to imagine any release of attitudes in a speech that was not preceded by entertaining, informing, convincing, or stimulating. The release of attitudes, therefore, may more readily be studied as a *part* of any of the four basic speech types.

Immediate Versus Delayed Release

Sometimes a speaker is trying to release an attitude immediately, as by calling for a vote at the conclusion of a speech at a club meeting. However, an immediate response may not be practical. If it is not, the speaker may try to release the attitude at a specific future time. For example, he may say, "And so next Tuesday when you go to your polling place be sure to vote for Sarracino for councilman"; or, "Go to your Red Cross blood-donor station tomorrow." That speaker is trying to get what we may call a delayed release.

TECHNIQUES FOR RELEASING ATTITUDES

Reinforcement

Very seldom does a speaker try to release an attitude in his very first words. You have doubtless attended a meeting where most of the audience sat in the rear of the room, leaving the front rows vacant. The chairman may have decided to ask the audience to move forward. If the chairman simply walked to the rostrum and bluntly said, "Will the people in the back of the room please fill those front rows?" he may or may not have got results. His chances for success would have been increased if he had preceded his request with a few remarks reinforcing the attitude that it would be better for all concerned if the audience sat nearer the speaker.

The first step then in releasing an attitude is to get the audience in the right mood. A listener has hundreds of attitudes but he can be aware of them only one at a time. The speaker must focus the listener's attention on the proper attitude before trying to release it.

Clarity

It is frustrating to hear a speech that gets us into a mood for action only to have the speaker conclude weakly that "something ought to be done," or "let us all firmly resolve." It is also confusing to have the speaker call for an action that we do not clearly understand; we want to act but don't know exactly what to do. Therefore, another technique for releasing attitudes is to make the audience understand exactly what they are expected to do.

One method of accomplishing this step is to describe what they are to do in concrete terms; tell them specifically when and how they are to act. Make the picture unmistakably clear. Examples:

> The ushers will pass among you with pledge slips. We ask *everyone* to take one of these slips. Take one whether or not you are able to contribute, etc.

> The wording of this resolution is complex. Do not allow that complexity to confuse the issue. When this resolution is put, vote *No*.

> When you go to the polling place next Tuesday, you will receive your ballot. In the privacy of a curtained booth, you will cast your vote. Look for Proposition Four—and mark that proposition *Yes*. I repeat—*Yes* on *Four*.

Stimulus

When you know that a listener has formed an attitude, when you are sure he knows what action is expected of him, and when you sense that he is in the mood to act, then is the time to provide the releasing stimulus. Timing is often of critical importance, but there is no formula to tell you when. An innocent remark at the wrong moment can wreck a perfect buildup. Suppose you are giving what you hope is the final pep talk to a prospective pledge for your fraternity. You feel sure that he has a favorable attitude toward your house; he knows what is expected of him to become a pledge; you are trying to create the right mood. Just as you have arrived at the psychological moment, in strolls an insensitive brother who yawns and says to your prospect, "Well, didjuh git registered today?" The magic moment is ruined.

A releasing stimulus can theoretically be anything—the howl of sirens for an air raid drill, for example. In public speaking situations, of course, a stimulus is usually verbal. Ask the audience to do something; suggest that they do it; predict they will do it; command them to do it. For example:

> And so, with deep confidence, I call upon the citizens of the state of Arkansas to assist in bringing to an immediate end all interference with the law and its processes.
> DWIGHT D. EISENHOWER

> I ask you to vote for Tom Bradley for Mayor of Los Angeles.
> THOMAS R. BRADLEY

> Give us the tools, and we will finish the job.
> WINSTON CHURCHILL

> No organization ever had a greater opportunity to do a greater service for America. No organization was ever better suited or better equipped to do the job. I know the Legion. I know what a tremendous force for good it can be. Now go to it.
> HARRY S. TRUMAN

Response

If you can get your listener to start the action you desire, he will usually go ahead with the remaining steps. It is something like opening a jar of olives—if you can get the first one out, the rest come easily. The same principle also applies when dealing with a group—if you can get one or two people to respond to your stimulus, the others are likely to follow the lead.

In releasing attitudes, therefore, it is a good rule to make the first step easy. Notice how Aimee Semple McPherson made it easy for people to raise their hands or stand up. Notice how advertisers say, "Just visit our great display of secondhand cars tonight. We don't ask you to buy—just come and look at them." Notice how political workers offer to provide transportation of voters to the polls.

This student describes and displays a questionnaire, and asks the class to give thoughtful anwers to it. She is completely successful.

Before a group, the speaker can sometimes provide the impetus for action himself. Opening a Liberty Bond Drive in World War I, for example, Woodrow Wilson publicly bought a fifty-dollar bond and challenged the people to match it.

If your cause is just, and if your speech has been well received, you can be certain that at least a few members of the audience will respond immediately and enthusiastically. If a few contribute, you can be sure that others will also. The sight and sound of others responding is a powerful stimulus in releasing attitudes.

Of course, no speaker can rightfully or safely call for an immediate and public response from his listeners unless he is sure that the requested action is reasonable and morally right. On the other hand, a speaker neglects his duty if he permits a worthy cause to die because of inertia. People like to build strong attitudes, based on evidence, reasoning, and decent motives, and they welcome the leader who will show them how to turn their beliefs into worthwhile actions. Nevertheless, whenever a speaker attempts to influence the behavior or beliefs of an audience, the question of ethics is likely to be raised.

THE SPEAKER'S ETHICAL RESPONSIBILITY

"I don't admire Barbara Graham at all—she's not my kind of a girl. But she's not on trial for that. She's on trial for murder." Thus spoke Attorney Jack Hardy to the jury. Mr. Hardy was the court-appointed lawyer defending the "beautiful blonde" with the "icy composure" who was accused of murdering and robbing an elderly lady. During the highly publicized trial the prosecution forced Barbara Graham to admit perjury and various other crimes and immoralities. While in jail she attempted to negotiate a false alibi, but the alibi man turned out to be a police officer who managed to get a voice recording of the negotiations. The recording revealed that Barbara Graham was asked if her lawyer knew about the attempt to fake an alibi. She said no, and added that she knew her lawyer would never approve. When the recording was played in court, Hardy was indignant that the police had questioned his integrity and had placed his professional reputation at the mercy of an admitted perjurer.

Now what would you say were Hardy's ethical responsibilities in that trial? He was outraged that anyone should even raise the question of his condoning false evidence. He knew, as all of us know, that a speaker's first responsibility is to speak the truth. Honesty is best because it is ethically right, but Hardy's experience illustrates also that honesty is best because it is practical. The penalties for false evidence are shattering. One detected instance can wreck the career of a lawyer, businessman, politician, teacher, or any other person. Dishonesty simply is not worth the risk.

Let us consider a second ethical question. Hardy was appointed by the court to defend Barbara Graham, a woman he did not "admire . . . at all." He was receiving no fee from his client, and he was endangering his professional reputation, as we have seen. Was not Hardy's first obligation to himself and his family? Should he not have feigned illness in order to avoid his duty? No. That would have been passing the buck to some other court-appointed attorney. In our country there are responsibilities that cannot be dodged by not speaking.

Here is a third question. What if Hardy had decided that his client was guilty? Should he then have pulled his punches in order that justice might prevail? No. In this country we believe that a person is innocent until proved guilty, and that he is entitled to have his case presented without prejudice in court. Hardy's responsibility was to present all the evidence there was in Mrs. Graham's favor, and to say everything that could honestly be said in her defense. The prosecution's responsibility was to present evidence and arguments against her. After hearing both sides, the jury's responsibility was to return a verdict. Such is the way of our system of courtroom justice. We extend the same principle to other controversies. We believe, for example, in the right of a minority to be heard. Usually, of course, a speaker defends people or causes in which he believes. Sometimes, however, it is necessary and ethical for a speaker to say, "I do not necessarily believe or disbelieve in this side of the controversy, but I do believe that its arguments should be heard."

It was Hardy's moral right and duty to introduce all the legitimate evidence he could find in his client's favor; to present legitimate reasoning in her behalf; and to try to relate his arguments to the legitimate motives of the jurors. "Motives?" you exclaim. Certainly. All speaking involves motives; our greatest and noblest speeches have motivated audiences. But notice that we said *legitimate* motives, *legitimate* evidence, *legitimate* reasoning. So you ask, "What is meant by legitimate?" There is no easy answer—each instance must be decided on its own merits, and often there is room for honest difference of opinion. For example, at one point in his closing plea Hardy was interrupted by a strenuous objection from the prosecution. Judge Fricke remarked mildly that "in the fervor of final argument" some allowances could be made. Hardy's responsibility for deciding upon the legitimacy of his words was shared by the judge, the opposing lawyers, and the jury. The ethical principles illustrated by Attorney Jack Hardy's defense of Barbara Graham apply to all speech communication.

In our nation freedom of speech is not only permitted, it is encouraged. A full discussion of common problems is necessary for the success of the democratic system. Each of us must expect to face situations where a failure to speak, and to speak well, will violate a moral obligation. Usually we can expect to speak only in defense of opinions in which we believe, but democracy sometimes requires that men present viewpoints that they do not necessarily share, but that would not otherwise be represented. Those of us who have the opportunity to secure sufficient training have an ethical responsibility to discharge the difficult task of the "court- (or conscience-) appointed" speaker.

Since we believe in this country that everyone has a right to speak his own thoughts, we expect in return that each person will respect the rights of others to be heard. We expect each group to check and balance opposing groups, but to do it responsibly, to uphold the principle of "Her Majesty's Loyal Opposition."

Finally, in this nation we impose on every citizen the obligation of being a vigilant listener. He must be willing to hear both sides. He must demand high standards of all the speakers. He must weigh the conflicting evidence and reasoning. He must decide whether motives are legitimate. He is the jury and must return the final verdict.

If you and I speak with honesty, if we respect the right of others to be heard, if we assume responsibility for our spoken words, and if we are vigilant listeners, we have earned the right to attempt to influence others' beliefs. Then there is nothing wrong with speaking to convince—it would be wrong not to speak.

SUMMARY

Sometimes a speaker's job is to build an audience attitude, or to reinforce one. Occasionally the speaker is expected also to release an attitude into overt action. He may want to secure either an immediate response or a delayed response. For either the methods are the same.

There are four ways of increasing your effectiveness in the releasing of audience attitudes: (1) Reinforce the attitude to be released. (2) Be sure the expected response is clearly understood. (3) Provide the releasing stimulus. (4) Make sure of a prompt response by one or more members of the audience.

The ethics of speaking to influence the behavior of others depends not on the speaking but on the speaker. The same principle applies when anyone fails to speak for a worthy cause.

The photo helps us to visualize the concept of interaction—the commingling of speaking and listening.

Speaker-Listener Interaction

TOPICAL PREVIEW

I Our noisy society

II Characteristics of listening
    A Activity
    B Multiple Stimuli
    C Selectivity
    D Interpretation
    E Rapidity

III Management of listening
    A Plan a program for practice
    B Be responsive
    C Listen purposively
    D Control your attention
    E Evaluate objectively
        1. Be wary of first impressions
        2. Cross-check your accumulated impressions
        3. Compare evaluations with other listeners
        4. Test what the speaker says against external facts

IV Summary

Listening

OUR NOISY SOCIETY

The first notable fact about listening is that we do so much of it. There are well over 100 million telephones in use in the United States, about 99 percent of wired households have television sets, the TV sets are in operation for an average of over six hours daily, and there are substantially more radios in America than people. In our increasingly urbanized, industrialized, and electronic era, we have indeed become a noisy society.

If you keep a log of your hourly activities during a typical week, you will probably be surprised at the amount and variety of your own listening activities. You will probably find that you spend far more of your waking hours in listening than in talking, reading, or writing (remember too that when talking you simultaneously listen to yourself). You will also become aware of the amount of listening that goes on during other ordinary activities—everything from driving a car to playing a game of volleyball.

CHARACTERISTICS OF LISTENING
Activity

In ordinary conversation the listening part may seem effortless because the expenditure of energy is not readily observable. Likewise it is hard to erase the public-speaking stereotype shown by the pictures below and opposite. The speaker is at the front of the room, actively moving about, gesturing vigorously, and doing all of the talking; the audience just sits there—passively receiving the message. *Passively?*

If you are a football fan listening on radio to The Big Game, you follow the sportscaster's words with intense concentration; simultaneously creating a mental image of the gridiron and the plays. You outwardly reveal your inner thoughts and feelings by your tense posture, your facial expressions, your clenched fists and other gestures, your groans or cheers, and your occasional exclamations. If you are a true football fanatic, you find that after listening to the broadcast you are emotionally wrung out and even physically tired. Yet all you have done is listen.

Multiple Stimuli

In football via radio the stimuli are all auditory, some verbal and some nonverbal. You derive most of your information from key words and most of the excitement from the sportscaster's voice. You do not hear a quiet monotone saying, "Hayden is throwing a pass. Swann catches it in the end zone." Instead you hear something like, "Swann's in the clear—in the CLEAR! Here comes Hayden's pass! Swann leaps up, and up, and UP! Did he hold on? YES, HE'S GOT IT!! TOUCHDOWN!!!" The crowd roars; the band blares!

Had the broadcast been on TV, you would have received additional

Stereotype 1: The speaker provides the "active" part of the communication process.

Stereotype 2: The listeners provide the "passive" part of the communication process.

nonverbal stimuli—visual ones, such as pictures of the play, the crowd, the band, and the cheerleaders. During half time you would see as well as hear the sportscaster interviewing one or more guests.

At this point you should pay special attention to the fact that these multitudinous stimuli are received by listeners as patterns (also called structures, configurations, or gestalten) imbedded in a context. You do not listen to a speaker phoneme-by-phoneme but by words, phrases, sentences. Nor do you listen to the marching band as a bombardment of discrete pure tones. The same is true of the visual stimuli: You do not see the speaker as thousands of unrelated light rays impinging on the retina—you see a whole, a person; the vocal cords do not speak, he or she speaks. There is no controversy among psychologists that we do experience multiple stimuli as patterns. There is, however, an intriguing theoretical question. Kurt Koffka, one of the leaders of the gestalt school of psychology, put the question succinctly, "Why do things look as they do?" Do we live in an orderly universe, or do we impose orderliness? Are perceived patterns "out there" or within us? The best answer seems to be an integration of the two viewpoints. Our present interest is focused mainly on what the listeners contribute to the patterning of incoming stimuli.

Selectivity

Many a conversation has never been held because one or both parties disliked the other. If you are not interested in Sociology 102 or if you do not like the professor teaching it, you do not enroll in Sociology 102. If you are a staunch Republican, you do not attend Democratic fund-raising dinners. Turning this illustration around, you seek out your close friends because you enjoy talking and listening to them. You enroll in your favorite courses. You attend a meeting to hear a speech by your chosen political candidate. This kind of selectivity frequently confronts you. If you want to listen to the evening news, you may have to make a forced choice among Chancellor, Cronkite, and Reasoner. People in the mass media call this "selective exposure," and it is obviously a serious bread-and-butter problem to many of them. To you, it illustrates one level of control of your own listening—you can sometimes select what you want to hear and what you want to avoid by deliberately choosing or rejecting entire communication events.

However, once you are in a listening situation, another level is reached—selective attention. When someone else is talking you can rarely avoid hearing the sounds, but you can significantly control your attention to them. Consider a few examples.

Suppose you utilize a bedside radio, tuned at low volume to an all-night music station, as a soporific that helps induce sleep. You hear the murmur of the announcer's voice but you are not bothered because, "I don't really listen to him—I sort of half-listen." You may go on to say, "I notice the names of composers but I mentally tune out the commercials." Similarly, you can survive a dull lecture by day-dreaming, or mentally planning a shopping trip, or reading a newspaper strategically located on your lap. In cases of this sort you are consciously controlling your attention, which means that you can heighten awareness of selected stimuli while reducing awareness of competing stimuli (see Chapter 12). Note that you can reduce, not eliminate, awareness of the unwanted stimuli.

An important variation is illustrated by the listening problems at a cocktail party. You can carry on a conversation with a companion despite the competing babel of the many guests crowded into the room—even when several nearby guests have louder voices than you or your companion. You perceive your private tête-à-tête as a pattern that stands out in contrast to the larger pattern or background context. You may suppose that you are completely oblivious to this background but if your name is mentioned within earshot, your attention is immediately captured. Obviously, you can dampen but not eliminate these other sounds, and your perception mechanism is ready to alert you to stimuli pertinent to your special interests or needs. This phenomenon was noticed long ago by Pavlov in his famous experiments on dogs, and he hypothesized an "orienting reflex" to account for it. Scientific interest in this hypothesis accelerated a few years ago when several neurophysiologists, independently and almost simultaneously, reported that an orienting function apparently characterizes a small area in the brain called the reticular formation. Incoming stimuli are routed through this area, which initiates an alert if any stimulus affects your interests or safety. Thus, you may pay no attention to normal traffic noises but you are automatically alerted by the angry screech of brakes.

Interpretation

If a friend talked to you for about two minutes and suddenly asked you to repeat verbatim what was just said, you could not do it. You do not listen like a tape recorder; you cannot rewind yourself and play back every word and syllable. You can give your friend your interpretation of what he said, including probably a few exact words and phrases. Your interpretation would not agree precisely with any other listener's version, nor would any such paraphrase agree precisely with what the speaker thought he said. The situation was wryly expressed by a sign reputedly posted in a New York publisher's office:

> I know you believe you understand what you think I said, but I am not sure you realize that what you heard is not what I meant.

When you attend a meeting to listen to a speaker, you bring with you in one human skin a whole bagful of your personal needs, motives, emotions, moods, mental abilities, attitudes, beliefs, habits, memories, purposes, and expectancies. All of these will influence your interpretation of a speaker's remarks. As pointed out in Chapter 1 and subsequently, the speaker provides patterns of stimuli that initiate intraindividual processes that only the listener can carry through to a conclusion. The end product represents an intermingling of the speaker's and listener's thoughts and feelings. Figuratively described, the speaker has the first word but the listener has the final word.

Rapidity

Research in listening has been stimulated in recent years by the development of an instrument called a speech compressor (pictured on page 324). This remarkable machine can speed up or slow down an audiotape playback without distorting vocal pitch, loudness, or quality. A major and rather spectacular finding is that selected informa-

The "speech compressor" in action: The student is listening to an altered recording of her own voice.

tional materials recorded at a normal speaking rate—about 140 words per minute—can be speeded up to 350–400 words per minute without significantly reducing listeners' comprehension scores; and some listeners given special training can score well at much higher speeds. This research has important theoretical value and has resulted in some practical applications (notably the compression of oral textbooks for the blind).

However, this research does not justify leaping to all sorts of hasty conclusions. It does not establish the speed of thought. It does not include the visual stimuli that are an important part of normal listening. Most of the experiments deal with only one listening purpose— the comprehension of informational materials. The basic fact to bear in mind is that the human hearing-listening mechanism can operate much more rapidly than the speaking mechanism.

Various other types of experiments also throw some light on the speed of listening. For example, there is some evidence to support the interesting hypothesis that people listen by means of "key" words and phrases. If true, this hypothesis might help to explain some of the speech compressor findings.

MANAGEMENT OF LISTENING

The sequence of pictures on pages 326–27 shows two students engrossed in a classroom assignment on listening, assisted by a set of instructions and printed guide sheets for note taking.[1] The listeners in this project have three duties: (1) to report objectively what they heard and saw (description); (2) to indicate how well the speaker said it (evaluation); and (3) to suggest how he might improve (prescription). Thus the listeners simultaneously fulfill three roles—reporter, critic, and coach. Class projects of this type help bring to life the discussion in the preceding section. A common remark by listeners: "I worked harder than the speaker." This remark can be translated into an overall proposition—you can improve your listening efficiency by working at it a little harder.

Most of us are lazy listeners most of the time, partly because we have never thought that listening (like reading, writing, and speaking) is a skill that can be improved by guided practice. With this in mind consider the following suggestions.

Plan a Program for Practice

The first thing to do is to start taking an inventory of your listening habits. Without consciously intending to, you have been acquiring listening habits for many years, mostly by accident or trial and error. To help recognize a "habit" when you see one, try starting with your radio-TV listening. What types of programs do you habitually choose or avoid? Think back over some recent phone conversations. Can you not spot a few telephone-listening habits? And you almost certainly have noticed that different students have different habits when listening to class lectures—but have you noticed your own? In similar fashion, analyze a variety of other listening situations in which you regularly participate. You will find additional cues of what to look for by checking through this entire chapter. Begin your inventory now and add to it later.

Your self-inventory will reveal that some of your listening habits are already good, but it will also include some habits that should be unlearned, replaced, or improved. The list provides a basis for planning a definite program to be put into practice. Some of these projects can be practiced in this class where you can have the benefit of feedback from your instructor or colleagues, but most of your listening experiments must be practiced in situations outside of class. No one can force you to listen well and no one can do your listening for you. You cannot become a better listener unless you *want* to.

[1] Milton Dickens and James H. McBath, *Guidebook for Speech Communication*, Harcourt Brace Jovanovich, 1973, Project 29, pp. 143–46.

This sequence of pictures shows the listening behaviors of two students while carrying

Be Responsive

A simple project for starting your practice program in this class is to become more responsive when listening to your colleagues. This does not mean going overboard. For instance, if you give the first classroom talk following the assignment of this chapter, and are confronted with exaggerated changes by all your classmates—everyone leaning tensely forward, putting on eager, smiling facial expressions, nodding vigorous assent to every statement, and applauding repeatedly as you proceed—you would either give up in dismay or break into hearty laughter.

So don't overdo. First, eliminate possible negative habits. For instance, a few students are likely to maintain a constant frown while listening. Inquiry reveals that they are not finding fault or disagreeing all the time, but have acquired the habit of frowning when interested and trying to concentrate. Other students habitually look out of a window or at an imaginary spot above the speaker's head when concentrating. And so on. Therefore you should find out if you have any annoying or misleading mannerisms. A good way to find out is by asking your fellow students—they have had to put up with you every time they have given a talk.

Since the central concern in speech communication is interactiveness, you as a listener want to assume your share of the responsibility. You can help the speaker by showing your reactions during his speech —degrees of interest or attention, understanding or puzzlement, agreement or disagreement. You can do this by small cues, such as posture, eye contact, nodding or shaking or tilting the head, and

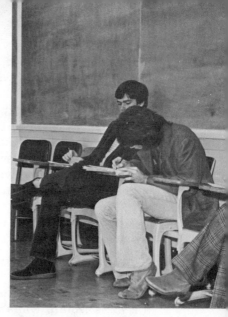

out an assignment to improve listening skills through guided practice.

especially by facial expressions. The speaker in turn is stimulated by a responsive audience to do a better job for you.

The you-and-I attitude can help make you a better listener, as well as a better speaker. A mutual goal in this class is better understanding of the process of interindividual communication, which throws a spotlight on the prefix *inter*. You form the habit of observing a "speaking event" as a "speaking-listening event." When you are a listener, therefore, you think of yourself as an equal participant in the process. You look at the speaker and mentally say, "You and I together are about to discover how your ideas relate to mine." As Norbert Wiener put it: Speech communication is "a game between talker and listener against the forces of confusion."

Listen Purposively

People listen to one another for a remarkable variety of reasons. However, the innumerable small variations and combinations may be reduced to a manageable number by classification. Here are most of the major purposes of listening: recreation (cocktail party), learning about a topic (lecture), getting information about a person (interview), experiencing an emotional or spiritual lift (sermon), strengthening beliefs (campaign speech by your preferred candidate), reaching a decision (conversation with a respected advisor), and putting a plan into overt action (briefing session).

In most listening situations you are guided by your purpose, consciously or subconsciously, and your behavior is strongly influenced by that purpose. For instance, when you listen to Bob Newhart,

Lucille Ball, or Bob Hope, your purpose is to relax, grin, chuckle, and laugh. Your enjoyment would be killed if you sat there taking notes as you would during a lecture in your American history class.

Listening purposes may also be negative rather than positive. Notice the differences between the *internalized* behaviors when conversing with your closest friend as contrasted with someone you dislike. All of us are occasionally caught in speaking-listening situations that we did not wish to be involved in. Usually this means that your listening purpose becomes, "I know I won't like this affair and I'll find a reason why." So you find it. Afterwards you may feel self-satisfied but you may have won a Pyrrhic victory. Habitual faultfinding is seldom listed as a social virtue.

Control Your Attention

You have long since learned to fake the appearance of paying attention to a class lecture while daydreaming or mentally reviewing for an exam to be given next hour in some other course. You know that as a result you will get practically nothing from the lecture. Thus experience tells you that you can control your attention mechanism by deliberately switching from "concentrated attention" to "minimal marginal attention." Roughly restated, you already know that you can pay attention or not pay attention. But let us pursue this matter further.

These three listeners reveal concentrated attention. If they were "faking," you could detect the difference.

Suppose you don earphones and try to listen to the same person talking on two different topics—one transmitted to your right ear and the other simultaneously to your left ear. You might suppose that you would experience an utter confusion of sounds. Controlled experiments have demonstrated, however, that most people can soon learn to follow instructions, such as "listen only with the left ear," and "now switch to the other ear." Variations on this experimental design have also been explored. You can roughly duplicate such experiments in the classroom or at home, using whatever electronic equipment is available—two tape recorders, two radios, a stereo, a TV set, or some combination. For example, two tape recorders may be placed side by side on the desk in front of the class and speeches by the same person on two unrelated topics played back simultaneously. Variations for practice may be introduced. Some possibles: move one of the machines to other locations in the room, increase and decrease the volume of the recorders separately and together, use two different voices or multiple voices, try different types of subject matter, vary the language level of difficulty, and so on. You will soon gather quite a bit of firsthand knowledge about the functioning of your attention mechanism as applied to listening.

Another line of research has been aimed at the listener's ability to shift attention from one thing to another while listening to a single speaker. For example, four groups listening to a speech were given four different sets of instructions: (1) listen for the content only, (2) listen for vocal and visual delivery only, (3) listen for both content and delivery, and (4) just listen. The test scores indicated that instruction (3) produced the best results.

The above and other researches show that you can consciously focus attention on one pattern of incoming stimuli while dimming competing stimuli, that you can shift your attention back and forth rapidly from one stimulus to another, and that you can improve this control by practicing. These abilities are subject to individual variations. You will consequently have to invest a few hours of experimenting in order to test how well you can control your own attention mechanisms. You will simultaneously find some individualized aids or gimmicks that work especially well for you. The practical value of improved control of attention to your listening effectiveness is self apparent.

Evaluate Objectively

There is no need to tell anybody to "listen evaluatively." For better or for worse, evaluation is a built-in part of the listening process. The stimuli provided by the speaker are processed by the attention-perception-cognition provided by the listener. As we have seen,

Modern mass communication: Who comprises the audience here? The three young people? The listeners shown on the screen? The millions of unseen listeners?

attention is selective and fluctuating; perception is a mirror curved by the listener's past; and cognition intermingles perceptions into the active ongoing thoughts and feelings of the listener. No wonder Democrats and Republicans can listen to the same speech and give completely contradictory evaluations.

The automatic portions of the attention-perception-cognition operations were evolved by Mother Nature to meet basic human needs, such as survival from danger. As we have seen, however, a significant share of these operations can be consciously controlled by the individual. The sounds of an explosion followed by screams of agony in a nearby room, should and do automatically dominate a listener's behavior. But a verbal description of explosions and screams in a classroom talk, no matter how vivid the words, produces behavior that is obviously under the listener's control.

Suppose that a student vividly describes explosions and screams while giving a talk on a current threat of a new war. Reactions of the different listeners may range from "ho hum" to signing a petition protesting war. These immediate responses may result from the listener's preconceived opinions or beliefs. The ho-hummer may already have evaluated the speaker: "He never knows what he's talking about; he's a fanatic"; or his way of speaking: "I detest that loud voice and that table-pounding"; or his main idea: "I'm tired of hearing platitudes about the horrors of war." Such prejudgments invite another platitude: "My mind is made up. Don't confuse me with facts." Of course, the same analysis applies to the petition-signer. He may be an intimate friend of the speaker, approve the emphatic delivery, and already have a deep conviction against war. So he listens avidly, reinforces his existing belief (which the ho-hummer would call prejudice), and is anxious to release his attitude by signing the petition. So here we have two examples of listening with a closed mind. Regardless of the merits of these listeners' beliefs, you and I may justifiably question whether either listener could give an accurate description, much less an objective evaluation, of the speaker, the speaking, or the speech.

Before casting stones at these hypothetical listeners, you and I should probably confess that we have at times committed the same sin. The most difficult problem in the management of listening is what to do about accumulated attitudes, beliefs, habits, memories, and expectancies. How can any human be expected to listen and evaluate objectively? For example, a few days after Vice President Spiro Agnew resigned his office, he addressed the nation in his own defense. The basic issues were morality and ethics—the very issues that involve the most deeply rooted beliefs and convictions of the majority of our people. By far the largest group of these people believed that Agnew had no defense; they either refused to turn on the TV or they listened in order to cut to pieces his anticipated excuses. A smaller group listened sympathetically; they expected to hear additional proof that he was betrayed, framed, victimized, and that he had resigned only to prevent national disunity. Both camps heard what they expected to hear. During this intensely emotional period, to have advised anyone on either side to "listen and evaluate objectively," would probably have been answered by "That's impossible" or "Why should I?" These are hard questions and legitimate ones. You cannot erase your past as you can erase words from a chalkboard.

> The Moving Finger writes; and, having writ,
> Moves on: nor all your Piety nor Wit
> Shall lure it back to cancel half a Line,
> Nor all your Tears wash out a Word of it.[2]

---

[2] Omar Khayyám, Rubáiyát, Stanza 71.

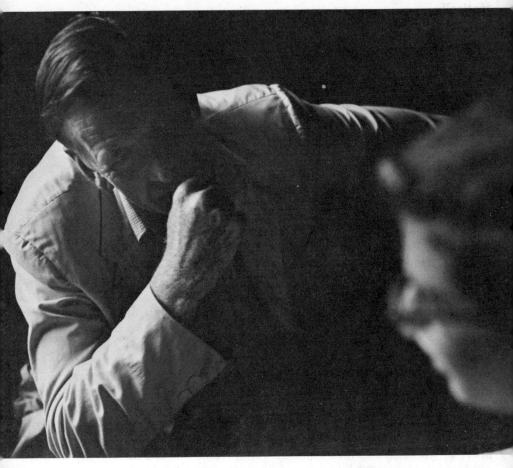

Here a professor provides a student with a visual model of good listening habits.

However, the very term *evaluate* means the application of standards, especially ethical ones. And the term *objective* implies a rational and systematic application of these criteria. So you do not try to forget standards. You try to improve them. You become more aware of them. You learn to use them better.

We will return to the turmoil of public issues presently. But the best place to practice listening and to form habits for future use is in this class. Therefore, consider the next four suggestions to help improve objectivity, and the discussion will be limited to classroom use.

1. BE WARY OF FIRST IMPRESSIONS   Hopefully you do not need this advice. However, some students listen to the first brief classroom talk of a colleague and immediately turn thumbs up or down so dog-

matically as to seriously delay and even prevent themselves from giving that student a fair hearing in his future talks. First impressions are nearly always based on insufficent data, mostly confined to appearance and voice.

2. CROSS-CHECK YOUR ACCUMULATED IMPRESSIONS Assuming
you suspend judgment of your colleague until you have listened to him quite a few times, you may then be justified in forming your first tentative opinions. You try to decide what kind of person you think he is, how well he thinks, and how well he expresses his thoughts. No one (except in movie westerns) is all good or all bad. So you mentally cross-check the speaker's assets and liabilities, keeping an open mind on his prospects for improvement. Furthermore, you should be alert to your own biases and, if necessary, make allowances because of them. For instance, "secret" envy of someone's attractive appearance or special talents can completely distort your judgment.

3. COMPARE EVALUATIONS WITH OTHER LISTENERS In this class
you can usually find out what some of the other members think regarding a given classmate. If you find yourself out of step regarding any particular judgment, it means that you should reevaluate that item or person. It does not necessarily mean changing your opinion. But you do have more data. Your objectivity is usually improved by an awareness of conflicting opinions.

4. TEST WHAT THE SPEAKER SAYS AGAINST EXTERNAL FACTS In
evaluating a classmate's use of evidence and reasoning you should review earlier portions of this book, including Chapter 15. The best criterion for verifying a speaker's accuracy of observation and reporting is of course firsthand experience of your own. If a classmate talks about objects, people, or events on or near the campus, you may already have firsthand information, or you can easily get it. You will perhaps find that to some extent you have approximately duplicated other experiences of colleagues—you have been to the same places or perhaps travelled by the same airlines. Finally, you can check many items when you are studying in the library. Of course time does not permit you to check everything said by everybody but the habit of spot-checking a speaker's verifiable facts is a good one for future use.

Let us go back over the above suggestions by applying them to community and societal speaking-listening events. Picking up where we recently left off, you will recall that soon after Vice President

Agnew's resignation President Nixon nominated Gerald Ford as successor. For the first time the new amendment to the Constitution on vice-presidential succession was put in motion—Ford underwent the process of congressional confirmation. The televized hearings were listened to by millions of Americans. Furthermore, the prevailing climate of political cynicism spawned *skeptical* listening by congressmen and public alike. It was a time for applying tests rigorously. No doubt a small percentage of citizens tuned in briefly and made snap judgments on such grounds as their liking or disliking Ford's appearance and gestures, or his voice and diction. But the polls indicated that most listeners listened longer and better. A good number of them wrestled with their consciences, trying to balance mentally and emotionally their many and sometimes conflicting impressions. People exchanged evaluations in conversations and informal discussions. Ford's past career and current testimony were checked against all sorts of external evidence by a miniature army of investigators from the FBI, IRS, and other government agencies.

This entire chapter has treated the often neglected skills of listening. Useful habits have been described or implied. As you well know, the formation of lifelong habits should begin early. College students are at the right age and in the right place to begin forming the listening habits that are so important to becoming better communicators in our society.

SUMMARY

The most used and least understood of the major skills of human communication is listening.

Important characteristics of listening include the following. (1) The process is not passive but active, sometimes extremely so. (2) The sensory stimuli that initiate the process are normally both auditory and visual, verbal and nonverbal. (3) The listener can usually select or avoid the stimuli, subject to occasional veto by the automatic functioning of the reticular formation of the brain. (4) The listener cannot duplicate exactly what a speaker says or means; the listener imposes his interpretation on everything he hears. (5) The human hearing-listening mechanism operates much more rapidly than the speaking mechanism.

The management of one's listening may be assisted by the following guidelines. (1) Plan a program for practice; listening is a skill that can be improved. (2) Be responsive; the you-and-I attitude assists the listener as well as the speaker. (3) Listen purposively; appropriate and positive purposes increase both the enjoyment and the profit.

(4) Control your attention; this ability can be improved more than most people realize. (5) Evaluate objectively; listeners who habitually approve of only what they already know and believe have frozen their personal development and denied a responsibility to their society.

TOPICAL PREVIEW

18

Group Discussion

DEFINITION OF GROUP DISCUSSION

Group discussion is a form of speech communication in which two or more persons talk and listen to one another in alternation, and think together interactively.

Perhaps the only term requiring comment is "in alternation." This implies a minimum of orderliness; when participants speak simultaneously the result can sometimes be pandemonium rather than discussion.

DIFFICULTIES AND DANGERS OF DISCUSSION

You will see that the definition can apply equally to a group of philanthropists planning their next charity ball or a gang of thieves planning their next burglary. The definition intentionally describes what group discussion is, not what it ought to be. Thus group discussion ought to be a device by which several persons pool their knowledge. They may, however, merely pool their ignorance. Discussion ought to be a process of cooperative deliberation, but frequently it is neither cooperative nor deliberative. Discussion ought to exemplify the process of reflective thinking, but often it is dominated by highly emotional thinking. Discussion ought to be an

Congresswoman Bella Abzug and Governor Nelson Rockefeller exchange pleasantries during an open forum discussion. It appears that they forgot the basic rule to "speak in alternation."

unbiased search for the truth, but many times it is a political maneuver to put something across. Discussion ought to be a technique for securing joint agreement on the solution of common problems. It may instead become a process wherein unnecessary antagonisms are bred and avoidable stalemates achieved. Discussion ought to be an orderly proceeding, but it may become an acrimonious brawl. Discussion should rise to the level of the best minds in the group, but it may fall to the level of the poorest. These difficulties in group discussion should not be concealed. They should be frankly faced so that the student may learn to do what is efficient and ethical, yet also learn to detect and to counteract what is inefficient or unethical.

TYPES OF DISCUSSION

If group discussions are classified on the basis of the major purposes for which discussions are held, four broad categories emerge: social groups, learning groups, problem-solving groups, and decision-making groups.

A social group gathers for purposes of recreation, getting acquainted, observing social amenities, or just for entertainment. You have participated in many discussions of this type: dinner parties, visits with friends, rap sessions, teas, cocktail parties, receptions, coffee hours. You have also enjoyed listening to the discussions on TV talk shows and game shows, such as "What's My Line?" The importance of socializing informally should not be underestimated. It is by far the most ubiquitous and common type of group discussion; it contributes vitally to basic personal needs for companionship and happiness; it provides the cohesiveness required for community survival. Without it, each of us would be condemned to a dreary, lonely life, bordering on solitary confinement.

The purpose of a learning group is to exchange information, to explore ideas, and to seek understanding. You have participated in class discussions since kindergarten days; and perhaps you have been in study groups, panels, or open forums. You have heard of group therapy, where discussion is used to help people develop better personal insights and adjustments in their mental and emotional lives. You have participated in interviews. And of course you have gotten information about many subjects from TV and radio discussions, such as "Washington Week in Review," "Issues and Answers," "Face the Nation," and "Meet the Press." The unique values of group discussion as a teaching-learning tool have been recognized for many years by leading educators.

The purpose of a problem-solving group is to analyze problems, to develop and recommend solutions. Examples are plentiful: committees (there are many kinds), conferences, juries, boards, councils, task forces, cabinets, staffs, vestries, commissions, judging panels, supreme courts. Most of these committee-like groups are small and are appointed or elected by a larger organization to which they submit reports or recommendations.

The purpose of a decision-making group is to receive, debate, and make final judgments on policies recommended by its committees or individual members. When a problem arises in a democratic organization, the usual procedure is to refer the problem to a committee as an open-ended question, "What should be done about this?" The committee may review a dozen possible solutions from which it evolves a recommendation. The larger group then makes the final decision on the restricted question, "Should this particular policy be approved?" The significance of these two question-forms will be further developed presently.

Looking back, you will see that the four categories are by no means mutually exclusive. No airtight classification of discussion types has yet been proposed by anybody, nor is one necessary. It is of course possible, at a given discussion meeting, to achieve all four of the purposes in varying degrees—you may have a good time, learn something, solve a problem, and make a decision. Usually, however, one of the four is the predominant group purpose, and the others are incidental or subordinate.

Social Groups

1. SELF-EVALUATION By far the largest amount of your experience in group discussion has occurred in ordinary conversations in small social groups. You have chatted almost daily with other people since your early childhood. One result is that by now you have formed many conversational habits, most of which have "just growed" without much guidance or much realization of the importance of such habits to your future happiness, satisfaction, and success. You should try to make an inventory of such habits. Perhaps you have a reputation among your friends and acquaintances as one who seldom says much in a social group and never assumes the initiative. Or perhaps you have the opposite reputation as one who talks too much and tries to dominate or monopolize. Hopefully, however, you have already learned to achieve an appropriate balance between talking and listening. A more difficult task is that of evaluating yourself in terms of what you customarily talk about and how well you express your ideas during spontaneous conversations.

In making a self-inventory, you must become your own best critic. You may be assisted by asking for frank evaluations of yourself from a few selected friends; or your instructor may take an anonymous poll by which class members interchange personal impressions of one another, based on social conversations out of class. Your best guidance, however, can only be secured from experience. And you will learn little from experience unless you have sufficient social sensitivity to profit from it.

2. SOCIAL SENSITIVITY Social sensitivity can be developed and improved. A good way to begin is by observing the social behaviors of other people. Suppose you are a guest at a dinner party. It takes only one insensitive person to spoil the enjoyment of everyone (except himself). He may introduce a subject and enlarge upon it with relish, oblivious of the facial expressions revealing that the topic is unpleasant to other guests. He may be insensitive to obvious verbal efforts to change the subject. Or suppose you encounter the egocentric person who reduces practically every topic to its relation to "my son . . . my daughter . . . my job . . . my house . . . my car. . . ." When you are subjected to the conversation of insensitive persons, the thing to do is watch your fellow listeners. Watch for their conscious or unconscious visual and auditory cues—facial expressions, glances, muscular tensions, restlessness, unusual silences, careful

Social sensitivity is developed by observant participation in ordinary conversation groups.

choice of words, or tone of voice when interjecting something like, "very interesting" or "you certainly have your problems."

You should also deliberately observe individual behaviors during good conversations. Of special value is the study of the leadership function. The fact that by their nature social conversations are unstructured and have no "official" chairman, does not mean that leadership is nonexistent or unnecessary. It means that leadership is psychological and unobtrusive, and that the role of leader shifts from person to person during a normal conversation. You should learn to sense when others expect you "to take the lead," and also to sense when it is time to pass the baton to someone else by changing the subject or asking an appropriate question.

You also learn by experience to summate the individual signs so as to develop sensitivity to the prevailing mood or trend of the group as a whole. For example, a group of friends has gathered to enjoy a sociable evening; the conversation is lively, all participate actively, everything runs smoothly, and everyone is happy. But can you sense when the time comes for the party to break up? If nobody senses this inevitable "moment of truth," the party will slowly drag to an anticlimactic ending. (And pity the host and hostess if there is that one couple who hang on interminably after all the others have departed.)

Group sensitivity carries over into all types of discussions. You can learn by experience, for instance, to sense when a committee is working together harmoniously. You are aware of a common feeling of satisfaction and progress. You can also learn to detect underlying discontent, frustration, or other negative trends. In assessing the prevailing mood, you must evaluate the small overt cues in context. A spirited argument between two members can be courteous and constructive, or it may reveal animosity, fatigue, or a possible stalemate. A period of silence may mean concentrated thought, or it may, in context, mean disinterest, disapproval, or anger.

Social sensitivity, then, is most readily developed and improved during your ordinary daily conversations; keep its value in mind while reading the next three sections.

Learning Groups

1. VALUES AND LIMITATIONS   The traditional college lecture has been defined as "the process by which the notes of the professor become the notes of the student without passing through the minds of either." Lectures are the most widely used teaching-learning method on most college campuses. The method has many virtues, especially in classes with large enrollments. However, students rightfully complain if they have too many lecture courses; they demand personal conferences and small group interchanges with the professor. Lectures via closed-circuit television or electronic teaching machines (see picture below) also have their virtues. But an inherent weakness is that a student cannot discuss the subject matter with a machine.

Group discussion as a teaching-learning method also has a long tradition—you may immediately think of Socrates' dialogs in ancient

This ingenious machine plays a taped lecture and automatically displays accompanying pictorial materials, usually coordinated with assigned readings. But the student cannot discuss the subject matter with the machine.

Here is another type of "teaching machine"—a professor talking with students after a class meeting.

Greece. Fortunately, many professors recognize that, when properly used, discussion methods have educational values such as the following:

1. Attention is improved by a variety of class procedures.
2. Motivation to learn is stimulated.
3. Mislearning is reduced by immediate corrections.
4. Understanding of some types of materials is improved by slowing down the presentation time.
5. Teaching of selected topics may best be achieved by allowing students to learn from one another.
6. Professors are forced to think harder, to stay out of ruts, and to "give more of themselves."

On the other hand, discussion has its limitations. The most common one is that it may require more time than is available. It can be dull if overused or poorly used. It may be inappropriate for a given topic. And it usually requires a reasonable amount of special skill on the part of both the instructor and the students.

2. CLASS DISCUSSIONS You are probably taking and will take courses (besides this one) where some type of class discussion is used as one of the teaching methods. Since participation in such discussions is an immediate and practical activity in your academic training, we will now pursue that topic.

Successful participation requires that you first analyze and evaluate each professor's version of "class discussion." There are many possibilities, some of which entirely eliminate traditional lectures.

However, a combination of lecture-discussion is the most common approach; the number of variations is limited only by the ingenuity of the individual professor. Almost automatically the leadership function is exercised by the instructor. The basic goal of the lecture-discussion should be teaching-learning, and most instructors probably interpret this to mean "I teach" and "students learn." This interpretation is workable even though it leaves out the fact that students can learn from one another while the instructor can learn from the students. Furthermore, the lecture portion tends to dominate. Thus a professor says, "I provide for student participation at every class meeting." Observation may reveal that at the close of a forty-five-minute lecture he says, "Any questions?" During the remaining five minutes, two or three students ask questions, sometimes merely to make a good impression on the professor.

If lecture-discussion is to be fully effective, at least three things are required of the teacher. First, he must plan the lecture partially in terms of the discussion format he intends to use. For example, he may:

Present part of materials—group completes them.
Present materials—group applies them.
Present materials—group analyzes them.
Present materials—group reinforces them.

Second, he must allow adequate time for student participation. He has several choices of time distribution: Lecture for about half of the period (or some other proportion) and then have class discussion for the remainder; divide lecture into segments, each followed by a discussion period; or encourage students to interrupt frequently and at any point during the lecture. He may divide the coverage of a unit of subject matter into larger chunks, such as straight lectures on Monday and Wednesday followed by class discussion on Friday. Third, he must have considerable skill in guiding group discussions. He must be able to encourage and stimulate student participation; he must prevent a few overaggressive members from dominating the time; he must head off time-consuming digressions from the topic.

Regardless of the educational methods used in the classroom, college students seek and have a right to expect that the professor will supplement the course by means of informal discussions outside of class. The photo on page 343 suggests the pervasive influence of this type of teaching-learning on any college campus.

3. PANEL DISCUSSIONS The panel format is a small-group discussion presented before an audience. You have observed many variations of this format on TV and radio. Advantages of this format in broadcasting (as compared with one person lecturing) include the

use of multiple voices, multiple personalities, and multiple points of view. The same (and other) advantages are often observed when student panels are used in the classroom.

If a round of panel discussions is assigned in your speech communication (or other) class, you will more likely be a participant than a moderator; and at proper times a moderator may shift into the role of participant. Therefore, a set of guidelines for effective participation in panels is presented below. With adaptations these guidelines apply to participation in class discussions, as well as most other forms of group discussion.

4. GUIDELINES FOR PARTICIPATION When you are a participant other than the leader, in a learning group or problem-solving group, the suggested guidelines look like this when put into perspective:

a. Come prepared.
b. Take an active part.
    (1) Contribute facts.
    (2) Contribute opinions.
    (3) Ask questions.
c. Control your participation.
    (1) Be relevant.
    (2) Be brief.
    (3) Be courteous.
    (4) Be cooperative.

We will next briefly discuss each of the above suggestions, focusing on learning groups, and anticipating that you can adapt the guidelines to participation in problem-solving groups later in this chapter.

a. Come prepared. Your first duty begins before you arrive at the meeting. You should think through the topic or problem, trying to delimit the scope and envision a realistic goal for the discussion. You should gather pertinent information needed to improve your grasp of the subject—some of this information will be offered at appropriate times later on in the discussion. You should prepare notes of such data, but do not prepare set speeches. If the subject includes controversial issues, you will probably reach some conclusions about them, but try to keep them tentative so that you will not join the group with a closed mind.

Do not suppose that you can avoid advance research unless you are willing to accept the penalties. Lazy preparation and subsequent bluffing become conspicuous in a panel or similar class project, especially to the majority of your classmates who have been working hard.

b. Take an active part. Remind yourself that active participation means talking, listening, and thinking interactively together. There should be ample give-and-take, some of it rapid-fire. By prearrangement the discussion may sometimes begin with a brief statement from each member. But interaction is minimized if a symposium format is used, that is, if most or all of the time is devoted to the presentation of lengthy individual reports. Lively interaction gives the effect of several alert inquisitive minds rubbing against one another, each mind being sharpened and honed by the contact. So don't just sit there. If you have an idea, speak up.

(1) Contribute facts. If a topic or problem is to be productively explored, the discussion must have a solid basis of facts. When all members of the group have done their homework, one function of the discussion process is the pooling of that information. You have probably discovered some pieces of information that none of the others has found; be sure to contribute them at appropriate times. Occasionally you may use notes or documents: "I found some statistics that may help us on this point. Let me quote from. . . ."

(2) Contribute opinions. During your reading you may have written down a few opinions quoted from authorities on the subject. If one of these is pertinent to a point under discussion, read the quotation; if necessary, identify the source and mention the author's qualifications.

Express your own personal opinions and judgments; this is both your right and your responsibility. Even a faulty judgment sometimes helps by stimulating the group to find the flaws. In stating your opinions avoid a dogmatic manner. ("This conclusively proves my contention.") Avoid abuse of the first person pronoun. ("I may be wrong, but I'll tell you what I think.")

(3) Ask questions. As you listen to the others during a group discussion, all sorts of questions are likely to come to mind. You may be afraid to ask any of these questions for fear they will reveal your ignorance. So you abide by the dictum, "It is better to remain silent and be thought a fool, than to speak and remove all doubt." On the other extreme you may have the habit of blurting out an almost steady flow of questions. To assist your selectivity, study the following question-purposes which are especially appropriate in a learning group: to elicit further information, to secure clarification, to test the validity of information, to test the reasoning of a colleague, to divert the talking from one person to another.

c. Control your participation.

(1) Be relevant. An efficient discussion group follows an outline or agenda in a reasonably systematic and orderly way. The responsibility for preparing this outline is the moderator's—although he should usually consult beforehand with the others so that the out-

line will reflect a consensus, if possible, rather than come as a surprise just before the discussion begins. Ideally, the points should be in proper sequence, and each point should be settled before proceeding to the next. But this requires a "perfect" agenda and requires that every member will always speak to the point and stick to the point. This ideal is rarely achieved in practice—there are going to be occasional digressions, and they are sometimes helpful (by relieving tensions, for instance, or promoting an atmosphere of goodwill). But the discussion degenerates if someone is almost constantly digressing, and then someone else digresses from the digression. An efficient group seldom wanders too far afield; seldom has to go back and rediscuss a point; seldom leapfrogs over important items in its preplanned agenda. Vice versa, an inefficient group frequently jumps backward ("If you don't mind, I'd like to go back to a point Donna Murray made a few minutes ago.") or forward ("As far as I'm concerned, we are wasting time. Let's get to the main point. Here's what should be done.").

(2) Be brief. Most discussions have time limits; there are several points to be covered, and everyone in the group has a right to be heard. Have something worthwhile to say but say it as briefly as is consistent with clarity. Do not reminisce ("And that reminds me of an incident that occurred last summer when I was visiting the Grand Canyon."). Or belabor the obvious (an example here would violate the advice). Or give more evidence than needed. Or insist on bringing up the same idea over and over. Or keep talking because you like to show off. Or keep talking because nobody stops you.

(3) Be courteous. Courtesy is the most basic rule in all group discussions: give the others a chance to speak. One aggressive individual can hog much of the allotted time, and he will reap boredom, irritation, or antagonism. A courteous individual will temper his talking with plenty of careful listening and thinking; he will often go further, helping the chairman to restrain the overtalkative and draw out the reticent ("We haven't heard from Art Fear on this question. Art, what is your opinion about this . . . ?").

(4) Be cooperative. Cooperation is fostered by using first names or nicknames, by listening attentively when other members of the panel or class are speaking, by asking questions focused on the subject matter, by avoiding questions that put a colleague personally on the spot, by answering questions frankly (even when the answer is "I don't know" or "I was wrong"), by complimenting others when credit is deserved, by showing appreciation or agreement at appropriate times, and by assisting the moderator as he tries to guide the group toward its common goal.

The suggestions above need not be overdone or insincerely done when the goal of a class project is to learn about a topic by interchanging information. The panel members should try to function as a team or partnership; the measure of success is accomplishment by the whole group. Differences in interpretation of some of the facts may well occur, but the group objective is not to argue these differences, only to clarify them.

Cooperation is equally necessary in problem-solving groups, but it is more difficult to achieve because the topics are controversial and the discussants may have opposing points of view. The cooperative resolution of conflicts, therefore, will be a major concern in the following sections.

Problem-solving Groups

1. CHARACTERISTICS   Problem-solving groups are most frequently called committees, although there are many committee-like groups identified by other names—a partial list was given on page 339. All

At first glance this may appear to be a casual rap session. A second glance shows that it is a problem-solving group.

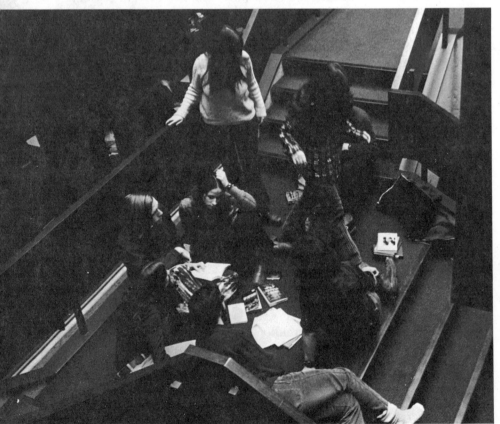

such groups have several commonalities: Their goal is to solve problems, they make recommendations to some larger body, they have someone designated as the leader, they rarely have written rules of procedure (nor should they), and they are relatively small—usually three to seven members.

The relation between (a) an official chairman and (b) a set of written rules of procedure, should be studied. The presence of either (a) or (b) would contradict the very purpose of social gatherings. A learning group needs a leader, but avoids formality. Therefore, in treating social groups and learning groups the emphasis was upon suggestions for effective participation. In this section (and the following section) a shift of emphasis will be made. A problem-solving (or decision-making) group inherently needs a leader who is given at least a modicum of authority and responsibility. Without any leadership or with ineffectual leadership a committee is either crippled or unable to progress at all. When you were called on the first time to chair a committee, you undoubtedly sensed that something was expected of you. You may have wished that you had some standard set of instructions spelling out the rules. A few minutes of reflection will demonstrate that the creation of a set of written procedures, similar to *Robert's Rules of Order Revised,* suitable for any and all committee-type groups, would be impossible. Any such rules, written or unwritten, must be created by the committee itself in terms of its particular task. A sorority rushing committee needs fewer and quite different procedures than the finance committee of a business corporation. The lack of a universal set of rules puts a premium on the leadership qualities of a committee chairman. Therefore, the emphasis of this section is upon leadership.

2. GUIDELINES FOR LEADERSHIP

Do not suppose that leadership is a mysterious quality that cannot be learned and improved, or that committee leadership operates without regard for logical procedures. On the contrary, a practical chart is presented, listing general principles and specific techniques of discussion leadership in committee-type groups. You should refer frequently to this chart (on next page) while reading the remainder of this section.

If you now look at the chart and study the left hand column, you get a perspective on the principal duties of a committee's leader. Looking next at the right hand column, you see a list of some suggested techniques. The usefulness of the chart will become increasingly apparent as we examine several of its implications, and as we consider how it can be adapted to a variety of committee-like situations. During the commentary following the chart we will assume that you are a committee chairman.

Leadership of Problem-solving Groups

What the leader does	Methods he may use
1. Make opening statement	a. State the problem and/or purpose of the meeting. b. State rules of procedure. c. Define goal clearly and concretely. d. Present agenda (or chairman's outline).
2. Get the discussion started	a. Secure agreement on agenda. b. Hand out written materials. c. "Let's go 'round the table." d. Have someone prepared to lead off.
3. Keep it moving	a. Ask leading questions. b. Contribute stimulating facts or quotations. c. Assist participants in expressing themselves. d. Restrain the overtalkative (including oneself).
4. Keep it relevant	a. Gently enforce agenda. b. Make transition statements. c. Use charts or chalkboard. d. Restate the problem.
5. Facilitate resolution of conflicts	a. Do not try to avoid or suppress conflicts on basic issues. b. Try to prevent or abbreviate unnecessary conflicts. c. Suggest or request constructive compromises. d. Be impartial.
6. Promote and conserve progress	a. Summarize occasionally to show progress. b. Remind group of time limits. c. Call for formal vote if necessary. d. Keep track of the Minutes of the Meeting.
7. Make closing statement	a. Summarize exact progress made. b. Be sure responsibility for action is assigned. c. Indicate points for future consideration. d. Declare adjournment within the expected time limits.

When making your opening statement try to accomplish two things as early as possible: (a) aim the thinking of the members toward their common goal, and (b) define the limits of your own authority and responsibility. The two go hand in hand. Before the meeting ask yourself, "What can this particular group expect to accomplish at this particular meeting?" The answer may be either easy or difficult. In the former case you simply remind them; in the latter case you mention the difficulties. You try to establish the group's goal as a criterion for judging the relevancy and progress of the coming discussion—you will need this criterion later.

Suggested procedures usually grow from the nature of the group's task. For instance, suppose this is the nominating committee of some organization. The goal is obvious and so is the agenda: The committee must recommend a slate of nominees for president, vice president, treasurer, and all other officers. You will immediately think of several alternative procedures for accomplishing this task. As chairman, you might foresee only one potential danger—an acrimonious argument over one or more "controversial personalities." In that case you may think of a procedure to reduce the danger in advance and to assist you to maintain the peace if the difficulty develops.

Usually, however, a committee is expected to review a problem and recommend a policy. Ordinarily the problem can be stated as, "What should be done about . . . ?" If you merely state the question and immediately say something like, "Does anyone have any ideas on this?" the most likely response is, "Yes, here's what I think should be done." Unless the matter is so simple as to require no discussion, this is a poor way to open the meeting—it puts the cart before the horse ("Well, folks, here is the solution. Now, what's your problem?"). Therefore, well in advance you should study the subject matter open-mindedly and prepare a chairman's outline. In doing this, you may be assisted by the following design.

I. Analysis of the problem
    A. Wording the problem: Do any terms need defining or clarifying? Possibly reword the question to "aim" it more directly at the group's goal? What are the upper and lower limits of authority and responsibility delegated to this committee?
    B. Nature of the problem: How big is it? How serious? How difficult? What are the obstacles to solution— money? time element? special-interest groups?
    C. Causes of the problem: What are the symptoms? What are the immediate causes of the symptoms? Are there more fundamental deep-rooted causes?

II. Finding a solution
    A. Determining criteria for evaluation: What symptoms and causes must be dealt with? What should be the scope? What obstacles must be overcome? Should relative weights be given to the criteria?
    B. Listing suggested solutions: Which ones should be discussed? Are we already agreed on any of them? Do we lack time to discuss any of them?
    C. Evaluating suggested solutions: What are the advantages and disadvantages of each proposal? How well does each meet the agreed-upon criteria? What would be the consequences if any given proposal is adopted?
    D. Making a final choice: Is there a consensus or majority favoring any one of the proposals? Is a compromise on a given one needed to secure agreement? Should two or more of the proposals be combined?

III. Putting the solution to work
    A. What steps are required to put the chosen policy into operation? Is a time table needed? Has responsibility for action been clearly indicated?
    B. In what form should the committee's report be presented?

Seldom do *all* the above details apply to any single discussion or meeting. You use the form as a check list to prevent forgetting or failing to foresee details that might be crucial to the success of your particular committee.

Unless there is good reason to the contrary, you should present a brief version of an outline to the committee during your opening statement. Do not try to force the outline upon them, but indicate the importance of having *some* such guide. Ask them for suggested modifications or alternative plans. The objective is to secure early approval (before they have a chance to get into arguments with one another) of a general plan and its implied procedures. You are securing authorization to lead them through a series of steps, within certain time limits, toward a specified common goal. If difficulties arise later, you have the psychological advantage of being able to say directly or indirectly, "You agreed upon a set of rules—they are yours, not mine. I'm only your servant whom you authorized to enforce your own rules. Let's not change them in the middle of the game."

In presenting your outline you may already have gotten the discussion started. However, sometimes the agenda is accepted nonverbally (by nods, perhaps). At this juncture some groups are timid or cautious—they require a bit of encouragement or prodding. One useful technique is to say, "Let's go 'round the table and each of us give a brief statement on the committee's problem as we see it." Some groups need no prompting; they may be willing or even eager to talk. In that case, your concern is to get them to discuss the problem before committing themselves prematurely to solutions. A suggested method on the chart is to ask someone in advance of the meeting to lead off the talk by analyzing an aspect of the problem.

It is important that you keep the discussion moving. Both beforehand and during the early stages of a meeting, try to analyze each member in terms of talkativeness. You must adapt to whatever mixture you find. On one extreme, you can have a group of aggressive prima donnas, each trying to dominate the others. On the other extreme, you can have a reticent group who expect you to present a proposal for solving the problem, do all the talking, and receive their dutiful ratification. Of course, most groups fall between these extremes. But even in a classroom practice project you may have difficulty with one or two colleagues. On the chart you notice several ways of drawing out the reticent member. A more difficult task of chairmanship is restraint of an overtalkative person. First, you can fail to "see" him when he is signaling that he wants to talk some more. Or you may say, "Bill, I wonder if I might interrupt and get the group to react to that point before you go on?" Or you may break in and summarize quickly, "In other words what you're driving at is . . . Joan, what do you think of Bill's idea?" (Extreme as it may seem, in order to interrupt you may have to watch Bill's breathing and catch him at the instant of inhalation!) Another technique: "Bill, I notice that our time is growing short. Shall we set a thirty-second limit on everybody's remarks?" As a last resort you may have to be blunt, "Bill, you've been talking more than your share. I declare a moratorium on you until the others have a chance to catch up." Your success with any technique goes back to social sensitivity—you must sense the degree of irritation aroused by Bill's garrulousness.

It is the chairman's responsibility to keep the discussion revelant. Your most effective help in doing this is the agreed-upon outline or agenda. In general, you simply remind them from time to time of which item on the list is currently under consideration. Do not hope to keep every remark strictly serious and pertinent ("Oops! I goofed." "Is it all right to smoke in here?"). Nor is perfection necessary—in fact, sometimes digressions are needed to relieve periods of hard concentration or to release tensions. On the other hand, it is your responsibility to prevent the group from meandering completely, wasting time, or turning the meeting into a legalized rap session. As the chart indicates, transitions help, "We seem to have covered the second point. The third point is. . . ."

You must facilitate resolution of conflicts. Probably the most severe test of chairmanship comes when members of a committee

Chairman Sam Ervin (Democrat) and vice-chairman Howard Baker (Republican) co-ordinated in a superb job of leading the potentially explosive Senate Watergate Committee during many difficult weeks of nationally televised meetings. Personal or partisan conflicts could have bogged down this committee from the start.

express strongly opposing views and perhaps reach a deadlock. You should not try to dodge or suppress fundamental conflicts. If you do so, any "agreement" reached is merely a postponement—it will fester and erupt later. However, you should try to prevent or abbreviate unnecessary conflicts, such as those that can arise from a clash of personalities. If there is a serious disagreement regarding facts, you might phone a library or similar source. But basic disagreements usually arise from differences in philosophy, attitudes, convictions, and opinions. Such conflicts should be expected. Lay a foundation early for handling them. Both the chart and the suggested design for a chairman's outline show how to lay such a foundation. Thus, you try to prevent members from stating strong positions prematurely. After someone has committed himself he tends to hang on stubbornly ("My mind is made up: I don't care what anyone says!"). You should try to avoid formal motions and votes—begin with straw votes or informal expressions of opinions. Set a good example yourself by being impartial. You are entitled to join in the discussion, but as chairman you must exercise self-discipline. Do not talk too frequently or lengthily. State your ideas objectively and in the spirit of making constructive contributions, helpful to the whole committee. You may even speak on both sides of a dispute to prevent either side from overlooking or overemphasizing a fact or argument. And you must certainly allow equal opportunity for opposing viewpoints to be heard. In general, you violate your responsibility and undermine your authority if you reveal prejudice or unfairness.

In foreseeing, sensing, and resolving conflicts, one broad chairmanship strategy involves your concept of group goals. You start off with the hope that the committee will gradually evolve a consensus—meaning new ideas will be hatched during discussion that will transcend differences so that a mutually satisfactory solution will emerge, containing contributions from all. If and when you find that a consensus is unrealistic, you then "lower your sights" and try to help work out a compromise—which means that no member is completely victorious, none is completely disappointed, and all or a majority can agree upon something in between. If you sense that compromise is no longer a realistic goal, you may suggest that the two segments work separately to prepare majority and minority reports. If your committee is so divided that no proposal commands even a bare majority (a situation that only rarely occurs), then all you can do is make a frank statement of their predicament and suggest a progress or no-progress report (at the least they can agree to disagree). The above four goals are presented in descending order of desirability; they provide one kind of practical perspective on the process of group problem-solving.

As chairman you should promote and conserve progress. Progress means that a group has covered an agenda item and is ready to proceed to the next. You may detect such a forward step (a) when the remarks show that there is no real controversy; (b) when the arguments become repetitious; (c) when an informal majority is achieved; (d) when the discussion of the item begins to lag; (e) when there remains only one dissenter and he has had fair enough opportunity to state his case; (f) when time-limit pressure demands that the committee speed up the pace; or (g) when opponents reach a point where a formal vote is obviously required. Whenever a forward step is achieved, briefly summarize that step and record it in your notes, in the minutes, or on a chalkboard. If you rely on memory you may later forget or distort an item.

Make an appropriate closing statement. Here the suggestions on the chart are self-explanatory; use any or all that fulfill your needs. Properly done, the closing statement can give the participants a satisfying sense of achievement.

Decision-making Groups

1. CHARACTERISTICS We now turn from problem-solving by small groups to decision-making by larger groups. Even in a small committee, freedom of speech for each member must be restrained in the interests of efficiency, orderliness, and fairness to other members. And as the size of an organization increases, so does the difficulty of maintaining a balance between the rights of an indi-

vidual and the rights of a whole society. To maintain this balance, written rules are needed; usually there is a constitution and bylaws (dealing with matters peculiar to the particular organization), and a specified manual of parliamentary procedures. The most widely known American reference book is *Robert's Rules of Order Revised* (although there are at least half a dozen other excellent manuals).

Parliamentary rules are designed to restrict the scope of a problem to a definite proposal and to restrict the speaking to the question, "Should this proposal be adopted?" The resulting form of group discussion is called debate. The essential rules are as follows: (a) a proposal must be put in the form of a motion, (b) the speakers argue for or against the motion, (c) the motion must be accepted or rejected (with or without amendments) or otherwise disposed of (e.g., postponement), and (d) only then can any other proposal be introduced.

2. GUIDELINES FOR USING PARLIAMENTARY LAW

a. The chair. A parliamentary meeting cannot be held without a presiding officer—who should refer to himself or herself as "the chair," as a constant reminder to be impartial in exercising the powers of the office.

The most fundamental power of the chair is derived from the right to give or refuse recognition (who shall "have the floor"). Theoretically the chair could refuse to recognize anyone at all (!) or could grant recognition only to members on one side of a controversy; in practice, a dictatorial chair may exercise this power more subtly, but such tactics will boomerang in the long run. One good way to handle a debatable motion is to state, "The chair will recognize, in alternation, speakers for and against the motion and no member may speak twice so long as others request the floor."

A second major source of power is the right of the chair to interpret the rules. If a member thinks that the chair has made a procedural error, he says, "I rise to a point of order," the point is stated, and the chair makes a ruling. The member may say, "I appeal from the decision of the chair," and the point is settled by a vote. Sometimes a member wishes to have the chair explain a rule, saying, "I rise to a point of parliamentary inquiry," and the chair explains. The chair has important discretionary powers; for instance, the chair should sense when to require strict adherence to "the book" and when to overlook unimportant niceties.

The chair also has psychological or moral influence that can set the general tone or atmosphere of the meeting. The basic objectives of efficiency, orderliness, and democracy are heavily dependent upon the personality, knowledge, skill, and impartiality of the chair.

Congresswoman Yvonne Burke, vice-chairwoman of the 1972 Democratic National Convention, shared with chairman Larry O'Brien the task of presiding. She provided a model of chairmanship—a no-nonsense mastery of the rules, a strict impartiality, and the plus values of vivacity, flashes of humor, and graciousness.

b. Order of business.   You should begin by getting a perspective on an entire parliamentary meeting. The customary (but not mandatory) Order of Business proceeds as follows:

1. Call to order
2. Minutes of last meeting
3. Reports of standing committees
4. Reports of special committees
5. Unfinished business
6. New business
7. Announcements
8. Adjournment

c. Main motions.   A main motion puts a substantive question to be debated and disposed of. This may be contrasted with other types of motions dealing with procedural matters (see Appendix D). The proper handling of a main motion is as follows:

1. Rise and address the chair.
2. Be recognized by the chair.
3. State the motion, "I move that (or to). . . ." ("I make a motion that" is not recommended.)
4. Another member seconds the motion.
5. Chair states motion to the group.
6. The motion is discussed (debated).
7. Disposal of the motion is determined by voting.
8. Chair announces results of the vote.

d. Voting.   There are five methods of voting:

1. By voice
2. By show of hands
3. By rising ("division of the assembly")
4. By secret ballot
5. By roll call

The criteria for choosing the method of voting include speed, accuracy, and anonymity.

When to vote is usually easy to determine: A motion has been adequately debated, and the chair says, "If there is no further discussion, we will now vote upon the motion to. . . ." Sometimes, however, a few diehards want to keep on arguing repetitiously. The way to stop them is to secure recognition and say, "I move the previous question." This traditional phrasing often confuses people; the meaning is, "I move to close this debate and vote immediately on the pending motion." The chair should at once say, "The previous question has been moved and seconded. Those in favor, say 'aye' . . . Those opposed, say 'no.' . . ." If *two-thirds* of the members vote in favor, the chair should say, "The ayes have it. We will now vote on the pending motion which is. . . ." Thus two votes are taken in quick succession—the first vote is to *close debate,* the second vote is on the *main motion* that was being debated. Your vote on either of these motions need not agree with your vote on the other.

e. Amending.   You may propose a change in the wording or substance of a main motion in any of these ways: by inserting (or adding), by striking out, or by striking out and inserting (or substituting). Your amendment should apply to words or paragraphs of the motion; it must be pertinent to, but not necessarily consistent with, the motion. Example of correct wording: "I move to amend the motion by striking out the words . . . and substituting the words. . . ." Your amendment may in turn be amended, but the road ends there. (Memorize: "An amendment to an amendment cannot be amended.") If your amendment carries, the debate is resumed on the motion *as amended.*

Usually amendments are intended to improve a motion by clarifying the wording, by including an overlooked item, by deleting an unnecessary or undesirable item, or by providing a constructive compromise.

f. Strategems. Someone has said, "As soon as you get three people together, politics begins." Most organizations have from fifteen to hundreds of members, and it is difficult to imagine any of them making decisions on controversial questions without politics playing some part. And when an organization holds a parliamentary or semi-parliamentary meeting, the opposing factions almost always develop strategies involving the rules of procedure. There is nothing inherently wrong with this; in fact, these inevitable strategies are desirable *if* the opposing groups try to be fair to one another. Fairness requires a belief in three fundamental principles: the will of the majority should prevail, the minority has a right to be heard, and all individual members enjoy equal rights and obligations. These principles are built into the standard rules of parliamentary law; safeguards for fairness are provided to the fullest practical extent. But you must always be alert to the possibility of deliberate misuse of the rules. Furthermore, unfair strategems can be employed by either the majority or minority groups.

An ethical strategy for the majority members should be based on the fact that they can sometimes strengthen their policies by borrowing minority ideas, and the fact that in the long run they will need the minority's goodwill. Hence, the majority group should allow ample time for opponents to express their arguments, and parliamentary procedures should be used only for intended purposes (efficiency, orderliness, and fairness).

An unethical and shortsighted strategem is to use steamroller tactics. Thus, for example, all attempts by opponents to introduce amendments are promptly tabled and, if the majority numbers two-thirds, all debate is suppressed by moving the previous question. Such undemocratic tactics are not only sure to alienate the minority, but are likely to shake the loyalty of some majority members who may have a deep sense of fair play.

An ethical strategy for minority members is to make maximum use of their most persuasive speakers, to exercise their ingenuity in creating amendments that provide an opening wedge and have a chance of securing the majority's approval, to be content with a reasonable amount of time for debate, and to join with the majority in using parliamentary procedures only for the intended purposes mentioned above. The minority should accept with grace the principle of majority rule *if* they have a fair opportunity to be heard, and thus try to transform their minority into a majority.

Public discussion of public questions by public-minded citizens at a Town Meeting in Brookhaven.

An unethical and shortsighted minority strategem is to use obstructionist tactics. For example, minority members can sometimes bring the progress of the meeting to a grinding halt by constantly raising points of order and appealing from each decision of the chair, by demanding a standing vote or a roll call vote on everything, by repeatedly moving to postpone or lay on the table or refer to committee, by making parliamentary inquiries about innumerable items, by moving to adjourn, by offering an endless series of amendments, and by launching into a discussion of anything, including undebatable motions. This kind of nightmare (which theoretically can be produced by a minority of only two members) can best be curbed by the chair who can fail to "see" or to "hear" the obstreperous members, or refuse their requests for recognition, or declare them out of order for various legal reasons, especially the customary rule against "dilatory" motions. (In an extremity, a truly "disorderly" member can be legally ejected from the meeting.) Finally, you will note that clearly obstructionist tactics almost inevitably create a backlash among fair-minded members on both sides.

The Table of Motions and the brief discussion of the basics presented in this section should provide enough guidance for your instructor to assign a classroom practice project in parliamentary procedures. Experience in such a project will soon demonstrate the need and the value of additional study of *Robert's* and other references that explore this subject matter.

JOINING IN PUBLIC DISCUSSION

As you near the close of this basic speech course, you may well look back over the entire term and then look forward to the future. You have improved your communication abilities by speaking before the class. Do not lose your momentum. You can continue to improve not only in future classes, but also by participating in extracurricular activities within the campus community. You have learned that good public discussion is an interaction that occurs when both the speaker and the listeners are participating knowledgeably, responsibly, and communicatively. These criteria apply not only to success in your future career but also to your contribution to the democratic society in which you will live.

A recurring theme throughout this book has been that your goal is to improve yourself as a member of a community. Looking beyond your immediate campus community to the years after graduation, you should give high priority to evaluating the public discussion of public issues by public servants. Do not restrict yourself to samples of these on television and radio. Actively seek firsthand observations —attend open meetings of the local Board of Education, City Council, County Board of Supervisors, and other community groups. If you find examples of neglect, inefficiency, or dubious ethics, do not cynically shrug them off but "ask what you can do for your country." A good place to begin is at the community level. A good time to begin is right now. What you should do tomorrow depends upon what you can do today—a thought provocatively expressed by the poet Rainer Maria Rilke, "The future enters into us in order to transform itself in us, long before it happens."

SUMMARY

When classified by major purposes, four types of group discussion emerge: social groups, learning groups, problem-solving groups, and decision-making groups.

In addition to enjoying recreation in social groups, you can consciously practice to improve your conversation and your social sensitivity to groups.

In class discussions, panels, and other learning groups you should deliberately practice methods for effective participation: Come prepared; take an active part by contributing facts, opinions, and questions; control your participation by being relevant, brief, courteous, and cooperative.

In committees and other problem-solving groups you experiment with methods for accomplishing the duties of leadership: Make an opening statement; get the discussion started; keep it moving; keep it relevant; facilitate the resolution of conflicts; promote and conserve progress; make a closing statement.

In decision-making groups you focus on the customary parliamentary rules for such meetings, learning what the most basic rules are and making a start toward applying them in practice.

Appendixes

TO THE INSTRUCTOR

Appendix A presents a suggested sequence of tested and successfully used classroom activities, assuming a one-semester, three-unit course with an enrollment of approximately twenty students; a class hour means fifty minutes. The format is intended to provide perspective and to save time for both the instructor and the students. If the enrollment is smaller, say twelve to fifteen students, you may want to add or expand classroom projects; if the enrollment is larger, or if the school is on the quarter system, you might delete or condense projects.

You may wish to rearrange the sequence of chapters and accompanying activities because of your personal preference or the special needs of different classes. Also, the suggested choice between projects 3ab and 4ab in the schedule will probably hinge on your preference for an interview or a small-group discussion; in either case, the teaching objective is the same: to provide a bridge between conversation and public speaking (see pages 21–26). A fuller discussion of the educational philosophy underlying this and other projects is given in the Instructor's Manual, which is available without charge to teachers using the textbook. Most of the projects in these appendixes, plus a number of others, are presented in detail, together with form sheets for student use, in Milton Dickens and James H. McBath, *Guidebook for Speech Communication,* Harcourt Brace Jovanovich, 1973.

The schedule specifies very few lectures. My own teaching and research have indicated that the instructor's contributions are most effective if they are woven into class discussions or oral critiques of students' work. However, the activities labeled "class-discussions" may just as easily become "lecture-discussions." Furthermore, if facilities are available, lectures may be taped for students to listen to outside of class. This provides a self-paced listening exercise for students, as well as a way of providing special materials without using classroom time.

Written assignments are not included systematically in the schedule because choices and due dates depend so heavily on the instructor's own preferences and the school's grade deadlines. Most instructors will want to include quizzes and midterm exams, written outlines of classroom talks, written critiques of off-campus speeches, and bibliographies or note cards showing the students' research in developing speech topics. Some materials for such assignments are given in the Instructor's Manual.

The textbook has been kept to a moderate length to permit latitude in outside readings; students must be encouraged to read in depth on their chosen speaking topics. Use of the *Guidebook for Speech Communication* or a similar workbook can help the progress of the entire class. Anthologies of model speeches, or a group subscription to *Vital Speeches of the Day,* are valuable sources of collateral reading.

The degree to which the schedule is followed, and the amount of rearranging the sequence of chapters and projects, depends, of course, on the experience of the instructor. The book has been kept flexible by tight internal chapter organization, so that each chapter is a self-contained unit that can be used in a number of combinations. However, it is suggested that inexperienced teachers adhere to the schedules rather closely for a term or two before experimenting with changes. In the long run, though, a successful course in speech communication must reflect the talents and preferences of the individual instructor.

Appendix A

SUGGESTED CLASS SCHEDULE

APPROXI-MATE HOURS	CLASS ACTIVITIES	INSTRUCTIONS NUMBER	READINGS COMPLETED
1	Preview of course; grading; getting acquainted	1	
1	Class discussion of Chapter 1	2	Ch. 1
1	Organize and plan interviews	3	Chs. 2–3; and pp. 377–78
	or		
1	Organize and plan panel forums	4	Chs. 2–3; and pp. 344–48
4	Presenting interviews	3	Chs. 4–5
	or		
4	Presenting panel forums	4	Chs. 4–5
1–2	Class discussion of "The Speech Unit" and "Speech Materials"	5	Review Chs. 3 and 1
3	Demonstration talks	6	Ch. 6
3	Anecdote talks	7	Ch. 7
1–2	Class discussion of "Speech Outlining"	8	Review Chs. 4–7
2	Action talks (video tape recorder, if possible)	9	Ch. 8
3	Informative talks	10–11	Chs. 9 and 13
2	Manuscript talks (audio taped)	12	Ch. 10
1	Class poll	13	Ch. 11
1	Class discussion of "Audience Analysis"	14	Ch. 12
3–4	Audience interest talks	15	Review Chs. 8–13
3–4	Indirect argument talks	16	Ch. 14
2	Class discussion of "Listening"; informal experiments	17	Ch. 17; review Ch. 10
3–4	Direct argument talks; listening assignment	18–19	Chs. 15–16
1	Planning and organizing parliamentary sessions	20	Ch. 18
5	Talks to persuade	21	Review Chs. 14–16
3	Parliamentary sessions	22	Appendix D; Review pp. 356–60
1	Lecture-discussion on "The Speaker's Ethical Responsibilities"		See Index, "Ethical responsibilities"
2	Final written examination		Review Chs. 1–18

INSTRUCTIONS

1. Introductions

At the first (or second) class meeting each student will introduce himself, standing at his chair. He will give his name, a suggestion that may help others to remember his name, his hometown, and his major field of study. Since the purpose is simply to get acquainted, these introductions can be put in the form of a memory game. After the first student introduces himself, the second student should name the first before introducing himself. The third student should name the first and the second, and so on. It is surprising how many names can be learned in this manner.

2. Class Discussion

The subject for this class discussion is Chapter 1, "Communicating Through Speech." The chapter introduces the student to communication theory and communicative practices. To get the discussion started, compare some of your previous attitudes and beliefs about speech communication with points of view suggested in Chapter 1. Clues revealing some of your basic past attitudes are provided by taking the following test. Your score will have no bearing upon your grade in this course.

Look over the statements and mentally indicate your present opinion as to whether each is true or false. Answers to this test can be found on page 377, but first try to answer them yourself.

T F 1. The study of speech communication dates back to ancient times.

T F 2. The most important test of speaking effectiveness is *always* in terms of audience response.

T F 3. By and large public speakers are born, not made.

T F 4. The aim of a speaking course is to teach the student to speak at any time, on any subject, with a minimum of preparation.

T F 5. There are several fundamental differences between public speaking and conversation.

T F 6. *How* you say a thing is more important than *what* you say.

T F 7. There are five vowel sounds in the English language (and sometimes two more).

T F 8. Most of our greatest speakers and actors still experience a great deal of stage fright.

T F 9. There is only one absolutely correct pronunciation for any given word.

T F 10. "Gestures" should be defined as movements of the arms and hands.

T F 11. An extemporaneous talk is one given without preparation.

T F 12. A good speaker should never lean on the rostrum or other furniture.

T F 13. In reading poetry aloud, the reader should pause at each comma, period, or end of a line.

T F 14. The first step in the efficient preparation of a public speech is to write a manuscript or at least an outline.

T F 15. The proper way to close any given speech is to say, "I thank you."

3. Interviews

The class will be divided into "interview groups" of four or five members each. So that each member will know the others in his assigned group and how to reach them, names and telephone numbers of group members should be recorded and distributed:

Members of Group

A._____

B._____

C._____

D._____

E._____

INTERVIEWS OUTSIDE OF CLASS The first round of interviews will take place outside of class. Each person will engage in two out-of-class interviews; he will interview one person, and then he himself will be interviewed by one other person. The person interviewing should attempt to learn as much as possible about the person he interviews.

4-Way Interview Group

A interviews B
B interviews C
C interviews D
D interviews A

5-Way Interview Group

A interviews B
B interviews C
C interviews D
D interviews E
E interviews A

INTERVIEWS IN CLASS The second round of interviews will take place in class. In each case, the original interviewer is himself interviewed about his subject (for example, A interviews C about D). Each interview session will run about fifteen minutes. Approximately ten minutes will be devoted to the interview, during which time the other class members should not interrupt. In the remaining five minutes the class may offer comments or questions, reserving a final brief opportunity for rejoinder from the "victim."

4-Way Interview Group

A interviews C about D
B interviews D about A
C interviews A about B
D interviews B about C

5-Way Interview Group

A interviews C about D
B interviews D about E
C interviews E about A
D interviews A about B
E interviews B about C

CLASS DISCUSSION   At the end of the last interview, the class may discuss generalizations that can be made about the interviewing process.

4. Panel Forums

The class will be divided into about four groups of five or six students each. Each group will present a panel discussion before the other members of the class. This project will give the instructor a chance to hear the students "think out loud," and will give them practice in extemporaneously putting their thoughts into words in an informal, conversational situation.

The project will require from three to six class meetings to plan and to present, depending on how extensive the instructor wishes it to be.

PLANNING FOR THE PANELS   Each group will meet separately in a different part of the room and will immediately elect one of its members as the chairman. Their second task will be to choose a discussion topic, and each student should come prepared to suggest one or more topics that he would like to discuss or hear discussed. Topics should be timely, controversial, and interesting.

Each group will then plan its attack on its topic. One way of doing this is to subdivide the topic so that each member is responsible for one phase or aspect of it. The panel may plan to open by having each member give a brief (one-minute) summarizing statement of his phase of the topic. After these opening statements the whole group may engage in a give-and-take discussion on the topic as a whole.

PRESENTING THE PANEL DISCUSSION   Chairs for the panel should be placed in a semicircle facing the rest of the class. If a table is available, it should be placed in front of the semicircle. The names of the panel members may be written on the chalkboard behind the chairs. The chairman should sit at one end of the semicircle. During the discussion, members should remain seated. See pages 377–78 for further instructions.

OPEN FORUM PERIOD If only one panel is to be heard at each meeting, the thirty-minute discussion may be followed by a ten-minute forum, permitting the rest of the class to join the panel with questions or brief comments. The chairman of the group should preside over the open forum and enforce the following rules. Questions should be addressed to a specified member of the panel through the chairman. The chairman may permit one or more members of the panel to answer, but a question and an answer together should be limited to one minute—he should not allow dialogues between a questioner and an answerer. He should encourage maximum participation, get questions from as many members of the audience and answers from as many members of the panel as possible. The chairman has the right to restate questions that he thinks should be made clearer, or to overrule questions that are irrelevant.

Each panel should, of course, have a different topic from the other panels. The following list is suggestive only; you may think of a better topic for your group.

What should be done to control pollution of rivers and lakes?
What changes are most needed in our secondary schools?
How should the federal government administer its program of financial aid to college students?
What should be the foreign aid program of the United States?
Can we improve our methods of selecting presidential candidates?
To what extent can a scientist be religious?
How effective is student government on this campus?
How can TV advertising be improved?
What should be America's role in the Middle East?
What ethical standards should the public demand of candidates for public office?
What should be the policy on this campus regarding national social fraternities?
What should be done to prevent the hijacking of aircraft?

5. Class Discussion

The goal of this class discussion is to clarify and stress the importance of "the speech unit," and the gathering and recording of research materials. These topics are covered in Chapter 5 (also review pages 43–47). Your instructor may require you to bring sample cards of materials gathered for projects 6 and 7. Prepare these cards in accordance with instructions given on pages 97–99. You should have one card each from the following sources: a book, a periodical, a newspaper, a pamphlet, an encyclopedia, a book of quotations, an almanac, an atlas, Who's Who, and either the Statesman's Yearbook or the Statistical Abstract of the United States.

6. Demonstration Talk

In this four- to five-minute talk you will present one point and then support it, largely by means of visual aids. Supplement what you *say* with something the audience can *see*. Don't rely entirely on the chalkboard—consider the list of possible visual aids in Chapter 5 and try to make an ingenious choice.

Follow this sequence:
1. *Opening.* State the main point of the talk.
2. *Transition.* Get from the statement of your point into the supporting materials.
3. *Development.* Your main task is to clarify, reinforce, or prove your point. If you use some explanation or description, keep both brief, simple, concrete, and interesting. Weave in your visual aids so that they are an integral part of the talk.
4. *Transition.* Get from developmental materials into your concluding statements.
5. *Conclusion.* Summarize or restate your point.

Your delivery of this talk should be concerned with just three things.

1. *Handling visual aids.* Try to handle them easily and meaningfully without excess or random movements. Be sure the audience can see them.
2. *Directness.* Talk *with* your classmates. Look at them. Think in terms of their reactions. Be friendly and communicative.
3. *Animation.* Show by facial expression, mood, and manner that you are alert, interested, enthusiastic.

You may use notes but do not rely upon them too heavily. You will find that the visual aids themselves become "a set of notes," reminding you of your planned ideas. Study Criticism Chart 6. Suggested topics:

Surfing
Practicing to be a drum major
How to perform magic tricks
Finger painting
Photography
How to set a table
Hitting a baseball
Anatomy of the eyes
Marriage and divorce rates
The art of theatrical or other
  make-up
Trends in women's (or men's)
  fashions
Freeway (or other transportation)
  networks
The population explosion
Optical illusions

How to read blueprints
Urban planning
How a communications satellite
  works
Polishing a car
Flower arranging
Modeling in clay
Good form in bowling
Handling a firearm
Proper form in tennis or golf
Our gross national product (GNP)
How to use home electrical tools
Color mixtures and combinations
The speech and hearing
  mechanisms
Human communication models

Criticism Chart 6 Demonstration Talk

Name_____Time____to____Total_____
Topic_____Visual Aid_____

OPENING 1 2 3 4 5[1]
Main point: stated—not stated; clear—not clear enough; too brief—wordy, abstract, technical, involved
TRANSITION 1 2 3 4 5
Adequate—fair—lacking; brief, smooth, appropriate—wordy, awkward, inappropriate
DEVELOPMENT OF POINT 1 2 3 4 5
Explanation and/or description: brief, simple, clear, adequate—wordy, complicated, hard to understand, inadequate; concrete, specific—abstract, vague; interesting—dull; compact—rambling
Use of visual aid: an integral part of the talk—partially appropriate—mostly superfluous; clearly visible to audience—not clearly visible to audience; helped clarify the point—distracted from the point—too complex or detailed
CONCLUSION 1 2 3 4 5
Summary or restatement: adequate—fair—lacking; appropriate—inappropriate; smooth—too abrupt
DELIVERY 1 2 3 4 5
Handling of visual aids: skillful—fair—distracting; too much physical movement—too little physical movement; appropriate—inappropriate, awkward, blocked view of visual aid; movements coordinated—jerky; relaxed—tense; vigorous—limp—too vigorous; meaningful—random; "fiddled" with _____
Directness: excellent, partial, lacking; looked at audience, at floor, ceiling, walls, out of window, over the heads, at notes, at visual aids, at one person or part of audience; eyes shifty, faraway look; general manner: aloof, condescending, reserved, passive, impersonal, uncertain—friendly, poised, communicative, forceful, intense
Animation: facial expression: excellent—fair—lacking—overdone—inappropriate; general manner: lively, enthusiastic, alert—listless, colorless, stolid

7. Anecdote Talk

In this three- to four-minute talk you will develop one point, principally by means of anecdote. You may include either one or two anecdotes, depending on time limits. If two are used, each should develop the same point. Follow this sequence:

1. *Opening.* Just start telling the anecdote. Don't state your point.
2. *Anecdote.* Review the suggestions regarding the choosing of anec-

---

[1] On the rating scale, 1 means far below average; 2, somewhat below average; 3, average; 4, somewhat above average; 5, superior.

dotes, pages 80–85 and 234–36. While telling the anecdote(s), imply your point, but don't state it.

3. *Transitions.* Get from the anecdote into the second anecdote if you have one. Lead into your statement of the main point.

4. *Conclusion.* State your point.

Four aspects of delivery will be practiced. Directness and animation remain the same as in the previous criticism chart. Appearance and bodily action will be added. Study Criticism Chart 7 regarding these additional aspects of delivery. Try to include the appropriate details as you practice your talk aloud. Don't memorize and don't overuse your notes.

Criticism Chart 7   Anecdote Talk

Name_____Time_____to_____Total_____
Topic_____

OPENING 1 2 3 4 5
   Began with illustration: well done—fair—weak; stated the point—used extraneous materials—"hemmed and hawed"
ANECDOTE 1 2 3 4 5
   Style: narrative—not narrative
   Detail: well done—too many—too few
   Arrangement: clear, easy to follow—unclear, vague, confused; built to climax—"ran down"—no climax—anticlimax
   General effect: pointed, appropriate, interesting, in good taste—pointless, inappropriate, insufficiently interesting, in poor taste, tended to "drag" in places
TRANSITIONS 1 2 3 4 5
   Adequate—fair—lacking; brief—too brief; smooth, appropriate—wordy, awkward, inappropriate, abrupt
CONCLUSION 1 2 3 4 5
   Main point: stated—not stated; clear—not clear enough; brief—too brief—wordy, abstract, technical, involved; appropriate—inappropriate; smooth—too abrupt
DELIVERY 1 2 3 4 5
   Directness: excellent, partial, lacking; looked at audience, at floor, ceiling, walls, out of window, over the heads, at notes, at visual aids, at one person or part of audience; eyes shifty, faraway look; general manner: aloof, condescending, reserved, passive impersonal, uncertain—friendly, poised, communicative, forceful, intense
   Animation: facial expression: excellent—fair—lacking—overdone—inappropriate; general manner: lively, enthusiastic, alert—listless, colorless, stolid
   Appearance: dress appropriate, well-groomed—distracting; posture alert, at east—tense, stiff, formal, slouchy, stooped, listless, swayed, leaned on _____
BODILY ACTION:
   Platform position: no change—paced, restless; moved about easily—

awkwardly—mechanically; moved at appropriate times—at inappropriate times

Feet: well-managed—fair—distracting; jiggled, teetered—straddled—at attention—weight on one foot—shifting

Basic hand positions: satisfactory—constantly shifted—the same; behind back—at sides—in pockets—in front of body—on lectern—twisted or rubbed together; fiddled with _____

Gestures: lacking—seldom—frequent—too many; natural—appropriate—not carried through—lacked variety

8. Discussion of "Outlining"

Be prepared to ask questions and discuss chapters 5, 6, and 7 as they apply to the structure and content of your informative talk (project 10). If your instructor requires a first draft outline of the informative talk, turn it in at this class session. If he does not, the full-sentence outline is to be turned in on the day your talk is delivered.

9. Action Talks

In this two- to three-minute talk you will come out from behind the classroom rostrum or table and discuss some topic that permits you to use lots of bodily action, especially broad and vigorous gestures. Try movements that require the whole body; do not be timid or halfhearted but remember the advice to *carry through.* Study the pictures in Chapter 8. If your instructor has a video tape recorder available for use, he will use it during this talk and arrange for you to see yourself as others see you. Much depends on your choice of topic. Here are some suggestions:

How to do a given dance step
On being attacked by bees
Movie stuntmen's tricks
How to play tennis or table tennis
Various swimming strokes
Modeling clothes
Dribbling and shooting in basketball
Body-building exercises
The most awkward person I've known

Fencing
Different ways of walking
Cheerleaders' routines
Orchestra conducting
Measuring the size of this room
Shadowboxing
A football referee's signals
Military marching

10. Informative Talk

You may select any subject on which you wish to inform the audience. The topic should be one on which you have personal experience or have gained special knowledge, and one that serves a clarifying function for listeners. The subject should be delimited thoughtfully in order to meet the time limit of five to six minutes. The materials of this talk should be outlined in accordance with the suggestions in Chapter 6. Study Criticism Chart 10 for a sample of how the success of the talk may be evaluated by the instructor. Suggested topics:

Air, water, or noise pollution
Invention or discovery of something new (laser beam, DNA, radar for the blind)
Birth control
Computer assisted instruction (CAI)
Charisma of renowned personalities
Biodegradable soaps, detergents, pesticides, fertilizers
Political elections: analyzing the outcome
Preventing or fighting forest fires
Peacetime uses of atomic energy
Funding local or state government
Fraudulent advertising through mass media
Perceptual distortions (optical illusions, distances)
Stereotyping (races, personalities, religions, social institutions)
Controlled usage of automobiles on freeways (e.g., odd and even license numbers)
Controlled boating on inland waterways and lakes
Legalized gambling
National and world demographical trends
The Delphi method of forecasting the future
Dieting
Intercultural communication
Race relations
Bunko artists (confidence men, investment funds, sales)
Social class and educational achievement
Safety engineering (automotive, color TV, home appliances, toys)
Solar energy
Inflation or depression
Organized crime
Prison reform

Criticism Chart 10   Talk to Inform

*Name*_____*Time*____to____*Total*_____
*Topic*_____

INTRODUCTION 1 2 3 4 5
    Did the opening catch audience attention?
    Did the speaker establish his right to inform upon this subject?
    Was the audience motivated to want to learn?
    Did the speaker lead into subject matter effectively?
    Was a preview of main points given?
BODY 1 2 3 4 5
    Was the central idea clear?
    Did the main points and subpoints clarify the central idea adequately?
    Did the main points and subpoints form an easy-to-remember pattern?
    Did the body of the speech employ aids to learning?

CONCLUSION 1 2 3 4 5
    Was the entire speech focused on the central idea?
    Were the main points summarized?
    Did the closing words give an appropriate, rounded-out effect?
DELIVERY 1 2 3 4 5
    See Criticism Chart 7

11. Impromptu Responses

To assist you in becoming a better listener and a more fluent speaker, your instructor may wish to make a supplementary assignment beginning with informative talks and becoming a "continuing" practice for selected projects during the remainder of this course. On days when several class members are scheduled to give prepared talks, everyone else will listen with a view to giving a brief response to one of the speakers. One way of handling the assignment is as follows.

At the conclusion of all of the prepared speeches the instructor allots a period of time for responses. The instructor chooses at random from the audience, first one student and then another who rises and gives his impromptu remarks directed to any of the speeches he has just heard. Thus, when you are among the listeners you will not know on what days or at what moment you may be called on. But each day you must be ready. This means that you must listen to your classmates attentively and purposively; often you will want to take some notes. When you give a response, you may either agree or disagree with the speaker; you may want to strengthen one of his points or to criticize his facts or logic. In any case, try to be constructive, and at least let the speaker know of some of your thoughts which ordinarily would have remained internal and unsaid.

Thus during the rest of the term you should get at least one and probably several chances to "talk back" to fellow students whose speeches have aroused your admiration or, sometimes, exasperation. Also, when you are one of the prepared speakers, you will get some overt feedback revealing the kinds of reactions that run through your listeners' minds and thus suggesting ways for you to become a more effective speech communicator.

12. Manuscript Talk

Prepare a three- to four-minute talk to be read aloud from the printed page (manuscript). Your major forms of support are selected quotations. The quoted materials should make up 30 to 40 percent of the whole. Quotations should be drawn from more than one author, and from more than one type of material. Consider poetry, speeches, plays, essays, short stories, novels, general nonfiction, textbooks, technical reports. For suggestions on reading from manuscript, study pages 205–07. Criticism of this talk will be focused on voice, articulation, and pronunciation. Your instructor may wish to audio-tape the talk and to use Criticism Chart 12. Suggested titles:

Voice of History
Political Campaign Slogans: The Quickie Appeal
The World of Ogden Nash (Johnny Carson, W. C. Fields)
The Masculine Mystique

Yo Soy Chicano
Revolt of the Consumer
Literature of Protest
The Jargon of Bureaucracy
I Am Frightened by the "Brave New World"
Irish Eyes Aren't Smiling
To Be Black in America
What Is a University?
Can the News Media Be Trusted?
Your Government and You
New Approaches and Interests in the Arts
The World of Sports Today
What's Happening in the Field of Medicine
The Money Crunch (Personal-National-International)

Criticism Chart 12   Vocal Communication

*Name*_____*Time*_____to_____*Total*_____
*Topic*_____

AUDIBILITY 1 2 3 4 5
Suggestions
_____faulty breathing (see page 178)
_____inattention to audibility (see page 178)
_____poorly adapted to acoustics (see page 178)
_____endings trailed away (see page 178)
_____muffled (see pages 178–79)
_____pitch level too low (see page 179)
_____other difficulties of audibility (consult instructor)
DISTINCTNESS AND PRONUNCIATION 1 2 3 4 5
Suggestions
_____careless, lip-lazy (see pages 180–81)
_____slurred, mumbled (see pages 181–82)
_____muffled (see pages 181–82)
_____too precise, affected (see page 182)
_____regional or foreign accent (consult instructor)
_____faulty sounds (see pages 179–82)

mispronounced words (see page 183)

other inaccuracies (consult instructor)

MEANINGFULNESS 1 2 3 4 5
Suggestions
_____insensitive to meanings (see page 184)
_____rate too fast (see pages 184–86)
_____rate too slow (see pages 184–86)

_____ rate monotonous (see pages 184–85)

_____ phrasing jerky, illogical (see pages (185–86)

_____ pitch monotonous (see page 186)

_____ general vocal quality monotonous (see pages 183–84 and 186–87)

_____ other difficulties of meaningfulness (consult instructor)

Additional comments

13. Class Poll

Mimeographed questionnaires similar to those appearing below will be distributed. To encourage frankness in answering, the poll will be anonymous. Fill out the questionnaire accurately and rapidly. When all students have filled in their answers, the papers will be collected and redistributed at random to keep the poll anonymous. The instructor will then read each item, and call for a show of hands—students voting according to the anonymous papers before them. The instructor will announce the count of hands for each item, and everyone can record the count on the margins of the ballot.

After the results have been tabulated each student will have a reasonably complete and accurate picture of the audience he will be addressing throughout the term. If time permits, immediately following the tabulation a class discussion of significant trends and exceptions may be conducted, together with a discussion of how these data can help each student in planning future talks. The record of the tabulation should be kept by every student, for it will be useful in future assignments.

This poll is anonymous. Do not write your name on this sheet.

Part One—Composition of Audience

Place check marks in appropriate blanks. (*Code* _____)

1. My age.

   a_____ under 18   b_____ 18–20   c_____ 21–25   d_____ 26 or over

2. Urban-rural background. I spent most of my life before 21 in:

   a_____ farm community or village   c_____ city of 25,000–100,000

   b_____ town under 25,000 population   d_____ city over 100,000

3. Geographical background. I spent most of my life before 21 in:

   a_____ this immediate locality   e_____ South; Southeast; Texas

   b_____ Pacific Coast area   f_____ East Coast or New England

   c_____ Southwest; Mountain   g_____ outside continental U.S.

   d_____ Midwest

4. National background.

   a_____ at least one parent or grandparent born outside U.S.

   b_____ language other than English is native tongue for at least one person in immediate family or grandparents

5. Economic background. To the best of my knowledge, parental income up to time I was 21, except for unusual periods, probably averaged, on a yearly basis:

Answers to true-false questions on page 366. The first two statements are true; the remaining thirteen statements are false.

a___$5,000 or less	c___$10,000–$20,000
b___$5,000–$10,000	d___over $20,000

6. Marital, parental status. I am now:

a___married	c___single
b___parent	d___divorced or widowed

7. Political preferences. Most of the time I tend to favor:

a___Democrats	c___third minor party
b___Republicans	d___none in particular

8. Religious preferences. (Check one or more.) I tend to favor:

   a___the Roman Catholic faith
   b___the Eastern Catholic faith
   c___a Protestant faith
   d___the Jewish faith
   e___the Moslem faith
   f___no church in particular (although I hold religious beliefs)
   g___agnostic, "free-thinking," or atheistic beliefs
   h___attending church regularly
   i___attending church irregularly
   j___attending seldom or never

9. Membership in certain groups.

   a___I am a member (or pledge) of a social fraternity or sorority
   b___I am or have been a member of a labor union
   c___I am or have been or hope to be a member of a recognized business or professional organization (such as the American Bar Association, the American Management Association, the National Association of Manufacturers, the American Medical Association)
   d___I am a member of a veterans' organization

10. Vocational aspiration or connection _____

Part Two—Audience Attitudes on Contemporary Affairs

Directions The purpose of this poll is to supplement course materials on audience analysis. Its value depends on the frankness and accuracy of your answers. Please draw a circle around the *A* if you tend, in general, to *approve* of the ideas represented by the person, group, or statement; around the *D* if you tend to *disapprove;* around the *X* if you *are not sure to whom or to what the item refers;* and around ? if you are *uncertain* or your feelings are divided.

A D X ?   1. Spiro Agnew
A D X ?   2. Hubert Humphrey
A D X ?   3. John F. Kennedy
A D X ?   4. Queen Elizabeth II
A D X ?   5. Billy Graham
A D X ?   6. Henry Kissinger
A D X ?   7. Hugh Hefner
A D X ?   8. Cesar Chavez
A D X ?   9. Willy Brandt

A D X ?   10. Richard M. Nixon
A D X ?   11. Mrs. Golda Meir
A D X ?   12. Edward (Ted) Kennedy
A D X ?   13. Martha Mitchell
A D X ?   14. Ronald Reagan
A D X ?   15. George Wallace
A D X ?   16. American Legion
A D X ?   17. John Lindsay
A D X ?   18. Movie censorship
A D X ?   19. NATO
A D X ?   20. WCTU
A D X ?   21. DAR
A D X ?   22. NAACP
A D X ?   23. NAM
A D X ?   24. NASA
A D X ?   25. Jacqueline (Kennedy) Onassis
A D X ?   26. Neil Armstrong
A D X ?   27. Walter Cronkite
A D X ?   28. AFL–CIO
A D X ?   29. AMA
A D X ?   30. United Nations
A D X ?   31. The present administration has been successful in its domestic policy.
A D X ?   32. The Voice of America is a waste of money.
A D X ?   33. The United States should reduce its defense budget by at least $10 billion.
A D X ?   34. Blacks, on the whole, have a square deal in the United States.
A D X ?   35. Russia and China apparently intend to conquer the world.
A D X ?   36. College fraternities and sororities are, in general, satisfactory.
A D X ?   37. A reemphasis on fundamental religion is greatly needed in the world today.
A D X ?   38. Medical care today is too expensive for most Americans.
A D X ?   39. The Communist party in the United States should be outlawed.
A D X ?   40. There is too much emphasis on nuclear weapons in present defense plans.
A D X ?   41. Labor unions, in general, are beneficial to the American way of life.
A D X ?   42. There is an overemphasis on big college athletic programs.
A D X ?   43. The United States should extend reciprocal trade agreements to cover more nations and more products.
A D X ?   44. Congressional investigating committees are doing a very good job.
A D X ?   45. The American public-school systems are doing an adequate job of educating American youth.
A D X ?   46. Farm price supports are unnecessary and wasteful.
A D X ?   47. The present administration has been successful in its foreign policy.

A D X ? 48. The average American is overtaxed.
A D X ? 49. Voting in the United States should be made compulsory.
A D X ? 50. Pornography should be more strictly censored.
A D X ? 51. Candidates for public office should be required to publish their personal financial status.
A D X ? 52. Successful participation in politics usually requires dubious ethical standards.
A D X ? 53. Social Security deductions are too large.
A D X ? 54. The present process of procuring military personnel for the armed forces is effective and fair.
A D X ? 55. The world population should be numerically and genetically controlled.
A D X ? 56. Wiretapping is an appropriate method for controlling crime.
A D X ? 57. Scientific technology should be able to solve the majority of our environmental and sociological problems.
A D X ? 58. Smoking in public places should be prohibited by law.
A D X ? 59. Homosexuality should be a socially accepted lifestyle.
A D X ? 60. There is an "unwritten" double standard of justice practiced by the United States system of jurisprudence.

14. Discussion of "Audience Analysis"

The tabulation of data provided by the class poll may be analyzed to discover trends and exceptions; this analysis should be discussed in terms of how the data can help each student in planning future classroom talks.

The class discussion should then be broadened to off-campus audiences that students are likely to encounter after graduation. Discuss ethical implications of the statement "Adapting to an audience does not mean surrendering to it."

15. Audience Interest Talk

Prepare for a three- to five-minute talk on "What This College (or Community, or State) Needs More Than Anything Else." Adapt the talk to the immediate interests of the audience, and make that adaption clear by references to places, persons, or events within the personal experience of the audience. Be guided by the class poll (Instructions, 13) in choosing a topic and planning the talk.

16. Indirect Argument

Prepare an eight- to ten-minute talk in which you take a side on a controversial issue. A subject must be chosen so that some of your audience will be undecided or opposed to your point of view. Your general purpose will be to convince, that is, to build new attitudes in those classmates who are undecided or opposed. The talk should be of indirect design, following suggestions in Chapter 15 with particular reference to pages 296 and 298–99. Study Criticism Chart 16 for more detailed guidelines on how the talk should be constructed. Suggested topics:

Traffic congestion
Unwed mothers
Improving postal services
High cost of textbooks
Television commercials
Privileged information given to reporters
Moratorium on space exploration
Additional superhighways and toll roads
Universal fingerprinting
Voiceprints in legal evidence

Criticism Chart 16   Indirect Argument

Name_____Time_____to_____Total_____
Topic_____

INTRODUCTION 1 2 3 4 5
 Did the opening words get favorable attention?
 Did the speaker establish personal prestige?
 Did he begin on common ground?
 Did he reveal his purpose and central idea too soon?
 Was the transition into the body of the speech smooth?
BODY 1 2 3 4 5
 Was the central idea revealed gradually and tactfully?
 Were the purpose and central idea sufficiently narrowed?
 Was the problem-solution sequence followed?
 Was the idea sequence adapted to audience opposition?
CONCLUSION 1 2 3 4 5
 Were the main points restated?
 Did the conclusion focus the whole speech on the central idea?
DELIVERY
 Appearance 1 2 3 4 5
  Dress; posture
 Bodily communication 1 2 3 4 5
  Change of position on platform; basic position of hands; gestures
 Vocal communication 1 2 3 4 5
  Audibility; distinctness; pronunciation; meaningfulness
 Language 1 2 3 4 5
  Meaningfulness; simplicity and precision; concreteness; figurative
  language; fluency
 General impressions 1 2 3 4 5
  Directness; animation; friendliness; sincerity; poise; other

17. Discussion of "Listening"; Use of Equipment

Discussion should center upon the major points in Chapter 17 (amount, characteristics, and management of listening). Some of the unstated implications should be tested against your daily experiences, including informal experiments. For example, the time differential between speaking behaviors and listening behaviors (page 323) raises the intriguing question: "Can you utilize the 'slack time' to improve your listening efficiency?" Or compare speaking-listening with writing-reading: "Who controls the pace in each of these communication processes?"

The class discussion may be stimulated by demonstration and informal experiments or by using available electronic equipment, such as a speech compressor, a teaching machine, a video tape recorder, or a pair of audio-tape recorders (pages 328–29).

18. Direct Argument

The class will be divided into pairs. The students of each pair will take opposing sides on a controversial question, giving six- to eight-minute talks in immediate succession. Each pair will thus present a semidebate. Each speech will be presented as a direct argument, following the suggestions in Chapter 15 but with particular attention to page 297. Criticism Chart 18 shows more precisely the specific details that may be evaluated in each speech. Suggested propositions:

We should have pay-TV.
Tax money should be allotted to private schools.
Recipients of welfare payments should be put to work for the state or city or county.
All college courses should be elective.
The United States should adopt compulsory national health insurance.
Modern advertising is detrimental to society.
Prayer should be restored to public schools.
Capital punishment should be abolished.
Labor union membership should be a condition of employment.
The sale of pornographic literature should be forbidden.
Welfare benefits to the poor should be increased.
Student health services should dispense birth control pills.
Laws against use and sale of marijuana should be abolished.
Students should be bused to schools to achieve school integration.
Every American should be guaranteed a minimum wage.
Stricter gun control legislation should be enacted.

Criticism Chart 18   Direct Argument

Name_____Time_____to_____Total_____
Topic_____

INTRODUCTION 1 2 3 4 5
   Did the opening words get favorable attention?
   Did the speaker state his point of view early?
   Did he give a preview of his main points?
   Was the transition into the body of the speech smooth?
BODY 1 2 3 4 5
   Was the central idea (proposition) clear?

Were the purpose and central idea sufficiently narrowed?
Did the main points suffice to prove the central idea?
Were there too many or too few main points?
Were the main points persuasively worded?
Was each main point supported by evidence?
Did the evidence include authorities, instances, and statistics?
Was the reasoning from the evidence sound?
Was the speech adapted to audience interests?
Was the speech adapted to audience drives and motives?
Was the speech adapted to existing audience attitudes toward related topics?

CONCLUSION 1   2   3   4   5

Were the main points restated?
Did the conclusion focus the whole speech on the central idea?

DELIVERY

Appearance 1   2   3   4   5
Dress; posture
Bodily communication 1   2   3   4   5
Change of position on platform; basic position of hands; gestures
Vocal communication 1   2   3   4   5
Audibility; distinctness; pronunciation; meaningfulness
Language 1   2   3   4   5
Meaningfulness; simplicity and precision; concreteness; figurative
   language; fluency
General impressions 1   2   3   4   5
Directness; animation, friendliness; sincerity; poise; other

19. Classroom Listening

You will be assigned a student speaker on whom to practice listening. Study the Listener's Report Chart 19. As listener, notice that you are to provide three things: description, evaluation, and prescription; you are a reporter, critic, and coach. The speaker will notice, at the bottom of the chart, that he may talk back to you.

The largest amount of space is for description. Try to give a reasonably complete and objective report of what you saw and heard. Occasionally this may best be done by complete sentences (for example, his central idea), but key words and phrases (often quoted from the speaker) will usually suggest what ideas and behaviors impressed you the most as you listened. To guide your reporting, some familiar captions are supplied in the left-hand column. On the right-hand side is space for your evaluations, paralleling the items being criticized. You may use a grading system for some items, but usually your comments will be more instructive. For instance, suppose that under description you note "explains costs—$50,000 total"; under evaluation you might comment "too many confusing statistics" or "statistics clear and convincing." In general, evaluations should include both the favorable and unfavorable; it is almost inconceivable that any student talk would be either perfect or without a redeeming virtue. Some evaluative comments are sufficient in themselves; others require suggestions on how to improve (prescription). Thus, it is frustrating to read only that the speech organization was "unclear" or "incohesive." Just what could the speaker do about it? Perhaps you have a constructive suggestion: "Change from spatial to temporal sequence," or "Give preview of main points."

In accomplishing the above tasks, one problem is rapid notetaking as you listen to the speech. A good procedure is to use scratch paper for these notes so that you may employ your own system of abbreviations and shorthand—a little later you can translate them to the chart, making them more meaningful and legible.

Criticism Chart 19　Listeners Report

*Listener*_____*Speaker*_____
*Topic*_____ *Date*_____

I. DESCRIPTION   II. EVALUATION
A. Content and organization
   Opening:
   Body:
      Central idea (state fully):
      Main points (list them):
      Supports (identify a few):
   Conclusion:
B. Delivery
   Appearance:
   Body communication:
   Vocal communication:
   Language:
III. General impressions
   (Animation, directness, friendliness, poise, preparedness, other)
IV. Prescription
   (Suggestions for improvement: Things speaker can do.)
Speaker's comments
   (Regarding above description, evaluation, and prescription)

20. Planning the Parliamentary Sessions

The choice of a significant current problem for use in the parliamentary project should be made several weeks in advance, so that by this time the class will have done a substantial amount of research. The topic should be of current community, state, or national concern. At the time of this writing, for example, current problems include presidential impeachment, reform of election laws, and the energy crisis. The chosen topic should be of sufficient scope to deserve more than a one-sentence motion or resolution.

At this class meeting any student may submit a tentative written draft of a resolution, or an oral sketch of one that he would like to prepare and present (at the opening of project 20). In any event, arrangements should be made for one or more students to prepare one or more resolutions in advance of project 20. Each resolution should be restricted to one page (or less) and duplicate copies should be supplied to the entire class as soon as possible (during the progress of project 19, for instance). Suggested form is as follows:

Line 1: A RESOLUTION recommending methods for dealing with the energy problem in the United States.
Line 2: Submitted by (name or names)
Line 3: Be it resolved by this student group,
Lines 4 ff: 1. That the ...
          2. That also ...
          3. That ...

Election of officers for the coming sessions should be conducted. To spread the experience of chairmanship, the class may wish to elect three persons to preside over the three days of project 20; by informal agreement each of them may appoint a chairman pro tem for part of his session. One or more person(s) should also be elected as the clerk(s) (or secretaries) of the meetings. Duties of officers are discussed in Chapter 18 and *Robert's Rules of Order.*

The instructor should probably prescribe time limits for speeches and other special rules needed for project 20.

21. Persuasive Speech

The term *persuasive speech* cutomarily includes any speech where the purpose is to stimulate (reinforce attitudes), to convince (build attitudes), or to actuate (release attitudes). For this final speech your instructor may grant wide individual latitude in choosing the purpose and subject. On the other hand, he may wish to provide detailed instructions for one or more specific types of persuasive speeches. In any case your ultimate goal is to influence behavior through speech.

Criticism Chart 21   Persuasive Speech

Name_____Time_____to_____Total_____
Topic_____

THE ATTENTION STEP 1 2 3 4 5
   Did the opening get attention?
   Was the attention favorable?
   Was the attention directed naturally and quickly toward the subject?
THE NEED STEP 1 2 3 4 5
   Did the speaker give the audience reasons for believing or acting?
   Were the reasons logically adequate?
   Were the reasons presented in terms of audience motivation?
   Was this step effective, that is, did the speaker actually arouse feelings of need?

If not, what may have been his trouble?

If so, were his psychological techniques ethical?

THE SATISFACTION STEP 1 2 3 4 5

Did the speaker present a proposal or plan?

Was it directly and clearly related to the "needs"?

Was the proposal logically adequate?

Was it psychologically sound?

THE ACTION STEP 1 2 3 4 5

Did the speaker give a specific and concrete picture of what each individual should do, think, or feel?

Did he include a definite "call for action" appropriate to the audience, the occasion, and the speaker's goal?

22. Parliamentary Sessions

At the first session, the chair will call the meeting to order, announce special rules, and say, "The floor is now open for presentation of resolutions or other pertinent motions." Someone will present a resolution (since written copies have previously been distributed, to save time he need read only the title) and move its adoption; the proposal will be handled in the fashion described in Chapter 18 relative to "main motions." (At subsequent sessions the chair may call for reading, correcting, and approving abbreviated minutes of the previous meeting.) During these sessions you will be guided by the suggestions in Chapter 18, the brief table in Appendix D, and *Robert's Rules of Order* (or other manual).

A suggested goal for this project is that you evolve a resolution of sufficient merit to justify sending a copy (perhaps signed by the entire class) to your councilman, congressman, mayor, senator, governor, or other appropriate public official. You may be surprised to receive a letter of personal comments in reply.

Appendix B

SAMPLE SPEECH OUTLINE

INTRODUCTION

Here is a remarkable piece of rock—just look at it. I found this rock right here on our own campus, and there's a story behind it which I will presently tell. Maybe that story will interest you in the hobby of rock-collecting. You will discover that this hobby is enjoyable, inexpensive, and instructive. You might even make a fortune from it!

BODY

Central Idea: Collecting rocks and minerals is a desirable hobby.
  I. It is enjoyable.
   A. You will enjoy hiking.
      1. Last weekend two friends and I enjoyed some beautiful scenery, a mineral find, and a mild adventure with some with animals. [Anecdote]
      2. After our return we found that we were relaxed, refreshed, and pleasantly tired. [Description]
   B. You will enjoy identifying and mounting specimens at home.

Milton Dickens and James H. McBath, *Guidebook for Speech Communication*, 2nd ed. (New York: Harcourt Brace Jovanovich, 1973), p. 32. Quoted by special permission of Harcourt Brace Jovanovich, Inc. See pp. 29–33 for a description of how this outline was developed according to the recommended six-step method.

      1. Here is an interesting specimen; let's identify it together. [Visual aid; explanation]
      2. Here is a mounted collection—let me tell you about it. [Visual aid; description]
II. It is inexpensive.
  A. You can buy the needed tools for about $6.
      1. Here is an inexpensive rock pick. [Visual aid; statistic]
      2. You probably own other necessary tools—magnifying glass, pocketknife, a penny, etc. [Instances]
  B. You can buy a beginning book for less than $1.
      1. Here is a paperback by Paul Shaffer which sells for only 59 cents. [Visual aid; statistic; perhaps read a brief quotation]
      2. Here are two longer books by Pough and by Pearl; each is authoritative; they sell for about $6 and $7. [Visual aids; statistics]
III. It is instructive.
  A. You will immediately acquire an unusual topic for conversation. [Have we time for subpoints? Or shall we just support by an anecdote?]
  B. You will soon acquire some surprising information about local geology.
      1. The soil is ... [Possible supports: description, quotations]
      2. Our water supply depends upon ... [Possible supports: now you supply a few appropriate possibilities]

CONCLUSION

This morning I have sought to show that collecting rocks and minerals is a desirable hobby. It is enjoyable; it is inexpensive; it is instructive. Why not give it a try? Almost every weekend I go rock hunting. Let me invite you to come along. Maybe we'll discover a uranium treasure. More certain, and more important—we'll have a wonderful time.

Appendix C

SAMPLE SPEECH OUTLINE

The following sample outline is more detailed than is necessary for an ordinary speech. The parts, the forms of support, and the transitions have been labeled in italics, and the gist of anecdotes is given. These details were added to enable you to follow the thought more readily, to show the relationships among ideas, and to show the logical relationships between the thought and the mechanics of the outline form.

Title: "Is Silence Golden?"
Subject: Speech training
Purpose: To convince my listeners that they should take speech courses

INTRODUCTION
  I. *Quotation:* The other day in my speech class Professor W. Charles Redding raised this question for discussion, "Is silence golden?"
     Transition: That question struck a chord in my memory.
 II. *Brief anecdote:* Last summer the boss gave a dinner party ... Jack Reader was tongued-tied ... Leaving party, Jack was discouraged. I said, "Well, silence is golden." "Golden!" Jack snorted, "it's humiliating!"
III. *Brief anecdote:* My Uncle Luther, a businessman ... his chance to run for president of Chamber of Commerce ... turned down chance be-

cause afraid of public speaking ... his silence isn't golden—it's expensive.

IV. *Brief anecdote:* Mrs. Warner, a neighbor ... children now grown up ... she needs constructive community activities ... she has money, talent, education but no speech training ... her silence isn't golden—it's a penalty on her community.

>*Transition:* People like Jack, and Uncle Luther, and Mrs. Warner are typical. They demonstrate that silence is often not golden. With most people the problem is not how to remain silent but how to talk effectively. This semester I have discovered that effective talking can be learned. I got my nerve up and enrolled in a speech class. And tonight I want to recommend that class to all of you.

BODY

Central idea: Tonight I want to show that speech training is golden. It makes you a more effective person, a more effective wage earner, and a more effective citizen.

>*Transition:* Let us consider the first of these.

I. *Main point:* Speech training makes you a more effective person.
  A. *Quotation:* Lowell Thomas once remarked, "I can think of nothing that is more likely to add cubits to your stature than well-rounded training in public speaking ..."
  >*Transition:* The truth of his words is well illustrated in an actual speech class.
  B. *Anecdote:* At the beginning of the term Tom was a social hermit ... he has now learned to like people.
  >*Transition:* Tom is no isolated case. A dozen others in the class have obviously improved their personalities. For example ...
  C. *Instances:* Loreine is less gushy; Paul has been developing confidence and poise.
  >*Transition:* But speech training not only makes you a more effective person ...

II. *Main point:* Speech training makes you a more effective wage earner.
  A. *Statistics:* According to the *Statistical Abstract,* here are the professions and vocations that pay the highest incomes ... Notice in how many of them public speaking is a necessity for success.
  B. *Statistics:* The National Council of Teachers of English made a survey of 2,615 adults from 253 different occupations ...
  C. *Quotations:* The national societies of such professions as engineering and medicine have recommended that public speaking be ...
  >*Transition:* Thus speech training is golden in a literal sense—it means money. That brings us to the third and final value.

III. *Main point:* Speech training makes you a more effective citizen.
  A. *Explanation:* In a democracy free public discussion is the basic technique ... contrast Russia where basic technique is propaganda ... under a dictator silence often *is* golden ... but democracy ...
  B. *Anecdote:* A group of taxpayers in my hometown held a meeting last year ...

C. *Quotation:* Woodrow Wilson summed up the importance of speech to responsible citizenship when he said . . .
   Transition: And now to summarize . . .

CONCLUSION

I. *Summary:* I have shown that speech training makes you a more effective person, a more effective wage earner, and a more effective citizen.

II. *Quotation:* John Morley has said, "I hope that your professors of rhetoric will teach you to cultivate that golden art—the steadfast use of a language in which truth can be told; a speech that is strong by natural force, and not merely effective by declamation; an utterance without trick, without affectation, without mannerism."

III. I am sure our professors can teach that golden art. The only question is: Are you and I, the students, willing to learn it?

Appendix D

BRIEF TABLE OF PARLIAMENTARY MOTIONS

These motions are listed in order of relative priority: the lowest in rank i listed first (except incidental motions, which have no order of precedenc among themselves).

MOTION	USUAL PURPOSE	INTERRUPT SPEAKER?	REQUIRE SECOND?	DEBATABLE?	AMENDABLE?
I. *Main Motion*	To introduce business	No	Yes	Yes	Yes
II. *Subsidiary Motions:*	Used to modify or dispose of the main motion				
Postpone indefinitely	To suppress consideration of main motion	No	Yes	Yes	No
Amend	To change a resolution	No	Yes	Yes	Yes
Refer to committee	For study and recommendations	No	Yes	Yes	Yes
Postpone definitely	To postpone to a certain time	No	Yes	Yes	Yes
Previous question	To vote immediately	No	Yes	No	No
Lay on the table	To lay pending question aside temporarily	No	Yes	No	No
III. *Incidental Motions:*	Pertain to the motions being considered				
Parliamentary inquiry	To learn procedure or information	Yes	No	No	No
Point of order	To correct a parliamentary error	Yes	No	No	No
Withdrawal of motion	Remove motion from consideration	No	No	No	No
Division of assembly	To secure an accurate vote	Yes	No	No	No
Division of question	To divide motion for separate consideration	No	Yes	No	Yes
Appeal decision of the chair	To reverse ruling of the chair	Yes	Yes	Yes	No
IV. *Privileged Motions:*	Do not pertain to pending motions, but to the members				
Question of privilege	Comfort or convenience of members	Yes	No	No	No
Recess	For a brief intermission	No	Yes	No	Yes
Adjourn	Dismiss session	No	Yes	No	No

Index

Verbal communication, introduction to, 5–19; and audience, 15–19; and silent thinking, 9; basic concepts of, 6, 15–17; communicative attitude, 15–17; definition of, 6; eye contact, 17; learning to talk, 5; process of, 11–15; signs and symbols, 8; societal, 8, 10–11; verbal attacks, 8

Vest, George Graham, *quoted*, 269

Visual aids: check list of, 89–91; handling, 162–63; *pictured*, 90

Visual communication, 150–65; importance of, 150–52; nonverbal communication, 151–52; personal inventory, 152–56; program for improvement, 156–63

Visual communication, program for practice, 157–63; characteristics of effective gestures, 161–62; conventional gestures, 160–61; handling notes, 162; handling visual aids, 162; platform movements, 162; posture, 159; spontaneity in gesture and movement, 163–64

Vocabulary, 207

Vocal chords, 171; *pictured*, 169

Vocal communication, 166–87; articulation inventory, 173–76; determining potential ability, 176–77; practice for, 176–77; *see also* Voice, Voice improvement

Voice: accuracy and, 174–75; and articulation, 172; audibility, 173–74; loudness, 186; meaning, 184; meaningfulness, 175; monotony, 183; phrasing, 185; pitch, 186; pleasantness, 175–76; rate, 184; variety, 186–87; versus correction, 167

Voice improvement, program for practice, 177–87; articulation exercises, 178–83; audibility exercises, 177–79; meaning, 184; phonograph records, use in, 177; vocal monotony, 183–84; vocal variety, 184–87; voice (tape) recorders, use in, 177

Voice production, 168–72; articulation, 172; phonation, 171; resonation, 171–72; respiration, 168–70

Watson, John B., 9
Watson, Thomas J., *quoted*, 139
Weaver, Warren, *quoted*, 6
Webster, Daniel, *quoted*, 199
Weinberg, Arthur, *quoted*, 132
Welles, Orson, 177
Wells, H. G., *quoted*, 19
Whitten, Mary E., 198
Wiener, Norbert, *quoted*, 327
Wiggle meter, 229
Wilde, Oscar, *quoted*, 87
Wilson, John J., *quoted*, 223
Wilson, Woodrow, 91
Wise, Claude Merton, *quoted*, 168
Words: as symbols, 191; beginning advice on, 9; concrete, 198; correct usage, 197; figurative, 198–200; meaningful, 193; precise, 195; simple, 194
Wrenchley, Elma D., 28
Wright, Donald, *pictured*, 283
Wriston, Walter B., *quoted*, 118–19
Written speeches, 205–07

Young, James Douglas, 207
Young, Owen, *quoted*, 42

A 4
B 5
C 6
D 7
E 8
F 9
G 0
H 1
I 2
J 3